BOYCE PN1031.E32
Eastman, Max,
Enjoyment of poetry
30392000016246

D1000188

BOOKS BY MAX EASTMAN

ANTHOLOGY FOR
ENJOYMENT OF POETRY

ENJOYMENT OF POETRY

THE LITERARY MIND

THE SENSE OF HUMOR

POEMS

CHARLES SCRIBNER'S SONS

ENJOYMENT OF POETRY

WITH

ANTHOLOGY

FOR

ENJOYMENT OF POETRY

ENJOYMENT OF POETRY

WITH

ANTHOLOGY

FOR

ENJOYMENT OF POETRY

BY

MAX EASTMAN

ONE-VOLUME EDITION

CHARLES SCRIBNER'S SONS
NEW YORK

H-4.67[H]

Printed in the United States of America

PREFACE TO THE COMBINED VOLUME

THE PUBLISHER's decision to issue a new edition of *Enjoyment of Poetry* with my anthology adjoined is not only joyous news to me, but also, I like to think, a good omen for poetry. Poetry was still singing, and was still clear, when this book was written. Poets were still talking to us. They were not, at least conscientiously and as a matter of devout principle, mumbling to themselves. The anthology, too, was selected in a mood of resistance to what I called the Cult of Unintelligibility. Max Perkins and I even thought of calling it "Anthology of Intelligible Poetry." So it may not be unreasonable to interpret the demand for this combined edition as a sign of an approaching change of poetic climate. Perhaps the skies are clearing—as ultimately they are bound to. The human race is too social, and communication is too much fun, for this introvert phase in the life of poetry to last forever.

No doubt values have been added to poetry by this ingoing adventure. Though it is, from the standpoint of the reader, a consecration of the mental blur, and that must be condemned on moral and political grounds when Western Civilization is fighting for its life, it is not that to the poets. They know what they are saying; they merely won't tell. And the reason they won't tell is not always an unpoetic one. The best of them are trying to come closer to the pure essence of their experience and its realization through language. They are following to its extreme the definition of poetry, and the distinction of poetry from practical speech, which I expounded in this book. They find that communication interferes with that. And of course it does, for it is only by using language as a practical instrument that we communicate. Grammar and syntax are practical, punctuation is practical. These are instruments, not of realization, but of social discourse. They do not help, as poetic words do, to crystallize our experience. When E. E. Cummings, for example, tries to use punctuation as poetry, he ceases to use it at all. It no longer is punctuation, but merely a series of specks and blotches on pages that would otherwise contain some of the purest lyric poetry we have.

At times, to be sure, another cause operates besides poetic extremism in this mystification of the reader. Instead of an excess in the direction of pure poetry, it may be a more or less deliberate surrender of the essence of poetry to the habits of an age of practical achievement. It does, in frequent effect, convert poetry from an imaginative experience into a logical and grammatical puzzle upon which practical minds can exercise their ingenuity. Instead of living the experience a poem offers, they can assemble their calipers and diagrams, their code-indexes and textbooks of stored knowledge, and triumphantly figure out what the poem means. This is an ingenious way of sugar-coating the pill of poetry for the hopelessly prosaic, and I think the poets are not all of them entirely unaware of it. Instead of a feat of sensitivity, it becomes an engineering enterprise to dig the meaning out of their lines. And this enterprise has certainly nothing to do with the enjoyment of poetry.

It will be a happy day for poetry when these facts and distinctions, so obvious to simple minds, begin to be recognized by those who go in for "intellect." No doubt I am in too big a hurry for that day to come and exaggerate the significance of this new edition of my own book. I might content myself with hoping that the book will help a little in bringing the day forward. A scientific (and that means only valid) general conception of what poetry is—one, at least, that a psychologist can read without tearing his hair out of his head—can hardly fail to have a clarifying influence so far as it travels. And a conception which understands the unintelligible poets, and accepts, when it is genuine, their poetic motive, lamenting only that slight exaggeration of this motive which renders them futile and foolish, their readers muddled, and their critics insincere, ought to be more helpful in clearing the air than an undiscriminating polemic.

MAX EASTMAN

January, 1951

PREFACE TO THE NEW EDITION OF ENJOYMENT OF POETRY

THE SUGGESTION from the publishers of a new and enlarged edition of *Enjoyment of Poetry* comes to me as rare good news, for I have been longing to bring all my essays on Æsthetics into a single volume.

Enjoyment of Poetry was my first book, written while I was lecturing on poetry in a course listed both as philosophy and psychology at Columbia University. It was, I think, the first time literary criticism had been regarded as a branch of psychology, and I was very proud of Professor Cattell's willingness to give credits to students in his department who took my course. In my enthusiasm for the further march of science into realms occupied by "the humanities," I made in my preface a rather wild statement about literary criticism, which I have now removed. Otherwise the text of *Enjoyment of Poetry* is unaltered. It used to be my child, but it has lived its own life too long to be corrected by a fussy parent.

One thing always troubled me a little about *Enjoyment of Poetry,* and that is that in my zeal to avoid being academic, I failed to convey the fact that I was propounding, for better or worse, a theory of art. I sketched a little casually, too, the explanation of metaphor, and of figurative language in general, which is the axis of my theory. In the essays "What Poetry Is" and "Art and Biology" (first published in *The Literary Mind* in 1934), I tried to be a little more technical or explicit on these subjects. And in the essay on "I. A. Richards' Theories of Poetry" I have defended my own view as profoundly as I know how. It is a defense, not only of poetry against moralistic impositions, but of the sovereignty of the mind in morals. I doubt if Mr. Richards realizes the horrors of obscurantism to which his theories of poetry conduct—or rather contribute, for in half the world these horrors are upon us.

John Dewey, in his recent book, *Art As Experience,* while generously endorsing my account of the æsthetic experience, tries also to bring into his own account a little of that "preparation for action" which Mr. Richards regards as the definitive thing. I am for introducing into *art* all the preparation for action, meaning, practical utility, etc., that may at any time suit the wish of the artist, but to introduce them into the *definition* of art is, in my opinion, bad psychology, and leads to bad criticism, bad morals and bad politics. In a brief reply to John Dewey's criticisms I had tried to make the logic of this disagreement clear.

The essays which I call "The History of English Poetry" and "Art and the Life of Action"—the latter now considerably revised—present my view in its historic aspect. So far as I know, no æsthetician has adequately grasped the fact that his problem has arisen as the result of a long process of evolution. An increasing division of labor, and of play also, between poetry and science, between art and artisanship, a discrimination of attitude and function, not only among minds, but within minds, is inherent in all cultural progress. The division has of course always existed, but advancing knowledge and technique extends it to ever new subject-matter. I hope some day to devote a book to this, and to some of the problems raised by it. Meanwhile the general fact is sufficiently indicated in these two essays, one first printed in *The Literary Mind* (where it was called "Division of Labor in Poetry"), the other as the title essay of a book published by Alfred Knopf in 1935. These two essays complete what I have to say—as yet!—about the psychology of the serious arts.

MAX EASTMAN

June, 1938

CONTENTS

CONTENTS

PREFACE AND SUMMARY

THE PURPOSE of this book is to increase enjoyment. That the poetic in every-day perception and conversation should be known for what it is, and not separated from the poetic in literature, is to my mind essential to the full appreciation of either. And that poetry in general should be cut off from those unhealthy associations that a leisure-class decadence has given to the word, is of value to the enterprise of enjoying life.

I have drawn the distinction between the poetic and the practical as it appears in my own experience, with little respect for academic or literary classifications. In this way I believed I should stay closer to my chief purpose; I should also be more likely to contribute to scientific truth.

A misfortune incident to all education is the fact that those who elect to be teachers are scholars. They esteem knowledge not for its use in attaining other values, but as a value in itself; and hence they put an undue emphasis upon what is formal and nice about it, leaving out what is less pleasing to the instinct for classification but more needful to the art of life. This misfortune is especially heavy in the study of literature. Indeed, the very separation of the study of literature from that of the subjects it deals with, suggests the barren and formal character of it. As usually taught for three years to postgraduates in our universities, it is not worth spending three weeks upon. The best lovers of literature know this, and the academic world will some day know it and will cast about for a real science which they may teach to those who are going to read literature to the young. That science will be psychology in its widest sense. For psychology is a knowledge that is general without being merely formal. It will reveal and explain, not the scholastic conventions about literary structure, nor the verbiage of commentators, but the substantial values that are common to the material of all literature. I hope that my book may add impetus to this change in education.

Perhaps, also, by emphasizing the fact that things are, and continue to be, what the poet calls them, whatever else they may be or be named by the scientist, it will add some strength to that affirmatively sceptical philosophy upon which it is founded.

But these aims are all secondary. The chief purpose is to extend to others the service of a distinction which has made the word more enjoyable to me.

In chapter one I have shown how this distinction first appears in the attitudes of different people, or the same people in different moods, toward their experience—toward actions, things, emotions, images, ideas. I have shown that the poetic attitude prevails in childhood.

In chapter two I have shown how the distinction appears wherever names are newly applied, in the origin and growth of language, in slang, in expletives, in conversation, in books, and in the disputes of metaphysics.

In chapter three I have pointed out the two acts, choice and comparison, which are discoverable in every new application of a name, and distinguished practical choice and comparison from poetic.

In chapter four I have explained why choice and why comparison assist the poetic impulse, the impulse to realize.

In chapter five I have shown that realization is often more poignant in the absence than in the presence of things.

In chapter six I have explained how choice and comparison appear in pure poetry, which is the verbal realization of things in their absence, and in poetic discourse. I have related the "figures of speech," so called, to the common poetic use of modifiers, they all being examples either of choice or comparison.

In chapter seven I have shown what I believe to be the primitive and basic relation of rhythm to the mood of realization.

In chapters eight, nine, ten, and eleven I have explained in detail how the technique of poetry applies to the realization of distinguishable elements in imagined experience—actions, things, emotions, ideas. I have introduced examples of poetry that has given me the greatest enjoyment, and I have illustrated the application of psychological, instead of rhetorical, concepts to its analysis.

In chapter twelve I have set forth values which poetry may have, not as a realization of other things, but as a thing to be realized for itself. I have done this briefly, because it contributes little to what is already contained in other books.

In chapter thirteen I have related the knowledge of poetry to the art of enjoying it. I have dwelt separately upon the poetry of experience and that of imagination through language, and I have stated that the best path to the enjoyment of the latter lies through the creation of it.

In chapter fourteen I have given the general principles that I think relate to the creation of rhythmical English.

In chapter fifteen I have praised poetry for its practical value, pointing out both its accidental value as an enhancer of meanings, and the value that pertains to its own essence. I have suggested that the latter will increase in proportion as we draw more perfectly the line between knowledge and mythology, and compel ourselves to resort for exaltation to an enthusiastic welcome of the world as it is or as it may be, and for religion to a consciousness of the final mystery of its being.

ENJOYMENT OF POETRY

I

POETIC PEOPLE

A SIMPLE experiment will distinguish two types of human nature. Gather a throng of people and pour them into a ferry-boat. By the time the boat has swung into the river you will find that a certain proportion have taken the trouble to climb upstairs, in order to be out on deck and see what is to be seen as they cross over. The rest have settled indoors, to think what they will do upon reaching the other side, or perhaps lose themselves in apathy or tobacco smoke. But leaving out those apathetic, or addicted to a single enjoyment, we may divide all the alert passengers on the boat into two classes—those who are interested in crossing the river, and those who are merely interested in getting across. And we may divide all the people on the earth, or all the moods of people, in the same way. Some of them are chiefly occupied with attaining ends, and some with receiving experiences. The distinction of the two will be more marked when we name the first kind practical, and the second poetic, for common knowledge recognizes that a person poetic or in a poetic mood is impractical, and a practical person is intolerant of poetry.

We can see the force of this intolerance too, and how deeply it is justified, if we make clear to our minds just what it means to be practical, and what a great thing it is. It means to be controlled in your doings by the consideration of ends yet unattained. The practical man is never distracted by things, or aspects of things, which have no bearing on his purpose, but, ever seizing the significant, he moves with a single mind and a single emotion toward the goal. And even when the goal is achieved you will hardly see him pause to rejoice in it; he is already on his way to another achievement. For that is the irony of his nature. His joy is not in any conquest or destination, but his joy is in going toward it. To which joy he adds the pleasure of being praised as a practical man, and a man who will arrive.

In a more usual sense, perhaps, a practical man is a man occupied with attaining certain ends that people consider important. He must stick pretty close to the business of feeding and preserving life. Nourishment and shelter, money-making, maintaining respectability, and if possible a family—these are the things that give its common meaning to the word "practical." An acute regard for such features of the scenery, and the universe, as contribute or can be made to contribute to these ends, and a systematic neglect of all other features, are the traits of mind which this word popularly suggests. And it is because of the vital importance of these things to almost all people that the word "practical" is a eulogy, and is able to be so scornful of the word "poetic."

"It is an earnest thing to be alive in this world. With competition, with war, with disease and poverty and oppression, misfortune and death on-coming, who but fools will give serious attention to what is not significant to the business?"

"Yes—but what is the *use* of being alive in the world, if life is so oppressive in its moral character that we must always be busy getting somewhere, and never simply realizing where we are? What were the value of your eternal achieving, if we were not here on our holiday to appreciate, among other things, some of the things you have achieved?"

Thus, if we could discover a purely poetic and a purely practical person, might they reason together. But we can discover nothing so satisfactory to our definitions, and therefore let us conclude the discussion of the difference between them. It has led us to our own end—a clearer understanding of the nature of poetic people, and of all people when they are in a poetic mood. They are lovers of the qualities of things. They are not engaged, as the learned say that all life is, in becoming adjusted to an environment, but they are engaged in becoming acquainted with it. They are possessed by the impulse to realize, an impulse as deep, and arbitrary, and unexplained as that "will to live" which lies at the bottom of all the explanations. It seems but the manifestation, indeed, of that will itself in a concrete and positive form. It is a wish to experience life and the world. That is the essence of the poetic temper.[1]

Children are poetic. They love to feel of things. I suppose it is necessary to their preservation that they should be, for by random exercise of their organs of feeling they develop them and make them fit for their practical function. But that is not the chief reason why they are poetic; the chief reason is that they are not practical. They have not yet felt the necessity, or got addicted to the trick, of formulating a purpose and then achieving it. Therefore this naïve impulse of nature, the impulse toward realization, is free in them. Moreover, it is easy of satisfaction. It is easy for children to taste the qualities of experience, because experience is new, and its qualities are but loosely bound together into what we call "things." Each is concrete, particular, unique, and without an habitual use.

Babies have no thought, we may say, but to feel after and find the world, bringing it so far as possible to their mouths where it becomes poignant. They become absorbed in friendship with the water they bathe in. The crumple noise of paper puts

[1]There is a poetic attitude to the practical life, and no poet is complete without it. It is expressed in these words of Peter Kropotkin:

"Struggle! To struggle is to live, and the fiercer the struggle the intenser the life."

But it is not that attitude which keeps the majority struggling, or keeps any man incessantly struggling. They are not concerned to receive the experience of struggle, but they are concerned to achieve their ends. This general tendency to achieve, to adjust—a primary impulse of life—is set off against the tendency to receive, to realize—a different and also, I believe, a primary impulse of life. Like all things in the world these impulses are rarely found pure, but they can be analyzed out and isolated for purposes of understanding.

them in ecstasy, and later all smells and sounds, brightness, and color, and form, and motion, delight them. We can see them discover light by putting their hands before their eyes and taking them away quickly, and again, at a later age, discover sound by stopping their ears and opening them again.

Who does not remember in his own childhood testing the flavors of things—of words, perhaps, saying them over and over until he had defeated his own wish, for they became pulpy and ridiculous in his mouth? Anything which invades the sense like cinnamon, or sorrel, or neat flowers, or birds' eggs, or a nut, or a horn, is an object of peculiar affection. It is customary in books about children to say that they care little for the actual qualities of an object, and are able to deal with it as though it were anything that they choose to imagine. But I think only the positive part of this statement is true. Undoubtedly their imaginations are active in more various directions, and they draw the distinction between the real and the ideal in perception less clearly than grown-up people do. But the most pronounced characteristic of children is that they are perfectly free to feel the intrinsic qualities of things as they merely are. What we call objects are for the most part practically determined coordinations of qualities. And what we call the *actual* quality of an object is usually the quality which indicates its vital use. When we say actual, therefore, we really mean practical. But so far as actuality from the standpoint of the things is concerned, the children come nearer to it, and care more about it, than we do. To us a derby hat is for covering the head, and that is about all it is; but to them it is hard, smooth, hollow, deep, funny, and may be named after the mixing-bowl and employed accordingly. And so it is with all things. The child loves a gem with its pure and serene ray, as the poet loves it, for its own sake.

Nor is it only such qualities as may be said to give pleasure that he seeks, unless pleasure be defined as seeking, for he wants all experience. He wants all that he can stand. He is exploring the whole world of sense, and not rarely upsets his stomach, and his entire system, in a zest for the reception of sensations that are instinctively abhorred. Two children of our neighborhood will wear to their graves the brand of a red-hot scarf-pin as a testimony to that first love of experience. They did not want torture, I suppose, but they wanted to see what it is to be tortured. And so it was in varying degrees with us all. It seems to me, when I look back, as if we were forever out behind the barn finding out what something or other was "like."

It has been a vast problem for those concerned with æsthetic and other theories, why people love tragedy when they are not in it. But if their theories would only allow that these organisms of ours, which have been gnashing and struggling together God knows what billions of years for a chance to live, have really an interest in living, there could be no problem. The problem is, seeing this wild zest for life, and life so tragic—the problem is, why people do not love tragedy when they are in it. And in truth they do. From the pure sweetness of early romantic sorrow to the last bitter comfort of an old man bereft, who mutters to his soul, "This is a part of the full experience of a man!" —from first to last, up to the cannon's mouth and down to the midnight grave, the poetic impulse survives. We love to taste life to the full.

In energetic but idle hours it survives joyfully. And in youth these were the predominant hours. At all times we were ready for exuberant realization. We were not indifferent to the morning. We did not wake at the greeting of a last night's proposition in commerce or knowledge, but at the smile of the sun. The stuff of our thoughts was not sentences and numbers, but grass and apples and brown honey. Such excellent objects parading before our minds in a thousand combinations and colors left us no time to develop these general conclusions with which we are now filled. We could not banish our prairie thoughts from the school-room, though they liked it as little as we, and the hour of recess was the hour of life. And in the hours of life how greedy we were! Every sense was open with indiscriminate material flowing in. Our eyes trained for every seeing, our ears catching the first murmur of a new experience, we ran after the world in our eagerness, not to learn about it, but to taste the flavor of its being.

"Oh, the wild joys of living; the leaping from rock up to rock,
The strong rending of boughs from the fir-tree, the cool silver shock
Of the plunge in a pool's living water, the hunt of the bear,
And the sultriness showing the lion is couched in his lair.
And the meal, the rich dates yellowed over with gold dust divine,
And the locust-flesh steeped in the pitcher, the full draught of wine,
And the sleep in the dried river-channel where bulrushes tell
That the water was wont to go warbling so softly and well.
How good is man's life, the mere living! how fit to employ
All the heart and the soul and the senses for ever in joy!"

This agility and fervor of realization extends early to the exercise of all the senses. And then as we grow a little older it comes inward, and we tremble to catch our own emotions on the wing. Fear, for instance, is a being of intense fascination, and even so impelling a power as the instinct of self-preservation is suspended by the poetic impulse—suspended in order that its own very nature may be experienced in feeling. Can you not remember the keen edge of a venture into the barn-yard, a tumultuous dash across to the corn-crib which offered a refuge impregnable to those mild-mannered cows? Anger is a moderate pleasure to most healthy persons, but in youth it is a thing to thirst after and brag of. It is life itself. Mulishness is an engaging state of being. Cruelty and mercy have often the same original charm.

I remember discovering insolence with exactly the same happy spirit of gratification with which I see babies discover light. I was profoundly interested in Nancy Hanks, who had broken the world's record by trotting a mile in 2.04. I believe that I *was* Nancy Hanks most of the time, and anybody who wanted to converse with me or put me in a good-humor would begin upon that topic. But at last I became aware that I could do something quite different from being gratified by all their talk, and I was carried away by the discovery. My opportunity came during supper, at the gracious hands of a maiden aunt:

"Do you know who Nancy Hanks was named after?"

"No," I shouted, 'I don't know and I don't care a *darn*—see?"

My memory of the punishment which followed, and how I became aware that there are limits to profitable exploration in such fields, is dim, but of the excited pleasure of the adventure, and my underlying friendliness toward the old lady throughout, I am quite certain.

They are great days when we first discern these powerful creatures in us, unnamed and meaningless monsters to challenge forth. Ghost-terror, and dizziness and sickness at the sight of blood, are among them. Imagine the mind of a young man who knows that there lies a pile of corpses the other side of a smouldering factory wall, and he both hastens to them and flees away from them, until finally this lust after the intense conquers, and he goes and gazes his fill. Do not call that morbid, but an act of exuberant vitality. For there is high-spiritedness in those that are young, not for sensation only, but for emotion. And this too they carry with them, some more and some less, throughout life. Rancor and magnanimity, lust and romance, rapture and even melancholy—drink them to the dregs, for they are what it is to be.

"No, no! go not to Lethe——"

It is not only things of the sense and body that a child loves for their own sake, but at a certain age he learns to watch with wonder the paintings of his mind. When he is condemned into his crib, and has to face the loss of the whole lovely world in sleep, then this is the last resource. As long as God lets him he will devote his somnolescent power to sensuous memory or anticipation, or just the circus-antics of grotesque and vivid-colored creatures that dance in before him unbidden, uncreated, unexplained. Even if sometimes he does honestly try to think, he finds that he cannot very long cling to the meaning of his thought, because he is all curious to examine those garments of imagery that it wears.

To most adults, I suppose, it is a bare mechanical or rational process to count from one to a hundred; but to an alert child it hardly ever is. It is a winding and bending over a plain, over a prairie, a slow climb, a drip-drip, or an odd march of marionettes, or perhaps it is just the queer sound of the words at his ear. At any rate, the engrossing thing is to estimate the unique character of the process and of each member in it. Eight is a jolly fat man. Six is sitting down. Some people say that they never had any of these pleasures, that they have no mind's eye at all. They cannot see six sit down. Let them try to comfort themselves with the idea that they are more scientific than the rest, not having vivid images to confuse their meanings in the serious business of reaching a conclusion. They are like the people on the ferry-boat who stay downstairs where there are few distractions and they can be perfectly sure to get across. Luckier than they are the people who can enjoy the scenery of speculation, who bring with them out of childhood a clear and spirited fancy.

"—Great God! I'd rather be
A Pagan suckled in a creed outworn;
So might I, standing on this pleasant lea,
Have glimpses that would make me less forlorn;
Have sight of Proteus rising from the sea;
Or hear old Triton blow his wreathèd horn."

The final appearance of the poetic impulse, its intellectual appearance, is also at its height in youth. It is well known that at a certain period, if they are healthy and have a little self-dependence, young persons fall in love with all kinds of unusual ideas. They come forward with an amazing belief, a wise or foolish theory, which they attach to for its own sake, and not out of regard for its practical or real consequence. They take a taste of Atheism, Anarchism, Asceticism, Hindoo Philosophy, Pessimism, Christianity, or anything that offers a good flavor of radical faith. This is only the same zest for experience. And it will need but a glance at life and literature to prove that such attachment to ideas, with small regard for their meaning in conduct, is not confined to the young. It is a poetic pleasure that people bring with them perhaps farther than any of the others. For most of these pleasures, and especially the more simple and innocent, they soon leave behind, as though it were somehow unworthy to be childlike and love things for their own sake.

We have a superstition prevailing in our homes that the first thing to do upon the appearance of a child is to bring it up. And we see children brought up in the utmost haste by persons who have purchased their own maturity at a cost of all native and fresh joy in anything available. But could we only realize how far the youthful pleasure in every poignant realization is above the accidents of fortune, we should take as great pains to preserve that, as to erect the man in our offspring. We should ourselves long to be born again, and maintain for the future a more equable union of the practical and poetic in our character.

That such a union is attainable, the lives of the greatest show. It is possible to keep throughout a life not wholly disordered, or idle, or cast loose from the general drift of achievement, a spirit fresh to the world. The thought brings us back to Æschylus, a man of heroic proportions who achieved, in an age of turmoil and war, a life filled wonderfully with realizations that were final, the fruit of evolution, and yet not wanting the excellence of great action directed toward a further end. With the participation of that poetic hero in the campaign of defence against the Persians, and in the battles of Salamis and Marathon, it seems as if Nature had indeed achieved her aim. There experience was at its height, but purpose was unshaken. The little library and piazza poets and esteemers of poetry in these days of art will do well to remember the great Greek, who died the most renowned literary genius of his age but had carved upon his proud tomb only this boast, that "The grove of Marathon could bear witness to his good soldierhood, and the long-haired Mede who felt it."

It would be foolish indeed to question whether or not the poetic are capable of purposeful achievement, and the practical capable of intense experience, for we are all, except those lost in apathy, in some degree both poetic and practical. But the example of the hero proves that it is possible for a man, who can think clearly and command the differences that lie within him, to be both poetic and practical in a high degree.

If we could but free our minds from a contamination with certain modern people who teach themselves that they are presided over by a pretty demon called an Artistic Temperament, we should not only cease cherishing by suggestion the tickle-brain condition into which they decay, but we should have for ourselves a sounder estimate of the place and dignity of the poetic. It is not an attribute of special, exotic, or disordered types, but a universal quality of our nature. No live man is without an arbitrary passion for some experience. Indeed, the defect of many of those most scornful of poetry is not that they are strong in the practical life, but that the attachment to some single state of being has got the better of them. There are fifty thousand morphine-takers in Paris, and all over the face of the earth how many million chewers, and breathers, and swallowers of what, far from being of practical value, is both costly and deleterious, bearing unconscious witness to the poetry of human nature.

The greatly poetic differ from them only in the healthy variety of their loves, prevailing everywhere and always. They are those who live variously as well as vividly in the present. This alone distinguishes them from the millions. This alone distinguishes them from all those excluded by our experiment at the beginning, who confine their enjoyment to smoke while they are crossing the river. They are not without realization.

But it is only the childlike and the poetic who make the innumerable intimate acquaintances that are to be made, who welcome all living qualities and perfect them, and finally, perhaps, in a supreme moment of morning sunshine and mist over the city, realize what we may call the essence of crossing a ferry. Their breast thrills, and their eyes drink with rapture the million moving and dancing details of that pageant of life——

"—the white sails of schooners and sloops,—the ships at anchor,
The sailors at work in the rigging, or out astride the spars,
The round masts, the swinging motion of the hulls, the slender serpentine pennants,
The large and small steamers in motion, the pilots in their pilot-houses,
The white wake left by the passage, the quick tremulous whirl of the wheels,
The flags of all nations, the falling of them at sunset,
The scallop-edged waves in the twilight, the ladled cups, the frolicsome crests and glistening,
The stretch afar growing dimmer and dimmer, the gray walls of the granite storehouses by the docks,
On the river the shadowy group, the big steam-tug closely flank'd on each side by the barges—the hay-boat, the belated lighter,
On the neighboring shore, the fires from the foundry chimneys burning high and glaringly into the night,
Casting their flicker of black, contrasted with wild red and yellow light, over the tops of houses, and down into the clefts of streets."

II

NAMES PRACTICAL AND POETIC

It is not in words that the distinction of the poetic from the practical begins. It lies not in books but in the protoplasm. And no doubt, if we knew enough, we need not begin even with people, but we could trace this cleavage of two motives back into the very birth of alertness in matter, and there see the one current scorning the other as to-day. For poetry is an attitude of the body. Both anteceding and transcending speech or idea, it is a way of experiencing realities.

And yet the realities that men experience are in their nature very much determined by words; their names are a part of them. And this it is important for those who estimate poetry to understand. It is important for them to understand the nature of what we call "things"—that they are all, as we perceive them, unions of an external impression with something that memory contributes. A mere glimmer of flame through the air, for instance, and we have an *oriole flying;* an odd-shaped parallelogram with a white blotch upon it, and we perceive the *polished, square surface* of a *table.* Stand too near an oil painting and you can see how few daubs are required, so they be the right ones, to present to us an entire panorama of external reality. Nature herself presents, at any one time, little more than those same few daubs, and her whole triumphal evolution would be to us only a rank flux and confusion of fragmentary qualities if we did not perpetually amplify her intimations, and respond to them as things. Perhaps no one ever saw a farm, or a country, but a farm or a country can be both perceived and dealt with if the mind is active.

Yet either to perceive it or deal with it, without a name, is not easy. Names are a vital part of the contribution that memory makes to things. They determine and carry with them all the rest—the imagery, the mood, the attitude, and activity. The right word is magic; it evokes for us out of the eternal fog whatever object is potential there, and puts us face to face in direct current of communication with it. It does this as no other power under the sun can do it. Is it not a question whether there could really be such a thing as a country until after there was a word for it? Take off the name, and I am not sure but the whole British Empire—that vast world-power—would vanish like a speculation, and you would have merely a number of people living some here and some there. Annihilate the word "love," and you would alter for many the quality of the very fabric of their lives. Such is the importance of names; they are close constituents of real things.

And every real thing has, or may have, two different kinds of names. It may have names which indicate a suitable adjustment to it, and names which engender a strong realization of it. The practical are always seeking the former names, and the poetic are always seeking the latter, and the distinction between them is eternal. It is rooted in the origin of tongues, and it branches in the highest apprehensions of metaphysics. Wherever a name is newly applied, we may ask and answer the question, Is it applied with a predominantly poetic or a predominantly practical intent?[1]

Doubtless we have in ourselves experienced something like the original birth of a poetic word. We first got acquainted with cows by mooing, and with the wind by howling up his chimney, and sometimes still, when a blue-bottle circles round us on

[1]It will be understood that by names I do not mean single terms only, much less nouns, *but any word or group of words identified with an experience.* Only five of the nine parts of speech—nouns, pronouns, verbs, adjectives, adverbs—can alone be called names of things. The rest are things in their own right, mental acts which serve in the creation or manipulation of names. *Horse* is a name; so also is *trot;* so also is *this horse that trots as though his fore and hind quarters were operated separately.* But *that* and *as though* standing alone are not names.

a summer noon, if we have nothing else to do we say "buzz," for no better reason than because he said it. And in some such way as this, thousands of years ago, upon the tongues of idle but appreciative savages, many little words and parts of words must have been born. Other little words are reported to have jumped right out of the mouths of these savages, when they were surprised or shocked by anything. And probably many of these too, when they were afterward applied to the object that produced them, were applied with a poetic intent, an intent to renew that experience for its own sake. But of those words which arose—as it has been held that all speech arose—out of a song or grunt of action in unison, a kind of "yo-he-ho," naming the action first and then extended to the object acted upon, probably the majority were children of a practical necessity.

It is not poetic to extend the name that is part of an act to the object acted upon, because the object is not like the act. I believe that this is why the Teutonic languages retain, in defiance of the dictates of utility, a certain number of "strong verbs," or verbs which change their character radically by the time they reach the past participle, where they become names of an object. To *kill* is a vivid act, but to die is quite opposite, and therefore the associative flavor of the word *killed* is wrong. It is very weak, and we always want to help it; we want to say "killed *dead,*" or something like that. *Shot,* on the contrary, sounds different from *shoot,* and is fit to receive the impact of it; it is a strong participle. The word *break* is intact and active, and *breaked* would be very much the same, but *broken* is in the condition it describes.

These are producings and modellings of the substance of words, but we must follow our distinction forward into another kind of creation—the creation of names by the new application or combination of old words. "Fire-water" is the name that the American Indians invented for whiskey. And it is, when you pause to receive it, a very wonderful and quick metaphor. Yet we can hardly say whether it illustrates better the practical or poetic motive in word-making, whether it was given in prudence or delight. In the name that some Polynesian savages gave to an explorer's watch which curiously pleased them, we have surer signs of a poetic perception. "Moon," they called it, and when they were questioned why, they said that it was "round and stayed awake all night." But for examples of such poetry in the transfer and recombination of words we need not go beyond what is obvious in our own language to-day, for within its recent history many names have been born, and still older ones retain the quality of their birth. *Buttercup* is a word of this kind. *Blue-eyed grass, golden-rod, fire-bird, dovetail, sky-scraper, ocean greyhound, pinchpenny, rakehell, swashbuckler, spit-fire, kill-joy, slipgibbet,* are words of more or less rapt appreciation; while on the other hand *winter squash, Canada fox, ball-and-socket, office building, steamboat, railroad, money-saver, motor-cyclist,* justify themselves only by their utility.

Even the plainest-looking words will sometimes reveal, to one who likes them well enough to look for it, a lucid perception out of which they sprang. Sarcasm is "a tearing of the flesh." And we may contrast it, for our purpose, with *irony,* which means "saying little—saying less than you mean," one conveying an acute experience, the other a practical analysis. *Gymnasium* is "the place of nakedness." *Retort* is "a twisting back." *Enthusiast* is "full of God." *Night* is "death." And *nightingale* is "singer-in-the-night."

Such is the poetry which you find in the dictionary, the unpremeditated art of men for ages dead, whose utterance in a vivid moment rose to the heights of genius and could not be forgotten. It is the supreme model for all poetry, vital, democratic, inevitable, embodying the native forms under which man has beheld his visible world, and the subtle work of analogy by which he has blended that with the widening panorama of the spirit.

The same process will go on forever. In our own times every little while, out of a body of names which all suffer the flavor of disreputability and are called slang, the language stoops and picks up a gem. "It's a peach" is an expression peculiarly akin to much of the poetry that already lies hidden in the forms of words. We can look forward to a time when in a changed language the fruit may have another name, but still a perfect thing or person will be a peach, and no one will know why. *Squelch* and *grouch* and *butt in* are words which might, either for practical or poetic reasons, be lifted into good repute. In the dialect of special cliques or professions, thieving, sailing, baseball, journalism, as well as in general slang, new names of both these kinds are continually born. A *hit,* and a *two-base hit,* and a *home run* are simply useful terms; but to *lean against the leather,* to *rap out a two-bagger,* to *zip it to the fence,* are superfluous and poetic expressions.

It is said that only those slang words which fill a vacancy are taken up into reputable discourse, but in reality literature is ever on the watch for terms which are peculiarly poignant or akin to their objects, and ready at any day to exchange for them an equivalent synonym. *Lurid* is a word exactly expressing the character of modern cheap newspapers, but it is not altogether living, and so in the first flush of their realization a new name came to the birth. They were *yellow.* And yet so strange is time, and so eternal is the perfection of a metaphor which is perfect, that if we turn back to the days when the word *lurid* itself was born and when it too joyfully lived, we find in it exactly the same poetry. It is *luridus,* a Latin word for "yellow."

The enduring character of the poetic instinct is further proven by the luxuriance and similarity in all ages of the language of vituperation. Poetry is the art of calling names, and, in the art of calling people bad names, not Homer, nor Shakespeare, who is the master, can excel the folk-lore upon which he builds. For acute realization of the vile qualities of men, and for scenic effects of the same character, we need not turn to our libraries. Though the scenic oath is scant among Anglo-

Saxons, the scantness is more than compensated in southern Europe. Imagine a race which put as much energy of genius into the verbal realization of the tragic or sublime as the Spaniards or Neapolitans do into the nauseous and irreverent—most of our poetry books would have to hide their heads. And as it is, I believe that their authors could better learn their art here—in the language of loose wrath among the unlettered—than anywhere else, unless perhaps in the dictionary of etymology.

Some people think that the poetic are always talking symbolism and endowing the sod with spiritual meaning. They do that, to be sure, because that is a great way to realize the sod and the spirit, but they also do the opposite. They daub the spirit. The most baneful degeneration to which names lend their aid is a poetic one. It is an excessive love of the imaginative realization of what is normally repulsive. Millions of so-called "stories" are current among men and women and children of which the climax is not humor but poetry, a vivid filth. And as the evening progresses you can observe this corruption creep into a group of story-tellers, while their humor expires.

Perhaps the reason why so many people will resent our calling these things, and others, poetic, is that they have got poetry sentimentally attached in their minds to a mysterious conception of the beautiful. They think that it implies a gush of harmonious numbers upon appropriate occasions, having especial regard to cliffs, maidens, hair, waves, pine-trees, the sea, the moon, and the ethereal significance of each. And the reason for this is that, excepting a few, the most variously poetic people do not write poems. It is usually only those of a certain romantic turn who care to separate names from their objects, and round them into the lyrical shape, and make of them a new object. But these objects when they are made are called *poems,* and thus the whole meaning of the word *poetic* is influenced by the preference their gentle authors have for such topics. In few minds to-day does the word poetic sit clear of this misfortune.

But once learn to apprehend as such the poetic in every-day talk, and you will see that it is unlimited either to any range of objects or to any sweetness in handling them. It is simply the giving to any object, or thought, or event, or feeling, the name that makes its nature shine forth to you.

To call whiskey "fire-water" is poetic, but it is also poetic, although with an admixture of humor, to say that Club Soda is "the water that tastes like your foot's asleep." Both are true names. And in such lively expressions, words which perhaps never permanently unite with their object, but are called once or twice and then forgotten forever—in them, poetry is living continually before us.

Imagine that there are two people walking along the beach in leisure where the sea resounds. "It sounds like eternity," says one. "Well," says the other, "it sounds to me more like shovelling coal down a chute." The contrast is perhaps sharp, but it is not extreme, for each has sensed and conveyed to the other in language the intrinsic quality of his experience. The deeper difference lies between them both and the man who, walking by the sea, does not name it for its sound at all, does not pause to receive the sound into his mind, but names it *brine*—water with a three and one-half per cent solution of natural salts which he might precipitate with a distillery and put to a profitable use. He is the practical man.

The conversation of the poetic is acute and exhilarating, waking you to the life and eminence in reality of all things. The conversation of the practical is instructive, interesting, sometimes full of surprise and a feeling of supreme possibility. For in its highest reach the practical application of names is nothing less than the external substance of scientific knowledge.

Those who are engaged in the quest of such knowledge, and who call it Pure Science, and scorn the application of its results to those purposes recognized in the popular use of the word "practical," will resist the appellation. But, nevertheless, their activity in the laboratory, or in their own minds, comparing, classifying, naming, is always directed toward an end, however arbitrary, which they have set before them, and is subject to the test of their achieving or failing to achieve that end. Wherever it is not mere mythology, science is to some degree practical in the accurate sense of the word. Even in those discursive studies which appear to be but a description of the species that occupy the earth, the classifications are made and the names applied always with a view to conduct, even though that conduct be merely mental. And it is only this that distinguishes their language from the language of the poetic.

Once more, imagine two people walking in leisure, and this time along the roadside. It is summer and the yellow-birds are holding their sprightly revels among the milkweed blossoms there, dancing along before them as they go.

"Regular little *butterflies,* aren't they?" says one.

"Yes," says the other faintly, and then, with emphasis: "It is the *American goldfinch,* you know—a *grosbeak.*"

These are the two ways of being, as we say, interested in the birds. They are the two ways of being interested in everything in the world, and calling it by name. But in no other place will you find the opposition of poetic and practical terminology more exquisitely set forth than in the bird-neighbor books and wild-flower guides of modern times. There, side by side, you may read them—on the one line, labels picked from a language whose poetry is dead, and applied by earnest minds to serve the business of intellectual manipulation and accurate reference, and, on the other line, names bestowed in living syllables by the hearts of rural people in happy moments of carefree and vivid experience. Trailing Arbutus, Bouncing Bet, Dragon's Blood, Beggar's Buttons, Nose-bleed, Gay Feather, Heart-o'-the-earth, Ruby-throat, Firetail, Hell Diver, Solitary Vireo, Vesper Sparrow—these are the words for those who care but to feel and celebrate the qualities of things.

And in the lavish persistence, and in the truth, of these meadow names, holding their own against so much Latin, there is a lesson in humility for all science. It is about twenty-three hundred years now that scientific people have been constructing a world in systematic opposition to the world of the poetic, until in certain communities things have become exceedingly strained, and communication between those living in the two worlds is wellnigh impossible. Here is so simple and commonly regarded an object as water, for instance. The scientific have named it "H_2O." The poetic name it "wet"—not to say "babbling," "wild," and so forth. Each professes to name it with regard to its intrinsic and most real and final nature, and hence arises the central problem of modern philosophy, and the great task of modern philosophy—to discover a mode of sociability between the extremes of the poetic and the practical world.

Is the right name of water *wet,* or is it H_2O? That is the great argument between them. And only in our own times has it begun to be clear that unto eternity neither side will ever give in, and that the only thing for persons to do who are in a hurry, or wish to be larger than either science or poetry, is to confess that it is probably both. Yet, after acknowledging this, those who came from the poetic side of the argument might be permitted to stipulate that, if there is to be any doubt allowed as to the correctness of either name, that doubt shall cling to the scientific one. For since science arises out of the impulse to alter and achieve, and poetry out of the very love of the actual, there is more danger that science will build too much intellectual stuff into things, than that poetry will. Science inevitably idealizes; poetry is primarily determined to realize. The poetic name points to the object, the practical name points from the object. And if there were to be a crisis between them, if all feeling and all endeavor were suddenly to cease, and the dispassionate material of each long-suffering reality somehow to move forward and declare itself, I think that the name this one would most surely declare, upon that day of the death of metaphysics, would be "wet." It might even be "babbling," not to say "wild."

One thing is certain, however, and that is that we need not

soon anticipate such a day, nor hope for the death of metaphysics. And in the meantime, which is forever, the key and the solution, the only one that mortals will find, of the conflict within them between these two kinds of names, is to decline to regard them as rivals, but, taking their difference to be a difference between two impulses of life, to avail themselves upon the appropriate occasions of each.

"Effulgence of bright essence increate" is a name that John Milton gave to light. He gave it, perhaps, in the pain and ecstasy of vivid remembrance, in blindness. At least he sought with all his power to convey, enriched by intellect, the naïve sense of the being of light. In the same century a different but equally supreme genius, Isaac Newton, following the Greeks, gave to light the name "corpuscular emission." He gave it in his laboratory, in the mature activity of an intense mind bent upon learning the terms in which the world is to be dealt with. Now, both these high efforts, Milton's as poetry and Newton's as science, may be said to have failed. Milton did not convey a sense of the being of light, fundamentally because light is not similar to the Latin language; and Newton did not learn entirely well to deal with light, because it is not very similar to corpuscles. But does not this make all the more obvious the folly of our becoming exercised over the conflict between them, as though the world were not large enough and time long enough to hold both Milton and Newton, and others who shall in part supersede or excel them both?

Only when the practical usurps the empire of the poetic, or the poetic denies an ultimate sanction to the practical, do they become rivals—rivals for a supremacy that no real names can have. For there is a large democracy in nature. The world itself is not dogmatic. It both lends its support to a number of practical assumptions and consents to be in some measure what any poetic mind perceives it. The mind, in truth, does not impose itself upon a world of other things, but is itself a part of things so far as they engender experience. The poetic impulse is a love of that experience for its own sake. Poetic creation begins in us when we marry, with such love, the images of memory to the impressions of sense, and when to this union we set the seal of a vivid and communicable name we are poets in the full and divine sense. We are makers of a world. For if there is any creation in all history, poetic names are creators. And the man who lives his life in apathy or expeditious indifference to them—the world will never attain a full being in that man's experience.

III

THE TECHNIQUE OF NAMES

It is to be hoped that this too continuous iteration of "poetic" and "practical" has begot a degree of antagonism in the reader, because now he will need some emotional momentum to carry him through a heavy passage. We cannot fully celebrate the possibilities of poetic names, until we have made clear and easy to our understanding the mental functions that all names in their first application perform. It is just this amount of analytic psychology the lack of which, in literary critics and others who write books about books, is so disastrous to our love of literature. It is the thing that will some day save us from that disaster; therefore let us study and learn it.

Experience is a continuous process of choice and comparison, selecting one thing and correlating that in the mind with another. I believe that choice and comparison are in some degree present every time that any one is really conscious of anything. It is easy to show that choice is always present; you have only to go somewhere, and stand still, and reflect how many things there are about you which you are not seeing. Existence is too full for you. You see only the things that your tastes and purposes determine, and of these you see sharply only such features as affect those tastes and purposes. Other persons will see other things, and other features of the same things.

Suppose that you are standing by the side of the road, and a horse and wagon jogs by. You see the horse and wagon, and you observe that it is picturesque. The horse is shaggy, a strawberry roan. But suppose that there is a farmer standing beside you, and he sees it too; he observes that the horse is lazy, ewe-necked, pot-bellied, has a ring-bone on the left hind foot, and other features which relate to the purposes of agriculture. How different is your perception from his, though you are looking the same way and standing almost in the same tracks! It might be, indeed, if you chose to look a different way, and if you happened to have that genius for concentrating yourself upon what you do see which is called absent-mindedness—it might be that you would never be aware there was a horse there at all, or so much as the noise of a wagon. Thales of Miletus, the father of philosophy, owes the half of his reputation to the fact that he once walked out into the yard in a state of such rapt examination of the stars that he fell into his own well, and imparted a kind of ridiculous dignity to the pursuit of scientific knowledge that it has never lost.

To show that comparison or correlation, as well as choice, is present in consciousness, may be a little more difficult. But if we remember that "shaggy" and "picturesque" are ideas which, derived from other horses and other experiences, were stored away in our minds, and that it is now these ideas themselves which step forward and select the features of this horse and join with it to constitute a perception, and that without the ideas no clear perception, and no clear horse, could be—if we remember that, we shall see that comparison is only a little hidden in the very act of choice itself. In *strawberry roan* it is not even hidden, for we have brought out into our memories the very thing with which the horse is compared. He is like a strawberry—in color, at least, something like a decayed strawberry. In *picturesque* he is "like a picture." But in *shaggy* also, he is "like other things that have given us the idea of shagginess." Always the mind is thus fitting materials chosen from the present into patterns which it brings with it out of the past. And this activity when it becomes explicit we call thought, and when it becomes articulate we call it naming things.

Therefore, in every fresh application of a name we can discern two acts: first, the choice of a detail in the thing named, and second, comparison in that detail of the thing named with other things. These two acts are always in a certain sense one, for it is the memory that makes the choice. Naming things is like cutting doughnuts: here is an undifferentiated mass of dough, upon which the cutter, which remembers the character of other doughnuts, descends and makes after that character a definite excerpt. Exactly thus a word descends into a general impression and selects out a clear experience. It selects an experience similar to the ones which it remembers. But since in this process sometimes the act of selecting, and sometimes the act of remembering, is emphasized, we can divide names accordingly into two classes. There are names which predominantly choose, and names which predominantly compare. The words *shaggy* and *lazy,* for example, *choose* a feature of the horse, but they leave those memories with which it is to be compared, undefined. *Pot-bellied* and *strawberry roan,* on the other hand, not only choose the part and the color, but they also declare the comparison to a remembered pot and a remembered strawberry. All names are of one or the other of these two types.

With this much technical wisdom, then—if anything technical can be called wisdom—let us return to our distinction between the poetic name and the practical. We observe that their technique so far is the same; they both of them choose and compare. But practical names choose different features in an object from poetic names, and they compare the object with different memories.

Poison-flower is a practical name which chooses; it chooses the feature of its object which is of vital importance to conduct. *Scarlet-berry* is a poetic name for the same plant. *Ruminant,* as naming a lamb, is also practically selective, although its importance is for intellectual more than physical conduct. *Blunt and woolly,* on the other hand, gives you no scientific indication but a feeling of the lamb's being here.

Undulations is the name which, since Newton's attempt failed, the scientific have given to light. It is a name which not only chooses from its object features discovered with great labor and ingenuity, but compares that object with another in which the same features are more simple and obvious. It compares light to the motion of waves in a disturbed fluid. It does this in order to enable us to deal with light, and adjust ourselves to it the better. But light may truly be compared to a great many other things. It may be compared to the high notes of a flute, it may be compared to knowledge, or to the idea of perfection, or to joy. If I call light "the joy of morning," I have a name which compares and correlates two things as well as "undulation," but it does so with a different motive and a different result. It does not enable you to deal with light any better, but it promotes your realization of its intrinsic nature. It is with this aim that poetic names choose and compare.

Homer could never seem to speak of dogs but he would allude to their "white teeth," choosing that sharp feature to generate a sense of their presence. He would never say the sea, but it was "the wine-dark sea," comparing it for intensification with something else so richly luminous. The feature of Hector is "the beamy helm," and the inevitable comparison for Juno is "her ox-like eyes." But we need not go to Homer, nor to any poetry book, or book whatever, to find the world enriched with names. People with this propensity to stimulating choice and comparison, and the gift of speech, are not wanting in any village of the earth to-day. "Ye came over that hill like a greased mouse," was Jerry Chambers's greeting to an automobile party that stopped for a drink of water at his well. And "Ain't this a singin' mornin'!" is a word from the same source, "You feel as if you was gettin' born!"

Poems did not arise in books, nor in closet ecstasies either, but they arose upon the tongues of vagrants. Souls whose way was to take a wandering taste of all the toils and sorrows and battles and festive delights of the people on the earth, and talk and sing as they went—they were the poets. And they were the teachers too, for in those days there was no sense of the difference between the words of poetry and those of practice. Beautiful unions of a brave attempt at scientific nomenclature with insuppressible poetry looking through occurred commonly then, as they still occur and will always in the language of childhood.

Children are often intolerant of poetry in books, because they have it in the reality. They need no literary assistance in getting acquainted with the live qualities of objects, or endowing them with their true names. Their minds are like skies full of floating imagery, and with this they evoke the inmost essences out of common things, discovering kinships in nature incredible to science and intolerable to common sense.

The toast is a "zebra."

"Nothing with a tail" is a snake.

The cat purring is a "bumblecat."

The white eggs in the incubator have "blossomed."

But education soon robs them of this quaintness. They are taught that they must get understanding, they must not linger and behold. After education has thus reduced them, however, and taken away their many-colored world, they will often recall with pathetic pleasure a few of the phrases that fell from them in those lost days of contact with things as they are. In the same way we recall the names that were bestowed when all the world was young, and men devoted to science itself had not lost a sense of those first-hand realities whose enrichment will ultimately give to science the only sanction that it can have. Heracleitus the Dark, the greatest of the Greeks who first devised momentous new words for the world—imperious and passionate genius in the childhood of thought—he knew the world both as it lives and as it may be dealt with, nor ever clearly distinguished them, but his science is poetry and his poetry is science, carrying both conviction and fire of reality into the hearts of men to the end of time.

What shall be the true name of the soul? he asks himself. The soul is Flame! That is the living principle, the poignant instant of all nature, union of change and constancy, both terrible and beautiful, and, like thought, supremely real. Not only a stirring epithet is this, to wake you into poetry and life; it is also a vital union of two things upon which the integrity of his science and his working faith depends. You must be temperate, he says, because of this flame substance that illumines you; you must be temperate especialy in drink—keep dry within. "A dry soul is the wisest."

Such writings are no more. We are grown up and sophisticated, and we have acquired the knowledge of science and poetry. We call these noble perceptions "mere figures of speech"; by which we mean, or ought to mean, that they create unions which, although contributing to the wealth of immediate experience, cannot to any extent be acted upon. Our ideal in maturity is not to confuse with them the unions which indicate conduct, nor ever to mistake the one kind of speaking for the other.

In the pursuit of practical knowledge we apply names which select in an experience the details that are *important,* whether for our special purpose or for general human purposes; and we unite that experience through such names with other experiences that are familiar and toward which we have an established attitude or reaction. The purpose of it all is adjustment. In the pursuit of poetic expression we apply names which select in an experience details which are *salient,* offering a good focus for the receptive attention, and we unite that experience through such names with other experiences which are surprising or stimulating, which give pause and alertness to the mind. The purpose of this is realization.

IV

THE TECHNIQUE OF POETIC NAMES

Terms are commonly supposed to perform the two functions of indicating things and suggesting their significance in human economy. But besides indicating things, and without relating them at all to human economy, they continually perform this third function of enriching the very experience of the things. Until this is understood, the natural origin of poetry will not be understood. We add the names to the things in order to enhance our participation in their being. Here is the expression, from a nature utterly poetic, of the state of mind which such a use of names fulfils:

"When I am in a room with people, if I ever am free from speculating upon the creations of my own brain, then not myself goes home to myself, but the identity of every one in the room begins to press upon me [so] that I am in a very little time annihilated. Not only among men; it would be the same in a nursery of children."

". . . if a sparrow come before my window, I take part in its existence, and pick about the gravel."[1]

It is marvellous to know that mere words, with their little acts of selecting and comparing, could contribute anything to vivify the experience of one so sensitive to reality. Yet it is true that he could hardly look upon a thing he loved without longing for the poetic name and searching it out, whether in the language of others or in his own mind. It is marvellous, indeed, because words are such tiny dry bits of things compared with the great flush objects that the world is full of. And yet if we remember how intimate and strong a part these little words have played in the very making of those objects what they are

[1]Quoted from letters of John Keats. W. M. Rossetti's *Life,* pp. 154–155.

in our experience, we shall understand how it is that the poetic love them. They love the appropriate name—whether it be a name that selects or a name that compares—because through it they are able in a way to encompass with consciousness the object to which it is applied.

As for the first kind, the selective poetic name, its value for this purpose is simple to understand. It guides the attention to a focus. And this service, though it may seem slight in the proposal, is in fact very great, and for the majority indispensable to the acute realization of anything. Even to that lucky few who are by nature awake when their eyes are open, the living word is no superfluity. He who can speak it, who can sometimes catch the humor of their sensibility and crystallize it upon a point, is as dear to them as he is tedious who can neither select a focus nor remain silent, but spreads adjectives all over the face of nature.

It is difficult to exemplify this gift, because in life the applicability of the choicest name is so often transient and specific. Some old white horse may look exactly "as if he had been used to scratch matches on," but this would be one out of a million white horses. Certain water-weeds in a swift stream may be called "yearning," but not so all water-weeds in all streams. Perhaps you have heard some one speak of the "sucking utterance" of a person, or the "dancing" of a voice, or the "shadowy haste" of a gray cat, and while the suitability of the word at the moment was so great as to make a little crisis in experience, it could hardly be reproduced after the moment was gone.

And yet poetic words which are generally, or again and again, applicable, abide in the memories of some people, and come out at the appropriate times to help them see. How many there must be wandering in the world who can never look at minnows in a brook but they see them stay "their *wavy* bodies 'gainst the streams," or listen to the gray flies but they hear them wind their *"sultry* horn." Doubtless there is a special passion for the word in some, and others just as poetic are less articulate in their modes of realization. But the average man is so deeply social that some part of the machinery of communication is present in his simplest perception. The more alive he is, the more likely is a word hovering near his lips.

"Million-footed Manhattan" is not the name to guide you in making your way to the metropolis, but if it chances to echo perfectly in your mind, it gives a gift to the journey.

> "Million-footed Manhattan, unpent, descends to her pavements."

So of the minnows—when you watch them now, those "wavy" bodies, and—

> "How they ever wrestle
> With their own sweet delight, and ever nestle
> Their silver bellies on the pebbly sand"—

you know them as they existed for one with the supreme gift of realization. You know them more intimately, and you like them better.

"Here are sweet-peas," he said, "on tip-toe for a flight"—a phrase which will give grace, better than water, to your garden. For words make the world grow—not, I think, because they express a feeling, for that means that they relieve you of it, but because they give to the feeling locality and distinct body. It comes down like dew out of the general air and alights here in a bright drop.

Even without a word, it is thus that we make what we love our own. Notice how specific you become in the presence of a loved object, and how all your tenderness or your delight seems to distil itself and hang upon a certain motion of that object, or a certain pencilling, or shining glance, or shadow. It is no strange, ancient, or bookish trick to greet things with epithets; it is the way the mind always welcomes an experience. And the more hot and electric its passion for that experience, the more it narrows itself to a single item and condenses there the whole ecstasy. In the midst of such passion, to be able to select with perfect intuition or judgment the item that will support and enhance it, is the first half of the poetic gift.

The second half, and that which is more susceptible of cultivation, is the power to evoke into the clear light of thought those specific memories of similar things that hover above every acute perception. The chambers of all minds are stored with them; they are latent in every common noun, or verb, or adjective, or adverb; so natural to us that in childhood we have trouble to distinguish them from the sensible reality, and yet for most of us in maturity blurred into non-existence by custom and the pressure of affairs. But linger to taste the flavor of any moment in your experience, and you will find vistas opening backward into other experiences which clarify and intensify it. They determine its being.

So essential is this union of two things similar in difference to the very existence, or definition, of human consciousness, that we cannot help believing it describes all consciousness, both in its essence and in its origin. It is the comfortable fortune of a clam to be so limited in sensations that the experience of today is almost exactly the same as the experience of yesterday, and may be dealt with in the same manner. Hence almost his whole life must be as unprovoking to him as the little daily act of buttoning and unbuttoning is to us. He is hardly ever roused into awareness of his environment at all. Nothing will rouse him, indeed, but an accident—the discomfort of an unfamiliar sensation. This he will have to attend to, and in some flickering adumbration of genuine perception, decide to which of the old sensations it is most similar, and respond to it accordingly. His being conscious in that moment depends upon the shock of difference and the need of similarity. It is an act of uniting or identifying two things that are similar although different.

And so is all consciousness, in a profound way of speaking, a uniting of two things that are similar in difference. In the practical or onward course of evolution it was only thus, as a detector of similitude, that consciousness ever arose. And since we are all, by the continuing irony of nature, essentially practical and onward, it is still only thus that consciousness appears in us. As soon as we become genuinely aware of anything, we are already receiving a hint or intimation of its likeness to something else. We are uniting the present with the past; for this function our minds exist.

And therefore it is no great exaggeration to say that one who cannot perform this function, and who never responds to an intimation of similarity, has no mind at all, but belongs among the mollusks or the dead. Only we must not make the mistake of identifying with one who does not respond to any similarity, one whose response is to abhor all those that are poetic, or presented for the sake of consciousness itself. He is not a clam but a practical man. A clam, indeed, would be more likely, upon the stimulus of some boisterous morning current, to glance round among certain irrelevant sensations of his just to "see what they are like," than would the practical man to contemplate for the wink of an eye-lash a poetic similitude. He calls them mere metaphors, and thinks that in so doing he has relegated them to a region as far off as possible from the righteous business of scientific, effective, or "real" identification.

Yet they are exactly the same thing, with the same basis in reality, only free from the domination of prospective conduct and employed for the sake of reality itself. They are correlations proposed, without reference to action, by those who desire consciousness for its own sake. It is as though the poets, seeing that we are all so blindly practical—we are made like tops to go to sleep running unless something upsets us—had determined to rouse us out of this too mechanical condition, and show us the world. And they have discovered an adroit and profound method for accomplishing this. Instead of interrupting our operations and making us wake only to the interruption, they insert into our minds direct the very essence of wakefulness—similarity in difference—and make us wake to anything under the sun that they choose. And that is the explanation, if for so original a fact explanation is possible, of the value to poetic perception of the names which compare.

It is customary in books about rhetoric and prosody to state, as an elucidation of certain figures of speech, that the cultivated mind takes a peculiar delight in apprehending a similarity in difference—a statement which is accepted in silence by the obedient pupil, and harbored in his true heart as one more evidence of the triviality of the cultivated mind and the great foolishness of having one. But we ought to state the case in this way: that mind, so far as we can distinguish it, *is* similarity in difference, it is a state of comparison, and what it takes delight in is the experience of the nature of things. Such a statement, besides approximating the truth, would have the advantage of suggesting to the pupil that his mind is probably a good deal more poetic than that of his cultivated teacher.

Imagine that we hear, or rather we are seized by, a loud and prolonged whistle-blast from across the river. It ends abruptly, and while some are trying in a maundering way to say that the change seemed very sharp, one whom we will call the poet, or the namer, states that "you feel as if you had been over there and got back." Will this be a special delight to the cultivated only, or will it be the common pleasure of all those who are fond of a sensation and want to get the full savor of it? Whatsoever they were fond of, they would love to have their vague, fumbling, and yet unique, awareness of it suddenly set forth for them articulate, and consummate, and clear, in a climax of the essence of consciousness. And that would be the manifestation not primarily of a love of "similarity," but of a love of the qualities of things. And that is the love that is fed by the utterances of the poet or the child.

He will say that the clouds are *like pop-corn,* and every one will pause and look up at the sky with pleasure. Or he will say that sumach-trees are *like poor people,* or that a peewee's note comes to you through the air *like an arrow*. Or, even in a more conventionalized and common way, he will call a man *goatish,* or *half-baked,* or *off his trolley;* or he will say that he has *butter-fingers,* as they do in baseball. A boy *gets jumped on* by the teacher; a girl is as *gay as a merry-go-round.* These are all, in their various ways, utterances of the poet among us, increasing our taste of the reality by selective comparison.

He it is that all down the path of human experience has been speaking, and has established such poetry in the heart of language. Nor can we in any way better understand him, and these two gifts of his, than by turning again to the dictionary and looking into the story of the births of words. *Gymnasium,* "the place of nakedness," was the work of a poet who *chose;* and I think he chose the best, as well as the most striking, feature of his object. *Sarcasm,* "flesh-tearing," was the creation of a poet who not only chose but also compared. He united an experience which is spiritual with one which is different in being physical but similar in the sheer quality of pain. We said that he might call a man *goatish,* and ages ago in the word *capricious* he has done so. In the word *insult* he has said that he "got jumped on." He has called men *half-baked* also, or at least *cooked too quick* in the word *precocious;* and in the word *delirious* he has called them, not *off their trolley,* but what is the same thing in an earlier state of civilization, *out of their furrow.* More beautifully in a word like *moss-rose* he has made his choice and comparison, and in *ruby-throat,* and *fire-tail,* and all those names of flowers and wild birds, uniting them always with something of invasive individuality, and usually with something beautiful because they are beautiful.

Birds were the first minstrels, and their notes slip like clear joy into the heart. Who has not a "Hail to thee, blithe spirit!" for the least of these aërial beings! Feathered voices, who can thrill with tiny energy acres of the dull air, and set quivering even in man's heaviest breast vague hopes of an eternal spring. Commonly and of old they have been named with words of subtle discriminating affection, brief perfect utterances, a poetry of the people. And rarest among them all, perhaps, in adoring realism—rarest of all, to one who knows at twilight the place of her wild and tender rhapsody, the swamp-angel.

Crests of nature's loveliness, thus tuned, thus dyed, and thus proportioned, the birds and blossoms have won out of all tribes a treasury of poetic names. And they who have the genius or desire to make poignant through language beings that are less easily or less quickly loved, will not alter the method here simply revealed. They will select in each a certain part or quality, and in a strong revery of the mind unite it with something they remember that is different, but in that high quality the same. They will name it after that. And a world that is sufficiently drab and monotonous to one whose mental indolence is great, or who has sophistication for an ideal, will be rich and wonderful to them.

V

IMAGINATIVE REALIZATION

In expectation and revery realization is often more perfect than in the too obdurate presence of things. And with this observation we pass into a domain more commonly called poetic. Yet it should be with regret that we take farewell of reality, in the perception of which poetry arises, and to the developed perception of which it descends again for sanction and for praise. Ideally poetry would always be a vivifying, through the magic of imagery and syllable, of present experience in an adventurous world. But the limitations of time and space and individuality are too tight, and therefore, provided we are healthily rooted in our own now and here, it becomes a thing of joy and benefit to us that we can so vividly remember and imagine, and through the clear medium of poetic language realize in dreams the experience of others.

Yet never let us pass to a consideration of those dreams without a protest against the opinion that makes their unreality the essence or the excellence of them. On the contrary, their essence and their excellence is the contribution which they make of poignancy and breadth and life and celebration, to the actual wherewith each dreamer re-engages. And no more than science can hold sway over the minds of men except as it contributes to their purposes or enlarges them, no more can poetry strongly survive in any individual except as it gives enrichment to the real presence of the world before him.

That this gift of realization can be given in the absence of things often better than in their presence, however melancholy it may be, and again suggesting an irony in nature, is a very manifest truth. Greedy people eat fast instead of slow, because their heart's enjoyment lies always in the next bite after the one that they have in their mouths. If sensual stimulation were really equal to their expectations, I suppose you could hardly induce them to swallow at all. Such hyper-æsthetic anticipation is a part of the onward or practical mechanism of nature, and so it may be explained. But reminiscence also is frequently better than experience, as is shown in the wonderfully rich and adventurous past that most dullards are able to enjoy. How dear to our hearts are the scenes of our childhood, and with what exquisite satisfaction we recall the old-fashioned winters that are no more, and the reckless skaters we used to be in those days. In the city we complete our love of the country and long to greet it again; in the country, some afternoon under a tree, we get the full flavor of our energetic life in the city, and think we but half realized the great drama we were taking part in all winter.

Here we are free from those practical necessities which were ever whipping us forward from one thing to another; we can loiter over the same course with a more discursive enthusiasm. A man in the pressure of affairs bent upon taking life poetically is like a mule trying to browse while he is driven; his mouthfuls will be hasty and unsatisfying, and at the same time his progress slow. This is one of the reasons why the poetic cultivate their power of reminiscence, and even learn to enjoy the finest savors of an experience after it is past.

Not only do they outwit necessity by this means, however, but they get free from a distraction which disintegrates the experience of anything actual. Actual things are never isolated and framed for our enjoyment as things are in revery. Things in memory are finely focalized and made seizable, unified, and indeed perfected, by the narrowing of their space and time extent, and the omission of whatever opposes or derogates from the feature chosen to be the apex of our attention to them. For as in the perception of things there is always a favored point, still more in the remembrance. In fact, the mind does not remember things at all, but retains mementos of them

—images, we say, of some little, perhaps trivial, detail, about which clings a diffuse sense of their presence. And even as a crucifix or a warmed jewel can sometimes more than console us for the absence of the thing we love best in the world, so can these dyed fragments that the mind collects revive the thrill of our bodies, revive and concentrate it upon themselves, so that they seem to equal or surpass the reality.

Perhaps it will be a fairer explanation, or at least a truer statement, of this superiority of the past, to say that in memory, since there is so little left of the sense-quality of the object, there is more room for emotion in our consciousness of it. And this is true also of anticipation and pure imagination. Our body joins in the apprehension of a thing better when the thing has no body of its own. That is why ghosts are extremely terrible, because they are almost never seen; but when they are seen, if we can believe the reports of those acquainted with them, their presence is not half so effective. And naked bodies are like ghosts in this respect. They are not seen often enough. The carnal appetite is sometimes intolerable, like a scourge, until it comes into the bare presence of its object, when, whether satisfied or not, it becomes quite simple and manageable. So does anger in some people faint at the encounter; and humiliation, and reverence, and love, and wonder appear to die away before a fact, as many proverbs attest.[1] Palpable reality is a kind of sedative, and as such it is often avoided by those who wish to become and remain excited over the qualities of things.

Not only can they realize many things better in their absence, indeed, but they can *enjoy* the realization of more things. Our zeal for being is immensely extended in the

[1]Absence makes the heart grow fonder.
No man is a hero to his valet.
Distance lends enchantment.
Familiarity breeds contempt.
A prophet is not without honor save in his own country.

thought of it. We call that "adventure" in the retrospect which in the event we called fright; we call that "pathos" which we called pain; and we call that "life" which was sharp agony to be shunned with all our force. The quality of these experiences is recalled and even intensified, but without that organic oppressiveness which drowned the poetic impulse. We are free to love them now with the original love of being.

And this freedom that we have in revery is excelled only by the freedom of sympathetic imagination, in which we transcend even these limits of individuality and drink in the experience of others. Here our realization is both fine and utterly catholic. If these others chance to be quite outside the place and time of our living, as usually the poets are, we rejoice in the possession of their utmost pains and passions. That enthusiasm of our childhood for every impress of the existing world that was endurable and accessible to us is now extended to embrace all things that ever presented themselves to the apprehension of a man. If our stomachs are strong—or our imaginations not too strong—we are attracted to the contemplation in this way of things disgusting and lecherous and full of murder, things that issuing or appearing before us in solids and liquids would sicken us to our entrails. We are attracted to all vivid realization whatsoever, as though we were some kind of blessed gods who, having made the world, were satisfied that it was good in every part.

This opportunity to behold and praise the universe we most of us owe to the power of poetic words. For the faculty of creating realizations is limited and unusual; and it is through the names that others give to their own experience, or to enlargements upon their experience, that usual persons are enabled to escape from the prison of themselves and get tastes of the general world.

While, therefore, poetic names are valuable to the complete perception of a thing, and still more to the clear memory or expectation of it, to that free realization by imaginative sympathy in which we make all human experience our own they are absolutely essential. And their method in this culminating function is exactly what it is in the simplest apprehension to which they contribute. In naming an imagined thing they select parts or qualities upon which to rest the attention, and then compare that thing with others imagined, similar in those parts or qualities. "O you temples," says the poet, "fairer than lilies, pour'd over by the rising sun!" And to the responsive heart comes a sense or vision of these ancient wonders, more poignant and more memorable, perhaps, than if they had been actually seen and examined, with no poet there to speak the magic syllables.

VI

CHOICE AND COMPARISON IN POETRY

POETIC choice is not a choice of things to be realized, remember, for to this end anything may be chosen. But poetic choice is a second choice, within the thing to be realized, of a focus that will intensify the realization. Suppose that we are gazing with a kind of vague affection toward a summer sky; any one by uttering the words "So near!" or "The nearness of it!" can be pleasing to us. These little words precipitate the thing we had in solution. And theirs is the simplest articulate poetry, just that single naming of a quality or part in the whole presence of a thing.

When, however, the thing is absent—when we are not gazing at a summer sky at all, but still the poet wishes us to realize it, he must say more than a single word. He must say enough both to indicate the sky as a whole, and then also the focal part or quality. "The sky so near," he must say, or "The nearness of the sky!" And that is how poetic choice appears in what we may call poetry proper, or imaginative realization through language. Everywhere its words are doing two things, they are indicating experiences in general and then suggesting specific details.

> "The old pond, aye! and the sound
> Of a frog leaping into the water,"

is the literal translation of a classic poem of Japan, one that they say every Japanese has by heart. I quote it because it reveals the act of poetic choice so simply. The general environment, one very full and rich with beautiful or moving details, is named, and then immediately the most characteristic of these details.

"The end of autumn, and some rooks
Are perched upon a withered branch."

"Aye! New Year's day, with a clear sky,
And conversation among the sparrows!"

These little utterances—*Hokku* they are called—consisting of seventeen syllables arranged in lines of five, seven, and then five, are the characteristic poetry of Japan. They are without rhyme or reason—just each a single act of poetic choice or comparison, to stand or fall by its own merits. And in most of them apparently the act of choice is accomplished, as in the examples above, by placing a general term first and then the specific details in co-ordination.

The general term does not always stand in the body of the work, but may appear as a title. The following little motion-picture is the winning poem from a public competition in which the general term was proposed by the arbiter. I quote from an English critic:

"The subject has been a 'Spring Breeze,' and to understand the significance of the verse we must remember that in Japan carpenters plane their wood in the open air, and that the curling wood-shaving is the exact shape of the Japanese letter 'no.' Here is the poem:

"'As I walked past the carpenter's, the no-letters chased me down the lane.'"

Sometimes, however, the realization is all conveyed in a simple declarative sentence as though it were information, and in these cases—as in our own poems, where the impulse to realize is hardly ever isolated—it is a little more difficult to trace the poetic act. Here the chief detail of what we might call a "sea-picture" appears as a solitary statement of fact:

"There, by the crescent moon, the shark
Has hid his head beneath the wave."

More often the chosen detail is subordinated still further, and appears as an adjective, or adverb, or phrase, or clause, modifying the general term.

> "*Without a word of warning,* there
> In th' autumn sky, Mount Fuji stands."

> "How *carefully* begin to bud
> In winter the camellia-trees."

These are rather serene and quiet pictures, where the name of the detail is subsequent and subordinate to the name of the thing. But as the poetic impulse grows intense the detail is more and more elevated, and the general term sinks into subordination, or if it can be somehow understood, it disappears altogether.

This is the tiny threnody of a Japanese mother, Chiyo, at the loss of her child:

> "Where may he have gone off to-day,—
> My dragon-fly hunter?"

She does not say, as the others would:

> "My boy who used to chase dragon-flies."

No, she makes the detail, the dragon-fly chasing, *be* the boy. That is the intenser art.

Here, in a different vein, is even a more incisive etching:

> "Spring Shower—an umbrella and rain-coat walk along conversing."

In this poem the detail of two covered people walking down the street together is chosen from the general aspect of the shower, and placed in a subordinate phrase; but afterward, within that detail, a more exquisite choice is made, and it is made sharply. There is no mention of the people at all, just those two *parts of them,* the rain-coat and the umbrella, walk along conversing! Such effects are produced by a man who is not afraid to let the poetic impulse dominate him, making his logical import ridiculous.

"They have slain the servants with *the edge* of the sword."

"There came a great wind from the wilderness, and smote *the four corners* of the house."

That is how choice utters itself when realization is intense. And almost throughout our English Bible it is intense. Poetry exists there in the old stories and songs, poetry of the very strongest, without metre, without metaphor, and even where the translator has lost all rhythm of speech. It exists in the choice of practically superfluous but poignant details, which irresistibly invade the mind.

"Woe unto them that devise iniquity,
And *plot evil upon their beds*."

"Bring out the prisoner from the dungeon,
And *them that sit in darkness* from the prison-house."

That parallelism of phrases, which is the structural feature of Hebrew verse, lets appear the true motive of poetry almost as nakedly as the Japanese Hokku. With them the whole poem is mere realization; with the Hebrews there is a practical intent, there is discourse, but that intent being more than fulfilled in the first line, the second, or the second two, are pure realization of the subject discoursed of. And in them therefore this almost fanatical specification of the minute detail.

"I will not suffer mine eyes to sleep,
Nor mine *eyelids* to slumber."

"Let not them that are mine enemies wrongfully rejoice over me:
Neither let them *wink with the eye* that hate me without a cause."

"He heard my voice out of his temple;
And my cry before him *came into his ears*."

"All they that see me laugh me to scorn:
They *shoot out the lip*——"

It is not really a long step from this flaming poetry to the modern utterances of Walt Whitman, a mystic too, forever hinting at something behind, or beyond, and yet in the depth of his soul loving the inevitable and temporal qualities of things here.

There is no better place to learn the difference between poetry and practical language than in his book, which is a grand mixture of the two. Take those lines beginning "What do you see, Walt Whitman?"—you can mark off whole blocks of them in which, being entirely satisfied with his own vision and himself, he makes no effort to let the reader see, he merely names things with their practical names. And then you can choose other lines and passages of supreme poetry, passages in which, as he himself says, he builds not with words but with materials:

"He puts things in their attitudes,
He puts to-day out of himself with plasticity and love."

Compare the two following sets of lines and you will feel this difference. You will feel the difference between words and things.

(1)

"I see plainly the Himalayas, Chian Shahs, Altays, Ghauts."

"I see the Brazilian vaquero;
I see the Bolivian ascending Mount Sorata."

"You Japanese man or woman! You liver in Madagascar, Ceylon, Sumatra, Borneo!
All you continentals of Asia, Africa, Europe, Australia, indifferent of place!"

(2)

"I see a great round wonder rolling through the air;

. . . .

I see the shaded part on one side, where the sleepers are sleeping—and the sunlit part on the other side,
I see the curious silent change of the light and shade."

"I see the battle-fields of the earth—grass grows upon them, and blossoms and corn."

"I see the place of the innocent rich life and hapless fate of the beautiful nocturnal son, the full-limb'd Bacchus."

"You beautiful-bodied Persian, at full speed in the saddle, shooting arrows to the mark!"

"You Austral negro, naked, red, sooty, with protrusive lip, grovelling, seeking your food!"

"You thoughtful Armenian, pondering by some stream of the Euphrates! you peering amid the ruins of Nineveh!"

"You Hottentot with clicking palate! You woolly-hair'd hordes!
You own'd persons dropping sweat-drops or blood-drops!
You human forms with the fathomless ever-impressive countenances of brutes!"

One reason why Walt Whitman, having this gift of conveying realizations to the very highest, mixed them with so much dead stuff is that he wanted his poetry to be like the world, to "tally nature," as he says, and have passages not beautiful nor conventionally poetic. But this ambition might have been satisfied by introducing in vivid reality things which are not usually introduced. It does not demand that things should be introduced without vivid reality. There are no abstract passages in nature. There are no catalogues of common names. Nature does not exist in classes—blacksmiths, carpenters, oil-works, white-lead works—but exists in the smoke and sweat of individual specimens. Nature does not signify by names but by qualities. And when, like her, the poet enlivens with an act of choice a certain member of his tedious processions, no matter what member it is, we are glad, and loath to depart from it. The energy of such a phrase is contagious, and for a little way on both sides of it the procession moves.

"I see the camel, the wild steed, the bustard, the fat-tail'd sheep, the antelope, and the burrowing wolf."

Observe how that "fat-tail'd" sheep emerges, gives you a sensation, and then lends a bit of his vitality to the whole parade. Leave that out and there is no parade, it is merely a list. But as it is, the camel and the wild steed both prick up their ears to see that fattail coming, and there is a real poetic quality in the whole line.

Turn from this poem, in which as in so much of his writing Whitman lacks abandon, there is too much of the conscious pulpiteer—turn from it to those poems in which he forgets. The psalm in realization of the death of Abraham Lincoln, the "Song of the Open Road," "Crossing Brooklyn Ferry," "Out of the Cradle Endlessly Rocking"—there where the poet loses himself in the things he names, the poetry is not failing. It is sustained, and moreover it is perfectly simple.

"Mighty Manhattan, with spires, and the sparkling and hurrying tides, and the ships——"

"The most excellent sun, so calm and haughty——"

"The high-spread sky——"

"The huge and thoughtful night——"

"The fragrant cedars and the ghostly pines so still——"

These are all seen in the sorrow of his great poem, just as in life a child first sees them, vividly and wonderfully.

"Day come white or night come black——"

is but the poet's, and the child's, way of saying "day or night." It is the act of poetic choice at its simplest, the salient quality being merely the most obvious of all—too obvious to be named anywhere but in the language of genius.

"Lithe and silent the Hindu appears."

"The friendly and flowing savage."

"The sagging moon."

"Immense and silent moon."

"Over the hoarse surging of the sea."

In these the choice of a quality is more subtle, and in the last one more emphasized also, for the quality begins to be elevated above the thing again. It is not, "Over the sea with its hoarse surge," but

"Over the hoarse surging."

And he might have omitted the sea altogether, as in this line he has omitted the flying:

"And every day the he-bird *to-and-fro*."

These highest degrees of the act of poetic choice, letting the attribute or part supplant entirely the customary name of the thing, have received from scholars some long names—metonymy and synecdoche—and have been classified by them in total separation from the poetic use of adjectives and adverbs and coordinate expressions. They have been called "figures of speech." And a figure of speech is defined as an *indirect* way of naming things.

"Spring Shower—an umbrella and rain-coat walk along conversing."

That is metonymy. Tell yourself that it is an "indirect" way of naming things.

"They have slain the servants with the *edge* of the sword."

That is synecdoche, also an "indirect" way of speaking.

The treatment in rhetorical theory of figures of speech appears to be one of the greatest blunders that an over-spectacled scholarship ever obtruded upon the world. It is due, I believe, to the fact that all discourse was assumed by Aristotle's scholastic successors to be practical in its primary intent; and from the stand-point of a practical intent it *is* indirect to say an umbrella when your logical subject is a man. From the stand-point of a poetic intent, however, an intent to put a man before the eyes *umbrella-foremost,* it is supremely direct. It excels exactly in directness the use of modifiers.

Yet that ancient classification and definition, important or at least interesting to one who studies the mechanics of connected speech, but of the least possible significance in the psychology of poetic inspiration or appreciation, is still forced upon the novice as one of the keys to the enjoyment of poetry. He must learn how lovely it is to be indirect, and when you set out to go somewhere, instead of going there, to back up and turn round and go somewhere else. This is so difficult for a plain man to learn that I think we may set it down as the chief academic obstacle to the enjoyment of imaginative literature. "Figures of speech"—"metonymy," "synecdoche," and other long-tailed monsters—are what bar the entrance of a simple human into the realm of poetry.

The reason for mentioning only two at this point is that we have now arrived at a suitable place to forget these two. It ought to be possible to obliterate them entirely from the mind, making room in their place for the simple truth that if a speaker's impulse is poetic, words that suggest salient parts or qualities of the things he mentions will stand out over the general names of the things. It is because he seeks to attain and convey to us a sense of the actual existence of those things. And for us things actually exist always with some part or quality thus predominant.

Some who have felt the poetry of the phrases we quoted will think that it lies rather in the choice of words than in the choice of qualities. We might state, for instance, that the moon is "near the horizon and convex at the bottom" instead of "sagging," that the savage "glides with a continuous grace of movement," instead of "flowing," and, while indicating the same qualities that the poet did, we should not convey the same realization. And that is entirely true, and it is due to the fact that the act of choice is altogether inseparable from the act of comparison. And every word which comes forth to name an experience in the present comes forth out of a past in which it has been the name of other experiences. And these it cannot forget. "Convex" compares the moon to what?—to lenses, to spectacles, to circles of paper. What does it remember? It remembers the school-room and the laboratory. And what have they, the school-room and laboratory, that they can bring as an offering to the pure perception of the moon late-risen upon a sorrowful evening? No, they are to be shunned earnestly, and that is why it appears that realization depends as much upon the choice of words as of qualities. It depends upon the comparison of things, and words are the bearers of comparison.

Suppose that we say,

> "Day come light, or night come dark,"

then we have nearly eliminated comparison, for *dark* is a word that remembers only other nights, and *light* remembers other days. Therefore, while these words, by their very superfluity, bear witness to the poetic impulse, the poetry that they generate is very watery indeed. But "black" and "white" have other memories, and much incipient or potential comparison will therefore enrich that day or night in which they choose the quality.

"The flowing savage" is a name which contains choice and comparison in high equilibrium. To one who already knew and loved the fluid motion of an Indian's body, it would be difficult to say which is the more perfect, the instinct that caught it, or the art that could just intimate rivers, melodies—its true companions.

Every line of poetry is pregnant with such latent comparisons;

it is a kind of menace. And just as with rapture the act of choice overtops the meaning, and the customary name is omitted, so also with rapture the act of comparison. The menace is fulfilled. Out of that imminence of vague memories suddenly shoots down into your very speech a concrete reality, and you utter, not the name of your logical subject, but the name of this other that is similar.

"The white arms out in the breakers tirelessly tossing."
"With angry moans the fierce old *mother* incessantly moaning."
"I will *toss* the new gladness and roughness among them."

Let this third example remind us that all we have said applies to verbs and adverbs, as well as to nouns and adjectives. "I will *generate with words,* will *stimulate by my presence,* a new gladness and roughness," would be a more practical expression, but *toss* comes forward inevitably and the sentence lives.

When comparison becomes as overt as this, it too is seized upon by the rhetoricians, cut off from the use of poetic modifiers or co-ordinate expressions, and called "metaphor." I am not sure but *the flowing savage* contains a comparison sufficiently manifest to fall under this misfortune. It might be called a "trope," or some other word to signify a shunting off, or blockage, of the general course of business. But I am sure that no essential difference for poety exists between its use and the use of any rich adjective, such as "lithe," or, upon the other hand, the use of two names and a particle, or copula, to express the comparison between them—"The savage who moves like a stream."

Say that a creature is *pale*—you have some comparison with other pale things. Say that he is *ghastly,* the other things emerge nearer; *ghostly,* still nearer; *ghost-like, ghost-pale,* they are imminent; and *pale as the ghosts of the dead,* they are upon you.

This is an essentially homogeneous list. But every rhetorician will make two abrupt divisions in it. *Pale* and *ghastly* he will let go as "direct," "normal," "literal" names. At *ghostly* he will make a great leap over nothing, and call it a "metaphor"; at *ghost-like* another leap, and call it a "simile." Moreover, if you say, "This creature is like a ghost," he will call it simile; but if you say, "He is a mere ghost," it is metaphor. These distinctions, which have to do with the small points of sentence structure, being pushed forward as something to watch for in poetry, greatly obstruct the natural love of it, and moreover occupy the place of a distinction which would really further its appreciation.

For there are, in the literature of realization, two very different kinds of comparison. There are illuminating, or intensifying, comparisons, where the things recalled only shed a light of strong reality upon the subject of discourse. Such are the metaphors we have been considering, and also both the similes and metaphors in the following lines:

"The words of his mouth were smoother than butter,
But war was in his heart;
His words were softer than oil,
Yet were they drawn swords."

"There is no faithfulness in their mouth;
Their throat is an open sepulchre——"

"But I am a worm, and no man——"

"Rottenness entereth into my bones."

"My heart is like wax; it is melted in the midst of my bowels——"

"I am poured out like water——"

On the other hand, there are comparisons in which the poetic impulse runs out into the things recalled, and you have a little excursion of realization away from the subject of discourse. And these we may call discursive or holiday comparisons, since they are so happily defiant of practical progress. They occur most frequently in the childhood of literature.

"The Lord is my shepherd;
I shall not want.

He maketh me to lie down in green pastures:
He leadeth me beside the still waters.
He restoreth my soul——"

"As for man, his days are as grass:
As a flower of the field, so he flourisheth.
For the wind passeth over it, and it is gone;
And the place thereof shall know it no more."

Here for a moment man is quite forgotten in the tragedy of that little flower; and before, I think, the Lord was almost forgotten in a pastoral idyl.

Such wandering in a simile from the original subject, while yet the original subject sustains and dignifies your enjoyment, is a special experience. It is poetically different from the purely illuminative use of comparison, because the realization lies for a moment in a new direction. Therefore the distinction of these two—although far less precise than the ones that the rhetorics draw—is of true importance to us.

"Allegory" and "fable" and "parable," and what has been called in Hebrew literature "direct metaphor," are poetry of this kind. "Direct metaphor" is simply an allegory with no overt transfer of names, no explanation of its symbolism. It is not more direct than other metaphors, but it is more extended. One occurs in Ecclesiastes beginning:

"Remember now thy Creator in the days of thy youth——"

from which it has taxed the generations to extract the proper meaning. The same kind of metaphor occurs in the poetry of primitive people, and the same difficulty arises when we try to enjoy, or even to perceive, the comparisons in this poetry. We do not understand its metaphors, and even after they are explained we cannot *feel* their appropriateness, because the objects named have so different a flavor to our affections from what they had to those who named them. This is a "Song of the Spirit Dance" among the Arapaho Indians:

"Wading passed I through
Yellow waters,
Wading passed I through
Yellow waters,
Ah, 'twas e'en, e'en the turtle lake—
Yellow waters—
Ah, 'twas e'en, e'en the turtle lake—
Yellow waters."

Dante has often this primitive quality. Allegory and extended metaphor are so natural to his mind that all his language, even in a prose translation, has a strange sound to us. He seems, almost like a bashful person, to shrink from naming the real subject of discourse, always intimating or indicating what it is by dwelling with a grave expression upon something else.

Now all these formal uses of comparison, being poetically different both in motive and effect, ought to be separated from the merely illuminative simile and metaphor. Only they ought not to be separated from discursive simile, which is the same thing in a far sweeter and more spontaneous form. The love of what lies at the *other side* of a comparison happens to carry us away, and we wander over there to look for a minute, before going on with the main poem.

"He shall feed his flocks like a shepherd.
He shall gather the lambs in his arm,
And carry them in his bosom,
And shall gently lead those that give suck."

Only from the point of view of practical discourse, of the pure effort to convey a meaning, can any of this language be called indirect, or out of the simple and natural. The moment the poetic impulse is acknowledged, and to the extent that it is acknowledged, any true comparison appears entirely direct and primitive. See it, as we saw poetic choice, in the second member of a parallelism, where the meaning is already satisfied:

"Whose confidence shall break asunder,
And whose trust is a spider's web."

Or see it in those verses from the Japanese, which have no practical motive, but are the atoms of poetry:

> "Fall'n flower returning to the branch,—
> Behold! it is a butterfly."

See it thus, and that sense of anything indirect, anything "turning aside," in poetic comparison, is impossible. Still more impossible if we look again to the very origins of formal poetry.

> "Beautiful, lo, the summer clouds,
> Beautiful, lo, the summer clouds,
> Blossoming clouds in the sky
> Like unto shimmering flowers——"

is the substance of a dance song among the Zuñi Indians. And this is a Hopi lullaby:

> "Puva, puva, puva,[1]
> In the trail the beetles
> On each other's backs are sleeping,
> So on mine, my baby, thou
> Puva, puva, puva."

Sometimes in our own literature this sense of a whole poem as pure poetry is conveyed through a device called apostrophe. And apostrophe, by the irony of rhetoric, means "turning away." It is turning away from the progress of your argument in order to realize something you have mentioned. But happily in certain cases there is no argument, and there has been none, and so there can be no turning away, but the whole poem is a pure turning toward. An example from William Blake is appropriate here, because, like the other poems we have referred to, it makes its appeal almost without the help of metrical music; it is poetry through the perfection of poignant choice and comparison.

"TO THE EVENING STAR

> "Thou fair-haired Angel of the Evening,
> Now whilst the sun rests on the mountains, light

[1]"Puva" is a verb meaning sleep.

Thy bright torch of love—thy radiant crown
Put on, and smile upon our evening bed!
Smile on our loves; and while thou drawest the
Blue curtains of the sky, scatter thy silver dew
On every flower that shuts its sweet eyes
In timely sleep. Let thy west wind sleep on
The lake; speak silence with thy glimmering eyes
And wash the dusk with silver.—Soon, full soon,
Dost thou withdraw; then the wolf rages wide,
And the lion glares through the dun forest.
The fleeces of our flocks are covered with
Thy sacred dew; protect them with thine influence!"

It will not appear, in this wrought harmony of realizations, so easy a thing to choose and compare poetically, as it may have appeared in the analysis. It is not a thing that every one can do well. The qualities that it requires are three, and they are three that rarely lodge in the same mind—sensitiveness, and self-knowledge, and sympathy. For the poet must receive the being of things with his whole nature, and yet he must know the motions of his mind in receiving them, and he must know the motions of all minds, lest his poetry be private and incommunicable.

VII

WINE AND SLEEP AND POETRY

THE joy of drunkenness to an Anglo-Saxon is that it gives lustre to his trivial experiences. He gets adventure without doing much. Having lulled with the narcotic those hereditary inhibitions which made him appear phlegmatic, he can come into that state of receptive exaltation which is native to the wine-souled Italian. Liberated from the tyranny of his own opinions, liberated from his self-esteem, his diffidence, or prudence, or good judgment, he is now able to taste life. And it was really for this same virtue that wine was anciently praised, for this purpose it was used—to heighten the flush of experience, and make one return, as Plato said, "into the state of soul in which he was when a young child."

The revels of Dionysus—perfections in the memory of some rural harvest carnival—reveal, through a glamour of mysticism, just this extremity of enthusiasm for the flavor of the world. Wild youths, and creatures with youth in them—satyrs, and fauns, and mænads, the lynx, the goat, the dolphin—a laughter of Bacchus falling upon them, hale each other forth with roses and ivy-crowns and vine-leaves trailing, snakes and torches and flutes and hallelujahs, to celebrate a fervent progress through the world. A triumph after no achievement, and a conscription leading to no deeds; a festive and terrific celebration of being.

Over the light blue hills
There came a noise of revellers: the rills
Into the wide stream came of purple hue—
'Twas Bacchus and his crew!
The earnest trumpet spake, and silver thrills
From kissing cymbals made a merry din—
'Twas Bacchus and his kin

Like to a moving vintage down they came,
Crown'd with green leaves, and faces all on flame;
All madly dancing through the pleasant valley . . ."

Akin to the spirituous insanity of these joyful creatures is a certain mood of the imagination in somnolescence, or midnight waking. Do there not sometimes, as you fall asleep, come swimming before your eyes, in vivid portraiture, shapes and scenes and faces, grotesque or beautiful, but of such speaking realness that they make you move? Or do you ever wake at midnight to find your soul naked to the touch of the world? Little things that you care for, yesterday's, or to-morrow's, or a lifetime's—they are too real. Sometimes the trees stand out this way before a storm. Each being is as though it had non-being for a background. In these hours none too sober, I think we are not far from the well-springs of poetry. Activity has ceased and the senses sleep, but there is energy of perception under the eyelids, and the world re-creates itself with fervor there.

Neither dreams nor the complete illusions of hypnosis, but just on the moonlight verge of them—the wakeful lethargy in which a creak of the floor seems an earthquake, and things with the special values of unreality acquire all the vividness of the real—this is the condition in which imaginative realization can vie in its intensity with the sensuous experience of a Bacchanalian. This is the condition into which the poet must bring us. He must lull us into our exaltation. And for this purpose, like a mother to her child in the night, he brings music. He cradles us in rhythm and soothes us with a perpetual and half-monotonous melody.

Music is wine to the imagination. And the essence of music, originally and in this respect, is rhythm, or the regular recurrence of a pleasant stroke. The trance-engendering power of such recurrence, however it may be explained, was anciently known and is easily verified. Patting and stroking are nature's anodynes. We rock our babies to sleep, we smooth the foreheads of the fretful, and we love to slide into oblivion ourselves, carrying with us the continual tirl of rain-drops on a roof, or beneath us in the darkness the murmur of a brook. Bernheim, the great scientific magician, hypnotized his patients usually by muttering "sleep—sleep—sleep," and stroking them with his hand; then, without altering the cadence of his voice, he could introduce imaginations into their minds, and make them realize vividly the presence of things even while they knew them to be illusory. This is an experiment which almost any two people may try, and in a few moments they will feel an original connection between rhythm and imaginative realization.

There is, perhaps, a yet more original and more broad connection between rhythm and all realization. It seems as if there must be, because rhythm is used, not only to lull the body and set free the imagination, but also, like wine itself, to excite the body to the last degree of the intensity of real experience. These are the two primitive uses of the recurrent stimulus, and somehow they both survive in poetry. The very metrical monotony that drowses us becomes, when we are lost to coarser things, a turbulent and stimulating stream along our veins. And no theory will ever adequately unfold the magic of such utterance that does not grant and reconcile these two effects. Until such a theory is devised, and commands us to the contrary, we can please our minds at least with the following analogy:

Suppose that we figure the nervous current which corresponds to consciousness as proceeding, like so many other currents of nature, in *waves*—then we do receive a new apprehension, if not an explanation, of the strange power over us of successive strokes. For to regulate a consciousness would be to regulate waves, and how else would that be accomplished than by a calculated rhythmic impetus? It seems to me that, in the entire lack of anything better deserving the name, we might almost call this analogy explanation, for it describes in physical terms what every one can say mentally—that rhythm seems to chime in with the very nature of his state of being and control it. Such an explanation will have this advantage too, that it does not demand an artificial separation of emotion from sensation, or imagination from thought, but it allows for the rhythmic elevation of all these kinds of experience. Whatever things occupy our attention—events, objects, tones, combinations of tones, emotions, pictures, images, ideas—our consciousness of them will be heightened by the rhythm as though it consisted of waves. And what is still more to the credit of the analogy, this effect will be strong, if not strongest, when the rhythm is not *perceived* at all, but the attention is directed elsewhere.

Shelley has expressed in a fragment, which is better information than poetry, a special pleasure of his which rested upon this fact.

"How sweet it is to sit and read the tales
Of mighty poets, and to hear the while
Sweet music, which, when the attention fails,
Fills the dim pause——"

Apparently he did not guess the truth, that the music acted while his mind was engrossed even more than in the pauses of the tale. But there can be little doubt of it. Music upon the inattentive ear is a most insidious stimulant. Perhaps it is for this that we so often beat a rhythm with our fingers when we think. At any rate, to many it is a pleasure not exactly "sweet," but better than that, to have some tune around them when their mind is steadily occupied upon anything. It need not be the tales of mighty poets, nor need the music be better than a hurdy-gurdy at the street corner. The effect is the same —a kind of high buoyancy of thought, with that accentuation of the reality of thought's objects. And I take it to lie, either like hypnosis in the lulling of the body and the prudential mind, the partial liberating of imagery from inhibitions of maturity and civilization, or, like the madness of dancers, in a general intensification of all experience. Some day both these things, the imaginative suggestibility and the physical ecstasy, the sleep and wine in poetry, may be harmonized together in explanation by a mature science, but at present we are free to speculate a while among them and leave them undetermined.

However it may go with the explanation, there is no undetermination of the fact that rhythm promotes every realization. A great new art of these days is the moving-picture show, and I have yet to find one in which the reality of the pictures is not enhanced with the beating of an old piano. Nobody notices the piano, nobody remembers what the piano played, or how badly, but there it is, always keeping up a *metre*. And even when the motion films give out, and there are thrown on the screen those old still scenes of true love by moonlight, still it pounds away, and the audience melts to the mood of credulous romance. Their voluntary mind is upon the canvas, but that music slips all the deeper into their being, and it makes them live the pictures.

The high and wide popularity of this art both makes plausible the rise of epics and gives assurance of the future of poetry. For poetry too is a series of pictures accompanied by appropriate music. The pictures are to the imagination, and not to its eye only but to its whole being; and the music is of a more subtle volume; but other than this there is no difference. Ages ago we can understand how those with the gift of seeing pictures, and the naming gift, availed themselves of the dance ecstasies of their tribe to get voice and ear for a little vivid utterance. We can imagine through centuries the gradual union of that poetic employment of speech which we have described as beginning when speech began, with the employment of rhythm to intensify experience upon festal occasions, until a custom and an art of poetry arises, and there are ballad-singers singing to the dance. Like speech itself into the earlier darkness of the tribes, a poet steps into the circle of these dumb carnivals and illumines them. Nor will it be long after that before he begins to gather his own circles, and sing to his own music or his own dancing, telling in metrical and poetic syllables the tales of the tribe. And the experience of his hearers will be purely imaginary. It will be pure poetry—a realization in the rhythmic trance of things that are absent and events that are not happening.

That is the origin, so far as we know, of the first poem, the metrical story, the ballad, the epic. And no one who sees it there, primitive and inevitable, and then sees it again here in our own theatres, the same thing only a little less tranced and more palpable—as adapted to a people who have their sophistication to overcome—no one who sees it so, or once so feels it in his own nature, will doubt that the union of rhythm and the language of realization was great and will be eternal.

VIII

REALIZATION OF ACTION

THE earliest poems were stories, and story poems are ever the most popular. Perhaps they are popular in spite of their poetry rather than because of it. For that onward voracity of the will to which a narrative appeals is different, and is almost always more compelling, than the inclination to realize. So compelling is it that often it makes us impatient of the delay and we resent poetry in a tale as much as we should in a book of technical science. "It is a good story," we say, "if you skip the descriptions." And while this may sometimes indicate that the descriptions are mere inventory, at other times it indicates a deep antipathy between the mood of anticipation and that of realization. A narrative poem is an unstable compound, and will generally fall out to be, in the reader's mind, either a good narrative or a good poem, but rarely both.

On the other hand, granted that the reader's mood is poetic, and that he is more eager to receive an experience than to find out a result, it will be easier to convey to him through language the experience of an action than the experience of an inactive thing. It is easier to make a series of words vividly suggest a series of events, than to make them suggest a collocation of objects. "He starts, he jumps, he runs!" gives a sharper touch to the imagination than "It is red, white, and blue!" And yet each is a mere list of practical names. I think the reason for this difference is that, in the first case, the words stand in the same relation to each other as the acts they name, they succeed each other in time; whereas in the second, the words succeed each other in time, but the qualities they name co-exist in space—it therefore requires a special kind of word to make us pause and receive them vividly.

This similarity of the utterance of words to the forth-striking of events has given rise to the celebrated opinion that the only proper subject for poetry is action.[1] But it would be truer to say that the first and easiest subject for poetry is action. Granted that the poetic intention is understood, it requires little technique of choice or comparison to make a succession of words conjure up a succession of events. A trimmed narrative is almost inevitably poetic.

"Enoch walked with God: and he was not; for God took him."

And when to this natural ease of creating and receiving the poetry of narrative we add the fact that unpoetic readers can ignore its poetry and eat up the narrative only, if they wish to, we have abundant explanation of the greater popularity of the story poem.

Ballad-singing is an art almost universally pleasure-giving. But the pleasure in ballads divides itself very sharply into these two kinds: on the one hand, that of persons not especially poetic, which may be described as a pleasure in finding their way to the end, and, on the other, that of poetic persons, a pleasure in viewing the whole as a single and simple jewel—a painting of action more poetic by the grace of nature than its author had the genius to make it. And melody adds to the first

[1]"If it is true that painting employs in its imitations entirely different means or symbols from those adopted by poetry—*i.e.,* the former using forms and colors in space, the latter, on the other hand, articulate sounds in time—if it is admitted that these symbols must be in suitable relation to the thing symbolized, then symbols placed in juxtaposition can only express subjects of which the wholes or parts exist in juxtaposition; and consecutive symbols can only express subjects of which the wholes or parts are consecutive.

"Subjects, the wholes or parts of which exist in juxtaposition, are termed bodies. Consequently bodies, with their visible properties, are the special subjects of painting.

"Subjects, the wholes or parts of which are consecutive, are generally termed actions. Consequently actions are the special subjects of poetry."—Lessing's *Laocoön,* chapter XVI.

kind of pleasure the excitement of suspense, while rhythm exalts the pure poetry of ballads.

"Hie upon Hielands,
And laigh[1] upon Tay,
Bonny George Campbell
Rode out on a day,
Saddled and bridled
Sae gallant to see.
Hame cam' his gude horse,
But never cam' he.

"Down ran his auld mither,
Greetin' fu' sair;
Out ran his bonny bride,
Reaving her hair;
'My meadow lies green,
And my corn is unshorn,
My barn is to bigg,
And my babe is unborn.'

"Saddled and bridled,
And booted rode he;
A plume in his helmet,
A sword at his knee;
But toom[2] cam' his saddle
A' bluidy to see,
O hame cam' his gude horse,
But never cam' he."

These ballads of the people, though they derive from the fingers of time a touch of perfection not their own, were none the less surely the work of poets. They have a discrimination of emotional atmosphere, an occasional poetic word used with exquisite regard to that, which proves the receiving mind. It proves that the purpose of this beginning was not merely to reach the end. We are permitted to pause at the sight of that

[1]laigh=low

[2]toom=empty

bonny bride "reaving her hair." Yet, upon the whole, there is a scarcity of these choices in ballad literature, and a repetition of conventional comparisons, which reveals in their authors a dilution of the poetic love with a too forward look. They have not that idle enjoyment of qualities which delays the action in great epics. The Iliad and the Odyssey were sung to an achieving people and they rely for popularity, like ballads, fundamentally upon their core of narrative suspense; yet they assume with a more royal assurance that their hearers will be hospitable to the individual nature of the events detailed, and that the world in which these events happen is itself worth looking round in.

Only a truly poetic fervor will endure the delays in Homer, or consider that the Iliad is not a cluttered narrative. The poet is never more alive than when he has stopped the action, and lined up his combatants, upon one excuse or another, to contemplate their aspect. I quote one of these instances for the simple poetic delight that it gives.

> "So, high in hope, they sat the whole night through
> In warlike lines, and many watch-fires blazed.
> As when in heaven the stars look brightly forth
> Round the clear-shining moon, while not a breeze
> Stirs in the depths of air, and all the stars
> Are seen, and gladness fills the shepherd's heart,
> So many fires in sight of Ilium blazed,
> Lit by the sons of Troy, between the ships
> And eddying Xanthus: on the plain there shone
> A thousand; fifty warriors by each fire
> Sat in its light. Their steeds beside the cars—
> Champing their oats and their white barley—stood
> And waited for the golden morn to rise."

Not only after night comes on, however, and while the actors sleep, does Homer make his lingerings and excursions, but even in the heat of battle and while spears quiver in the fists of heroes. Perhaps the most soul-surprising calamity that could befall the Greeks was that their bulwark Ajax, large of muscle and soul, should fall away before the horses of the car of Hector, which came crashing through the ranks like a storm of wind.

"Father Jove Almighty touched with fear
The heart of Ajax!"

Here surely is a situation of which we cry for the outcome! And yet for the length of fifty lines and more we are expected to drink in the spectacle, and not only that, but even to depart from it upon a tour of reminiscence. A hungry lion was driven off from the cattle-yards by a crowd of farmers; a gang of small boys with sticks went after a donkey that had broken loose into the harvest.

Nor only in these extreme demands upon our geniality does the epic poet reveal his scorn of mere getting there; but even in the swiftest passages he paints with a loving hand. He flashes a detail or a likeness before us as quick as a word.

"I followed on their flight *like a black tempest;* fifty cars I took,"

says boasting Nestor.

"Illustrious Hector sprang
Into the camp. His look was *stern as night.*"

"Down plunged
The Lycian, *like a diver,* from his place
On the high tower, and life forsook his limbs."

Deaths are the supreme things in the Iliad. Never a warrior falls but some acutely specific noise, or pose, or shuddering exposure of him, is made, that puts the event into your very marrow.

"The spear passed through and reappeared behind.
Down sat the wounded man with arms outstretched."

"The helm
Of massive brass was vain to stay the blow:
The weapon pierced it and the bone, and *stained*
The brain with blood——"

"It pierced the spine
Where the head joins the neck, and severed there
The tendons on each side. *His head and mouth*
And nostrils struck the ground before his knees."

Such intensity of specification reminds us, in a way, of the Psalms. And yet there is no felt delay of the action. It is surely the height of poetic narrative, when realization and suspense thus unite, not to exasperate, but to exalt each other. Homer was at times a master of such vividness in rapidity, but neither he nor any other poet has in this equalled Shakespeare. Look to Shakespeare for the poetry of verbs.

"He waxed like a sea."
"Struck Corioli like a planet."

"As weeds before
A vessel under sail, so men obey'd
And fell below his stem——"

"—from face to foot
He was a thing of blood, whose every motion
Was tim'd with dying cries."

"And to the battle came he; where he did
Run reeking o'er the lives of men, as if
'Twere a perpetual spoil."

Never was richer freight of sensuous and emotional experience hung on a swifter tale. Never, unless you could pack the whole original parturition of verbs out of nouns, and adjectives, and each other for prehistoric ages, into a single tumultuous volume, could you excel the metaphoric portrayal of action with which Shakespeare astonishes the world.

"Not Romans—" says Coriolanus, "as they are not,
Though *calv'd* i' the porch o' the capitol."

"And still to *nose* the offence——"

"With this ungracious paper *strike*
The sight——"

"This kiss, if it durst speak,
Would *stretch thy spirits up into the air*."

"Blow winds and *crack your cheeks!*"

Such a wanton manipulation of words could awaken nothing but wrath in a man like Tolstoy, whose terrific poetic enthusiasm seems to have been narrowed in his later years almost to the exclusive enjoyment of the moral emotions. We can imagine his saying, in one of his novels, that the wind was blowing round like a giant. But that would not do for Shakespeare; he must specify at once. He sees the giant as quick and clearly as he feels the wind. And that sudden, exaggerative realization, to the contemptuous destruction of grammar, logic, and all reliable sobriety, of everything under the sun that is mentioned, appeared to his sombre critic to be a ranting degeneration of the organ which exists for purposes of moral intelligence. Yet in reality that and no other quality has made centuries of men worship Shakespeare, in spite of all the sins and failings as an artist or a sage which Tolstoy more justly ascribes to him—and in spite even of the unperceiving adulation of his other critics. He is, with Shelley, the supremely poetic genius of the English language. And in the power of feeling action, he is high above them all.

It is doubtless this fact that made him so great a dramatist. Yet it must not be thought that by "the realization of action" we mean to recall that outworn distinction of dramatic from lyric and epic poery. Drama was regarded as a division of poetry by Aristotle simply because prose dramas were unknown to him. In all the Greek theatres the actors spoke poetry, and hence a distinction between the art of acting and this manner of speaking never occurred to him. The whole performance was covered by the term "dramatic poetry." For us, however, if we were not still tangled in the scholastic tradition that he started, the term would have no value whatever. Poetry is a kind of speech, and writers of drama may put this into the mouths of their actors, or they may not. When they do, it is not a different kind of poetry from what it would be in their own mouths or anywhere else. Therefore, when we say that Shakespeare is supreme in the poetry of action, we mean that when he makes one of his characters speak of an action, that action comes before you like a reality. In the language of his own prologue, you

> Think when he talks of horses that you see them,
> Printing their proud hoofs i' the receiving earth.

Let us illustrate the mental origin of this high-handed management of verbs which we attribute especially to Shakespeare. I suppose that almost any poetic man or child, if he were to say "I straddle the fence," would have some dim passing of the shadow of a horse through his mind. He might even say, if he were in a playful mood, "as though it were a horse," or "I pretend it is a horse." But if he said this in the midst of a stirring narrative, we should resent the delay. "I horse the fence," on the contrary, would both flash the comparison and make us jump forward all the faster. And yet it appears that nobody but Shakespeare ever wrote, who continually could and did solve these difficulties thus at a stroke. Upon the slightest hint from imagination, he interchanges verbs, he puts nouns or adjectives in the place of verbs. For poetry's sake, he disrupts all barriers between the parts of speech, reverting to practical barbarity—and it is this, the highest power of the poetic impulse in literature, that makes his language a distinct creation amazing in the way that language itself would be amazing to one discovering it.

It is not uncommon to hear a Shakespearian expression upon a child's lips, where language is truly being born. "The hurt blooded," for example, is vivid through a spontaneous transfer of the parts of speech.

Verbs are fewer than nouns; they are more highly generalized and more rigidly distinguished from each other. The truth is, they are of greater practical importance than nouns, a more finished instrument, and their conventional hold upon the mind is stronger. So it has hardly ever occurred to rhetoricians that verbs are subject to such liberties as Shakespeare took with them. They have regarded metaphor, or condensed comparison, as a function of nouns only. But if they had understood that metaphor is only an exaggeration of that comparison between two experiences which is intimated by almost any poetic name, they could hardly have made this error. When Burns says of the mountain daisy,

> "Yet cheerfully thou *glinted* forth amid the storm——"

he avails himself, only more instantly, of the same comparison that he uses when he calls the flower itself a "bonny gem." Both the noun and the verb are names that compare. And when Tennyson says,

> "Let the wild
> Lean-headed eagles *yelp* alone!"

he puts into that verb more power of the comparison with ranging dogs, or jackals, than he could with any overt metaphor that a rhetoric would recognize. He paints the action with the very word that names it. He paints for once as Shakespeare would.

Generally, however, the less drastic poets have been content to color actions by the use of simile or modifying clause or phrase. And they have been perpetually tormented by the fact that such modifiers, while they enhance the poetic effect in the accepted way, nevertheless tend to destroy with art that poetry which pertains by nature to a swift succession of names conveying action. In some form this problem is rarely absent from the deliberations of a narrative poet. How shall he realize a moving thing without stopping it?

REALIZATION OF ACTION

In those rare first stanzas of the poem "To a Waterfowl," by William Cullen Bryant, occur these lines:

"As, darkly seen against the crimson sky,
Thy figure floats along."

And Bryant is said to have originally written:

"As, darkly painted on the crimson sky,
Thy figure floats along."

He made the change, I believe, in fidelity to the poetry which nature, and not he, created—the trueness of the naked verse to motion. And that difficulty, that sacrifice, is symbolic for all writers of poetic narrative. When their art cannot exalt and vivify without delay, then they are better without the art, as Byron often was. Let their narrative be clear, and swift, and rhythmical—it is inevitably poetic.

Yet its poetry is never, for the common reader, the essence of it. For the essence of all high narrative is anticipation, and the essence of poetry is realization, and they are opposed. It was, indeed, the discovery of their difference, the separation of story-telling from the poetic art, that lost for poetry its universal place and influence. It was not industry, nor sanity, nor science, nor the greater generality of language—none of these things has so profoundly affected the prevalence of poetic language. But the common novel, and the prose drama, and the newspaper—made very meagre in specific qualities of experience, but full of general suspense—have supplanted poetry in people's idle hours. Poetic utterance is returning into the novel, as all the followers of Turgenieff witness; poetic utterance is even returning with popularity into the theatre. As for the newspapers—the world will yet recover from that mania. And meanwhile poetry will live beside them, if not loved so much perhaps, or by so many, yet loved more purely for itself.

IX

REALIZATION OF THINGS

WHEN people began to tell stories in practical words, the distinctive qualities of poetic words became more sharply observed. Colors and shapes, and smells, and sounds of concrete things, were seen constantly attracting the attention in the language of poets. It was sensuous language. It appeared to move somewhat slowly and be full of pictures. And so there arose among those who were seeking to catch and confine the essence of poetry, which is quicksilver, within the limits of a definition, the term "word-painting." With that they thought to sum up the whole difference between poetry and practical speech.

And when we turn from the swift and all too naked tale of some elopement, as it may appear in a popular novel, or in the morning paper, to such a poem as "The Eve of Saint Agnes," we may feel perhaps that "word-painting" is a true definition of the difference. In the poem it is not what happens—that can wait!—but to whom, and where, and in what light, among what draperies and music, with what warmth and cold, what weather beating on the panes—these are the interests that we dwell upon. The whole first stanza gives us little more information than would a glance at the thermometer, but it gives a view and a sensation that winter's self could not excel:

"St. Agnes' Eve—Ah, bitter chill it was!
The owl, for all his feathers, was a-cold;
The hare limp'd trembling through the frozen grass,
And silent was the flock in woolly fold:
Numb were the Beadsman's fingers, while he told
His rosary, and while his frosted breath——"

Lingering upon these words, receiving them into our veins, is it not possible for us to be entranced away from our too palpable surroundings, to shiver with the old man muttering there so long ago in futile piety, to feel our own fingers large, and see that swift white disappearance of the breath on frosty air? That is the mood in which the poem will be enjoyed. It is a serenely moving series of high portraitures. It seems a miracle that written words should ever have so richly painted on a page the full experience of the senses.

"A casement high and triple-arch'd there was,
All garlanded with carven imag'ries
Of fruits, and flowers, and bunches of knot-grass,
And diamonded with panes of quaint device,
Innumerable of stains and splendid dyes,
As are the tiger-moth's deep-damask'd wings;
And in the midst, 'mong thousand heraldries,
And twilight saints, and dim emblazonings,
A shielded scutcheon blush'd with blood of queens and king.

"Full on this casement shone the wintry moon,
And threw warm gules on Madeline's fair breast,
As down she knelt for Heaven's grace and boon;
Rose-bloom fell on her hands, together prest,
And on her silver cross soft amethyst,
And on her hair a glory, like a saint:
She seem'd a splendid angel, newly drest,
Save wings, for heaven:—Porphyro grew faint:
She knelt, so pure a thing, so free from mortal taint.

"Anon his heart revives: her vespers done,
Of all its wreathèd pearls her hair she frees;
Unclasps her warmèd jewels one by one;
Loosens her fragrant bodice; by degrees
Her rich attire creeps rustling to her knees:
Half-hidden, like a mermaid in sea-weed,
Pensive awhile she dreams awake, and sees,
In fancy, fair Saint Agnes in her bed,
But dares not look behind, or all the charm is fled.

"Soon, trembling in her soft and chilly nest,
In sort of wakeful swoon, perplex'd she lay,

Until the poppied warmth of sleep oppress'd
Her soothèd limbs, and soul fatigued away;
Flown, like a thought, until the morrow-day;
Blissfully haven'd both from joy and pain;
Clasp'd like a missal where swart Paynims pray;
Blinded alike from sunshine and from rain,
As though a rose should shut, and be a bud again.

. . . .

"Then by the bed-side, where the faded moon
Made a dim, silver twilight, soft he set
A table, and, half anguish'd, threw thereon
A cloth of woven crimson, gold, and jet:—
O for some drowsy Morphean amulet!
The boisterous, midnight, festive clarion,
The kettle-drum, and far-heard clarionet,
Affray his ears, though but in dying tone:—
The hall door shuts again, and all the noise is gone.

"And still she slept an azure-lidded sleep,
In blanchèd linen, smooth, and lavender'd,
While he from forth the closet brought a heap
Of candied apple, quince, and plum, and gourd;
With jellies soother than the creamy curd,
And lucent syrops, tinct with cinnamon;
Manna and dates, in argosy tranferr'd
From Fez; and spicèd dainties, every one,
From silken Samarcand to cedar'd Lebanon."

We cannot refrain from asking upon what principles a poet makes these choices and comparisons, that with their magic he creates out of that thin line of words a full environment. Upon what general rules could we be taught to say the "silver-snarling trumpets," or "twilight saints," or "azure-lidded sleep," or "jellies soother than the creamy curd," and so convey a presence to the ear, the eye, the tongue? We cannot refrain from asking such questions, but we can, if we are wise, refrain from answering them. We can say: Go to the particulars—there are no rules! Or rather: There is a new principle, and a new rule, for every act of greatness. They are Time's fools who summarize.

One of the principles at least is Beauty. "Azure-lidded sleep" is beautiful. But Beauty—even in this poem—is by no means supreme. "Snarling" as a name for trumpets is more surprising for its truth, a kind of outrage against beauty. Beauty pleads against whole pages of the greatest poetry. I think of Spenser's awful stanza where the dragon spreads her filth; no ingenuous mind would call it beautiful. I think of Shakespeare's execrations. I think of Whitman.

> "The malform'd limbs are tied to the surgeon's table,
> What is removed drops horribly in a pail."

> "The prostitute draggles her shawl, her bonnet bobs on her tipsy and pimpled neck."

No, not beauty, nor yet unbeauty—not truth nor untruth, nor simplicity, nor complexity, nor the sublime, nor the familiar, nor the thing whose name is rhythmical, nor the thing whose name gives welcome interruption to the rhythm, nor the exciting, nor the soothing, nor the characteristic, nor even the unhabitual, is a master principle for the art of giving names. There is no master principle for that art whose very nature is to shun generality, and cleave to the unique nature of each individual experience.

There is no master principle—but there is a principle that rises in its generality above the others, because it is based deeper in the nature of our consciousness. It is not the principle of the beautiful, however, but of the unhabitual. Poetry is the art of keeping us awake in idleness, and to that end it is almost essential that, however a thing be named, it should not be named with exactly the words that we expect. Habit is the arch-enemy of realization. No matter how poetic a name may have been in its first application, or when we first received it, let it grow common in that application, and, even though it should acquire no practical use, its life withers away. The choice and the comparison both die out of it. It learns to slide unnoticed through the mind. Homer's most awakening epithets became, with endless repetition, no better for the purposes of poetry than *Jack* or *John*. And we have killed with iteration in our churches half the living words of Hebrew poets. It was a daring realization of the believed nature of Christ to call him *Lamb of God;* it was still more daring a comparison to call him *King*. But to us these words are only faded labels, and we interchange, or mix them, indiscriminately.

> "Crown him with many crowns,
> The Lamb upon his throne!"

we sing, in sleepy oblivion of a ridiculous picture! Most of the hymns are dead. And to those piously reared, a great part of the Bible itself is beyond reviving. Its words have grown habitual, and their poetry has ceased to be.

The fact that poetic words are thus ever fading with use, and degenerating into mere designations, and the fact that it is not always easy to tell how far they have faded, gives rise to the old schoolroom tragedy of "mixed figures." A "mixed figure" is either the union of two incongruous comparisons—as in the example of the crowned lamb—or it is the use of a comparison accidentally inappropriate to its object, as when I say "he *landed* in the water." These are both errors of the lifeless imagination, and due to the fact that a name once poetic has grown habitual. "To *land* upon something" was at first a sufficiently living metaphor taken from the sea, but it long ago grew common, and the practical mood seized upon it, and now it can be applied even to its own poetic opposite without our feeling the incongruity. When poetic words have gone as far as that into the blight of custom, they may well be called dead, and dedicated to the use of science. For science is seeking to give permanent names, with fixed habits of reaction attached to them, whereas the names of poetry are by their very definition new and transitory.

Many a sharp divergence in poetry from the common usages of language has no other justification—and needs none—than lies in the fact that it is a divergence. It begets surprise, which is close kin to consciousness itself. There is an intrepid defiance of expectation in that poem of Edward Carpenter's, "Little Brook Without a Name"—one of the very precious poems of recent times. "The little mouse," he says, "the water-shrew, walks (*even like Jesus Christ*) upon the flood, paddling quickly over the surface with its half-webbed feet." The poet had, no doubt, a practical purpose—to intend by this comparison the kinship in divinity of all nature—but he was not blind, I believe, to the pure poetic value of our astonishment. Homer himself cannot be said to have been above an interest in shocking his readers, when he so unexpectedly announced that

> "Prayers
> Are the daughters of Almighty Jupiter,
> *Lame, wrinkled,* and *squint-eyed*——"

Such extreme measures are at times indispensable to the sustainment of poetry. Something has to explode. Our souls must be invaded and ravaged, so ponderous is their lethargy in which they apprehend only vague presences and general bearings of things. Sing "Lord! Lord!" forever, and you rouse no heart to repentance; but shout "Sky-Blasting Jehovah!" and some necks will move.

This, then, is a principle—if beyond the acts themselves of choosing and comparing there can be a general principle—upon which the poet makes his words, which are consecutive, paint objects which are juxtaposed. He makes the words surprise us, and we look around. "The very colors of her coat," he says of the virgin, "were better than good news!" And who can pass instantly from such a phrase, or from the contemplation of such colors? The invisible skylark singing is "like an unbodied joy"

—he brings the abstract into the contemplation of the concrete, reversing the customs even of poetry, and we cannot but pause there in wonder. Or he violates the very discrimination of our separate senses, the deepest habit of perceptual life: "The fire *cries* with light," he says. All possible disorganizations of the categories, not of grammar only, but of perception, and of thought, belong to poetry, because these too are habits, and in them our individual spirits sleep.

Surprise belongs to poetry. But let us say no more than that. Let us not try to make even the unhabitual an absolute or unqualified rule. It seems, indeed, that the greater a poet's experience, the more is his reliance upon this principle mitigated, or at least mingled with other considerations. Greater poets do not *merely* surprise us, but they surprise us with the true, the beautiful, the ugly, the distinctive, in a thing. They surprise us oftenest by telling us most exactly what we knew.

"The cat on the house-sill" strikes off to my thought a picture clear as day, and "the sun-warm cat" is a touch to my hand. Yet I am not sure but, if I took a glance over the world, I should find that a large majority of cats are both "sun-warm," and "on the house-sill." It is altogether inevitable, and yet signally characteristic of them, that they should be. There is no strained acuteness of perception in the poets whose poetry is nature. Their words are only the things they sing of.

"The chanting linnet, or the mellow thrush;
Hailing the setting sun, sweet, in the green thorn bush——"

Thus to awaken us with words that are only the surest words, is a high gift, which comports with all that we call classic. It was this that made the early fame of Robert Burns eternal. And I think it was this too—the simple, the inevitable, in her singing—that gave to Sappho the supreme place in antiquity and through time. She was called "The Poet," because her very looking upon a thing was poetry, and her poetry was but looking upon it. To Evening she said:

"Evening, you bring all things that the bright morning scattered wide,
You bring the sheep, you bring the goat, you bring the child to his mother."

Perhaps it requires some acquaintance with poetry to develop a high appreciation of what is so greatly simple in choice or comparison. Perhaps the whole joy of it is never felt except as a relief after the self-conscious astonishments that are delivered to us by less mature genius. When Homer tells us that Ajax gave ground before his opponent by "moving knee after knee," if we are old enough in the love of poetry to perceive that anything has been said at all, we perceive that the final word for the imagination has been said. It is not a word ingenious, weighty, significant, or suggestive of anything but its object. It is simply the exact truth of perception, conveyed with singleness and restraint. It surprises us with unsurprise—and that, if it be paradoxical enough to destroy itself, we may safely set up as a master principle. It is a final perfection of the art of painting things with words.

X

EMOTIONAL REALIZATION

"THE EVE OF SAINT AGNES" is wonderful, not only for the vividness of its pictures, but for the fact that they are made to move before us in a stream of romantic feeling. The feeling is pure and sustained; and therein the poet has revealed a great part of his genius. He has roused in us, besides an imagination of things, the real experience of an emotion. He has done this, however, by those same acts of choice and comparison. He has chosen, for vivid imagining, many things about which the emotion is wont to cling, and compared them with other things having the same quality. In many parts of the poem this has been the sole motive of his words.

The ode "To a Nightingale" is perhaps even more completely dominated by an emotion. Let us consider, without any context, one stanza of it:

> "Fade far away, dissolve, and quite forget
> What thou among the leaves hast never known,
> The weariness, the fever, and the fret
> Here, where men sit and hear each other groan;
> Where palsy shakes a few, sad, last gray hairs,
> Where youth grows pale, and spectre-thin, and dies;
> Where but to think is to be full of sorrow
> And leaden-ey'd despairs,
> Where beauty cannot keep her lustrous eyes,
> Or new Love pine at them beyond to-morrow."

As a realization of the sorrow of life, we can see—perhaps without the violation of a too minute analysis—the high conscious or intuitive skill of poetry with which this stanza was fashioned. Tired, feverous, and envious people, old people, young people growing old, beauty and love ceasing to be—

these are the things chosen to sustain the emotion. And they in turn are made vivid by a second choice of their piercing details—the pallor, the groaning, the gray hairs sad and few, the thinness of the sick, and those "lustrous" eyes—wondering tearfully at the promise of their own decay—and finally that newness of love, that in the morning is gone. And our sense of these things, our consciousness, is still further enhanced by comparisons and intimations of comparison too subtle to be told. They are like spectres, the thin people, and the eyelids are lead, and the thinking of it all is like a well filled full of sorrow.

It is ungrateful to explain a wonder, and fortunately it is not altogether possible. The stinging residual essence of every experience is individual, and not to be set forth in general language. The best of poetry is when it starts the old indefinable echo of reminiscence and hope. The quality of some vital instant in our past, or our ancestors', some tremulous balance of the affections, is just re-suggested and appears there only as fleeing from us for an instant, and then it is gone into the past again, and we into the future, forever.

For the attainment of these moments there are no rules, because they depend upon the things that make us different from each other. Each will have his own chosen poems. We can only generally declare this much—that wherever a poignant emotion is sustained, a sensuous memory sustains it. Even those passions that we call intellectual, or spiritual, seek always an image and cling to it. When God becomes a spirit, Christ is begotten. And when Christ is blended with God, we worship the cross that he died on. It is only thus we can hold our love and our pain. As Walt Whitman, in his psalm of the death of Abraham Lincoln, has merged the very body of sorrow in a trinity of sensations, the fragrance of lilacs, the pendulous star, and the quivering voice of a bird—

> "Lilac and star and bird twined with the chant of my soul,
> There in the fragrant pines and the cedars dusk and dim——"

so has the human heart always done with that which it would have eternal.

Poetry is not often written without strong emotion, and not often without a dim desire to eternalize emotion. And this again has persuaded men who love that quality of poetry to a limiting definition. They have held that to enjoy emotion without anxiety is the essence of poetic pleasure. This opinion was intimated in the writings of Wordsworth and Shelley, but reached its highest scientific expression in an essay of John Stuart Mill, who defines the natural poets as "those who are so constituted, that emotions are the links of association by which their ideas, both sensuous and spiritual, are connected together."

We can see the reason for this opinion by examining almost any lines of Shelley—to whose writings Mill himself refers, in distinction from those of Wordsworth, as the poems of a poet.

> "And like a dying lady, lean and pale,
> Who totters forth, wrapt in a gauzy veil,
> Out of her chamber, led by the insane
> And feeble wanderings of her fading brain,
> The moon arose upon the murky earth,
> A white and shapeless mass."

No ground of union exists between the two imaginations in these lines, except a potential congruity of the beholder's emotions. And this dangerous disregard, not merely of practical similarity, but of all the external senses, is characteristic of great modern poets. Whether their motive be specifically to realize an emotion or not, they continually bring these interior vibrations of the body into a realization, in order to make it full and personal and strong. They continually choose out for a focus the quality or the detail in things that relates them to our vital feeling, and they compare things together upon the basis of similarity in this feeling.

Those jewels in "The Eve of Saint Agnes" must have been full of lustre, a romantic lustre in the moonlight; they must have been richer even than the window-panes, more deep in hue; but for the poet of our hearts they were *warmed* jewels, they could not be more.

Emotion is the surest arbiter of a poetic choice, and it is the priest of all supreme unions in the mind. Let things be ever so kin in a sensuous or objective feature, as blood is to roses, but be the burdens that they carry to the heart opposed, they are precarious consorts. Let these burdens be the same, and it matters not how alien in all else, in space and time irreconciled, in act, in reason antipathetic as the poles, they flow together as if by nature.

> "Not so the eagle, who like thee could scale
> Heaven, and could nourish in the sun's domain
> Her mighty youth with morning, doth complain,
> Soaring and screaming round her empty nest,
> As Albion wails for thee."

In the face of such evidence and such authority, it is true, however, that emotion is not the essence, nor a definitive feature of poetry. The most practical language—like earnest achievement itself—can awaken the emotions. It is not the existence of these emotions, but our attitude to them, that distinguishes the poetic mood. We wish to experience them for their own sake. And in exactly the same way we wish to experience sensations, or actions, or ideas. It may be that we are not often attracted to experience anything whatever, when it does not contain for us some emotion, some feeling besides the mere attraction or pleasure. But this does not warrant our regarding the emotion as the exclusive object of attraction. It rather counsels us against so sharply separating it from all the other qualities that go to constitute a thing. Probably any theory which regards the laboratory analysis of our experience into emotion, sensation, affection, image, idea, and so forth, as a final truth, will itself prove but temporary. We are safer when we talk of experience as a whole.

Even in so far, however, as we *can* distinguish emotion from other elements in a perception, we can prove that it is not always the object of a poet's regard. If it were, emotional congruity would invariably characterize poetic comparisons; or at least we should find no comparisons that distinctly violate and destroy emotion. But these we do find in the greatest and most natural poetry. I have in mind the story of the wounding of Menelaus in the Iliad,—the poetic pleasure that is taken in the sharp mark of "purple" on his thigh, taken in brazen defiance of the hero's agony and peril which we felt. This is the idea that the poet associated with his plight:

"As when some Carian or Maconian dame
Tinges with purple the white ivory,
To form a trapping for the cheeks of steeds,—
And many a horseman covets it, yet still
It lies within her chamber, to become
The ornament of some great monarch's steed
And make its rider proud,—thy shapely thighs,
Thy legs, and thy fair ankles thus were stained,
O Menelaus! with thy purple blood."

Here, at least, we can truthfully distinguish sensation from emotion, because sensation leads the comparison in one direction, while emotion would lead it in another. And the poet's fidelity is to the sensation; he loves the pure color. In another passage of the Iliad, equally discordant for the feelings, he is faithful to his sense of sound. The shouting onslaught of armed hosts of war is compared to the clamors of a flock of sheep. The truth is that a poet's associations will depend, like those of his readers, upon that undefinitive and incalculable thing, his personal interest. If he happens to love color and love horses, and if we do, and we are in no hurry, then it is poetic that we should pause and recall to observation that Carian maiden—her own arms stained with the crying purple too—and consider the *illustrious* steed the work of such an artist must be reserved for. Let Menelaus bleed—we must see the horse!

Emotional choice and comparison are not distinctive of poetry from practical language, but they are in a certain degree distinctive of modern from ancient poetry. Only, indeed, by making this general distinction between the inner and the outer feelings, can we fully explain the lightness, the breadth, and health of early poets. Their choices are less personal, their comparisons more often purely sensuous, than ours. They are comparisons in shape, size, color, attitude, texture, motion—comparisons which seem very wide to us, because they hold things together which are not, and cannot be, blended deep in the crucible of the heart's passions.

> "Thy hair is as a flock of goats
> That lies along the side of Mount Gilead.
> Thy teeth are like a flock of sheep that are newly shorn,
> Which are come up from the washing;
> Whereof every one has twins,
> And none is bereaved among them."

We find also that early poets are more idle in their comparisons, less rich in metaphor, more given to the long simile, more given to the reduplication of similes, and to that simile that we have called *discursive,* because our enjoyment wanders in it away from the subject which it was to illumine, and we find ourselves in a different part of the world. Indeed, they do not always care to what object their comparisons are attached, and they repeat them like a refrain. I believe that all these characteristics of the poetry of the ancients can be comprised in the statement that it is more purely poetic, more purely child-like, and willing to love, than the poetry of later people. Having a less complex environment to which they must adapt themselves, and being irresponsible in their minds to a mature and austere science, they were habitually more free to enjoy all qualities of being. They required no profound organic disturbance, no hushed and tremulous utterance, to sanction their engaging in the enjoyment of poetry. They were ready at any time to suspend business and make an excursion into the world. Their love was free.

Theocritus begins in this sweetly wandering language a lyric which he calls "passionate":

"Hast thou come, dear youth, with the third night and the dawning; hast thou come? but men in longing grow old in a day! As spring than the winter is sweeter, as the apple than the sloe, as the ewe is deeper of fleece than the lamb she bore; as a maiden surpasses a thrice-wedded wife, as the fawn is nimbler than the calf; nay, by as much as sweetest of all fowls sings the clear-voiced nightingale, so much has thy coming gladdened me! To thee have I hastened as the traveller hastens under the burning sun to the shadow of the ilex tree."

We take delight in this free-hearted poetry as we might in the rippling of a stream where it spreads out among little stones. We take delight, thinking of it as something unusual and refreshing. But for ourselves, in our own world, we have all too little of it. We feel that the poetic attitude is not quite allowable in maturity, except when demanded by a deepening of the passions. And this is very unfortunate; because it makes people who have not deep passions, and yet are poets, feel compelled to simulate the language of exaltation, and construct studious verses out of strange, intense-sounding words, when they might sit down and write a little natural poetry with no great exhaustion, if we would only expect it of them.

With this tyranny of the inward feelings which culture, or self-consciousness, or just time itself has begotten, the loss has been far greater than the gain. For while we have hardly the tendency to enjoy—except as antique, or after we have named it "pastoral"—such an address of a lover to his beloved as these we quoted from Theocritus and the Song of Songs, still the writers of such poems did have the power we have of being deep and swift and true only to their passions. There are hymns of the ancient religions in which these wanderings are not possible, because the ecstasy has utter dominion. And even Theocritus, the poet of a pasture-land, has made as intense a lyric of impassioned love—save only the lost remembered songs of Sappho—as the world has record of. He has made also the high model for all songs of tears, the model upon which Milton formed his lament for Lycidas, and Shelley the poem "Adonais," which he deemed his greatest, and which is perhaps the most sublime and conquering expression of sorrow in the world.

Both early and late it appears that sorrow is the great mother of poetry. It is most fertile of all those streams of feeling out of which high realizations of the world arise, and which they seek to make eternal. America has not been rich in poems that are supreme, but she has risen in sorrow to the heights of language. Her poet Bryant is said to have grown up within view of a rural grave-yard; a circumstance that can alone explain his writing at the age of eighteen that final poem of the thought of death, and never again, save for a few re-echoing lines, a syllable of great poetry. "Thanatopsis" is a courageous realization of death. "When Lilacs Last in the Dooryard Bloomed," another universal poem of America, is a passionate realization of death. The fragments of Edgar Allan Poe are all mystical echoes of the beauty of death, or the death of beauty. We cannot write the theory of emotional realization without recalling some songs of love and sorrow. And with them we may well cease writing the theory. We may well ascend to the truth which is no theory in the poems themselves—"Lycidas," "Adonais," "Thanatopsis," "When Lilacs Last in the Dooryard Bloomed"—poems that not only realize, but elevate, and make perfect for us that universal sorrow of which only the very love of life's experience, pure poetry, can ever melt or mitigate the sting.

XI

REALIZATION OF IDEAS

PERSONS of intellectual rather than sensuous nature, persons who can say with the philosopher, "I do not mind a blow, sir, —nothing affects me but an abstract idea!"—will not think that all the talk about realization of action and word-painting and the enjoyment of emotion, comes very near to the heart of poetry. For they too have their definition, which is an expression of their taste. They think that the essence of poetry is to be found in its manner of expressing ideas or abstract judgments. And these it expresses in two ways—either by means of a symbol, or by means of a concrete example. "All is vanity," saith the preacher, and the poet adds "a striving after wind." "The shortest distance between two points," says the geometer. "As the crow flies," "a bee line," says the poet. And these ways of speaking are surely distinctive of him. But we need not be surprised to find that they only illustrate, in the intellectual world, those same two acts of choice and comparison which we have observed in the world of things, and that the poet's attitude to an idea is but a part of that attitude toward all being which we have ascribed to him. He loves the idea, as he loves the thing, not for its meaning, its indication into the future, but for itself, its content in the present. He wishes to realize the nature of that. And he does so, either by choosing among all the particulars suggested by the idea, one which can bear the whole flavor of its significance, or by comparing with the idea some being that is wholly outside its significance, but similar to it.

Suppose that the idea be *silence*. "The butterfly sleeps on the village bell" is a poem of this idea, a realization by means of the concrete particular. Or suppose the idea be *that our sins shall be forgiven*. We have for this an enduring symbol, a symbol so strong in native poetry that it begot rhythm in the heart of the translator:

> "Though your sins be as scarlet,
> They shall be as white as snow;
> Though they be red like crimson,
> They shall be as wool."

Thus to show forth in earthen dyes the thoughts of a spirit, to make what is ideal and impalpable assail the senses of the flesh, has seemed to some the high, and to some the low, essential service of poetry.

It has seemed high, because it makes ideas warm, and acceptable to those who can hardly enjoy them in a purer form. It colors and popularizes the life of meditation. We are not all capable of that intellectual love which is the invisible support of the philosopher's austerity. We must have in our ideas an admixture of the corporeal, before they appear to us a natural object for affection. I suppose that Immanuel Kant, who is the master of an intolerable prose, had within himself a more consuming passion for the process of thought than Ralph Waldo Emerson. But he could not make thoughts lovable to the people, because he gave them no body. Emerson was perhaps not the greatest creative thinker, but he was a great lover of the experience of thought, and a creator of that experience and that love for others.

Let us compare, as examples of the extremes of poetry and its opposite in the world of ideas, his statement that

> "Man is the façade of a temple,"

with this sentence from Kant which deals, for all we know, with somewhat the same subject-matter:

> "Now, as in order to cognize ourselves, in addition to the act of thinking, which subjects the manifold of every possible intuition to the unity of apperception, there is necessary a determinate mode of intuition, whereby this manifold is given; although my own existence is certainly not mere phænomenon (much less mere illusion), the

determination of my existence can only take place conformably to the form of the internal sense, according to the particular mode in which the manifold which I conjoin is given in internal intuition, and I have therefore no knowledge of myself as I am, but merely as I appear to myself."

These heights of metaphysical abstraction are obviously inaccessible to those who have something else to attend to, and yet there is a joy in being up there, as the existence of the book and all its arduous commentators attest. And I believe it is a joy not altogether different from that which Emerson extends us. For philosophy, even self-mutilated as it is by the wish to be also a science, is more truly, or more generally, a realization of the full nature of those ideas that are the technique of science. Emerson, with his serene genius of expression, perfected this realization. And he has thus had a more direct and wider influence upon lives of the nineteenth century, than the acceptance of any theory or doctrine can register. He has filled them with a high experience. He is—as he always quietly felt himself to be, in spite of the failings of his verse—essentially a poet. He is the poet of philosophic ideas.

By some minds this descent from what is called the "abstract rationality" of a concept into that world of accident and multiplicity whence it rose has not been considered a high experience. To the unhealthy morality of mediæval sainthood it was a positive evil. Together with all things that wear the colors of material existence, poetry was dismissed in those days as a temptation to the soul. It was named—with a stroke of poetic genius which must itself have appeared supremely sinful—"The Wine of the Devil." But even before and since then, by scientists and philosophers as well as by priests, it has been held that the highest attainment of the human spirit is the process of thought unadulterated with any recollection of sensuous life. Tradition reports that Democritus blinded himself for the sake of intellectual culture, and even so sensuous a Platonist as Shelley declared that "the deep truth is imageless." And so it has always seemed that, even though there be nothing sinful in the material symbol, there is at least something immature in depending upon it. With the cultivation of intellect, language has risen slowly away from the particulars, until now the names commonly used only designate, as with a wave of the hand in their direction, vast classes and common qualities of things. And this power of general designation is so vital to what we call civilization, that it cannot but appear retrogressive and primitive to be perpetually descending to the particulars, perpetually remembering individuals, perpetually specifying and symbolizing what is already understood by the mind.

It is primitive. Poetry is of necessity the language both of children who do not understand the general names of things, and savages who have not decided upon those names. The speech of uncivilized people is full of irrelevant specifications. They continually say such things as *red dog, white dog, curly dog, fat dog,* not because they wish to convey an impression, but because they cannot help it, they have no word for *dog in general*. The Cherokee Indians are without any verb meaning *to wash,* but they have verbs meaning *wash my head, wash another person's head, wash my face, wash my clothes, wash dishes, wash a child*. And this feature of early language is not due to the predominance in its originators of a poetic instinct; it is due to the fact that language arose, not in general reflection, but in particular experiences. The first words would naturally be names of special things. Probably most of them were proper names, the most special of all—names of but one object in the world. And whenever such names are extended to include a whole class of objects, the act, however practical in its author, appears poetic to us because we have a name for the class itself. When we call certain kinds of people *Judases,* we do so for the sake of vividness; but if we had no term *traitor,* we should be compelled to do so whether we wished to be vivid or not. And that is a frequent position of the savage.

Besides the significant use of examples, his speech is full of elaborate symbolism. And this, too, can frequently be traced to his lack of an abstract term. Let us imagine that a Navajo Indian has no such concept in his knowledge as *patience,* yet one day it comes to him in a vague meditation that the Moqui tribe, peaceable though they be, are not altogether contemptible. "Moqui is—" how shall he say it? How shall he express that notion that comes so easily to our tongues? "Moqui *sits down happy,"* perhaps—and to the civilized translator this will be a most poetic idea. But imagine further that after a week or two of reflecting upon it he decides that *to sit down happy* is a good thing! He wishes to express that too, but he has no such general term as *good.* He has *good hunting, good fire-building, good fighting,* but the idea of virtue in the abstract has never yet entered his speech. What shall he say? *"Sit-down-happy* is *good fighting,"* let us imagine! And that is still more poetic. What quality or real flavor, indeed, has our own proverb —*Patience is a virtue*—until you discover the military origins of the last word, which give it the power of a symbolic realization?—Patience is a good fight!

Such poetry, not consciously created, but a by-product of the growth of generality and abstraction, is rife among all uncivilized peoples.[1] And, moreover, their singing and their speaking are not so separate in their lives as ours, and their pas-

[1] I do not mean to imply that savages are not also intentionally poetic—more frequently and more purely so, perhaps, than we are. I do not know. But I know it is a profound error to suppose, because of these characteristics of primitive language, and their survival in Homeric and other early poetic dialects, that as language develops in the power of expressing abstract ideas true poetry becomes less natural or less possible. True poetry, arising from the pure poetic wish, becomes only more clearly distinguished from accidental poetry, arising from the quest of information. It is just as possible to specify, it is just as possible to symbolize, as it ever was. Indeed, the resources for symbolism are richer than ever, for one abstract idea can now stand for another, or for a concrete thing. Only it is not so often necessary, and so the power is less cultivated among practical people. Poetry is left for the truly poetic.

sions not so subjected to the time and place, and there is therefore a continual poetry in living among them. It is not unlike the poetry of advancing science, the poetry of any mind that gropes beyond the confines of its present vocabulary.

The Persians have many anecdotes of the first appearance of poetry in their literary heroes, and one of them astutely attributes it to the young man's ignorance of technical terminology.

"The celebrated Abderrahman, son of Hissân, having, when a child, been stung by a wasp, the insect being one he did not recognize, he ran to his father, crying out that 'he had been wounded by a creature spotted with yellow and white, like the border of his vest.' On hearing these words uttered in a measure of Arabian verse, as elegant as natural, Hissân became aware of his son's genius for poetry."

To attribute to it the origin of great poetry is paying too high a compliment even to so valuable a thing as ignorance. But that there is a certain antithesis between poetry and general knowledge, and that poetry exists either before that is acquired or after it is surmounted, let us gladly acknowledge. Leaving out the accident of metre, we could discover these origins of poetry every day in the kindergarten. A little boy is trying to guess the name of his teacher's friend, and not having in his mind the name of the general concept *first,* he asks, "What is the letter that lives on the edge of it?" Another conveys his abstract notion of *height* in the words, "Nearest the sky."

We shall not impugn the genuineness of the poetry of children, nor that purity of their poetic love which we have insisted upon, we shall but strengthen the force of that insistence, if we also acknowledge that their poetry of ideas is frequently but a happy incident of ignorance. We might call it necessary poetry. The most practical adults are driven to it when by a reversal of circumstances, the general name being given, they are called upon to explain its meaning to one who is still in the primitive condition. They have either to recall particulars or to employ symbols. There is no escaping the picturesque. I find this memorandum of a bit of such instruction in the early diary of Helen Keller:

"Nancy was cross. Cross is cry and kick."

Now, if we could arrange so that all the children of the world should become teachers of the adults, telling them how to turn their talking into poetry, we should find exactly such memoranda in the note-books of the pupils. They would be taught that "Cross is *cry and kick.*" But in language, as in life, the prejudice prevails that instruction should pass in the other direction. The jewels of childhood's utterance are adventitious; the chief end of man is to acquire sagacity in the use of general concepts; his chief end is to be sensible or scientific.

In scientific thinking, we trim away from every experience all that makes it individual and astonishing, in order that we may give it a common name and establish it in a familiar class. Science deals with each reality as city people deal with a merchant, neglecting for a supreme expedience all that is of unique and immediate value in the relation established. It regards only the sameness of things. In books of science we get no taste of a particular existence, but things having some important similarity are referred to as though they were all exactly alike, and by a word stripped of every appropriateness to their nature, stripped of all individual quality whatever, save what is essential to distinguish it from other words. The culmination of this process is to abandon words altogether, as savoring too much of a reality, and let *a* stand for one concept, and *b* for another. Algebra is the extreme antithesis of poetry —so complete in its practical idealism that the real existence of various things is not even intimated as possible, but we deal only with terms and their relations in the mind, the last vestige of poetry sucked out of them. This is the true end and climax, not only of what we call pure science, but of that abstract intellectuality which the philosopher praises. It is an idealization of the practical uniformities of experience—a process which advances with such marvellous rapidity, especially in the absence of experience, that if we remain in our studies, we can be led to believe that all the world may one day be summed up in a single formula, and the perfection of science achieved.

By that time we shall need to remember that the world does not exist in the abstract, nor in general, nor in any classification, but in concrete and heterogeneous detail. The poet reminds us of this. Poetry is a countryman, and greets every experience by its own name. Books of poetry, no matter how abstract or general the ideas they convey, are filled with presences. Things are made to appear before us in rich multiplicity, and by words cunningly apposite to their unique characters, amid which the general meaning must find expression as it can. And no matter what that meaning may be, no matter how intellectual or how scientific his thesis, the poet is by his very speech engaged in exploiting against the spirit of science the varieties of the world. And as the extreme of science is the vanishing up of all generalization in a single truth, so the extreme of poetry is to descend from the generality proper to the very existence of language, and engage in the diversities of life. Poetry ushers us out of the library. It is a gesture toward the world.

And thus it is that, although primitive, poetry is also divine. It is a redeemer of the mind from the serious madness of abstraction. It is "the breath and finer spirit of all knowledge," as Wordsworth said; it is "the tuft and final applause of science," as Whitman said; not because it goes still higher up into the air than science and knowledge, but because it carries science and knowledge continually back into the specific realities out of which they arose, and whose illumination is their culminating function.

And yet this, too, we should remember—lest we be as foolish as the fools of science—that abstract ideas themselves exist, and are among the realities of experience. The realization of ideas is a part of the adventure of being. And a poet dwells upon the symbolic image, not merely because it is warmer than the idea, but also because it is the essence of the idea in so far as that has any substantive existence. The meaning is transitive, it is an act of the mind; there is no pausing upon it alone. But the image in which it dwells, and which it hallows with new feelings that are offspring of the power of generalization—that is a thing that can be raised up, and seen, and dwelt upon for its own sake. Through that, and through that alone, the poet can arrest and entertain a thought.

"Now, while the birds thus sing a joyous song,
        And while the young lambs bound
            As to the tabor's sound,
To me alone there came a thought of grief:

. . . .

"Our birth is but a sleep and a forgetting:
The Soul that rises with us, our life's Star,
Hath had elsewhere its setting,
        And cometh from afar:
Not in entire forgetfulness,
And not in utter nakedness,
But trailing clouds of glory do we come
        From God, who is our home."

This was not a new thought, nor was the proof offered of it convincing even in its own day; but it was the new realization of a thought as old as man, and dear to him. It was the bringing down of abstract immortality into the world of things and passions where it might be touched and felt. The day was long gone by when a philosopher could astonish men with the idea that our mind in childhood brings proof of some migration from a higher sphere. Plato thought in a far more scientific way of this. But the day was not gone by and never will be, when a poet could astonish us with the vision of this thought in robes of color and emotion.

"Trailing clouds of glory do we come!"

We consider such symbolic or visionary thinking to be very rare, and that a special star attends the birth of a poet. But no doubt these fires of imagery play in the firmament of every mind. It is not without initial effort that we learn to disregard them. Present to your mind, if you can, some naked meaning. Let it be that contained in the word *junction*. Unless you are content with the mere sound or appearance of the word itself as a bearer of the meaning, you will find in your imagination a vague picture of two things coming together, two undefined objects whose very lack of definition shall represent the generality of the idea. And if your mind is feverish, or electric with passion, the picture will be more defined. There will even appear a particular instance (perhaps that one in which you first learned the word), and this will stand for *junction* in the abstract, until a new concrete is given by the completion of a sentence. "Let there be a junction between your ideals and your daily life." Yet even here we are at a loss to attain a clear image, for the words *ideal,* and *daily life,* are also highly general. Something above reaches down upon something below, something light touches upon something drab-colored, or a vagueness from heaven swims over the picture of ourselves in practical costume—the difference depending upon how we have learned and used the word *ideal,* and the word *junction,* and the words *daily life*. Whatever form it takes, it is inevitably vague and unemerging—unsatisfying, because it leaves us all of the pictorial work to do. It is "prosaic." "Hitch your wagon to a star"—that is poetic. It gleams into the mind, scorning all three of those old words that were obscure and not compatible with each other, putting in their place one visual experience which abides. Poetry but dwells upon and perfects that significant imagery which is the natural instrument of all thinking. It perfects the individual nature of the idea.

And the poignancy of an idea so perfected is usually greatest when the image stands alone, when the meaning in its more abstract form is not expressed. We are given only the specific and concrete, yet with some shadowed intimation that it contains more than itself.

> "The Moving Finger writes; and, having writ,
> Moves on: nor all your Piety nor Wit
> Shall lure it back to cancel half a Line,
> Nor all your Tears wash out a Word of it."

We cross the bridge of comparison by ourselves, and hardly with words. We only inwardly feel that we have arrived in the presence of an idea. And so unique and magical is this, the experience through speech of what is unspoken, so wonderfully does it float and linger through the lines of all ideal poetry, that it has seemed to those who love above all things a miracle to be a kind of essence of the poetic quality. They, too, have wished to confine all poetry within the limits of their love. "Suggestion"—"intimation"—"nuance"—"meaning" in the occult sense—are what they wait for, and sail over the great seas of open poetry thinking they are but a passage-way for these vessels of mystery.

Let us acknowledge that though poetry is far wider and far more than they believe, yet this is among the sublimest of her powers. For we are sometimes led by her most fine suggestions, not only into the presence of ideas, but into the presence of what is beyond any idea. We are made to apprehend the being of things the mind cannot contain. In trigonometry, because we know the relation between two lines, we can measure the one which is beyond the span of our instruments, and we nail our diagrams to the stars; and in poetry, likewise, when we have experienced the reference of a present image to absent ones, we are awake to those references which pass beyond our minds, and we catch them on their way to the images that are eternally absent. There is poetry that runs along the verge of infinity. Repeatedly we span the universe by the juxtaposition of words, and as the architecture of these successive visions is piled before us, we are led almost to expect a revelation of the unseen. This power has hung the veil of sacredness upon the name of poetry

—that with these written syllables it can so bring over us the nearness of infinite and universal being.

Some shadow of this enduring wonder must have dwelt above all those bright gods of Greece, who were the children of the love of pure ideas. Realizations in that warmest symbol, personality, of the ideas of health, and courage, and wisdom, and some unnamable great beauty that was supposed to lie beyond them all—they dwelt like light among the citizens of Athens. And in the darkness of declining faith in their true being, there arose one who declared that though they fade, the symbols fade, the ideas abide forever and are real. Health and beauty and lightness, these abstract things, exist in perfection and can be seen, if not with the sensual eye, yet with the eye of the mind. So Plato's evening prayer was a prayer not to the deities, not to the beautiful and good, but to beauty and goodness. He sought to substitute the image of a word with its meaning, for the image of a god with his meaning, and so preserve for a little longer the high-hearted joys of a young religion. But he too failed, and died. The gods must all perish and be lost to us, until we have grown old enough in science to return to them and know that they are poetry, the symbols of ideas and of a universal mystery.

XII

POETRY ITSELF

POETRY is not only a realization of things, but it is also a thing itself. It contains present elements to realize and make perfect, or make poignant, for their own sake. Perhaps the finest of all these elements, the most magnetic to those who love life, is a great conflict. The spontaneous pulse of the speech is fighting the restraint of rhythm perpetually, and in the clash both are exalted. In some poems the established rhythm triumphs often; in others it is often wrecked. And they who value generality and law for their own sake will favor the first kind of poems, and they who value the general law only as an opportunity for individual rebellion will favor the second kind. This difference will always be. But for either of them to get the real food for his taste, it is necessary that both the rhythm and the spontaneous pulse should exist, that they should exist distinctly, that they should continue in that state of warring equilibrium which seems to define the very nature of existence.

Those who love liberty will enjoy this conflict as it fares in the blank verse of Shakespeare's mature years; those who love the established order will be better pleased with Tennyson. But even Tennyson cannot allow the order to prevail for many lines unbroken, as a quotation will reveal.

"So saying, from the ruin'd shrine he stept
And in the moon athwart the place of tombs,
Where lay the mighty bones of ancient men,
Old knights, and over them the sea-wind sang
Shrill, chill, with flakes of foam. He, stepping down
By zig-zag paths, and juts of pointed rock,
Came on the shining levels of the lake.
There drew he forth the brand Excalibur,

And o'er him, drawing it, the winter moon,
Brightening the skirts of a long cloud, ran forth
And sparkled keen with frost against the hilt——"

There are three variances in these lines against the formal rhythm:

"Shrill, chill, with flakes of foam,"

and

"Brightening the skirts of a long cloud,"

and

"Came on the shining levels of the lake."

And one might insert for *brightening the skirts of a long cloud,* the words, *illumining the skirts of trailing cloud,* and for *shrill, chill,* the words *all shrill,* and for *came on,* the word *beheld,* which would restore the rhythm to complete regularity; and by so mutilating a perfect thing he might see, if he cared to, how greatly its perfection depends upon a conflict.

Another element of poetry, as a thing itself, is that melody of letters on the lips and tongue—a melody less high and startling perhaps, but just as clear and eminent to those whose senses can discriminate with fineness as the clang of horns and cymbals. I call it melody because it gives no sounds in unison, but otherwise it has upon an elfin scale the whole diversity of symphonic music. It has a cadence that is almost formal melody; it has the change of tempo and intensity; it has a lineal euphony and dissonance of tonal qualities. Each vowel is an instrument, and each consonant a kind of stop. And all these stops and instruments can be conjoined in myriads of the ways of pleasing that we call beauty—more ways, indeed, than those of instrumental music. For it is not to the ear only, but to the sentient organs of articulation, and even to the eye, that the lettered syllables of poetry give music. Phrases, lines, and stanzas have each a distinct being, and all these beings can be built up together congruously into an architectural wonder.

In modern days, indeed, this building up of vocal wonders has become a great part of the art of writing poetry. Tennyson gave much of his creative attention to it. And it was truly a wonder that he built—a supremely soft, mellifluous wonder—

> "Music that gentlier on the spirit lies,
> Than tired eyelids upon tired eyes."

Sidney Lanier also loved this art, and wrote a science of it, and even exceeded Tennyson, if not in the melting away, at least in the intense sweetness of the linking of his syllables. They hardly allow themselves to be forgotten, they fall so velvetly out of the mouth with rhyme, alliteration, assonance, and every shade of conscious euphony. But of all the builders of the lingual melody, Edgar Allan Poe seems to have given it the least divided regard, and in the few perfected poems that he made, brought it to an extreme of limpid fluidity.

> "At midnight, in the month of June,
> I stand beneath the mystic moon.
> An opiate vapor, dewy, dim,
> Exhales from out her golden rim,
> And, softly dripping drop by drop,
> Upon the quiet mountain top,
> Steals drowsily and musically
> Into the universal valley.
> The rosemary nods upon the grave;
> The lily lolls upon the wave;
> Wrapping the fog about its breast,
> The ruin moulders into rest;
> Looking like Lethe, see! the lake
> A conscious slumber seems to take,
> And would not, for the world, awake.
> All Beauty sleeps!—and lo! where lies
> Irene, with her Destinies!"

Rudyard Kipling injected into this art a more heroic ring. His syllables raise a magnificent clangor that puts health into the pulse, and their sounding marks quite a crisis in the history of the music of English letters. "The ringing, stinging spindrift, and fulmar flying free!" seem hardly of the same genus as "The velvet violet cushions," and "The silken, sad, uncertain rustling of each purple curtain." Yet after all they are only a variation of taste in the same field of interest. They direct the attention, more or less explicitly, as Tennyson so often did, to the vocal materials of verse.

Poetry contains more essence of its own, however, than syllables and letters, or the wonders made of them. It contains words. And of all the jewels of Africa there is no one that can surpass, in concentration of intense being, a unique word. Suspend before the mind, but only for a moment lest its spirit flee, a word—the word *wraith,* or *vigil,* or *night-wandering. Ingot, water-nixy, preen, simoom*—are they not wonderful creatures? They bear all the charmed diversities of nature in a faery world. No poet ever lived, no vivid-minded child, but loved to know them.

And knowing them—or shall we call it tasting, feeling of them, loving to build them also into wonders—has been a second great part of the art of poetry in modern days. Consider, for example, those lines "To a Snow-flake," by Francis Thompson. Consider them, not because they lack all other poetry, but because they lack all other greatness in poetry, than the greatness of a creation in the flavors of words. A sensuous if delicate cloud is hung before us, hiding the snow-flake, or even the God, we may have thought of, but hiding it in order to ravish us away with a mystery of names. As a builder of these magic clouds, dwelling upon them forever, and even to the ruin of his melody and rhythm, Francis Thompson has hardly been excelled.

TO A SNOW-FLAKE

"What heart could have thought you?—
Past our devisal
(A filigree petal!)
Fashioned so purely,
Fragilely, surely,
From what Paradisal
Imagineless metal,

Too costly for cost?
Who hammered you, wrought you,
From argentine vapor?—
'God was my shaper.
Passing surmisal,
He hammered, He wrought me.
From curled silver vapor,
To lust of his mind:—
Thou could'st not have thought me!
So purely, so palely,
Tinily, surely,
Mightily, frailly,
Insculped and embossed,
With his hammer of mind,
And his graver of frost.'"

The poem is so moving, and yet withal so inevitable—so superior in that quality to others in its volume—that we might almost retract what we said of it. We might say, for one thing, that there is a kinship between the sensible nature of its words and of the thing they speak of. Both do curl and flutter, even if not in the same unconscious purity. And in so far as that is true, there is a higher poetry than lies in the mere realization of words. It is a poetry upon the borderland between word-conjuring and the imaginative realization of things—a special poetry to which the text-books have given the longest and most unpoetic name of *onomatopœia.*

This poetry contains similarity, but it is a similarity not between two things that are named, but between a thing and the very naming of it. *Buzz, bang, slap, grumble,* are words used to illustrate this, and they are always supplemented by these long-suffering lines of Tennyson:

"The moan of doves in immemorial elms,
And murmuring of innumerable bees."

No book about poetry is acceptable without a quotation of these lines; and few books about poetry fail to convey an indistinct impression that they contain the real, or at least the only seizable, quintessence of poetic language. This is unfortunate, because the lines are obviously unusual and had to be sought after, and we should not care to hear a great many like them even if we could. But, unfortunate though it is, it is the nearest that the text-books ever come to telling the truth about poetic language. It is a real intuition of the truth, and far less misleading than what they have to say about "figures of speech" in general.

The reason why the text-books talk about onomatopœia as though it were the quintessence of poetry is that their authors understand its poetic value, but they do not understand the poetic value of the other figures. They perceive, in an obscure way, that making an absent experience vivid to the mind is the very magic of poetry. And they can explain to themselves how an imitative sound makes an absent thing vivid. It is like saying "bow-wow" for baby at the word *dog*. But how the choice of a salient detail, or the comparison of one absent thing with another, makes it vivid to the mind, they cannot explain. And so they pass over these greater acts of poetry somewhat abstractedly, as we have seen, and they dwell upon this small incident of mimicry and these misfortunate two lines of Tennyson, as though they were a kind of special archetype for all poetry, and were achieved by a supernatural union of the poet himself with the objects he loves. But we need only glance back a little way in the same poem to prove to ourselves how much more utterly lost in his objects a poet may become, and yet make no sensible imitation whatever.

"But cease to move so near the Heavens, and cease
To glide a sunbeam by the blasted Pine,
To sit a star upon the sparkling spire;
And come, for Love is of the valley, come,
For Love is of the valley, come thou down
And find him; by the happy threshold, he,
Or hand in hand with Plenty in the maize,

Or red with spirited purple of the vats,
Or foxlike in the vine; nor cares to walk
With Death and Morning on the silver horns,—

. . . .

"But follow; let the torrent dance thee down
To find him in the valley; let the wild
Lean-headed eagles yelp alone, and leave
The monstrous ledges there to slope, and spill
Their thousand wreaths of dangling water-smoke,
That like a broken purpose waste in air:
So waste not thou; but come; for all the vales
Await thee——"

The language of Dante held people in so great awe that a tradition arose, and has survived among the credulous, that a foreigner can understand him to some extent by the very wailing of his words—a tradition which gives more credit to Dante in its folly, than it would if it were true. For how should a man descending into very hell, experiencing the universal horror till his mind was rabid and his bones were gaunt—how should he be attending to the trick of juggling some eight thousand words until they mimicked every noise or object he encountered? It is pardonable that we should speak of Dante with superstition, for he is probably the only man that ever fully went through hell. But I think we do light honor to the superhuman genius in him when we unite it with this magic of the languid study. We unite it with such achievements as Edgar Allan Poe's "Bells"—a poem which shows the love of onomatopœia, and word-tasting, and letter-music, in extreme and almost ludicrous dominance over the motives of universal poetry.

"Hear the sledges with the bells—
Silver bells!
What a world of merriment their melody foretells!
How they tinkle, tinkle, tinkle,
In the icy air of night!

While the stars that oversprinkle
All the heavens, seem to twinkle
    With a crystalline delight;
Keeping time, time, time,
In a sort of Runic rhyme,
To the tintinnabulation that so musically wells
From the bells, bells, bells, bells,
    Bells, bells, bells—
From the jingling and the tinkling of the bells."

One might almost regard these verses, with "The Raven," as a parody upon the tendencies of chamber-poets in the modern day—their consecration of the sensuous materials of language. It is but a step beyond them in affection for the palpable to devote the energies of creation—as at one time the poets of Persia did—to beautiful penmanship, and the coloring of the pages, and dusting them with live perfumes.

The poets of the world have not been dominated by any of these passions of the writing-room. For them poetry itself is an experience subordinate to those which it portrays. They have mastered the art of verbal melody much as they mastered the art of handwriting, in order to subject it utterly to the service of the imaginative realization of life. The pleasure in their syllables does not protest itself; the perfection of their utterance is supreme, but it is in the truest sense a negative perfection. It is but the clear medium through which a greater thing continually appears.

Two elements belong to poetry as a thing itself, however, upon which even the great poets have sometimes concentrated their best energy. They are the form, an intellectual element, and the unique emotion that words aloof from things can sometimes generate. I quote for illustration of the first a sonnet whose excellence, whatever elements of passion it may hold, is not separable from its totality. The passion and its images are wrought together on a rhythmic pattern into a high unity that becomes a being for the intellect—a poem.

"Remember me when I am gone away,
Gone far away into the silent land;
When you can no more hold me by the hand,
Nor I half turn to go yet turning stay.
Remember me when no more, day by day,
You tell me of our future that you planned:
Only remember me; you understand.
It will be late to counsel then or pray.
Yet if you should forget me for a while
And afterwards remember, do not grieve;
For if the darkness and corruption leave
A vestige of the thoughts that once I had,
Better by far you should forget and smile
Than that you should remember and be sad."

Thus to engender without loss of passion or simplicity a perfect form is an art which somehow stirs in us a greater admiration than does the mere music made of syllables. It is at least a more complete creation. A poem as a form is a new thing that language adds outright to what the world contained.

Perhaps to create out of the materials of life, by recombining them with names, a feeling that life itself never offered, a quality of passion that is the poem's own, is a still higher art. It seems both high and rare, and to partake of the divineness of nature's own spontaneous generation. And we need not wonder if those who dwell too much in reading, and too little in the world, should make a kind of idol of this power and almost wish to call no other utterance poetry.

"I saw pale kings, and princes too,
Pale warriors, death-pale were they all;

. . . .

"I saw their starv'd lips in the gloam,
With horrid warning gapèd wide,
And I awoke and found me here
    On the cold hillside.

"And this is why I sojourn here
Alone and palely loitering,
Though the sedge is wither'd from the lake,
And no birds sing."

An echo will recall the spell of this sad ballad, and remind us that such magical emotions are indeed a precious gift that words can make to the original wealth of life. They are at least a crowning attribute of poetry as a thing itself. And blended with all poignancy and beauty in the other attributes we have too crudely analyzed and separated from each other, they can easily become the object of supreme poetic love in days when art usurps the place of life. They are a culmination of what we may call the poetry of the poet's chamber.

XIII

TO ENJOY POETRY

Of all things poetry is most unlike deadness. It is unlike ennui, or sophistication. It is a property of the alert and beating hearts. Those who are so proud that they cannot enter precipitately into the enterprise of being are too great for poetry. Poetry is unconditionally upon the side of life. But it is also upon the side of variety in life. It is the offspring of a love that has many eyes, as many as the flowers of the field. There is no poetry for him whose look is straitened, and his heart lives but to the satisfaction of a single taste. He had the power of poetry and lost it.

Not variety alone, but idleness in variety pertains to the poetic life. Greed, anticipation, or the aspiration to achieve may branch a thousand ways. Even old necessity is not monotonous. But poetry cannot flourish where these things absorb the heart. Realization is a flower of leisure and does not blossom quickly. It is a flower of the mood of leisure, and that in these days is the possession of a few. Among the well-to-do it is a traditional possession of women only, and so poetry has there grown to appear feminine. Among the poor it is unattainable to any but degenerates, or the best rebels, and so poetry appears not to belong there at all, but to be almost an exclusive pleasure of those whom we call cultivated. Poetry has grown aristocratic. It looks into the future for its golden age, the age when it will again be loved by many kinds of people, and rise to its heights upon a wide foundation. They who cherish hopes of poetry will, therefore, do well to favor in their day every assault of labor upon the monopoly of leisure by a few. They will be ready for a drastic re-distribution of the idle hours.

Even a more heroic change they will have to see, if poetry is to prosper in those hours. For with the achievement of leisure as it is to-day, there spreads over the whole nature of man that baleful constraint, the ideal of respectability. And that is a more sure destroyer of poetry than even necessity or the absorbing ambition that is genuine. The privilege of maintaining a refined insulation from real contacts with the matter of life being possible only to the wealthy, it becomes the accepted token of wealth, and a stern requirement to those whose judgments of merit are determined by a pecuniary standard. They wrap themselves in fabrics and fine manners. They incase themselves in forms. They touch nothing to the quick. They are even more effectually sundered from the poetry of experience than those considered less fortunate who are occupied with a genuine problem of self-preservation. For they, when they do discover some hour of contemplation, look straight into the face of the world. They taste the sorrows at least. But these others dwell in their mansions of great aspect as in the tomb, forbidden by their ideal the realization even of the tragedy of their own deadness. I walk from Central Park eastward, and as I draw near to those quarters where poverty has kept off this malady, I draw big breaths again, as if I had issued out of a polished museum wherein were kept packages of human remains.

What wonder if the poets, the lovers of the sting of life, have revolted against this voluntary blight. A noble flavor of disreputability clings about the greatest of them. Nor does comedy err in presenting their type as clad in a rolling collar, a flowing tie, or some other symbol of rebellion against the demands of respectable opinion. They do not love these peculiarities for themselves alone, but they love them for the declaration that they make of public liberty for individual existence.

It it true that this revolt in manners cannot always be effected without a loss of that unconsciousness of self which is so justly valued. But this does not prove that the revolt arose from such consciousness; it proves the all-poisoning power of the ideal revolted against. It but extends to the man who defies it a further challenge. His defiance will not weaken, because it is grounded in the nature of his will. But the strange power of that ideal is grounded in a condition of extreme economic rivalry, and will diminish with a change in this condition. With a wiser distribution, not of leisure only, but of wealth, its tyranny, which is pecuniary at heart, will there rot. And a certain naturalness without respectability, the rarest jewel of our present leisure, will then be more abundant.

It would not be true, perhaps, to attribute all the unexpectedness of the poetic to their revolt against the anxiety or insulation of being respectable. For there is a certain contrariety between custom itself, whatever be the heart of it, and poetry. There is truth in the high opinion that in so far as a man conforms, he ceases to exist. He fails to launch that separate orbit into the sphere of being which the luck of birth allowed him. And, therefore, a divergence for its own sake from the common course receives the poet's sanction. To aspire forever toward the general type is—as even Plato in his world of thought acknowledged—a kind of death for the individual. The measure of experience is all too short for those who love it.

And if custom, or the typical, appears to them a kind of death, how much the more does individual habit, or the washing out of all acute impressions through mere repetition. This they cannot bear. They cannot settle down to any daily round whatever—to stay at home, or leaving home to cut always across the same meadow. They make new paths at every turn. They shun the clutch of habit as a wild hawk shuns the cage, knowing that it has more power than its bars. It has the power of conquering their wish to leave it. And here that other popular or comic apprehending of the poet's nature—that he is a little unreliable—finds also a measure of justification. He is not the best of neighbors, because you can never tell quite where to find him, or what you may expect of him when found. He is unreliable only in so far as you commit your fortunes rashly to the hope of his repeating yesterday to-day. That mode of living, in so far as mortal tissue and its preservation will allow, he has kept clear of. And in this way, as well as in the way of unsophistication, and variety, and idleness, and the disreputable, and the uncustomary, he has made the return to childhood. He has preserved the poetry of life.

The poetry of language is secondary to that. It will be found, mixed often with humor, on the tongues of those we have described; its best enjoyment will be known to them. And yet it is a different art, and there are further requisites of its enjoyment. The first and greatest of them is that we should know its character, and estimate it as itself. All lively things of nature, from the planets to ourselves so busy on them, are forever forward-looking, and unconsciously we draw all new things to this company, and judge them as they further or retard its progress. Far more than half our judgments, half our conscious being, half our speaking, is directed toward the future, finds its sanction there. And poetry is exactly otherwise. It aims to step aside from, and to stem, that everlasting process with a strong abiding in the present. And this is foolish mutiny to those who cannot understand; but to those who can, it is a fine rebellion. And that is all the difference.

What silly tassels "figures" can appear, when discourse is conceived as wholly occupied with interchange of meaning, we have seen. A studied row of metrical or rhyming syllables is equally absurd, if it be judged accessory to the conveyance of information or conceptual understanding. The entire technique of poetry is rejected with a contemptuous epithet by persons who have never caught the idea, even unconsciously, that there is a difference between the realization of being and the occupation of becoming. From their standpoint, the standpoint of practical sagacity, the statement ascribed to Tolstoy that *nothing was ever said in poetry which could not be better said in plain language,* is entirely true. But from the standpoint of one who wishes to experience the intrinsic nature of a thing spoken of, it is entirely true that *nothing was ever said in plain language which could not be better said in poetry.* When language is essentially practical, too much of the poetic is an intrusion; but when language is essentially poetic, too much of the practical is an intrusion. Whatsoever part of language *is* poetic, moreover, and aims to be so, will be judged and apprehended under the standard of its own aim, or it will not be really judged or apprehended at all.

When the essential difference is once fixed, however, and it is seen how all language parts away on one side or the other, what further relates to the art of enjoying poetry will be quickly understood. It will appear that poetry is not a mere digression, but a parallel of achievement. It requires the same energy of morning. You cannot sit down in the odd moments and snatch a bite of poetry. There will be words, but the realization will not come. It is the vigorous idleness that is so rare. And once it is attained, a childlike vividness of speech is almost inevitable, and the poetry of books rings wholly true. All those inconsequent details and qualities, those self-significant comparisons, those throbbing syllables, come like an inspiration to the mind. Their stirring and sustaining of pure consciousness exalts us. And the power of lingering, forgotten since the nursery picture-books were closed, returns, and these the picture-books of our maturity grow vivid with the colors of the world.

The power of lingering with energy—this is the second lesson in the art of loving poetry. The third, if we may steal a word from those who teach the love of God, is faith. For poetry is like religion in that it exists with glorious definition for those who have attained it, but for those who merely look upon it, there is little that appears. I believe that if we were to examine the whole field of poetry, from the first corybantic festival to the last polished rondel of a French artist, for some common characteristic *in the words themselves,* whereby the essence of poetry should be indicated, we should find one such characteristic and one only. It would not be rhythm. It would be the employment of certain particles of emotion or address which are wholly foreign to the speech of ordinary communication. The *Ahs,* and *Thous,* and the *Forevermores,* seem to be more universal in the language of realization than any other audible or visible thing. And are they not a result of the wish to establish a separation of the poetic moment, to beget in the hearer a change, a reverence, a kind of submission to the magic that invests the poet—a magic that will not exist for him until he yields? The trance of realization is a definite experience. It would be praised by many that are scornful, if they but knew it, this sacred charm that can swing down into the most wretched lives or circumstances and illumine them. And if we dwell upon its kinship with a vision or a waking sleep, let this not suggest unhealth, or unreality, or anything occult, for it is natural as laughter. Only let it give a doubt to those who now dismiss the poetry of rhythmic language from the things of their enjoyment before they ever have experienced it.

The surest path to its experience, if they should humbly wish to know, lies not through reading, but through making it. Better than faith or cherished idleness, better even than understanding poetry as a way to learn the enjoyment of it—and that without alienation from the better poem of one's own existence —is to create it for one's self. Let but a rhythmic utterance with the chosen name rise in some deep or vivid moment of our own experience, and the rhythms and designations of great poetry are then forever natural. We are of their kindred, and their speech is native to our minds.

XIV

TO COMPOSE POETRY

The knowledge needed to create an English rhythm, the only general knowledge there is upon that subject, may be acquired while one converses about it. There may be different ways of systemizing this knowledge, but one which flows from our hypothesis about the waves appears the most simple. Rhythm, according to that hypothesis, must be a repetition of similar effects at approximately equal intervals; and the similar effects repeated in poetry are, in the first place, *lines,* and in the second place, *surges of emphasis* within the lines.

Both lines, or short utterances separated by a pause, and the surges of emphasis within them, are found in primitive chants; therefore neither can be regarded as the more original unit. Poetic rhythm is almost universally a combination of the two, and its chief varieties arise from this fact. Nevertheless, the line has been simply taken for granted by most prosodists, as though it were tied across the page before the poet came there, and his verses were various ways of stringing syllables upon it. This is due, I suppose, to the fact that the line rhythm is *visible* to a reader, whereas the rhythm of emphasis is only audible, or to be felt, in the motions of articulation. But whatever may be the cause, it is a basic error, and the great reason, I believe, why no clear account of the nature of poetic rhythm has ever been given.

The recurrence of lines is often accentuated by placing rhymed syllables in a regular order at the ends. Without some such device, indeed, when poetry is read aloud as we read it in these days, the existence of lines is hardly to be detected at all. We may regard the audible rhythm of blank verse as almost purely accentual, and represent it by a single series of waves.

The incurrence of rhyme in this series might then be represented as scientists represent any merging of commensurable undulations, thus:

This strong intensifying of the line series arises naturally, I believe, only in poetry that is especially exciting. Milton was doubtless right in declaring it to be a troublesome bondage in the labor of composing or reading a work, part poem and part treatise, like *Paradise Lost.* But as a general dogma he has reduced his own statement to absurdity by writing greater poetry with rhyme inevitable. Rhyme reduplicates the metric pulse when feeling runs strong, as insuppressibly as a dancing darky begins to clap his hands with every so many clicks of his flying feet. A similar reduplication may be, and has been, accomplished in poetry by other means, and means less difficult to the composer, but rhyme is probably the final best of them. Its exciting and hypnotic power was discovered by the Chinese, by the Persians, and Arabic poets, and doubtless independently by the late Latins in Europe. It is neither a conventional ornament, nor a mnemonic device, nor esoteric, nor ephemeral, in poetry. It is as native to a rhythm that flows high as whitecaps to the ocean.

As for the accentual rhythm, the surge of emphasis within the lines—that needs no intensification, for once it is established, it can hardly be concealed. It is established by so arranging the words that their natural accents produce it. Examine, for instance, the following sentence:

When yóu have eáten all of yóur peánuts, yóu will nót be allówed to share míne.

Various emphases or accented syllables are here, but no metrical rhythm. The words must be rearranged until the emphases recur at *approximately equal intervals.*

When yóu have eáten all yóurs, my peánuts yóu cannot sháre. begins to suggest such an arangement. Yet it is unsatisfactory.

It sounds like the translation of a libretto. It can be improved as follows:

"You cán't have ány of mý peanúts when yoúr peanúts are góne!"

This possesses a rhythm so strong as to compel us to mispronounce a word without knowing that we have done so. We cannot say peá-nuts any longer, even when we try.

These three sentences will exemplify the process of producing an accentual rhythm. Each surge of this rhythm, each group of syllables containing an accent, is called a "foot." And the natural accent plays exactly the same part in the foot, that the rhyme, or the pause, or the turning back of the eyes, does in the line. It establishes and marks the crest of a rhythmic pulse. And these pulses, as well as the line pulses, might be marked off upon the page, if they were not already in danger of overemphasis.

"Oút of the/hílls of/Háber/shám,
Dówn the/válleys of/Háll—
I húr/ry amaín/to reách/the plaín,
Rún the/rápid and/leáp the/fáll——"

From this combining of the pulse of accent with the pulse of line into a single flow, there arise four general types of rhythm. That in which the accent occurs upon the first syllable of the line, and not upon the last, we might call a downward, or falling, rhythm.

"Lázy laúghing lánguid Jénny,
Fónd of a kíss and fónd of a guínea."

That in which the accent occurs upon the first syllable, and also upon the last, would be a down-and-upward, or a falling-rising rhythm.

"Swíftly wálk o'er the wéstern wáve,
Spírit of Níght!"

That in which the accent occurs upon the second (or third)

syllable, and not upon the last, would be an up-and-downward, or a rising-falling rhythm.

"Wee, sleékit, cówrin', tím'rous beástie,
O, whát a pánic's ín thy bréastie!
Thou neéd na stárt awá sae hásty,
  Wi' bíck'ring bráttle!
I wád be laíth to rín an' cháse thee,
  Wi' múrd'ring páttle!"

And that in which the accent occurs upon the second (or third) syllable, and also upon the last, would be a wholly upward, or rising, rhythm.

"Ye bánks and bráes o' bónny Dóon,
How cán ye blóom sae frésh and faír!
How can ye sing, ye little birds,
And I sae weary fu' o' care!

Thou'lt break my heart, thou warbling bird,
That wantons thro' the flowering thorn!
Thou minds me o' departed joys,
Departed—never to return."

These four ways of combining the line with the foot-rhythm are so different in effect that it is well either to make them alternate at regular intervals, or else to make one kind pre dominate enough throughout a poem to throw the mantle of its quality over the whole.

Two rhythms are so made to alternate in this supremely, and to me sadly, beautiful song of Tom Moore's.

"Come, ye disconsolate, where'er you languish,
  Come, at God's altar, fervently kneel;
Here bring your wounded hearts, here tell your anguish,
  'Earth has no sorrow that Heaven cannot heal.'

"Joy of the desolate, Light of the straying,
  Hope, when all others die, fadeless and pure,
Here speaks the Comforter, in God's name saying,
  'Earth has no sorrow that Heaven cannot cure.'

"Go, ask the infidel, what boon he brings us—
What charm for aching hearts he can reveal,
Sweet as that heavenly promise Hope sings us—
'Earth has no sorrow that God cannot heal.'"

In Charles Kingsley's "Song of a River," on the other hand, the spirit of a fall-and-rise rhythm is sustained, in spite of many variant lines, throughout.

"Clear and cool, clear and cool,
By laughing shallow and dreaming pool;
Cool and clear, cool and clear,
By shining shingle and foaming wear;
Under the crag where the ouzel sings,
And the ivied wall where the Church bell rings,
Undefiled for the undefiled;
Play by me, bathe in me, Mother and Child.

"Dank and foul, dank and foul,
By the smoky town in its murky cowl;
Foul and dank, foul and dank,
By wharf and sewer and slimy bank;
Darker and darker the further I go,
Baser and baser the richer I grow;
Who dare sport with the sin defiled?
Shrink from me, turn from me, Mother and Child.

"Strong and free, strong and free;
The flood gates are open, away to the sea.
Free and strong, free and strong,
Cleansing my streams as I hurry along
To the golden sands, and the leaping bar,
And the taintless tide that awaits me afar,
As I lose myself in the infinite main
Like a soul that has sinned and is pardoned again.
Undefiled for the undefiled;
Play by me, bathe in me, Mother and Child."

The variations possible from any of these rhythms are evidently unlimited. But a maker of poetry will usually have the swing of one or another of them definitely in his veins. And this, if he be an amateur, he can most easily acquire by "beating the time" with a pencil, or by simply repeating a monotonous syllable in the various ways.

Tá ta, Tá ta, Tá ta
Tá ta, Tá ta, Tá

for example, and

ta Tá, ta Tá, ta Tá,
ta Tá, ta Tá, ta Tá, ta.

Two such rhythms, even in this abstract form, will have a different effect upon his spirits. And by tasting this difference he will learn more than a whole book of Greek terms could teach him.

The only other general difference between rhythms is a difference in the length of their surges. Poetry may be made, that is, with lines of greater or less length; and it may be made with feet of greater or less length. The lines will hardly exceed six (or at the most seven) feet, because if they exceed that, they cannot easily be perceived in the reading as a single thing. Within that limitation, however, the variety in length of line, or arrangements of different lengths, among which a poet may choose is determined, not by any laws of prosody, but by the laws of combination and permutation, or his own wish. Only he must remember that if he mixes lines of different length, with entire absence of regularity in the recurrence of similar ones, he sacrifices the line almost entirely as an element of fundamental rhythm.

As for the length of foot—that, too, is determined by the poet's wish. He will find it impossible to pronounce more than three (or at the most four) syllables naturally, without placing an accent upon one of them, but within that limitation his choice is free. He may introduce whatever number of syllables between each recurrent emphasis he chooses. And he may use feet of different length in whatever succession he chooses. Only, as in the case of lines, if the length of his surge (the interval between his emphases) is not kept regular enough to maintain the general character of repeating similars in equal intervals, he will sacrifice the foot entirely as an element of fundamental rhythm.

There is little more than this to be said with truth of metrical utterance as a mode of sustaining realization. There is one thing more to be said, however, for those who wish to compose poetry. Rhythmic perception among the civilized races, and especially the musically civilized, is finer than it used to be when they shouted their poems to the accompaniment of a tom-tom. We no longer need the tom-tom's assistance in detecting a rhythm, and it only gives us a sing-song and monotonous experience, against which in itself we often react so strongly that it fails utterly to produce a rhythmic exaltation. We simply go somewhere else. And therefore amateur poets must beware of shouting to the tom-tom. They must beware of having the actual surge of their poetry, when it is naturally read, fall in too exactly with the rhythmic pattern. For the pattern will then dominate them entirely, and their bodies will appear to be swaying and swinging and their feet drumming time to their words, and while they may themselves enter in a truly hearty and primitive fashion into this performance, it will surely appear a little ludicrous to most of their audience.

We might express it in this way, that man has grown so perspicacious, and so vain of his perspicacity in these matters, that he will not tolerate having himself played upon by a too obvious device. He will not even walk up the street with a drum, unless it conceal its monotonous function under some flippancy, skipping a beat now and then, or throwing in a little superfluous thunder. He wishes to unravel his rhythm out of something else. He wishes here, as everywhere, to find a similarity in apparent difference by at least a semiconscious act. And this little vanity of his you will have to consider, even though you may not care to cultivate the conflicts between your pattern and your phrasal rhythm for themselves. You will have to remember continually to swing the natural utterance of your verse *out* of the channel of its rhythm, and yet swing it *in* again, and ever and ever again, so that the pulses of that rhythm, while they are not exaggerated, are yet abundantly sustained.

Remember that you are engendering and sustaining in the mind a flow of waves, and you will need no laws of prosody. Remember also that the words, and groups of words, you work with are not common names grown old in the conveyance of a meaning; they are surprising names, new-made by you, to choose fresh qualities and details in the things you speak of, and to join them in the mind with other things they never knew before, thus sending them alive and vivid into that stream of heightened consciousness the waves induce. You will need no laws of rhetoric. You will have the knowledge of the art of writing poetry, and the surest path to its enjoyment.

XV

THE PRACTICAL VALUE OF POETRY

Every little while the members of a young men's society debate the question whether poets or statesmen have had the greater effect upon history. They decide in favor of the poets, and then go and devote themselves to politics and practical affairs. If meanwhile a poet arises among them, he has attributed to him an unusually liquid and ineffectual character. It appears that a poet in history is divine, but a poet in the next room is a joke. Nobody demurs at our attributing power to Shakespeare, the supreme greatness of Anglo-Saxon life. Few feel that Bacon could uphold such greatness. And the farther into history we look, the more the statesmen dwindle and the poets shine. Lincoln's word of praise gives final honor to Walt Whitman, but poets are the very fame of Pericles.

This mixture of veneration with distrust toward poetry is not colloquial. It is the world's attitude. There are savages of Africa who give beads of wealth and honor to the singers that entertain them, but they bury them upside down in a hollow tree, to show that the honor is not unmixed with contempt. I sometimes think the singers of our own day have a similarly compounded attitude toward themselves. For while they consider a life of realization so self-justifying as to warrant their renouncing for it every aspiration of an acting man, they still descend from this to complain that they are not appreciated by others, as though they had not their own reward. Even the greatest have been affected by some double current of feeling, for they have been moved to defend poetry and write apologies for her, as though she were in contempt of men, but these apologies when they were written gave her such character as would make apology an impertinence. They defended her by declaring that she is above the need or possibility of defence, she is life and mind itself.

One supreme man in literature is reputed to have renounced poetry altogether. But he did in fact only dwell with especial emphasis upon each side of this paradox. Plato is magnificent both in scorn and adoration of the poetic gift. Poets, he declares, are foolish, they are an outrage upon the moral understanding, so insidious in their arts that he is all but ready to banish the whole tribe from his ideal Republic. For what are they engaged in? They are engaged in presenting to the affections, not ideas, but mere things, and these generally the most blood-heating kinds of things, over which they work us up into a wholly inconsequent madness. Nay, it is worse than that, for these things of theirs are not even real, they are not there at all, they are only imagined things! So why should we sacrifice our equilibrium to them? Have we not enough to exercise us in the conduct of genuine life according to intelligent principles? Such is the great question as to poetry. And I think that every poetic person who is well equipped for life has in him this platonic and vulgar contempt of conscious realization, and can taste the anathema in the term poet. "He who cannot rise above his writings that he has been long patching and piecing together, adding some and taking away some, may be justly called Poet!" says Plato, in high scorn of his own pursuits.

It seems as though a man ought to have something to do. Sitting in a hammock with a book of rhyme, realizing the intrinsic being of something, perhaps the west wind, when he ought to trim a windmill, and be starting up the pump—this is a poor picture of a hero. So poor is it, that it will probably bring those who adore poetry, if they have not been brought already, into open conflict with our opinion that it is essentially a realization. They will declare that poetry does promote achievement, does concern itself with practical truth and meaning. A man unacquainted with the *Book of Poems,* according to Confucius, is not only unable to see, but also unable to advance

—he is face to face with a stone wall. According to Philip Sidney, effective instruction is almost the definitive function of poetry. For Shelley all life's idealism, all progress of the spirit, all hope of high action, is contained in the word. And no one of these enthusiasts exceeds Plato himself, who declares, with royal inconsistency, that the character of a people depends so much more upon their songs than upon anything else, that we ought to make these the chief forces in education. Give them great poetry and the state will flourish. Did he say that poetry is madness? Yes—but the madness of poets is the most efficacious state of being that this world offers. Madmen are strong. They mould history and the earth. Is it not a kind of madness that the world exists at all, a kind of infatuation with the idea of being? And is not the madness of Homer more akin to divinity than the sanity of all your politicians? Would you not even rather join yourself with Homer, who so loved reality, and begot with her such children as the Iliad and the Odyssey, than be a husband and the father in respectability of a whole family of industrious citizens? Such is the other judgment of Plato, and his enthusiasm when he speaks upon the brighter side of this universal paradox.

We cannot but conclude that poetry is of high practical value; it is of value to purposive conduct and adjustment for the future. And yet we know that in some way it is also not practical, and of no value beyond itself. I think there would be no inconsistency here, if we were not too eager to generalize—if we were content to say that some poetry is of high practical value, and that other poetry is of no such value at all. Then we should be separating the general definition of poetry from the estimation of particular poems, as heretofore none of its lovers have been willing to do, and we could resolve that ancient paradox and subject it to the demands of rationality.

The poetic as such is not concerned with conduct or the conveyance of meaning. But when one who is concerned with conduct and desires to convey a meaning, conveys it poetically, he adds to his speech a great and separate power. He not only gives to our mind the indication, or the general information that he wishes, but he gives to our bodies an acute impression less easy to forget. To read in practical language is to be told, but to read in poetry is to learn by experience. And it is because of this, because imaginative realization can enhance the statement of a meaning and augment its practical effect, that poetry has become identified with meaning, and with truth, and wisdom, and morality, and all those things that look greatly into the future. Poetry but lends itself to them. It is of its own nature foreign to them all.

Suppose we say that life and danger and death are a great adventure, and it is best to know them and enter into them heartily—we should put into that statement almost all the meaning of this poem, but we should leave out the living realization of its meaning:

"Give me a spirit that on life's rough sea
Loves to have his sails fill'd with a lusty wind
Even till his sail-yards tremble, his masts crack,
And his rapt ship run on her side so low
That she drinks water and her keel ploughs air;
There is no danger to a man that knows
What life and death is—there's not any law
Exceeds his knowledge."

Does not such poetry add itself and its own efficacy, entirely new, to the meaning which we had expressed? And furthermore, if poetry can add efficacy to such a meaning, will it not also add efficacy to false or impractical meanings? I think that we should as rigorously condemn a poet for touching the torch of realization to an unheroic idea, such as this,

"'Tis not what man Does which exalts him, but what man Would do!"

as we should extol him for giving illumination to a great concept. But in either case the illumination is not the concept, and if opinions are ever to be consistent upon this subject, it must be distinguished from it by the understanding. No meaning properly so called has ever been expressed with poetry, which could not conceivably be severed from its poetry and set forth in practical language.

Perhaps this judgment does not give to poetry as such the most commanding place in men's esteem. For while they all respect the expression of a meaning destitute of poetry, calling this a culmination of their scientific spirit, but few give honor to any poetry that is unrelated to a meaning. Reading pure poetry is like gazing on the moonlight long. We wish we could receive it, but we cannot—a final proof that we are sadly practical at heart. We are but driven pilgrims through the world, the children of its evolution, and we must be going on. Pure being is too much for us. The best that we can ask of moonlight is that it shall shine upon our occupation. Perhaps the best that we can ask of poetry is that it shall attend the statement of a truth with glory. And yet there are great poems, poems universally called great, which are pure realizations. There is Keats's "Ode to Autumn." Let it be held a supreme achievement of his genius. For with all the world intent upon a future, eager for the word that indicates, it is not easy to withhold it and be noble. It is not possible for those mere lovers of their moods who oftenest elect to try it. But for those whose character and thought are deep, determined onward with the world, and who arrest us as the world itself sometimes arrests us for a moment only with the wonder of its being, it is possible. Pure poetry upon their lips seems even more divine than truth, more ultimate, more universal.

There is indeed, for those who recognize its aim, a value in such poetry that goes beyond the present. There is a value toward a goal not yet attained. Even the mere realization of autumn in its absence—unattended though it be by any moral or true meaning—looks somewhat to a future end. It looks to autumn. It is not only an imagination, but a preperception, and its value culminates in the more full experience of the very hours it dreamed of. Thus the poetry of words may be regarded as a means toward the poetry of life. It is to that end practical. It nourishes the waking spirit, nourishes the gift of vision, and the tendency to issue from the bondages of habit and receive the world. We recognize this value in our kindergartens, where we seek to train the mind in childhood for keeping awake during a lifetime. But poetry continues and renews this training always. We do not read Shelley and then return to the world, but we see the world through Shelley's eyes. Creative vision of the specific actual throughout all time—creative vision kindled by that flaming language, is an onward and immortal value of his songs.

The poetry of books prepares, and also it restores. To us the world grows stale, because in proportion as we become accustomed to a thing we are estranged from it. In proportion as we win the daily presence of our friends, we lose them. We come to regard life as a dry package of facts. We want the spirituous refreshment of another's vision. We want to have our eyes reopened, and our souls made naked to the touch of being.

This is the priesthood of art—not to bestow upon the universe a new aspect, but upon the beholder a new enthusiasm. At our doors every morning the creation is sung. The day is a drama, the night is an unfolding mystery, within whose shadowy arena impetuous life shall still contend with death. A world laughs and bleeds for us all the time, but our response in this meteoric theatre we suffer to be drugged with business and decorum. We are born sleeping, and few of us ever awake, unless it be upon some hideous midnight when death startles us, and we learn in grief alone what bit of Olympian fire our humid forms enwrapped. But we could open our eyes to joy also. The poet cries "Awake!" and sings the song of the morning. He that hath eyes let him see! Even now all around us the trees have arisen, and their leaves are tongues of the air in song—the earth swings on in drastic revolution—and we laugh and love perpetually—and the winds enlarge our goings and our comings with a tune.

The poet, the restorer, is the prophet of a greater thing than faith. All creeds and theories serve him, for he goes behind them all, and imparts by a straighter line from his mind to yours the spirit of bounteous living. His wisdom is above knowledge. He cries to our sleeping selves to come aloft, and when we are come he answers with a gesture only. In him we find no principle; we find ourselves re-born alive into the world.

So far from being past, or on the wane, this wisdom of the soul of poetry looks for the first time joyfully into the future. Man is now returning to his rights as an animal. He has now learned that morals is not meant for a scourge and a dry medicine, and that joy is its own reason. Existence was not perpetrated in malice or benevolence, but simply is, and the end of our thinking is that here we are, and what can we make of it? We have a planet to act upon, a sense of the drama. We will not squat and argue, nor balk, and try to justify God, but we will make with high hearts of abandon our entrance and our exit before the congregation of the stars.

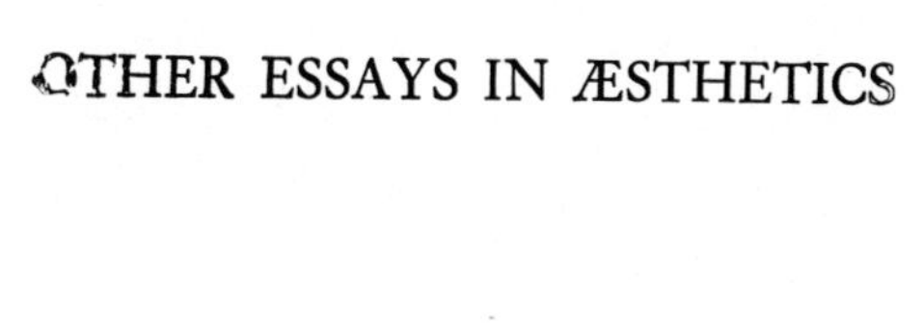

OTHER ESSAYS IN ÆSTHETICS

WHAT POETRY IS

I

THE conflict between science and religion was, or will be, adjudicated for intelligent people by a scientific study of religion. It has been so with magic. It will doubtless be so in the future with systems of metaphysical belief. Indeed I think the current "reconstruction in philosophy" might almost be described by saying that philosophy, having once vaingloriously set out to explain science, is now somewhat consenting to be explained by science. Undoubtedly the same thing will happen to literature, in so far as literature professes to have a validity in conflict with the findings of science. The scholarly defenders of "literary truth" will continue to hold their own in a dying fashion, until men have approached literature itself with the methods of trained observation and experiment, and learned to state in general terms what it is and how it differs from their own activities.

What *is* literature apart from science? What is the literary mind? What will it have left to do, thousands of years hence when trained investigators with statistics and laboratory findings under their bulging arms may conceivably have *some* tested and dependable word to say upon almost any problem that arises? These are the questions that demand answer, once we have penetrated the superficial commotion about romantic and classic, naturalist and humanist, tradition and experiment. And since it is quite obviously poetry, or the poetic ingredient, that makes literature deeply different from science, it is not too much to say that the central problem for those concerned about the future of literature is the problem of defining poetry.

The very idea will provoke a smile among the sophisticated, for it has become almost a commonplace these days that poetry cannot be defined. "Poetry," says Herbert Read, "is properly speaking a transcendental quality—an effulgence radiating from the sudden transformation which words assume under a particular influence—and we can no more define this quality than we can define infinity." "What is man," cries T. S. Eliot, "to decide what poetry is ?" Edwin Arlington Robinson defines poetry as an "indefinable." And even Professor Snyder, whose little book, *Hypnotic Poetry,* is the latest real contribution to this subject, remarks with a sigh that he does not look with much hope "toward the general controversies over 'What is poetry?' which have been carried on since the dawn of history." This agnosticism is a new thing, and testifies, I believe, not to a deeper or finer experience of poetry among our critics, but to a dawning apprehension among them of what it means to define a thing. They are ready to give up, because they see clearly that a million definitions have failed to define, but they do not see what help this very fact can give them in the task of definition

The world is indeed overfull of ingenious and sprightly essays which purport to tell us what poetry is, but really tell us what kind of poem the author likes, or upon what quality when reading he most fixes his attention. Poetry has been defined by estimable authorities as imitation of human life, glimpse of the divine, wine of the devil, as expression of emotion, sublime expression of truth, aspiration toward beauty, communication of pleasure, as speaking pictures, apparent pictures of unapparent natures, as reality, make-believe, as concrete, as abstract, metaphor, metre, madness, wisdom, sanity, trance—there is almost no way in which poetry has not been defined. There is no sphere in which "the best that has been thought and said in the world" shows a more bewildering disjointedness, a more total lack of focus and complete incapacity to guide the inquiring mind, than in this sphere of the essay on poetry. Our critics perceive this, but it does not occur to them to make the most simple inference from it—namely that the word poetry is an extremely general term, and must apply to something quite ordinary and wellnigh universal. If you can find poetry in all the situations by which sane and wise men have proposed to define its essence, then you can find it almost anywhere. And the only possible way to give clear sense to a word of such wide application is to find a very general definition, one which will include all those applications and yet also significantly exclude something.

Of course there is a voluntary element in all definition. If Herbert Read wishes to confine the word poetry to a few rare and ecstatic states of his being which he also calls transcendental effulgences, nobody can stop him. Such states of being exist, and the word poetry exists. But if we can find a clear and highly general distinction which corresponds to the uses of this word, or makes intelligible at least a large proportion of its important uses not only now but throughout history, and which provides the best as well as the most natural first step towards a useful classification of literature, then I think the voluntary part of the act of definition—the arresting of this particular word and conscripting it to this purpose—can safely be left to the practical good sense of mankind.

The attempt to define poetry was put on a wrong track at the beginning, owing to the absence in early times of novels and prose dramas. For Aristotle the term poetry included all kinds of fiction writing, and thus he thought he could distinguish poetry by its subject matter—call it "imitation of life," and regard the diction of the poet as incidental. The mere fullness of experience has displaced his use of the word poetry—confused enough in his own day, it seems to me—and to cling now to the antique idea of a "poetic subject," as Matthew Arnold did, is merely to stand stuck in the mud while history passes you by. It is poetic diction that we have to define. We have to describe what happens when a man who has something to say says it poetically, and how it is that this poetic way of speaking when concentrated and developed becomes poetry instead of prose. It is absurd to say that these questions cannot be answered; they can be answered as soon as we understand our minds. It is still more absurd to be afraid to answer them, as I think many lovers of poetry are, lest something be lost, as though defining a general term could exhaust or destroy the wealth and variety of the particulars.

The problem, I repeat, is to find a definition general enough to include all these particulars. To say that poetic diction is beautiful, or true, or divine, or devilish, or passionate, or sensuous, or effulgent, or pictorial, or indeed to attribute to it any other special quality of experience, may be a good way to lead someone into it, but will not serve as a general definition, for the moment you select one of these qualities, I can show you poetic diction which exhibits the opposite. Even if you become very matter-of-fact and "in despair of giving a serious definition of poetry," say with Professor Santayana that poetry is "metrical discourse," I can find you examples of diction which is not metrical, but is so vividly metaphorical that you will have to call it poetic. When Miss Edith Sitwell, wishing to tell us that the plants in her garden are bending down with their blossoms near the earth, says that they "begin to cluck," we do not have to have metre to assure us that this is poetic. On the other hand, if you regard metre as accidental, and say, as Miss Helen Parkhurst does in her recent book called *Beauty,* "The quintessence of poetry . . . is little else than metaphor," I can bring you examples of diction that is metrical but not metaphoric—a great part of the popular ballads, for example—and you can hardly deny that they too are poetic.

Metre and metaphor "belong together," and our definition will have to be general enough to include them both and explain their companionship. It will also have to include language that may be neither metrical nor figurative, but deliberately and as though with malice aforethought arouses our emotions. It is not poetic to shout, "Look out, there's a rattlesnake!" when there really is one, no matter how much emotion the words arouse. But to cry "Vipers and venom!" into the vacant air suggests that a poem is about to begin, if it is not perhaps already finished.

Emotion is, in fact, together with metre and metaphor, so commonly found in poetry that it too has been used as a defining term by matter-of-fact people, by people who understand that the problem is not one of ingenious invention but of adequate generalization. There are two reasons why poetry cannot be defined with the word emotion. One is that emotion is present in all alert states of being; to identify poetry with emotional speech would be almost to identify it with wide-awake speech, and that indeed is *too* general. The other reason is that as soon as you define emotion and really distinguish it from other elements in experience—or to the extent that you do so—it becomes easy to show that poets frequently violate an emotion and destroy it when they are interested in something else. Psychologists are not well agreed as to the nature of emotions; all men agree, however, that they belong among the inner as opposed to the outer feelings. They differ from sensations like color and sound which come directly in to us from causes in the external world. And the moment you have defined emotion even to this small extent, a glance over the field of poetry will show that poets are not at all exclusively preoccupied with it. I always like to prove this with that passage from Homer's Iliad, where Ajax, the great fighting man of the Greek army, their sole bulwark in the absence of Achilles, falls wounded in battle. He lies there bleeding and gasping, and the Trojans come ramping over the plain, and you would certainly think that if poetry were solely devoted to emotions, a supreme poet would not let pass this supreme chance. But just as though to disprove this too introvert definition of poetry, Homer catches sight of the blood flowing down on Ajax's thigh, and he becomes so interested in the mere color of that blood that he wanders off babbling about it as though he had never had an inward or deep feeling in his life. He babbles like a rustic—or what we call a pastoral poet. "Why, it was so darned purple," he says, in effect, "that it reminded me of those pieces of ivory—you know those girls over in Caria that dye little pieces of ivory to make ornaments for the bridles of those fine horses they have over there, awfully pretty girls, and they get it all over their arms. . . ." That single—and perhaps slightly irreverent—recollection of a great poet so preoccupied by a quality of external, or as they say, projicient, sensation, that he ignores and transgresses the feeling-tone of his own climax of tragedy, suggests the difficulty one would have in defining poetry by emotion, once one had really defined emotion.

I dwell on the impossibility of this definition, because the attempt has a certain scientific standing. John Stuart Mill made it sound very wise and technical by linking it up with the "association psychology" of his day. Ideas, according to that psychology, are associated on a basis of "resemblance," "contiguity" or "emotional congruity." And the poets, said Mill, are "those who are so constituted that emotions are the links by which their ideas, both sensuous and spiritual, are associated together." I have called Homer to witness that this definition will not hold, because it seemed well to have a big and respectable witness. But the case could be more easily proven by any of our very modern poets who have been so earnestly striving not to be romantic that they have almost a neurotic aversion to emotional congruity. When E. E. Cummings, in his delicately almost sublime poem of a cathedral at sunset, introduces the word *bloated* to describe the rose acres in the evening sky—a word sacred, so far as I can testify, to the memory of dead fish—this choice, or comparison, or whatever it may be, is certainly not "association by emotional congruity." Years ago, before Mr. Cummings was known as the inventor of the punctuational gymnastic, I sat with him and some others in a room where a cat was purring. In a pause of our conversation—which was a rather chilly one, he being a poet and I for the moment an editor—he suddenly exclaimed: "I have it—it's milking the cow, it's the milk scudding into the foam in the pail!" The emotional incongruity of this remark to the prevailing atmosphere was so great that everybody, as I remember, was a trifle embarrassed. But as a pure matter of auditory sensation it was so accurate that it remained in my mind—John Stuart Mill to the contrary notwithstanding—as the sure proof of a poet. It was, indeed, significant of a whole small epoch of poetry in which a meticulous and witty sensuousness has been more popular than inward feeling. With that epoch behind us, it should be obvious at least that poetry cannot be defined with the word emotion.

II

If the crucial word in our definition must be more general than the name of any element or quality in experience, then obviously it must be some such word as quality or experience itself. If I say that poetic diction has or conveys more qualities than prosaic—if I say it is more like experience, or more *of* an experience, to read it—I think everybody will agree with me, no matter what kind of poetry he likes. And that is, in fact, all that is possible and all that is necessary to say. Poetic diction suggests the qualities of experience; it does this more than prosaic diction does; it does it more than is practically necessary, or necessary to theoretic understanding. When a prosaic or practical companion would be content merely to point to something, a tree for instance to which he wishes you to attach a clothes-line, a poet will take the trouble to say "Hitch it to that old hickory," or perhaps he will say "that shaggy old hickory." He is interested in the quality of the thing, and not wholly focussed upon its use. And when, in the absence of things, a poet wishes to remind you of them, he again goes farther than is necessary for mere purposes of identification. He speaks of old trees, even when he is not talking about any particular ones, as "knotty, knarry, barren," because he likes to remember trees. And when he is talking about a whole woodsful of these abstract trees he calls it "some branchy bunchy bushybowered wood," because he wants to feel as though it were here. Even indeed when there are no trees in question, and no "thing" in question at all—only the poetry itself, as in these days seems often the case—the poet is still trying to convey the quality of an experience. And to make us clearly, or intensely, or richly, or vividly conscious of this quality is the whole of his effort. It is an effort, as Miss Edith Sitwell very accurately affirms, to *heighten consciousness.* Pure poetry is the pure effort to heighten consciousness; it is poetry spoken when a practical person would have nothing at all to say.

Prose, on the other hand, is merely the practical way of talking. It names things with the ordinary names through which we have become adapted to them, and indicated their important relations, and learned to use them, and it regulates our attitudes toward them with no more suggestion of their quality than is necessary for identification. It does not matter in the least whether the things in question are real or imaginary; it matters only how they are spoken of. There is not a purer example of naked prose style in English than that of Jonathan Swift in his extravagantly fanciful account of *Gulliver's Travels.* Indeed it is the complete absence of poetic realization from these tales—the fact that they are told in the perfected language of an inventory of goods or a text-book of information—which gives them their uniquely veridical flavor. Usually in literature fanciful events are recounted poetically, and therefore this extreme prose style induces an attitude of belief which, in view of the incredibility of the events, gives us a feeling like realization. A kind of inverse poetry thus results from the very practicality of the language. But the fact remains that our most fanciful classic is written in our purest prose. And there is no conceivable way to describe this prose except to say that in telling us things, it refrains from suggesting their qualities. If a real adventure were as prosaically described, we should consider the book somewhat lacking in color—which is to say, in intimations of what things are like—and we should be quite right. For ordinarily, and except for scientific or business purposes, a good prose style must contain its ingredient of poetry. Indeed absolute prose, or language used without a hint of the concrete existence of things, is to be found only in books of logic and mathematics.

III

People who have read a few thousand of the literary definitions of poetry will realize that the one I am advocating is not unfamiliar. On the contrary it is a view which has already, without any clear consciousness of the process of generalization by which it was arrived at, begun to prevail among the more alert critics and teachers of literature. Bliss Perry in his *Study of Poetry* urges his students to "remember that poets are endeavoring to convey the 'sense' of things rather than the knowledge of things." Robert Graves says that the virtues of verse are these: "Its rhythms, rhymes and texture have an actual toxic effect on the central nervous system. In the resulting condition . . . voices are heard, images are called up, and various emotions felt of a far greater intensity than in normal life." John Drinkwater in his delightful little book about *The Lyric* describes poetry as "the sign of that which all men desire . . . intensity of life or completeness of experience." "Extreme activity of the perceptive mood," he calls it. And with a tranquil innocence of technical terminology, he speaks of "the poetic emotion, or intensity of perception." He is pointing the same way as Miss Sitwell with her "heightening" of consciousness. Hart Crane, too, in defending some of his metaphorious sins, described the whole province of the poet's art as "added consciousness and increased perceptions." Even the philosophers, who have for the most part little attended to the real nature of poetry—using the word most often as a kind of scrap-bag for any old pieces of things that would not fit into their systems—are waking up to this clear and more general conception of it. Professor Whitehead takes it quite for granted when he says: "I hold that the ultimate appeal is to naïve experience and that is why I lay such stress on the testimony of the poets." He is wrong no doubt in laying stress on their *testimony* —especially to the existence of such things as "eternality"— for testimony involves interpretation. But he is right in looking to them for a *communication of the quality* of the naïve experience. I think it may be said that the literary mind as a whole —except where it has lapsed into an agnosticism that is indolence upon this subject—is drifting toward that conception of poetry which I propose that it grasp clearly and adhere to.

The manner and the course of its drifting—in England at least—may be indicated as follows. Coleridge, although in rapture he wove, like Wordsworth and Shelley, a power of knowledge into the very definition of the poet, nevertheless did in a cooler vein contrast poetry correctly with science. "A poem," he said, "is that species of composition which is opposed to works of science as having for its immediate object pleasure, not truth." The modern drift toward wisdom has consisted of putting, first "emotion," and then afterward "experience" or "intensity of life" or "the sense of things" or "added consciousness" in place of the word *pleasure* in making this distinction. And this great step forward has been taken because our more realistic psychology has taught us that "pleasure" is an abstraction not often pursued by any, and by some anxiously avoided. The poet is no more and no less concerned with this abstraction than the scientist.

But there is a further step forward to be taken—likewise under guidance of our better psychology. Not only is the poet not seeking pleasure in the naked and abstract way that Coleridge imagined, but the scientist is not seeking a "truth" quite so embracing and akin to a total report of experience as he and the essayists of his day conceived. In order fully to grasp the definition of poetry as a communication of the qualities of things, it is necessary to realize the extent to which science is not a communication of these qualities. We are in process of realizing this, and the realization is working a deep change in our attitude toward all mental problems—a change so deep that we may now even genuinely hope to succeed where so many have failed in comprehending the nature of poetic speech.

Science does not merely refer to things in our experience and state what they "are," but interprets them and states how they are to be "conceived" in relation to other experiences, and to the interests and modes of behavior of the conceiving mind. This fact, which had become apparent to those who studied the mind itself scientifically, has been driven home to all scientific students by the recent extreme developments in theoretical and practical physics. To take a simple example, it was once hotly disputed among physicists whether light consists of waves in a disturbed fluid, or of a stream of moving particles. This hot dispute over what light "is" has now dissolved away into a common agreement to conceive light in both ways, or in either that happens to be convenient in working out a given problem. Light as an experience could obviously not "be" both waves and a stream of particles. Indeed, I do not see how it could be either one or the other, for in order to see these waves or these particles you would have to have light shining on them, and it would have to be—begging the physicists' pardon—*real* light! But such remarks do not any longer disturb the physicists, because they so generally realize that the question what light "is," is not the one they are trying to answer. They are trying to find out how light should be conceived in order to generalize its important relations to other things, and enable them to predict or control its behavior.

This new understanding of science prevails so widely to-day that Clarence I. Lewis in his book on *Mind and the World Order* is able to speak of "the absurd prejudice—now happily obsolescent—that science is 'just a report of facts.'" What is not quite so widely understood—although even more important for the theory of poetry—is that long before science begins, the very language with which it begins has already accomplished a vast work of practical and theoretic interpretation. We are far from the experienced facts when we begin to talk about them. Professor Lewis has demonstrated as convincingly as Bergson, and without any ulterior motives of a mystical order, how persistently all words, and indeed all thoughts, interpret experiences from the standpoint of purposes and modes of behavior and social co-operation—so much so that it is impossible, he thinks, even to allude to an experience without so interpreting it. There is such a thing, he comforts us, as the uninterpreted *quale,* the "given-in-experience," but it is not to be communicated in language. To describe a thing as "edible" is quite obviously to interpret it for purposes of action, but to describe it as "an apple" also contains such interpretation. Even to call it "a thing" is false to the sheer "feel or quality." Trying desperately to suggest what the sheer feel or quality is, which being interpreted becomes an apple, Professor Lewis calls it "a round, ruddy, tangy-smelling somewhat," thus startling with one phrase of poetry the most strenuously prosaic volume I have read in years. It could not be otherwise, for poetry *is* the attempt to make words suggest the given-in-experience.

It is undoubtedly true that this goal is, in an absolute sense, unattainable. The given-in-experience in its purity cannot be spoken, and that is why the modernist poets, having resolutely set out to speak it, are going through such a variety of meta-grammatical contortions. The life of our race has been predominantly filled with strivings or anxieties; we have been all the time trying to adapt ourselves to the environment, or it to us; and our speech reflects this preoccupation with action and adaptation. But it is equally true that we cannot get away from the given-in-experience; some lingering image of it remains with us so long as we speak, and indeed so long as our thought is conscious. And I suspect that the growth of language has been influenced by the desire to communicate sheer qualities far more than Professor Lewis or any of his colleagues in the instrumental logic have happened to imagine. It seems to me sentimental and foolish to say, as Professors Greenough and Kittredge do in their text-book on philology, that "language is poetry." The growth of language must obviously be, like the use of it, partly poetic and partly practical. That word *ruddy,* for instance, has probably survived or been revived alongside its cousin *red,* because of its value in exactly the function to which Professor Lewis devotes it. With its more colorful vowel and that hard and yet dancing *ddy* at the end, it suggests a quality of experience whose difference from red would not often matter practically, but is worth communicating for its own sake. *Tang* also is a word to some extent, I think, intrinsically poetic. Poetry at any rate is not merely a trick that we have learned to perform with a practical instrument; it has played its part in creating the instrument.

Professor Lewis, then, in his eagerness to prove that words do not communicate the given-in-experience, has proven that to some extent, when chosen and employed to that end, they do. He has done this so well as to make it plausible that if he had a sustained passion for thus restoring a sense of the given, and for building up structures out of the experiences restored—such a passion as he has for clarifying our interpretations and unfolding the relations between them—he might be as distinguished a poet as he is a logician. Indeed I do not see that his "round, ruddy, tangy-smelling apple" is greatly inferior in its kind to Chaucer's "knotty, knarry, barren trees," or Hopkins's "branchy bunchy bushybowered wood." It is certainly the same kind of talk.

IV

When the words *poetic* and *prosaic,* or still better *poetic* and *practical,* have been identified with this most general distinction which can be made in the uses of language, the millions of literary "definitions" of poetry fall into their true place as indications of the various things that can be done with, or made out of, poetic diction. But it remains to show that the three almost universal attributes of poetry, those with which even scientific minds have tried to define it—metre and figure and a preoccupation with emotions—stand in a particular relation to poetic diction as so defined. They each enter into the technique of suggesting the given-in-experience and heightening our consciousness of it.

Let us consider first the mystery of the poet's addiction to an essentially monotonous rhythm. I cannot think of any other art besides poetry in which so much labor has been expended in the effort to be monotonous. If you go back to the early Anglo-Saxon poetry, you find that it sounds almost like beating a drum or a tom tom—or, as Andrew Lang says, "like blows of hammers on an anvil."

> "Icy in glimmer and eager for sailing."
> "With weapons of warfare, weeds for the battle."
> "Bold and battle grim brandished his ring-sword."

These two-stroke lines, each stroke repeating the consonant of the last, were strung together by the old bards or glee-men for hours and hours. It seems almost incredible that the most sensitive and intellectual men of the clan should have been so wilfully tedious in their public talk. They even left out the definite article most of the time in order to reduce their poetry as nearly as possible to a perfectly regular series of twin yells, grunts or shouts. In order to understand this strange thing, you have to remember that these glee-men were also jugglers and magicians, and that they danced too and banged on a stringed instrument, and that the whole performance was largely hypnotic.

The subtler poets of our day conceal the monotony of their metre by pushing it down underneath a more flowing growth of speech, decorating it with the delights not only of syncopation but of complete riot and rebellion against its iron beat. But although they rebel and riot against it, they never permit us to forget that beat completely. Verse is distinguished from prose exactly and only by the degree to which this monotonous mathematical drumming which lies in the heart of all rhythm forces itself upon our attention. As Edward Sapir has expressed it, "Verse is *rhythmically self-conscious speech*. . . . Verse rhythms come, or should come, to us; we go to the rhythms of prose." There is no other difference. And for my part I find it still incredible that intellectual and sensitive people, with no unkind motive in their hearts, should expend the most intense efforts of which the mind is capable in order to force this monotony upon us along with their most lively conversation, unless they are still trying to hypnotize us.

Professor Snyder insists that in order to read poetry wisely and criticize it well, we must learn how to distinguish hypnotic poetry from the poetry that he calls "intellectualist." He is right, I think, in emphasizing these two extremes, and advising us to approach and judge them differently. And since our poets at the moment are striving so hard if not altogether successfully to be intellectual, his book becomes a plea for the appreciation of poetic rapture with which I deeply sympathize.[1] To my mind it is the people who employ metre *without* the purpose to entrance—who dress out the most cold, sober and sophisticated of

[1]Professor Snyder makes one erroneous statement which I wish to correct. He says that in my *Enjoyment of Poetry,* where I first suggested that hypnosis explains the association of metre with poetry, I evinced "a certain timidity" about applying this principle, and merely left the matter to be decided by "a mature science." I was timid and disposed to await a mature science, not about the hypnotic effect of a rhythmic stroke nor its relevance to poetry, but only about whether that effect could be ex-

adult "propositions" in irrelevant sing-song—it is they, and not the poets of rapture, who may be asked to defend themselves against a charge of "intellectual immaturity" and of playing with a childish toy. At any rate Professor Snyder realizes that his distinction is one of degree, and he does not oppose my contention that the original and basic function of the rhythmic stroke in poetry—the reason why it got there, no matter what merely delightful objective patterns certain mental types of people may choose to make out of it afterward—is that it hypnotizes the reader, or brings him a little way into that hypnoid state in which any experience that the words suggest is realized with a completeness approaching hallucination. That a mild monotonous metric stroke is a means of lulling us into these states, is a piece of psychologic wisdom as old as the race of man. That it belongs naturally upon the lips of poets, if poetry is defined as making words suggest the experienced qualities of things, is obvious enough.

Another slight custom is so general among poets as almost to belong to the definition of their speech, and that is their use of archaic or liturgical forms of expression—the *thee's* and *thou's* and *for aye's* and *forevermore's* in English poetry, for example—which effect a separation of the poetic moment from the ordinary flux of life. They make entering a poem seem a little like going to church. Even when the poem is quite manifestly nothing but a glassful of the wine of the devil, and sparkles all through with the lewdest passions of this world, it still has often this kinship with the language of worship. It is the old kinship, never too close, between magic and religion. For these forms too are to be interpreted as a part of the baggage

plained by the assumption that the nervous current proceeds in waves. About that I should still speak without a great deal of courage, although it seems on the whole more probable to me now than it did then. The difference between us is that I applied the principle to metrical poetry universally, and Professor Snyder corrects me—without denying that it may have had originally this universal application—by showing that it is possible to distinguish poetry which is hypnotic from that which is not.

of the witch doctor. They are weird instruments of a wand-like nature which he lifts over us to get us transfixed and fit for the ritual slumber. They are somewhat out of fashion in these days when poetry, rather overwhelmed to see how much can be accomplished with straight talk and machinery, has been aping prose rhythms and trying to cover up all signs of its origin and true base in the practice of magic. Whether these wonder-working expressions will come back with the inevitable return to hypnotic rhythms, we shall wait to see.

Our next task is to show that a preoccupation with emotions belongs to poetry in the same special way as a disposition to put us to sleep. And this is perhaps the most difficult problem that a definition of poetry has to face, for there is nothing more indubitably associated with wakefulness than emotion. I remember that being kept awake by his own emotions was what led Professor MacDougall to his theory of emotional instincts as the very source of nervous energy and purpose. His theory is not widely accepted now—any more than any other theory of the emotions—but the agreement is universal that emotions accompany an aroused and active state of the body. In fact the assertion made by James and Lange thirty-five years ago, that emotions are merely sensations of bodily change and movement —they are how it feels to behave in certain ways—is still the underlying assumption of most attempts to locate or explain these inward elements of experience. It would seem, then, that our definition has the impossible task of reconciling two exactly opposite things, the stimulant and the sedative—or, as I like to call them, the wine and sleep—in poetry.

This impossible task will accomplish itself without the slightest effort on our part, if we but remember that poetic diction when it is metrical is employed in the absence of the external things of which it wishes to heighten our consciousness. The poet strokes us with his syllables and lulls us into a controlled slumber, in order to make us vividly aware of external impressions which we are not really having. A part of his "given-in-experience," that is to say, is not actually given—it is not there—and only in dreams or states of dreaminess or trance, can we be made vividly to perceive things which are not there. It is for the sake of this external part of experience that the poet resorts to the mesmeric arts, and literally tries to sing us to sleep. But there is another element in every experience, an element of inward feeling, which is present when things are present, and forms a part—often indeed the intensest part—of our experience of them, but which also remains available when the things are gone. To this inward element, which we so conveniently carry round with us—and which when it has a certain degree or kind of poignancy we call emotion—the poet has naturally a different attitude. He wants to evoke this, so far as he can, in reality and not in image. He is here no mesmerist or magician, but a lexical and social engineer. And we need not be surprised if, as we surrender to the somnolent monotony of his rhythms, we find him deliberately plunging words soaked with hot feeling into our hearts, and even pounding our blood-stream with that very rhythm which seemed only to be lulling our pulses to rest. He is impelled to these opposite tactics by an identical motive, the desire to convey vivid experience. Those inward feelings are a part of experience, and so belong to his effort as ends. But they are also that part which he can really and not only imaginatively evoke with words, and so enter into his technique as a means of giving intensity to the whole. That is the reason why, in spite of so many clear facts to the contrary, wise men continue to insist that poetic diction can be defined as solely preoccupied with emotions—as though a poet were of necessity introverted and romantically shut up inside his own viscera—as though, indeed, any such one-dimensional creature of feeling could exist.[1]

[1]The fact is that the word *emotion* as commonly used by writers on æsthetics does not mean emotion at all, but means an aroused but inactive consciousness. They use this word, not in order to distinguish an element in consciousness, but in order to distinguish that whole condition from an enterprising one.

V

When language is not metrical or wantonly emotional, we still call it poetic if it contains a luxury of surprising and rich adjectives and figurative expressions, particularly those swift figures, metonymy and metaphor, which do not help to explain like maps or illustrations, but rather obscure the meaning of the sentence in which they occur. If then we can explain these "figures of speech"—which no rhetoric or grammar-book ever has explained—with the same generalization with which we explain metrical rhythm and a preoccupation with emotions, we shall be entitled to call that generalization the beginning at least of a scientific conception of poetry.

So long as figurative speech is vaguely described as using words in "out of the ordinary" ways, calling a thing by an "unusual" name, or applying to it an adjective that is not "habitually" applied, its value to the art of heightening consciousness is obvious. The ordinary, usual and habitual slides through our brains without enough friction even to attract attention. We have heard the expression *sharp point,* for example, almost as often as *How do you do?* or *All aboard!* and that is reason enough for saying *thrilling point* or some phrase like that, if you wish to make us vividly aware of the dangerous end of a sword. However, it will not do to say *sky-scraping* or *loud-thundering* point. That might arouse a certain consciousness, but it would be of the author's dullness rather than the sharpness of the sword. In order to heighten our consciousness of any particular experience, figurative language must depart from the ordinary in certain special ways. These ways have been imposingly classified and given alarming long Latin names by grammarians who had not the slightest idea why any one should depart from the ordinary at all. And the names are so much like those of prehistoric animals that they have frightened a great many people away from poetry. But the acts themselves are simple enough, and quite harmless, and there are only two of them. One may, instead of calling an experience by its own proper name, call it by the name of some element within it; or one may depart from it altogether and call it by the name of some other experience that is similar. These acts might be described adequately as figures of choice and figures of comparison. Thus I may say "The sudden bulk of a man alarmed us," instead of saying "A bulky man suddenly alarmed us." That is a figure of choice, and would be called *metonymy* or *synecdoche* by the grammarians, just as fire was called "escaping phlogiston" by chemists who did not have the slightest idea why it occurred. Or I may say "A sudden mountain of a man alarmed us," and that is a figure of comparison, called *metaphor* by the grammarians. In the first case I have replaced the "ordinary" name of the man with the name of his own bulk; in the second, I have replaced it with the name of another bulky thing.

That figures of choice do heighten our consciousness of a suggested experience may be seen in the example of the "sudden bulk" of a man. And with a little reflection it may be seen how they do this. They emphasize, more sharply than the corresponding adjective would, a specific detail or quality in the experience. In actual life we always receive experiences, especially at moments of high consciousness, with some quality or detail thus dominant. We receive them with our attention focussed. Indeed, a "heightened consciousness" and a focussed attention are, in the language of many psychologists, but two aspects of the same thing. A low consciousness is a diffused one. Poetry keeps calling out the names of specific details and qualities in things, and even when possible lets these replace the general names of the things, because it is trying to arrest our attention. It was to this technique that Professor Lewis resorted in order to suggest that given-in-experience which practically interpreted becomes an apple. He abandoned the general name of the object and called it a "round ruddy tangy-smelling somewhat." He thus became a poet—but not quite, I regret to say, a pure one. For his habit of practical interpretation survived lamentably in that word *somewhat*. What has that to do with the given-in-experience? It is merely the most general interpretation Professor Lewis could think of, and really carries us still farther away from experience than would *apple* itself. With a little instruction from our modernist poets, Professor Lewis would soon learn to abandon these last survivals of the practical or prose habit. He would name his uninterpreted apple a "round, ruddy, tangy-smelling," and nothing more. And that would be a "figure of speech"—metonymy or synecdoche, or what you will—defined by the grammarians as "naming the part for the whole," "the container for the contained," "the author for the creature," "the attribute for the substance," and so forth. It should be defined as omitting (or subordinating) the practical name, which by immediately identifying an experience with a general class toward which we have established attitudes of action, reduces our consciousness to a minimum, and supplying a new name which, while suspending our tendencies toward action, selects a focus for the resulting heightened consciousness or attention.

To explain why figures of comparison inhere in the essence of poetry is a little more difficult, although the fact is most obvious of all.

> "Her paps are like fair apples in the prime,"

sings the old bard. And this seems so intrinsically and naturally to be the essence of song, that when he adds:

> "What need compare, where sweet exceeds compare?"

we find it difficult to regard this as a serious question. He is merely despairing of the essence of his art. It is, however, the most serious question that can arise for any one who wishes to make a definition of poetry. Why does comparing a thing with something else that is not similar in any practical way heighten our consciousness of it?

In order to answer this question it will be necessary to decide why we ever become conscious of a thing in the first place. And this is especially difficult because psychologists have no very fixed attitude toward the problem of consciousness—except for a few, at least, who have been reduced by the "Behaviorists" to a fixed attitude of fright. But I think most of those who feel free to concede that we do become conscious, and that also we become *more* and *less* conscious, will agree that what makes us conscious of one thing rather than another is usually some difficulty that it presents from the standpoint of our activities. We can dress ourselves from top to toe without once consciously perceiving a limb or a garment, provided the garments are in their proper place, and the limbs too, and all goes well. But if something obstructs the process—if an arm will not pass through the sleeve of a coat—then that situation automatically swims into our ken. Or suppose it has been dimly in our ken, it becomes more sharply so. It swims into the focus of attention. And as it does so the sleeve which our arm will not pass through becomes, let us say, a hole in the lining of our coat. As soon as we have perceived the experience in this way—and perhaps inwardly named it *torn lining*—the process of dressing is resumed with a correction, and may now go through to the end without further intrusion from the mind. I think that is a fair example of how consciousness arises, or is heightened, in practical life. And that use of the words, *torn lining,* in order to resolve a situation that was in doubt and enable us to resume an obstructed activity, is typical of the practical or prose use of words. It shows that practical words, in their simple and original function, not only do not heighten consciousness, but reduce it and get rid of it.

I do not know how you could better define consciousness in that case, than to say it was the process of resolving the experience of a coat-with-an-impenetrable-sleeve into the experience of a coat-with-a-hole-in-the-lining. It was identifying an unfamiliar experience with a familiar one for purposes of action.

And as soon as this identification was accomplished and action resumed, the consciousness lapsed. It lapsed because the identification was, as we say, correct. But that is little more than saying it was the one which permitted the action to be resumed and carried successfully through; it was the practical identification. It seems then that consciousness is, arises out of, or depends upon, two things—a blockage of action, and an identification of one experience with another so that action may be resumed. That being the case, what could a person do who desired to heighten consciousness, or intensify, or preserve, or prolong, or in any other way cultivate it for its own sake—what could he do that would be more fundamental than to suggest *impractical identifications?* Poetic metaphor is the employment of words to suggest impractical identifications. You may choose this or that identification for any one of a thousand reasons, all of them very interesting but none general enough to enter into the definition of poetry. *Any* impractical identification that you can induce somebody to listen to is poetic, because it is the essence of an attentive consciousness. It is mind suspended on the brink of action.

VI

If we could observe, not only introspectively but also objectively with a microscope, the exact situation in a nervous system at the moment when it becomes conscious of something, the next step in my argument would be to describe this situation and convince the reader circumstantially that it consists of delayed action and incomplete association. We cannot observe the functioning of the nervous system through a microscope; all we can do is to observe its structure and then guess at its functioning. But it is important to note that those who have made a life work of such guessing agree with the introspective account of the matter I have given.

Psychologists first began to realize the close relation between consciousness and action toward the end of the last century.

Out of a million impressions that fall continually upon our sense organs, we become aware only of a tiny few, and it seemed at first reasonable to say that these few are the ones about which we do something. In 1900 Hugo Münsterberg went so far as to maintain that an excitation of our brain centers by an incoming nerve current does not entail a conscious experience at all, unless the current passes out in the form of a motor discharge. That is, to put it crudely, we do not hear the hen cackle unless we go after the eggs. As soon as this statement was thoroughly made, however, it began to appear that exactly the opposite is true. The things we respond to with a complete muscular action —as a hand to the banister or an eye-wink to a drying eye—are just those of which we do not become conscious. It is only when one appropriate muscular response is blocked or hindered by some other, that we seem to pay any mental attention to it. And moreover the "degree" of our consciousness seems to depend upon the extent of the hindrance. Professor Montague of Columbia presented this view, and if you will forgive his rather technical language, he presented it very clearly and well:

"Perceptions are presumed to arise synchronously with the redirection in the central nervous system of afferent currents into efferent channels. When this process of redirection is prolonged by reason of the many conflicts with the cerebral association currents, then the consciousness is prolonged, keen, and complex. When, on the other hand, by reason either of innate adjustments or of long practice, the journey through the central labyrinth is quick, smooth, and direct, then the consciousness, if present at all, is simple, faint and brief."

The next chapter in this story was written by Professor Margaret Floy Washburn of Vassar College, who published a book in 1916 in which she showed that there is an element of truth in the assertions of both Münsterberg and Montague. A perception does not become conscious unless a responsive action is *initiated,* but it also does not become conscious unless the initiated response is *obstructed.*

"Consciousness," she said, "accompanies a certain ratio of excitation to inhibition in a motor discharge, and . . . if the amount of excitation either sinks below a certain minimum, or rises above a certain maximum, consciousness is lessened."

This may sound a little abstruse, but it is merely a statement from the standpoint of a person observing your brain, of something that you yourself can observe in your own mind. A world of things is continually within range of your attention; you commonly notice only those which impel you to action or have some relation to what you are doing, and of these you vividly attend only to those whose relation to your activity is not quite fixed and sure.

If you are really intent upon gathering eggs, for instance, you will pass right by the garden without noticing the flowers. But if a hen happens to make a noise under the flowers, you will notice that. And if the noise is *something between* a cluck and a cackle, you will become very clearly conscious of it. You will turn your attention to it because it contains both excitation and inhibition. A cackle would divert you into the garden to hunt for a hidden nest; a cluck would send you on to the barn where you normally gather the eggs. And moreover your consciousness will grow "less" in proportion as one or the other of these tendencies dominates. If the sound, as it swims into the focus of your attention, becomes emphatically a cluck—and is perhaps named a cluck with some phantom motion of your throat and tongue—you will pass on to the barn and hear it no longer. If it becomes a cackle, you will turn into the garden, and there too—unless perchance it suggests *two directions* in which you might go seeking the nest—it will slide away into the fringe of your attention. When you find the nest, the hen may still be exclaiming over her achievement, but you are no longer aware of the sound. You have interpreted that given-in-experience and fully responded to it, and it is gone out of your life forever.

Such is the dependence of consciousness on a "ratio between excitation and inhibition" in a person who is gathering eggs.

And if, on the other hand, a person is gathering flowers, a whole flock of hens may cluck and cackle themselves to death without his ever noticing that a sound has been made. But now let us suppose that a person is gathering neither eggs nor flowers, but, like Miss Edith Sitwell, a "heightened consciousness" of her garden—then the flowers have only to bend over hen-like on their stalky stems and they themselves will "begin to cluck." For a clucking flower—to a person properly equipped with both egg-gathering and flower-gathering possibilities of motor discharge—provides exactly that "ratio between excitation and inhibition" upon which a heightened consciousness depends.

Of course it is not only when he actually walks into his garden gathering consciousness, that a poet finds himself to be, as it were, in a state of metaphor. It is the same when he remembers or imagines a garden, or wishes to convey the realization of a garden to others. For not only external perceptions, but images and ideas, and indeed all conscious qualities, arise, if this theory is true, as a result of conflicting movements. The movements are usually minute, tentative, hardly begun, invisible to an external observer—unless in some tricks of "mind-reading" they are detected. But even so they must each one not only be aroused, but also checked and delayed, in order to give rise to any conscious experience.

"All thoughts and mental images," Professor Washburn asserts, "all the contents of consciousness, rest not simply on delayed full motor response, externally visible, but on delays in the system of tentative movements. When these systems run smoothly we have 'unconscious thought'; when delays occur we have 'sensations' and 'images.' "

That is about all that psychology has to say about the interior causes of consciousness. And even that cannot be said of course with a great and dogmatic certainty. It is a good circumstantial and faithful guess in a field where the appeal to observation is limited. It accords well, however, with the views of a group who are making valuable use of psychology, the Freudian physicians. To them the failure of a motor conflict to produce, or sustain, the consciousness in which it might be resolved, is almost the definition of functional disease in the nervous system. It accords with that operational or instrumental logic which views science itself, not as a mere "report of facts" but as a solution of problems in adaptation and behavior. Indeed, before ever Hugo Münsterberg started the discussion I have recounted with his "action theory" of consciousness, John Dewey had anticipated the outcome of it. "The sensation or conscious stimulus," he said in 1896, "is not a thing or existence by itself; it is that phase of a co-ordination requiring attention because, by reason of the conflict within the co-ordination, it is uncertain how to complete it. . . . It is the holding of the movement at a certain stage which creates the sensation, which throws it into relief."

The importance of this theory for our attempt at a psychology of poetry lies not only in the explanation of metaphor, but in the possibility it offers of describing the poet, or the poetic-minded person, from the standpoint of an external observer. If this person, as we assume, is not seeking some defined end under the drive of specific needs or tendencies, but is seeking a heightened consciousness for its own sake, he would be committed, not only to a continual series of impractical associations as the poets indubitably are, but also to a continual series of interrupted motions. He would be—however inwardly and invisibly—in exactly the condition which biologists describe, when writing the life-story of the lower organisms, as "general motility." The phrase belongs to Professor Jennings, who cites this account of the condition as it appears in the flatworm:

"Sometimes individuals are found which for a brief period (two or three hours) seem in much more active condition than usual. They move about rapidly, but do not conduct themselves like the excited individuals. As they move they keep the anterior end raised and wave it continually from side to side as if searching. Specimens in this condition react to almost all mechanical stimuli, whether weak or strong, by the positive reaction, turning toward the point stimulated. Experimentation failed to show that this condition was due to hunger."

In my opinion this tiny organism is the prototype of the poet, and the organic condition here described is the one with which every attempt to explain poetry should begin. It is a condition of search, and the search is for nothing more specific than increased or intensified experience. When this motive, or mode of behavior, is seen at the source of life as well as in the highest manifestations of mind through language, the full generality of our definition of poetry begins to appear. Poetic speech is not so much an art as a natural material in which artists may work. And the material is life itself, in so far as words can assist in making it conscious or communicating it.

THE HISTORY OF ENGLISH POETRY

If you take a glance back over English history, it is surprising to see how the rise and fall of schools or movements in poetry has been gaining speed. The first movement, that of the pagan alliterative minstrels, lasted longer than history can remember. The next one, that of the Christian legendarists with a leaning towards rhyme, lasted six centuries. The romantic movement under French influence held the centre of the stage for two or three centuries more. The new realism identified with Chaucer's name, and the proletarian poetry invented by Piers Plowman, divided the attention for another two hundred years. In the sixteenth century there were perhaps two schools of poetry. In the seventeenth, three. In the eighteenth, four. I am making it far more precise than it was—but the nineteenth century saw five full-sized poetical epochs. And the twentieth, unless my count fails me, has already given birth to six. In fact, in Moscow—which is affirmed by some to give us an image of our own future—I once attended an evening meeting of the Poets' Union, and listened to the reading of original manuscripts representing fifteen separate and distinct schools of twentieth-century poetry. I was carried home unconscious in the gray light of dawn, and I do not remember what any of that poetry was about, but I had the presence of mind to bring away a handbill, and here is the list of those fifteen different schools of soviet poetry: Symbolist, Imagist, Acmeist, Moscow Parnassiens, Father Damiens, Neo-Classics, Constructivists, Imago-Constructivists, Proletarian poets, Peasant poets, Futurists, Presentists, Nichevoki, Petersburg Parnassiens, and Acoitists. *Nichevoki* means "advocates of nothing," and the

Acoitists were a school of poets who renounced all physical contact between the sexes. There was only one member of this school, a beardless youth with a prophetic gleam in his eye—prophetic, I should say, of a large family of children.

History is moving faster and faster all the time. Machinery and education are speeding up history the way moving pictures speed up the blossoming of a flower. And they are speeding it up in a geometrical progression. The faster it goes, the faster its rate of acceleration. It seems a mere mathematical inference from the above figures that in another two thousand years schools of poetry will be popping off with the rapidity of bullets coming out of a machine gun. By that time it would seem inevitable that critical opinion will arm itself with some scientific terms and distinctions, more deeply valid and more clearly defined than the names of these successive schools of poetry.

It is in this somewhat millennial mood that I wish to approach the problem of the causes of the modern tendency. Not only would the word "modernism" be a nuisance here, but the words classicism and romanticism also, for even these solidly established abstractions are mere labels for certain particular groups of poets, and no guide to the causes of things.

"The word *classicus,"* as Sainte-Beuve tells us, "was used in a figurative sense by Aulus Gellius, and applied to writers: a writer of worth and distinction, *classicus assiduusque scriptor,* a writer who is of account, has real property, and is not lost in the proletariat crowd." In short it meant *classy,* and naturally became identified with "law and order," and with the idea of restraint. It is so easy to believe in law and order and to restrain oneself, at least from anything bordering on incitements to riot, when one has a little real property and is not lost in the proletariat crowd. It also became identified with a kind of objectivity or self-effacement, not because the classes are less interested in themselves than the proletariat, but because being well fixed they do not *have* to think about themselves, and are thus able to regard protrusions of the ego or protests in behalf of liberty or individuality as slightly vulgar. And finally it became identified with a decorous consideration for conventions and for what is somewhat naïvely called "society as a whole," not because the classes are more interested in society or social organization, but because they are well pleased and protected by the existing ones. Thus a certain loose association of traits, due not to hereditary character but to the influences of social status, became ticketed as *classical.* Robert Graves regards these traits as so mystically inherent in their class origin that speaking of the "dependence of English prosody on the political outcome of the present class warfare," he voices the belief that "A Red victory would bring with it . . . a renewal of the native prosody in a fairly pure form, as the White domination of the eighteenth century made for pure Classicism." He made this statement in 1928 when the red victory in Russia was already secure and it had become clear as daylight that the "proletariat crowd," once seizing the power, were far more vigorous about law and order, about discipline, about being objective, about suppressing the individual and about having a mind only to the whole of society, than their predecessors, the people of worth, distinction and real property, had ever dreamed of being. Art and literature in soviet Russia are submitting to the grip of a state regulation and regulation by party manifesto and administrative ordering of social opinion, that makes the days of Louis XIV look like a romantic revival. That shows the folly of resting in mere literary terminologies not based on a discrimination of the causal relations of things.

As for the word *romantic,* that too has a kind of class origin, having at first designated the vernacular—that is, 'domestic slave'—languages related to Latin, and so the kind of tales told in these languages. Nor is this origin inappropriate to its use as a label for all those who contributed to the vigorous reblossoming of poetry at the turn of the eighteenth century. But after tagging this vast and variegated multitude as an adjective, it obviously can do nothing as an abstract noun but save people the labor of stating in definite language what they are talking about. In Irving Babbitt's *Rousseau and Romanticism* I have counted upwards of one hundred and twenty different meanings attributed to the words *classic* or *romantic* or the distinction between them. It is such a fine book that I think it would make an excellent monument to leave upon the burial place of these Gold Dust Twins of criticism. They have done most of the work of the critical mind for now many years. Despairing of their further labors in the sphere of criticism, Rebecca West has suggested that they be brought inside the individual—this is, turned over to psychology—and employed to designate two different phases of the creative process. I venture to assert that psychology will decline the too generous offer with thanks.

In order to understand the tendency in modern poetry which lies deeper than any of its names, the tendency to cease telling us anything *about* life, and merely try to give us life, it is necessary to go back to the sixteenth century, and reconstruct the whole story from there. Most poetic readers would agree with Havelock Ellis that speech was "never more alive than in the sixteenth century," and they would agree that those times will not return. Rabelais and Shakespeare and their companions seem like a race of giants who inhabited the earth in times long past. There is an outpouring imperious sovereignty of utterance in them, not even to be asked of the modern species. This is usually explained by the fact that they were for the first time writing in the vernacular; theirs was not only a new literature, but literature in a new language. I think that is less than half the explanation. Those men lived on the brink of the division of labor. Not only does all art begin in those days to divide itself from handicraft—or rather all crafts begin to lose the character of arts—because of the introduction of the factory system, but throughout society there begins that increasing division of labor in all fields which has brought "crippling of both mind and body," as Karl Marx says, but which has brought also the colossal achievements of modern civilization. And in this process no element is more stupendous in its results, more fundamental and necessary to the whole, although it has been so little observed or ever commented upon, than the division between science and poetic literature. This inexorable process was at a new beginning in the sixteenth century, and that is a principal reason why they wrote then as perhaps no man ever will again. They experienced the stimulus of that birth of real knowledge which has created our modern world, but without feeling pushed aside by it—without losing the naïve conviction which emerged with them out of the Middle Ages, countersigned by Aristotle, that poetry itself is knowledge, and that knowledge can go no higher than the poet raises it. "Amongst all those rare ornaments of the mind of Man," says Drummond of Hawthornden, "*Poesie* hath had a most eminent place and been in high esteem, not only at one time and in one climate, but during all times and through those parts of the world where any ray of humanity and civility hath shined. So that she hath not unworthily deserved the name of Mistress of human life, the height of eloquence, the quintessence of knowledge. . . ." This was not a quaint hyperbole, but a very general attitude among men of letters in that "sixteenth century"—which, by the way, extends a good way into the seventeenth. It had not occurred to them then that any knowledge was either too large or too technical to be grasped by the poet if he wished to descend to it. Chaucer had been an astronomer, and Kepler was even then proving the Copernican hypothesis, not only by mathematical calculations, but by such arguments as this: "In the first place, lest perchance a blind man might deny it to you, of all the bodies in the universe the most excellent is the sun, whose whole essence is nothing else than the purest light, than which there is no greater star; which singly and alone is the producer, conserver and warmer of all things; it is a fountain of light, rich in fruitful heat, most fair, limpid and pure to the sight. . . . Since, therefore, it does not befit the first mover to be diffused throughout an orbit, but rather to proceed from one certain principle, and as it were, point, no part of the world, and no star, accounts itself worthy of such a great honor. . . ." How different it was to live an intellectual life in those times before science and poetry had so largely parted company, I think few people realize.

Sir William Osler began his famous address on assuming the presidency of the Classical Association at Oxford in 1919 by regretting that the meeting was not being held in 1519, when they might have had the pleasure of listening to "a real Oxford scholar-physician," Linacre, teacher of Greek and founder of the Royal College of Physicians. Doctor Osler's address is famous because of the opinion he expressed that science needs the humanities and the humanities need science, and their "unhappy divorce . . . should never have taken place." But he himself in apologizing for not being a modern Linacre—although indeed he came amazingly near it—gave the reason why this division of labor occurred and why it was inevitable. "In those happy days," he said, "to know Hippocrates and Galen was to know disease and be qualified to practise." That is not the whole reason, for knowledge grows intensively as well as extensively, and as it delves deeper it divides not only the laborers but the commodity also, and poets and scientists cease even to speak and write the same language. This too was pointed out by Doctor Osler, and although his address was ostensibly a plea for the union of science and poetic literature, it was in fact a demonstration that scientific progress had compelled their divorce.

He need not have gone back so far, however, as 1519—not so far indeed as 1619—to find science and poetry still married together in the same mind and the same book, unconscious of any incompatibility in their ways. He did find them, indeed, in Sir Thomas Browne's *Religio Medici,* his favorite book, and in Robert Burton's colossal and curious *Anatomy of Melan-*

choly, a veritable memorial museum of that unrecoverable age in the history of man's mind. Even Francis Bacon himself, the herald of scientific method, could turn with no sense of a change in pursuit or profession from puttering with bubbles in an alembic to studying out the hidden meanings of fables from antiquity. It was only as the achievements of Gilbert and Harvey and Galileo and Descartes and Newton and Robert Boyle became known to the educated world that science began both to seem, and so far as concerns astronomy and physics and chemistry and anatomy at least, to be, a pursuit and a profession wholly distinct from literature.

In 1645 "divers worthy persons, inquisitive into natural philosophy and other parts of human learning and particularly of what has been called *New Philosophy* or *Experimental Philosophy,"* agreed to meet once a week and each to read a paper or give a demonstration. They became the Royal Society, and it was not long before the Royal Society adopted resolutions on the style in which the reports of its members ought to be delivered—resolutions which effectively and forever drove poetry out of the books of natural science. "They have exacted from all their members," says Thomas Sprat, writing the history of the Society in 1667, "a close naked natural way of speaking, positive expressions, clear senses . . . bringing all things as near the mathematical plainness as they can. . . ." And Sprat accompanies this piece of great good news with a triumphant outcry against the "trick of Metaphors," which he thinks "may be plac'd amongst those *general mischiefs,* such as the *dissension* of Christian Princes, the *want of practice* in Religion, and the like, which have been so long spoken against that men are become insensible about them. . . ."

In the century to follow, poetry will be driven as ruthlessly out of the books devoted to political and economic science. Thomas Hobbes in his *Leviathan* is already warning the public against "Metaphors, Tropes and other Rhetoricall figures" instead of "words proper." "For though it be lawfull to say, (for example) in common speech, *the way goeth or leadeth hither or thither, the Proverb sayes this or that* (whereas wayes cannot go, nor Proverbs speak;) yet in reckoning, and seeking of truth, such speeches are not to be admitted." Thus Hobbes laid down the law against poetry in English political science, although he was himself among other things a poet, and although the very title of his book is a metaphor, and his prose style so well set out with tropes and rhetorical figures of speech and so little confined to "words proper," as to constitute another great monument of the days before this division of labor was really complete. From Hobbes' *Leviathan* through Mandeville's *Fable of the Bees,* to the solid prose labors of Adam Smith, is but another story of the gradual banishment of poetry from the pursuit of knowledge.

In the nineteenth century it is the "Science of Life" which ponderously separates itself from the general body of literature. Erasmus Darwin wrote what he knew about evolution in verse; Charles Darwin not only wrote practical language but confessed when he had done that the ardors of a life devoted to science had made it impossible for him even to keep an ear open to the arts. H. G. Wells, wishing to bring this science back a little way on its path, to make it accessible at least to readers of literature, is compelled to associate himself in a co-operative enterprise with two men who, not distracted by the poetry, have specialized in the knowledge, of life. And he describes this maturest form of the division of labor by saying: "The senior partner is the least well-equipped scientifically. His share has been mainly literary. . . ." Thus not only the word *poetry,* but the word *literature* itself, would seem to be losing all its old association with the enterprise of reliable knowledge. It is instructive to compare this use of the word *literary* with that of Thomas Thomson, writing the history of the Royal Society in 1812: "The only account of a Literary Society which can be at all valuable or interesting, is a detail of the efforts they have made to increase the stock of knowledge, and to promote the various branches of science to which they have directed their attention."

Throughout the twentieth century the same division has been defining itself with the same fateful rigor in all discourse about mental attributes and the nature and behavior of men. Here the men-of-letters and the professors of literature, fighting their last battle, will for a short time still persuade themselves that wisdom is something else besides completed and rightly applied knowledge, but in the end they too will surrender to that necessary condition of all human progress—co-operation through the division of labor.

These three centuries, then, since Shakespeare and the Elizabethans, have seen the division between science and poetic literature advance gradually throughout the whole universe of human discourse. It is obvious that this development is fundamental if we wish to give an account of the literary tendencies of those centuries in terms of cause. That does not mean, of course, that this development is the sole cause of everything that has occurred. It has brought other things after it, or come with them—industrial capitalism, the machine age, finance capital, democracy, sex equality, proletarian revolution, the World War. And there is always the dance of the chromosomes to remember. It would be metaphysics to exalt any one of these causes as prime mover above all the others. It hardly needs more than to be said, however, that the separation of all the sciences out of her body, one after another in the course of three centuries, has played a major part in determining the evolution of literature during those centuries. Professor Whitehead in his book on *Science and the Modern World* has touched this subject, but he imagines it is only the *results* of scientific study—the kind of knowledge acquired—which has affected the poets. Thus he is able to say that "so far as the mass of literature is concerned science might never have been heard of," and to imagine that what has affected literature in certain sensitive points is only the "mechanistic" view of the world at which science seemed to have arrived. I am afraid Professor Whitehead has no adequate idea of the egotism of poets. What troubles them, and what affects them, whether they notice it or not, is not that science proposes a "mechanistic" as opposed to an "organismic" formulation of knowledge, or anything else that science proposes. What troubles them is that this knowledge, whichever way it is formulated and whatever it may be, is formulated by scientists and not poets. It is science and not poetry. It is too complex and highly specialized to be mixed up with poetry, or find poetry a help either in its discovery or the expounding of it to adult minds. Into whatsoever field it advances it reduces poetry from her high throne as the "mistress of life" and the "quintessence of knowledge," to the position in relation to knowledge of a mere datum, or at best an object-lesson or method of teaching by means of imaginative experience what was discovered by other means and is known in other terms. And it advances inexorably into all fields.

It is because poetry has never been studied from the standpoint of this, the central event in her whole history, that there appears no intelligible order whatever in that history, and we find plausible such books as that of E. E. Kellett, in which the major changes in her character throughout history are described as a mere "Whirligig of Taste." I want to describe those changes in English poetry—in briefest outline, and with an eye mainly to explaining their end term, the modernist poets—as they appear from this vital point of understanding.

Milton still believed with unwavering mind that poetry is the highest science, its riches to be attained "by labor and intent study, which I take to be my portion in this life," and by "devout prayer to that eternal Spirit who can enrich with all utterance and knowledge, and sends out his Seraphim with the hallowed fire of his altar, to touch and purify the lips of whom he pleases: to this must be added industrious and select reading, steady observation, insight into all seemly and generous arts and affairs." Theology protected Milton from feeling the division that was far advancing in his life-time, or submitting to its effects; he remained, by the special grace of God, an Elizabethan. The first strong sign in English literature of the separate existence of science is to be found in the so-called "metaphysical poets." They were metaphysical only in that their most delicate raptures concerned thoughts rather than things. They were intrigued by science, by the astonishing things coming to pass at the hands of people who devoted themselves not to learning but to thinking. They seem to have felt towards thinking as towards an exciting adventure somewhat like discovering America, and they made poetry out of thoughts. That is to say, they made words reproduce thoughts, not with an eye single to the meaning as a scientist would, but with an eye to putting forth the whole inward being of a thought as a thing to be enjoyed for its own sake. You might describe the transition from the true Elizabethans to the metaphysical poets as a transition from poetry as an assumption of knowledge to poetry as a serious playing with ideas. And from playing with ideas in England it was a short step to toying with conceits in Italy and France, and from toying with conceits in Italy and France they were soon taking the words apart and putting them together in new ways in Spain. Thus the first reaction of poetry to the birth of science from her loins—the turning of so many eyes away in admiration to this new portent—was to accept and then even begin to over-emphasize, as though in a pet, her own resulting lightness and inconsequence.

This mood did not of course give a real equilibrium and could not last long. Poetry finally regained her self-esteem by discovering that she had never really had anything much to do with truth, least of all in its vulgar and mean form as natural science, that a refined intellectual pleasure is her essential preoccupation. She came to rest in a feeling of the elegance and acknowledged social superiority of this preoccupation. Within twenty years of Milton's mighty asseveration that the eternal Spirit could enrich and touch the poet's lips with all knowledge, John Dryden was declaring that "Delight is the chief, if not the only, end of poesy," and that "the court" is "the best and surest judge of writing." Another contemporary of Milton, Thomas Hobbes, introduces his translation of Homer to the readers of poetry—who, he remarks in a parenthesis, "are commonly Persons of the best Quality"—with the assertion that "the work of an Heroique Poet is no more but to furnish an ingenuous Reader (when his leisure abounds) with the diversion of an honest and delightful Story, whether true or feigned." Hobbes did not of course forget that this honest story might inculcate the moral virtues; the reader must not imagine that the idea of poetry as a learning died suddenly a complete death, and that of poetry as an elegant pleasure as suddenly rose in its place. The history is one mainly of emphasis. The element of "delight" was not ignored by the Elizabethans, nor the element of "instruction" forgotten by their successors. The emphasis finally arrived at by those poets who set the fashion for the period we call classical, is most neatly intimated in the saying of Alexander Pope that in poetry,

> "Blunt truths more mischief than nice falsehoods do."

It is somewhat more crudely stated by George Granville, Lord Lansdowne, in his *Essay upon Unnatural Flights in Poetry:*

> "Important Truths still let your Fables hold,
> And moral misteries with art unfold;
> Ladies and Beaux to please is all the task,
> But the sharp Critick will instruction ask."

Compare this with Sir Philip Sidney a hundred years before, making his noble boast: "So that the ending end of all earthly learning, being vertuous action, those skils that most serve to bring forth that, have a most just title to be Princes over all the rest: wherein if we can shew, the Poet is worthy to have it before any other competitor. . . ." And compare Edmund Spenser—"our sage and serious Spenser," as Milton called him, "whom

I dare to name a better teacher than Scotus or Aquinas"—speaking of poetry as "no art, but a divine gift and heavenly instinct not to be gotten by labour and learning, but adorned with both; and poured into the wit by a certain ἐνθουσιασμός and celestial inspiration." You will see what a wide difference an emphasis of this kind can make.

It is commonly assumed that for some mysterious reason deep organic passions disappeared out of the literary world for these generations called "classical," or were brought under restraint by men who loved order and moderation with a purely intellectual love. The fact is that these men were driven by the deepest and most fixed of human passions, the desire for invidious distinction. No longer able to find it as the Elizabethans had in the glorious position of poetry in the hierarchy of the sciences, human and divine, they sought it in the elegant association of poetry with the leisure hours of the people of quality. To this end, and driven by this unrestrained passion, they endowed poetry with those virtues which are supposed to distinguish these people of quality from the common herd. And those virtues—"the Vertues of an Heroic Poem, and indeed of all writings published," to quote the inimitably perspicuous Hobbes again, "are comprehended all in the one word Discretion." The whole proceeding might well be described as an effort of the literati, after having lost that exclusive superiority so long secured to them by the Latin language, to recapture it by building up a style in the vernacular that no downright and plain man with something important on his mind would use.

It was here that the phrase "polite letters" came in and played its part, and the phrase "belles lettres" came in also, and the phrase "good taste." And the word *wit* from having meant intelligence came to mean a ready tongue, and the word *virtuoso* from meaning a man of intellectual power came to mean a man of æsthetic talent, and the ideal of the *Savant* was replaced by that of the *Beau Esprit,* and the ideal of propriety and the obeying of established rules acquired the same prominence in literature that it possesses in the court or the drawing-room, where as "fine manners" it is an indispensable means of making hereditary leisure conspicuous. If poetry was not the quintessence of knowledge, it was at least the quintessence of refinement, and the proper intellectual recreation of a gentleman. And to this could be added the comforting reflection that even the Royal Society knew nothing except about the external world, and that after all "the proper study of mankind is man." In this study "wit" could still disport itself, even if not wisdom, and the poet still boast of "Reason" and of a "natural sense" that is better than systemized knowledge.

As to that boast of "Reason" which still deludes so many, I think it is time to remark that a poem which gives pleasure by an elegant dignity and restraint of diction is not one whit more reasonable than one which gives pleasure by sending a barbaric yawp over the roofs of the world. Reason has nothing whatever to do with the case. The confusion of the ideal of "Reason" with this cultivation of the social position of poetry is due to the insecurity of that social position. In the first place, natural science was steadily throughout these two centuries improving its status. Even in 1665 Joseph Glanville complimented the Royal Society on having so "redeemed the credit of philosophy" that it would soon be accounted "none of the meanest breeding to be acquainted with the laws of nature and the universe." In the second place poets had no title to their position; they were mere fashionable appurtenances of the lordly life, about as secure to perpetuity as the lace collar or silk breeches that it pleased the Lord to wear. Boileau unconsciously immortalized the humiliating inner truth of this phase in the history of poetry—and also gave a good glimpse of the kind of "Reason" which prevailed through it. In his *Art of Poetry,* which was translated by William Soames with the help of John Dryden and set the pace for the whole "classical era" in England, he advises poets *not* to make their art a trade or sell themselves for gold, and then to the question what they *shall* do to keep from starving, replies in all suave solemnity:

> "What can we fear, when Virtue, Arts and Sence,
> Receive the Stars' propitious influence;
> When a sharp-sighted Prince, by early Grants
> Rewards your Merits, and prevents your Wants?
> Sing then his Glory, Celebrate his Fame,
> Your noblest Theme is his immortal Name."

In this insecure position it is not surprising if poetry, besides looking down upon science and gently ridiculing its labors, also looked up to it, and showed a disposition to lick its boots and imitate its virtues, and pretend to be of a parallel nature. This phenomenon has appeared elsewhere—most notably perhaps in Zola's celebration of the "experimental novel." But in Zola's time science was in a more fact-gathering phase, and his boast to be himself a kind of doctor of research in the front rank of the advance of science led not to a display of "Reason" but of "realism." In the period called "classic," science was in a more mathematical or pattern-making phase, and it was a natural emulation for poetry to make a great matter of patterns too, and to call this pattern-making and this cult of cool elegance and restraint, except in praise of Princes, by the name of Reason.[1]

Such was the equilibrium attained by English poetry after the first shock of its separation from science. It became, as one might expect, a more trivial thing, but by dint of imitating science, and by bolstering itself up with a high and mighty

[1]It seems clear to me that the two types of creative mind, the one which loves to make patterns and the one which loves better the materials of which they are made—are to be found in both science and poetry. It is often remarked that the mathematical scientist is like a poet, and prophets of confusion are not wanting to tell us that he is a poet. He is interested in fitting the conceptions of things together in a vast logically consistent design, mending or modelling them often solely that they may fall beauti-

priggishness, and making a severe enterprise of good breeding and a nice behavior, it managed to save its face. As science pressed forward, however, assuming the form of an almost passionate love of "Reason," and a frenzy to apply "Reason" not only to astronomical and physical problems but to the problems of society and education—a proceeding which would most certainly and unceremoniously cast down those people of quality from that secure position in which they were enjoying the refined delights of poetry—the rôle of feeding out these delights to these particular people became a too precarious and too obviously trivial trade for a great poet.

A great poet happened to be born—two great poets happened to be born—and they signalized their arrival by revolting explosively against the foundation of this whole prevailing mode of speech, the division of labor between poetry and truth. Reason, we now hear, is a mere limitation of the energetic principle and father of all truth, imagination or spiritual sensation, which will ultimately triumph over Reason and in a second coming of Christ or Poetry save this world from deadness and from doom. "God's prophets are the poets who have the courage to take their own imaginings for truth." That is the "Art of Poetry" according to William Blake. And Wordsworth is little behind him in this embattled re-entry into the lost realms of knowledge. Not only is the poet alive to nature, according to Wordsworth, but nature is alive to the poet and by him only and his diligent sympathy to be reached unto and understood. If poetry is not perhaps "the quintessence," it is nevertheless the "breath and finer spirit of all knowledge; it is the impassioned expression in the countenance of all science."

fully into their place. The poet makes his designs of the experience of things, and his consistencies are not necessarily logical, and it is not helpful to confuse these two makers of designs. There is a similar analogy between the fact-gathering scientist and the poet who is more interested in the colors of experience than the patterns he makes of them, but it is equally erroneous to confuse "facts" in the scientific sense with the sheer qualities of experience as they interest a poet.

"Its object is truth, not individual and local but general and operative; not standing on external testimony but carried alive into the heart by passion; truth which is its own testimony, which gives competence and confidence to the tribunal to which it appeals, and receives them from the same tribunal. Poetry is the image of man and nature." It is this great and conscious declaration of war on the division of labor between poetry and science—this heroic attempt, by mysticism or by metaphysics, to return to the attitude of the Elizabethans that inaugurates the new era which we call "romantic" in English poetry. Shelley, a thousand miles from Wordsworth in every other motive and conviction of his mind, is at one with him in this. He is at one with him, and goes beyond him and beyond even his Elizabethan forebear, Sir Philip Sidney, who kept at least to the path of a sensible plausibility in his *Defense of Poesie.*

"Poetry," cried Shelley, "is indeed something divine. It is at once the centre and circumference of knowledge; it is that which comprehends all science, and that to which all science must be referred. It is at the same time the root and blossom of all other systems of thought; it is that from which all spring, and that which adorns all; and that which, if blighted, denies the fruit and the seed, and withholds from the barren world the nourishment and the succession of the scions of the tree of life." Is it possible to deny that in this reassumption of the scope and grandeur of an art of knowledge, this challenging of science to mortal combat for the whole universe, instead of sitting content with the petty superiority of good breeding and a special entrée as polite letters among the people of quality, lies much of the essence of the so-called Romantic Revival in English poetry? It was an effort to recapture the great speech of the Elizabethans by denying and destroying that very system of divided labors which has brought us down from it.

Shelley's revolt is unique in this, however, that he was irreligious and that he studied science and loved it. If he carried science and poetry both up into the flying clouds of his eloquence and confused them, it was only because his own mind and his own ardent hopes of humanity relied on and contained them both. He might have been quite happy to think of poetry as a winged herald and forerunner toward those great ends of joy and love and justice toward which he believed true science was to bring the race of man. This makes Shelley a modern poet in a sense that neither Blake nor Wordsworth is. And Keats—if I may speak out of a mere personal feeling of his mind—had a better sense of the underlying facts of the matter than any of them. Perhaps because he had set out to study medicine and turned from that to poetry, he felt without much thinking the depth of the cleft between this art and the art of acquiring or expounding knowledge. He was a man of keen and steady revolutionary convictions which he knew how to express with dramatic force and a hard humor, but you can read his great poems from end to end without ever hearing the echo of them. They were something else than poetry. I know it is now the fashion for the unbelievably virtuous people who preside over the growth of English literature, having denounced Keats as a mere sensualist for a hundred years, to try to make it up to him in the only way they know how, by attributing to him the very essence of the interior flame that keeps pure the soul of a Sunday School teacher. For this they make all they can of the confused idealism of his ungrown mind, the influence of his elders, the cry from his divided heart, "Beauty is truth, truth beauty." But I believe the steady and real thing in his heart was a consciousness of the division, and that when once, seized by a strong passion for knowledge, he expressed the thought that poetry may be "not so fine a thing as philosophy—for the same reason that an eagle is not so fine a thing as a truth," he said something right out of himself more sagacious than what others were teaching him. To me at least he seems to belong, with his pure poetry and his matter-of-fact mind and his *trouble* about the relations between poetry and truth, even more than Shelley, to our own age.

For of course the revolt of Wordsworth and Blake and Shelley, and their great attempt to recapture the kingdom of knowledge, failed. The movement both of poems and theories of poetry since then has been a gradual retreat, a reluctant acceptance of the steadily advancing division of labor, a search for some independent function and prestige for poetry, to replace in a democratic society that post of caterer of elegant delights which had kept up her complacence in the days of gentlemen and ladies. Browning, of course, and Emerson, stood by the banner of Wordsworth, and Walt Whitman believed with Blake that in some mysterious way too subtle for the books of logic, poetry arrives at, and is, if not indeed the "centre and circumference," and not even perhaps the "breath and finer spirit," yet at least the "tuft and final applause of science." In Tennyson an exquisite pure-lyric poet was buried and half lost in the big black hat and sombre cloak of the Village Preacher that a Wordsworthian tradition demanded he should be. Matthew Arnold prolonged the tradition with a sly compromise, dodging the words *truth* and *knowledge* altogether, and calling poetry a "criticism of life." In that dry slogan—distasteful to both sides, as a compromise upon essentials always is—the cognitive poets, so far as concerns a belief in their own mission at least, are clearly in the decline. Thomas Hardy keeps but a faint-hearted pretense in *The Dynasts* to make any criticism of those Napoleonic wars of which his poem treats. Certain "Impersonated Abstractions or Intelligences, called spirits," hover over the drama and make temperamental comments from time to time, but Hardy himself warns us that they are to be taken "for what they may be worth as contrivances of the fancy merely. Their doctrines are but tentative, and are advanced with little eye to . . . lift the burden of mystery of this unintelligible world." During Hardy's life a great part of the mystery was lifted from that particular episode by a study of the natural and economic forces underlying it. But he knows nothing of that; he regards it all as a "calamity . . . artificially brought about." He is a poet, and the attempt really to understand history has become an affair for prose thinkers. The formulæ of modern historic research would indeed fit awkwardly in the singing lips of those impersonated abstractions or intelligences called spirits. In those shadowy beings, uncertain of their function, uncertain of their thoughts, the Wordsworthian revolt, the grandiloquent attempt of poetry to recapture her place in the kingdom of knowledge, is approaching its end. Stephen Benét in his epic of our American Civil War makes no effort of understanding whatever—seems indeed to take for the moral of his tale a renunciation of understanding, of all purposive attitude, of all judgment.

> "Say neither . . .
> It is deadly magic and accursed,
> Nor 'it is blest,' but simply it is here."

Robert Bridges, in his *Testament of Beauty,* comes down to the desperate expedient of fitting pedestrian text-book instruction—the language of the foot-note—into the metrical forms of the Iliad and the Odyssey. And Alfred Noyes clings to the last flapping shred of the pretensions of poetry to have something of its own to do in the sphere of cognition by writing ecstatical gossip about the soul life of the men of science whom he acknowledges to be the "Torch-Bearers." That is the end of the life-story of poetry as "quintessence of knowledge."

Since the middle of the century poetry has lived most vividly in those who regarded themselves, not primarily as sages or priests or teachers, but as artists. The pre-Raphaelites abandoned themselves to a painting of the colors of emotions—of flesh and angels and emotions. And the definition of poetry as emotional language, formulated by John Stuart Mill, began rapidly to obliterate all memory of a day when poetry had been identified with truth. Swinburne, as though set in motion by the definition, poured out a liquid stream of language like tide running out through a channel, a liquid in which not knowledge only disappears, but frequently the meaning too, and in which a bold man may cast loose and swim far out borne rapidly until he is lost utterly to the solid earth, as Swinburne himself loved to do, or with a like abandon loved to tell everybody he did, on sunny days in the blue ocean. George Meredith made poetry of happy passion in "Love in the Valley," and of unhappy pain in "Modern Love," and though he was very intellectual, he had nothing to say to us about either one of them that we have been able to remember, except that there they were. John Masefield does a certain perfunctory preaching, but happily it burdens him as little as it does any of the readers of his strong unintellectual tales of action and emotion. Edna St. Vincent Millay has almost recaptured the language of the Elizabethans, but only to clothe therein her feelings and her fearless will to have them. Carl Sandburg is a kind of successor to Walt Whitman, but not the kind that looks back to him as he looked back to Jesus, comrades in a prophetic mission, "journeying up and down, till we make our ineffaceable mark upon time and the diverse eras." Carl Sandburg has rather left it to the Marxians—the socialists or the communists or the I. W. W., and without even quite assuming the task of deciding which—to look after that ineffaceable mark upon time and the diverse eras. Robert Frost has built him a little rustic philosophy with which he thinks to lift poetry back to her place among the ways of knowledge. "I have wanted of late years," he says in an essay on *Education by Poetry,* "to go further and further in making metaphor the whole of thinking. . . . The metaphor whose manage we are best taught in poetry—that is all there is of thinking." But his philosophy consists mainly of not asking himself the most obvious question: What is the difference between poetic and scientific comparison? Why, if metaphor is all there is, and it is best taught in poetry—why did science ever appear upon the scene at all? We do not go to Robert Frost for education. We go to him for the almost uneducated simplicity—the almost indolent simplicity—with which he communicates to us a kind of experience not elsewhere accessible and which we like to touch. Archibald MacLeish has a philosophy too, or a long dark poem at least about relativity, in which he seems to want to rescue some last little remnant of the universe, if it is only Einstein himself, from Einstein's understanding. "Something inviolate"—and I suppose he wants to keep it so for poetry. But to what end I cannot see, for he says elsewhere in the same volume that

> "A poem should not mean
> But be."

That at any rate is what a majority of poems do in this modern era—they do not mean but be. Edwin Arlington Robinson compares with Robert Browning much as Carl Sandburg does with Whitman—except that in his case we are gladder to be spared the homiletic element, the sentimental theological philosophy of optimism. The "imagists" made a stir with their vague and trite program only because underlying it, and implied in their very name, was the timely assertion that poetry need not do any more than paint a picture. And so it is in varying degrees with all the standard poets of this day. Although they are not conscious, any more than Keats was, of the break with an antique tradition, they are taking their place more and more among the artists rather than the priests and teachers of mankind.

And we need not be surprised if beside these "standard" poets—poets, I mean, who have moved into the new position gradually, and not completely, and without giving the sense of an abrupt outrageous change—we find a group of extremists, excitedly modern, making a veritable crusade and consecrated glorious life work of the art of telling us nothing in their poems. These "modernists" are in truth merely an extreme manifestation of the position of all poetry in our time, the retreat before science. But that is not the whole explanation of them. They are so extreme, and so ingenious about it, for historic reasons of their own. They belong to a different tradition. They derive from a different source. They do not look back, or carry our minds back, to John Keats, who wrote pure poetry but struggled to believe it was identical with truth. Their direct forebear and mind's ancestor, although they are separated from him by a long journey both in time and space, is Edgar Allan Poe, who first among modern poets boldly accepted the total separation of poetry from truth.

"It has been assumed," Poe wrote in one of his astonishing little essays, "tacitly and avowedly, directly and indirectly, that the ultimate object of all poetry is truth. . . . We have taken it into our heads that to write a poem simply for the poem's sake, and to acknowledge such to have been our design, would be to confess ourselves radically wanting in the true poetic dignity and force:—but the simple fact is, that . . . there neither exists nor *can* exist any work more thoroughly dignified—more supremely noble than this very poem—the poem *per se*—this poem which is a poem and nothing more. . . ."

In that cool declaration of independence—declaration of the dignity of poetry without truth, the *nobility* of poetry in a new society where nobility meant intrinsic worth, and not titles and land or the glamour to be gained by hanging around people who possess them—in that is to be found the key, I believe, to the unique and crucial position Poe has come to occupy with his few frail lyrics in the history of poetry both English and French. For Baudelaire was enraptured with Poe and transported and translated him, essays and poems and all, into France, where he came to appear a kind of fountain source of the whole modern tendency.

In France there had been no such revolt and rallying of poets to regain the world as had occurred in England. It is significant that the French Revolution, so often held responsible for what is called the romantic revival in English poetry, produced no glimmer of such a revival in France. What happened in France at the same time—and, if my view is right, in the same connection—was the conscious attempt of André Chénier to combine poetry with science, to overcome this division of labor by himself studying science and writing with his own hand as poetry a whole series of volumes titled with the names of gods, but which we in our matter-of-fact way should describe as the Outline of History, the Outline of Geography, the Outline of Biology, the A B C of Astronomy, the Elements of Chemistry, the Foundations of Economics, and the General Principles of Political Science. . . . Only a few fragments of these labors of a Herculean Lucretius were ever composed, and they were neither poetry nor science but only a kind of rhymed oratorical eloquence. That in order to make poetry of the law of gravitation, Chénier felt obliged to give it an occult influence upon his own soul—exactly the kind of pre-scientific astrological influence which the accurate study of gravitation had displaced—may serve to suggest the inevitability of his failure. "Just the same, there was something there," as he himself said, tapping his head meditatively when sentenced to the guillotine. It has been a matter of dispute among French critics whether André Chénier was the last of the "classics" or the precursor of the "romantics." He does indeed occupy a unique position in the history of poetry, and may prove to have been the precursor of something that lay far beyond them both. His effort, at any rate, occupies the place in French literature that is occupied in England by the revolt of the poets against science, their effort to reassert, as poets and by divine right, their sovereignty in the realms of knowledge.

When France came to her break with the refined tradition, she had this gigantic undertaking behind her, the fragments of it lying in her hands. Her "romantic movement" was, therefore, in the main not a revolt against the division of labor but an acceptance of it—an heroic assertion of the importance of literature as an art, and as one capable of commanding prestige on its own merits, and without imitating rationality or putting on the fine manners of a lordly class. They talked about "truth" and "nature" in 1830, but what they meant by truth here was reality and not knowledge about it. Their central tendency was toward realism, or the mere painting of experience, and they emphasized those aspects in which the artist's experience is unique and so escapes from among the objects of understanding. The pith of their excitement, or the most advanced point reached by it, is contained in the exclamation of Gautier: "Radiant, resplendent words, rhythm, and melody—these are poetry; Poetry proves nothing and tells nothing"—and in his celebrated formula "l'art pour l'art." It was to a literature which had arrived at this mature stage in the division of labor that Poe came over the sea as a herald of something new and wonderful. I do not know what that new and wonderful thing was, unless it was a scorn for the prophets, and a very deliberate perpetration, engineered with an ice-cold purposiveness that is scientific, of ecstatical conditions sufficiently extraordinary in their beauty, or sufficiently bizarre, to raise poetry once more to a high place in life without feudal snobbery on the one hand, or on the other the pretense to prove anything or teach anything. That was the equilibrium at which poetry arrived in France in the days of Baudelaire.

And if the "symbolist" poets added any deeply new thing, it was certainly not that they made these word-conjured ecstasies symbolic of some truth, or suggestive of some generalization into which they might enter. On the contrary they delved deeper into the unique character of the individual ecstasy. All words are symbolic; it is only through a common agreement as to the signification of a whole system of symbols that communication becomes possible. These poets were trying in spite of the practical symbolism involved in the very nature of language to make words come down close to the unsymbolizable thing, the individual thing in each experience. As Edmund Wilson says in his delightfully sympathetic book, *Axel's Castle*: "Symbolism may be defined as an attempt by carefully studied means—a complicated association of ideas represented by a medley of metaphors—to communicate unique personal feelings." Mr. Wilson regards this as a swing away from the "mechanistic" tendencies of science. But unique personal feelings are no more opposed to mechanism than are the most universal social feelings. Unique personal feelings are opposed to science itself. They are what refuses to enter a generalization. They are what is left over when science has done its worst. In moving from that preoccupation with words and that taste for the indefinite which in Poe and his companions had brought poetry so near to music, towards an exact faithfulness to whatever is unique in the experience suggested by the words, a trait which has brought it nearer to painting, these poets were only taking a new and boldly brilliant step in the development of poetry as an art now totally distinct from the art of general knowledge. That some of them ran close to madness, and that one of the most audacious, Rimbaud, after touching the outside circumference of pure poetry, stepped back into the practical life and died a merchant and a man of action, are most natural results of the intensity with which they consecrated themselves to this pure art.

It is necessary thus to travel with Poe across the water to France in order to give even a spare outline of English poetry. For our movement of the nineties, associated with the word *decadent* and the phrase *art for art's sake,* and with the names of Walter Pater and Oscar Wilde and Arthur Symons, was a kind of homecoming of this wanderer. It was a reflection in England of the complete and conscious acceptance by these French poets of the distinction between being a poet and having knowledge, their cultivation of poetry as a pure and sensitively deep trance of realization. The highest fruit of this exceptional moment in English literature—and one of the rarest jewels in all literature—is Walter Pater's formulation of the ideal of pure poetry as an ideal not of art only, but of life. What an arduous ideal it is, to "burn always" with a "hard gemlike flame." How much more arduous than "decorum" or to behave always like a gentleman with a proper amount of money in the bank.

An impression prevails that there was an effective moral reaction, or reaction of social intelligence, against those devotees of art for art's sake. But I think the opposite is true. There was a realization that in their preoccupation with sin, their exaggerated delight in a freedom from moral meanings, these exceedingly British young men were feeble in their own impulse and superficial. They were exemplifying the very bondage to morals which they denounced. Even Walter Pater tinged with a color of naughtiness his sublime expression of an ideal—an ideal as needful to man as any other of the many that he needs—by withdrawing it from his book at the bidding of some thin-flanked prudes of the frightened bourgeoisie. They were in bondage to morals, those men of the nineties, and they were unaware, moreover, that morals is but one kind of practical thinking. The deeper tendency, of which their sinful and delightful excitement was a mere top-ripple, is the tendency of art to acknowledge itself independent of, and if it please irrelevant to, all practical thinking and all general truth, and yet to flourish and live universally and cultivate with ardor its own domain.

It is this deeper tendency—inevitably involved in the progress of human culture—that underlies the poetry of our contemporaries which we call modernist. They are a still further development—not of that movement of the nineties, which was but a belated echo in moralistic Britain of Gautier and the mood of the thirties in France—but of the consecrated effort of Poe and Baudelaire and Mallarmé and Rimbaud and all those desperately poetic Frenchmen of the last half century to explore every corner of the mind and every device of language, seeking values which poetry can have without pretending to have general knowledge. And it need not surprise us, if besides their prepossession with the "symbolists" in France, these pure poets should incline back toward the beginnings of the seventeenth century and find a companionship of intellect with the "metaphysical poets" of their own country. For the startling and absorbing development of psychology in our times, the invasion by science of the last citadel of humane letters, has naturally produced an effect not unlike that of its first incursion—its first birth, I should say, as an independent speech and profession. Zola could still pretend to himself that his realistic art of literature was possessed of the honors of science, that its purpose was "to solve scientifically the question of how men behave when they are in society"; he could do this because it was still possible in his time to ignore the existence of psychology. "If the experimental method leads to the knowledge of physical life," he said, "it should also lead to the knowledge of the passionate and intellectual life. From chemistry to physiology, from physiology to anthropology and to sociology. The experimental novel is the goal." With the best will in the world to deceive ourselves, we could no longer accept this construction. We know that the goal of that progression is not novels of any kind but the text-books of psychology.

We are confronted throughout the entire universe of human discourse with the division between scientific and poetic literature. Where our own parents consulted the poets for direct guidance in the unmanageable crisis of their lives, we consult the nerve-specialist or the psychoanalyst, or some technical expert in education, or household economy, or the theory of business cycles, or the economics of the class-struggle and the seizure of power. To "know the best that has been thought and said in the world" rings false to the ardent spirits of our day; we want to know what, if anything, has been found out to be true. We see that just as in the seventeenth century the Galileos and Newtons and René Descartes, eloquent men as they were, drove poetry out of the books which convey knowledge about the external world of nature, so in our time the Pavlovs and Freuds and Marxian Lenins are driving poetry out of the books which convey knowledge of man. And to them we are turning for guidance in all matters upon which they have a verified opinion. That, I think, is why the modernist poets make a cult of not expressing opinions.

Poetry of course does not end with these modernists, nor does it follow from this history that "nothing is left for poets but to sing." Singing is a great deal—but other things are left. There is no law which prevents a poet from understanding science, which is nothing after all but informed and disciplined good judgment. A poet possessed of such judgment can, besides making us more alive to the varieties of things, present them in more vital aspects and with more fruitful emphases. He will inevitably reflect back into the particulars of experience rays from the general understanding of it. He may indeed to some extent illuminate and teach that understanding, and even, if he be great as Goethe was, advance it. Moreover verified knowledge, although it now exists in almost every field, is limited in scope. There is a vast friendly ocean still of ignorance in which the poet has as good a right to make emotional guesses as the scientist. Indeed he has a better right, for he will not be misusing the authority of science, which derives from a contrary procedure, in order to give more weight to his personal guesses than they deserve to have.

The division of labor we are discussing is, in short, not absolute, and never can be, either among people or among books. You can not say: These men are wholly poets, these scientists; these books contain no knowledge about experience, these communicate no experience to the imagination. You can only say that the two functions, distinguishable within the mind, have become more and more distinct in literature, and that their increasing separation is inherent in the progress of human knowledge. The very great poets of the future, whatever they may undertake, will be intelligent enough to understand this conditioning fact and accept it.

ART AND THE LIFE OF ACTION

I

THE IMPRACTICAL IN ART

All men distinguish works of art from utensils by the fact that they have an eminent value in themselves, apart from the uses they may serve. Even those who pretend to "define" art as some form of utility merely try to show that the objects so distinguished from utensils differ also from mere playthings by serving a certain purpose. And the variety of the proposed purposes shows that their object is not usually to define art, but to advocate or celebrate a certain employment of it. Education, recreation, revelation of God, representation of nature, relief from pain, diffusion of pleasure, compensation for reality, integration of reality, propagation of emotion, purgation of emotion, escape from emotion, embodiment of reason, objectification of will, manifestation of law, liberation from law, organization of attitudes, elevation above attitudes, prophecy, recollection, purification, publicity, propaganda—it is clear that men surrounded on all sides by objects of art, and agreeing when they point to them, could not disagree in all these extreme ways when merely trying to tell what common property they possess.

The communists, in asserting that art "is" propaganda because they wish to use it so, are thus not a new thing in the earth. They mean to say that things possessing a value in themselves, no matter how great, will be regarded by them as mere idle pleasures unless they also serve a propaganda purpose. Or if they are philosophical, they mean that the "class essence" of man is so pervading, that even those objects which he greatly values for their own sake do work upon him in the manner of propaganda. In either case, the word art continues to denote those acts or created objects whose mere experience or perception—whatever other ends it serves—has a high measure of value to somebody.

There is, however, a sharper difference than this between art works and utensils. For in order to bring into eminence that immediate value, it is necessary to suspend the tendency to practical action. It is necessary to arouse and heighten consciousness. And consciousness is a function of the blockage and suspense of action, not of its smooth flow. This may be seen in any poetic metaphor—and such metaphors are perhaps the simplest works of art. I will take one from a book by S. Tretiakov, who advocates a "literature of fact" and thinks it will be the poet's function in the future merely to "formulate" the practical information assembled by the scientist. In his "bio-interview" of a Chinese student, Tretiakov speaks of the *bursting pod* of an overpacked suit-case. Now, in so far as "fact" is concerned, a suit-case, no matter how fully packed, does not become nor acquire a bursting pod. The scientists would not report it so. Why does the literary "formulator" falsify the scientific fact? It is because the suit-case "looks like" a bursting pod, of course. But does it not also look like a suit-case? Then there must be some further reason for calling it a bursting pod. And the reason is that besides *looking like* a bursting pod, it *is not* a bursting pod. It cannot be so handled and dealt with in action. It cannot be so dismissed, therefore, in the onward practical rush of the mind. The metaphor provokes the brain function with its truth-to-perception, but inhibits it with its untruth to action. . . . All of which is, of course, merely a thoughtful way of saying, what is quite obvious, that Tretiakov employs the metaphor to make his style vivid. Metaphor is, indeed, the primary means of making the "literary commodity" "explode like a dynamite bomb in the stomach of the consumer"—to quote a prospectus of his Left Front group. Science employs metaphors also, and sometimes far-fetched ones, but they can always within some limits be acted upon. A poetic metaphor is an *impractical* identification of two experiences, and its function is to arrest action and arouse consciousness. Thus while Tretiakov's ultimate purpose in giving artistic form to the information gathered in China may be to convey facts and organize attitudes-of-action, his art consists essentially of arresting people in their action in order to heighten their consciousness of those facts.

I think that this coincidence of stimulus with inhibition, which can alone explain poetic metaphor, will be found to explain much that is similarly taken for granted in other arts. It is a commonplace that an expression of feeling does not rise to the dignity of art until it assumes what is called "form." But what is the mystery behind this word form? Everything that has material existence has a form. The forms that elevate mere impulses of expression into works of art are *interesting* forms. That is, they are inhibitions of those impulses by others equally authentic, so that instead of being successfully expressed and lost, they are in-pressed and the feelings attending them brought into vivid being and sustained. It may be that the persistent belief in some real distinction pointed to by the words *classic* and *romantic* also finds its reason here; it refers to the proportion kept up between the response to a stimulus and its inhibition. Both must be present. All works of art must find some way to stand up against the stream of action. A cup or beaker, if it is to be artistic, must not only satisfy our eye and hand and lip, but must stop us from drinking.

That is why I say there is a sharper division between art work and utensil than that mere eminence of the immediate value which distinguishes the art work and enables us to talk about it at all. And this more distinctive attribute, this arresting of the brain's purposive flight while consciousness itself spreads wings, is what distinguishes art from the mere purveyance of a pleasure. It may be a pleasure which art holds vividly before us;

it may be, in the narrow sense, a pain. But even when it is a mere confection or a juggler's trick, art lies in making us stop still and dwell upon its quality. There is no distinction more unreal than that between the so-called æsthetic and unæsthetic senses. The eye and ear are distinguished primarily by their association with a more complex technique of practical adjustment. But it is exactly that complex technique which, when aroused and yet arrested in its action, expands the thin stream of practical consciousness into a deeper lake of realization.

To me it seems obvious that such realization, or heightened consciousness of life, is desired for its own sake. It is not possible, perhaps, to have a "pure" realization of anything—one quite unmixed with attitudes of action or of practical conception. Moreover, by deftly managing these attitudes, and by carefully selecting the kinds of things to be realized, the trance of realization can almost always be made to serve some end—as many ends as there are philosophies of art. But that men love art regardless of the attitude it inculcates, provided they are endowed with or instructed in the gift of loving it, and providing the attitude involved is not *too* sharply hostile to some quick passionate purpose in their hearts, is proven by innumerable facts. It was proven to us not long ago by the Rockefellers' patronage of Diego Rivera's painting. Almost all Rivera's art is in its attitude, or motive, revolutionary, but that does not impede their admiration of it—not, at least, until a head of Lenin appears in a building where offices are to be rented. Lenin himself is described by all who knew him as the "goal-pursuing" man, yet Lenin read the Russian classics, Pushkin, Lyermontov, Turgeniev, who had no leaning toward his goal, in preference to lesser artists who were bent on it. He read because he loved experience, and not only knowledge, and not only action towards an end. So do all complete men love experience. It is just because of this, and because they value art as sheer experience, that art becomes so apt a vehicle for propaganda.

There are two reasons for the strong resistance to this obvious fact. Life is, at large, and must be if it will survive, purposive. And men of art feel deeper sunk in life, more of the body of it, than mere entertainers. They have not thought up any vital way to distinguish art from entertainment, or affirm the sovereign value of a complete consciousness. Public life, besides, is too anxious about measures of provision and defence to concede this sovereign value, even if the artists knew how to affirm it. Society has not yet freed itself, except in tiny groups and moments, to realize with energetic idleness the stuff of life and call this a *good deed*. Even to grasp boldly the fact that art does this, and *is* by definition this, whatever else it does—an intellectual duty since the fact is clear—is denounced by the common run of critics who dare not stand up on two feet without a moral sanction, as a "feminine" or "passive" view of art. This we must blame upon our precocious adulthood. Man was a pinched and undernourished child, and he has still to find his youth.

There is another reason, however, for the stubborn feeling, stubborn frequently among artists, that art has some social function that is practical and proper to the definition of it. The reason is that in the past creative art was sanctioned by utilities and bound up with social purposes far more than now. There has been in this respect a vital evolution. The division of labor, the factory, the development of the power-machine, the decline of faith in magic and religion, and the growth of scientific knowledge, have pushed art steadily into a position of greater independence. The art for art's sake slogan, however meagre as a program, was unimpeachable as a statement of fact. Art had in the early nineteenth century arrived at a point where it could be created by serious professionals, and enjoyed by large masses of people, without either the existence or the pretence of a practical function. "Art for art's sake" as a Bohemian battle-cry on the lips of Gautier was quite a scandal in the world, but the same idea formulated as an act of understanding by the God-preserving philosopher, Immanuel Kant—"purposiveness without a purpose"—seemed right enough and proper to the age.

The two most momentous artistic events perhaps of modern times, the discovery of the high value of antique and prehistoric art, and the development of symphonic music, exemplify and prove the truth in these formulas. You cannot pretend that art has no value in itself when you stand humiliated before the perfection of a carved image whose goal outside itself was some funny trick of necromancy dead six thousand years. Nor can you keep up this pretence in face of the intensity with which orchestral music in its purest forms is loved, and loved by all kinds and classes of people, who throng out as though to a religious or patriotic revival or a gladiatorial arena, to drink the experience of it. In the light of these facts, to dismiss "pure art" as a decadent indulgence of the bourgeoisie is mere cant and nonsense.

2

THE SANCTION OF PERFECTED CRAFTSMANSHIP

IN DISCUSSING any question of cultural evolution it is necessary to have in mind the scientific ideas of Karl Marx. It is equally necessary to dismiss from mind the Marxian metaphysics. For that metaphysics, by identifying theoretic knowledge of the past with purposive program for the future, makes it impossible to give an undistorted account of any cultural development. And since the program for the future demands a change in the economic foundations of society, the distortion of the past consists always in attributing to these foundations a mystic force "determining" whatever has occurred. That economic factors *condition* in a fundamental way all cultural developments is an unescapable inference from the fact that "human beings must have food, drink, clothing and shelter first of all, before they can interest themselves in politics, science, art and religion." The realization of this simple fact, and its far-reaching implications, is the scientific contribution of Marx both to history and to artistic criticism. It no more "explains" art and literature than it evaluates them. But it enters as a basic factor into any explanation and any thoroughly circumspect evaluation, and we shall not forget it. We shall not, however, confuse *condition* with *determine,* as all orthodox Marxians are compelled to do, and thus reduce the infinitely various and little-comprehended problems of historic causation to a mere catalogue of "cases" in which the "economic relations are . . . ultimately decisive."[1]

Art has, we may assume, almost as many "origins" in savage tribes as it has in our own breasts. I can count eight or ten dis-

[1]Plekhanov, who taught Marxism to the Russians, is supposed to have established a "Marxian æsthetics." How far it is from modern anthropology may be seen in his assertion that when an individual admires with genuine disinterestedness an object of art, he is, unknown to himself, expressing an "instinctive" judgment of its social utility. This statement has no ground either in cultural history or the biology of instinct, and can be disproved with a single fresh glance at the commonest objects of art. How credulous a good mind may become when committed to this system of economic self-persuasion about history may be further seen in Plakhanov's statement that "if we want to understand a dance performed by Australian indigenes, it suffices that we should know what part is played by the women of the tribe in collecting the roots of wild plants."

Plekhanov has himself explained why, in spite of his great learning and fertility, he failed to arrive at a wise attitude toward artistic questions. It is because, being a believer in the Hegelian-Marxian philosophy of dialectic materialism, he was unable to examine the history of art with an objectively inquiring mind.

"A disciple of Hegel," he said, "can become a socialist only in case a scientific investigation of the . . . economic structure brings him to the conclusion that its inner lawful development leads to the birth of the socialist order." A disciple of Hegel, then, may "become a socialist," or he may "conduct a scientific investigation," but he cannot do both. For scientific investigation is not investigation conducted with a view to proving that the world is on our side in a social struggle. Plekhanov's "Marxian æsthetics" is entirely dominated by the necessity of arriving at this foreseen result, and in spite of many fruitful thoughts, is therefore fundamentally unscientific.

tinct motives which have impelled me to compose poetry, and the poems were, so far as I can gather, equally artistic and sincere. I do not believe that savages differ in their fundamental thought and motivation from myself. They do differ, however, in their traditional beliefs and understandings, and the conditions in which they live. As a result of these beliefs and conditions, early art as a public institution was commonly associated with magic practices, and as a private occupation it was associated with the perfecting of an industrial technique. A war dance or a hunting dance designed to weaken the resistance of the enemy, or swerve the wild beasts in the jungle, or a springtime festival where the seeds by force of gesture in excitement were compelled to swell and burst and leap right out of the ground, is one at least of the great origins of art. And a serious preoccupation with the lovely, or grotesque, or fancy, or symmetrical, or neatly rhythmical, design or color of some box, or cooking bowl, or moccasin, or pitcher, is another. In both these conspicuous and universal forms of early art, the purposive element, the sense of practical endeavor, is involved.

Professor Boas tells of Indian designs on leather boxes which were carried out with complete care on flaps of leather to be invisible in the finished object—a pleasure in pure "form," he thinks, since not even social approbation could have been the aim. Other anthropologists might draw perhaps the opposite conclusion, that the pattern had an occult function to perform. In either case, however, the purposive sanction was not far removed. The box was useful, its perfection, broadly speaking, practical. And if its maker's love of it, and of himself, his fine and wonderful technique, *spilled over* the strict bounds of practicality, that was incidental. Art was still at large an enterprise with ends outside itself.

It needs but a glance at social evolution to see how this art which arose as the by-product of a skilled technique, a serious creative playfulness in artisans, has become separated from its matrix in purposive life. This has been an automatic result, first of the division of labor, then of the power-machine industry. For the purpose of walking in them, shoes can be made as well by many hands ignoring the pattern, or by machines unable to conceive it, as by an artist half-hypnotized with some apprehension of what a shoe in its most inward individual being is. The creative art of designing, modelling and painting moccasins has been split up into a variety of functions exemplified in the "machine-minder" at a shoe-factory at one extreme,[1] and the artist at the other, who has hung up some savage moccasin or picture of it in his studio, to gaze at for its own sake and weave its "primitive" spirit into paintings called abstract, which have no function, either, but to hang beside it on the wall.

It is often said by communists defending the view that art is but a "propaganda implement," that in the great days of the renaissance the artist was regarded as a craftsman only. Even were this wholly true, it might remain a puzzle why the "Marxo-Leninists" should want to stop the course of evolution and go back four hundred years to find the model of a future civilization. But it is not true. Leonardo tells with high contempt how "not infrequently the lust for gold brings even a good master down to the level of a mere craftsman." The truth about those days is not that art was craftsmanship—it was predominantly still a votive offering—but that craftsmen were still to some extent artistic. The division of labor and the machine had not yet divorced completely the purely practical from the creative-minded making of utensils. Karl Marx himself described this fact, and in a language which shows plainly that he had no premonition of the "Marxian æsthetics."

[1]"For the mass of the workers attending this or that machine which performs this or that one of the two or three hundred separate processes in the making of a shoe, they might just as well be working in a tobacco factory or at steel-pen making or any of scores of other occupations for anything of shoemaking craftsmanship there is in their particular job. They are machine-minders of the type now common to all power-machine industries."—Fred Henderson in his illuminating book on the *Economic Consequences of Power Production.*

"Every one," he said, "who wanted to become a master had to learn all the secrets of his trade. Therefore among the craftsmen of the Middle Ages there is to be observed a certain interest in the special labor and in the art of labor, which could rise to the level of a certain limited artistic taste. But for that very reason the mediæval worker merged himself wholly in his work. He had to it the relation of a kind of sentimental dependence, and was far more subjected to it than the modern worker who is indifferent to his work."

Remember that this mediæval worker with his "limited artistic taste" stood halfway between the modern worker who is "indifferent to his work," and the worker of the primitive tribe, whose work was so dear to him that, to quote Professor Boas again, "most objects of everyday use must be considered as works of art." You will see how the mere progress of human culture has inexorably pushed that art which was conceived as perfected craftsmanship into a position of independence.

Professor Boas, almost as though directing his remarks to the new advocates of "collective creation" and "mass organization" in the arts, describes the damaging effect of these innovations upon the early art of pottery. "The vessels show plainly the effect of factory production and of the resultant slurring . . . ," he remarks. And again: ". . . The painting is almost always slovenly: evidently the result of mass production." And he makes this extreme statement: ". . . there is no slovenly execution among natives who make utensils for their own use." With modern machinery, it is not, of course, inherently impossible to multiply a work of art and produce it for the market without slurring. That is indeed the very function of the publisher of poetic literature. But to confuse that practical enterprise with the creation of the work is not progressive; it is a blind, limping and encumbered effort to crawl back into the past.

The art of pottery in our society is pursued by people quite without illusion as to the social practicality of what they do. Practicality is to be found in the china store. Their quite superfluous plates and dishes, even when purchased by the very rich, are usually hung up like pictures on the wall. Their art is all but "pure." And this purity is an intrinsic item in the general march of human culture, not to be wished away by any theory —not to be wished away by any communist Politburo or fascist Minister of Enlightenment.

3

THE MAGIC SANCTION

A SIMILAR evolution has occurred in the sphere of ceremonial, and the making of those objects whose purpose was not to serve man directly, but to coerce for him the powers of nature. Here we feel, perhaps, that we are among the more proper origins of art—of Art, at least, when spelled with a capital A. But here too we must beware of exaggerating the differences between civilized man and savage. Many of the little carvings and trinkets made by primitive people, which serve no overt practical purpose, serve no occult purpose either. Some of those, too, which are conceived to serve an occult purpose have doubtless had this dignity read into them—a kind of social sanction— after they were made. The important fact is that the sanction was at hand, and was accepted. The magic ceremonial and the practical enterprise were not discriminated in the public mind. The hunting dance was an integral factor of the hunt. The spring festival, the leaping "dithyramb," was a part of the technique of agriculture. Jane Harrison tells us that the Tarahumares of Mexico have the same word for *work* and *dance*.

"An old man will approach a young man, saying, 'Why do you not go and work?' (nolavoa). He means, 'Why do you not dance instead of looking on?'"

A startling picture of the origins of art—a picture too of art's most golden age. For what could better solve the problem of the artist's pride and seriousness, his need to be a social dignitary, a competitor of engineers, than to believe that his intenser sense of things, his raptured consciousness produced by gesture, symbol, image or rhymed metaphor, does with its very vividness or its perfection coerce reality and make it serve the ends of man?

Is not this, indeed, the very state-of-being which our modern "serious" and "noble" artists—noble enough to sacrifice both truth and independence to the wish—are groping after with their overfervent cry that "art is propaganda and if it is not propaganda it is not art"? Are not these extreme partisans of progress and the future only making a most frantic effort to get back into the past? They do not care what "propaganda" means. Is it factual instruction? Is it emotional persuasion? They care as little as the reactionary artist cares what "beauty" means or "elevation of the soul." They want to recover that blessed state of being in which their own orgiastic exaltation—their high impulses continually aroused and carried to the point of gesture, but balked of downright action and so pitched up to frenzy—can be *believed in* as a vital part of action.

Nothing more clearly reveals the character in art which distinguishes it from all provident or prudent enterprises than that Greek Bacchic frenzy, or dance of the Mænads, which has its counterpart in many other tribes and regions of the earth. Not only do these dancers cherish joy at the expense of every practical consideration, but they cherish pain with the same reckless infatuation. It is consciousness of life that they are infatuated with. Yrjö Hirn, telling of these facts in his chapter on *The Enjoyment of Pain,* departs a little from his own definitions, and lays down the principle which can alone really explain the origins of art.

"In every conscious life," he says, "there operates a dim instinctive craving for fuller and greater consciousness, or, if the expression be preferred, for the most complete self-realization." "In pain as in pleasure, in suffering as in voluptuousness, we attain a heightened and enriched sensation of life. The more we love life, the more must we also enjoy this sensation, even if it be called into existence by pain. . . . By noise, roaring and loud cries, by frenetic dance and wild actions, the Mænads strive to preserve and recover the fading sense of life, which ever baffles their exertions. And as the last infallible means of excitement, resorted to when all other stimulations have proved unable to stir up the dulled senses, we may explain the tortures which the partly insensible Bacchante inflicts upon herself."

So long as the distinction between self and non-self is not too steady-clear, and it is verily believed that what floods us with a realization of life will flood nature too, or swerve the heavenly beings in their courses, so long art was indeed a "preparation for action"—art was "moral." But when that conviction dropped away, then art became a substitute for action, a drunkenness upon the verge of action—art became "immoral." The common sense of modern man, penetrating all ethico-deific rationalizations, has long been aware of this "immorality" and has condoned it. Only the too solemn artist, determined still to have prestige and virtuous importance in his crime of being all alive, and his too educated critic, that dupe of practicality whose reason faints at the mere thought of an escaped rapture, fail to face this fact.

4

THE SANCTION OF RELIGION

As THE business of conducting proper ceremonials and knowing how to coerce the powers of nature, that business of "making" things by uttering their perfect names whose memory survives in our word *poetry,* became the attribute of a caste, and priests were born—the gods perhaps most often as their afterbirth—a task of propitiation began to replace the more direct attempt to work upon the world by magic forms and rituals. Art here became a votive offering. A temple is an invocation of the deities, a tomb a place where every effort must be made to meet their supernatural wishes and supply the other-worldly needs of the departed. Around the temples and the tombs all the supreme art in long ages of the world was concentrated. Dance and music and painting and sculpture and poetry, even the art of cracking jokes on a grand scale, was directed towards, or sanctioned by, these super-earthly purposes. "All the statues and everything else equally on the Acropolis at Athens," said Pausanias, "are votive offerings"—a pious exaggeration, but not an untruth.

Only one artistic purpose, in those ages, could vie with this of bringing gifts to God, and that was celebrating kings and heroes. When Plato says that in his ideal republic he will have no poetry except "hymns to the gods and praises of famous men," he is accurately looking back to the epoch which preceded his in art. In that epoch, moreover, famous men usually found it expedient, sooner or later, to become gods; and therefore the distinction is not deep. The superhuman and the socially ascendant, when not identical, were in close alliance.

Art was, therefore, in its predominant character throughout very long ages, a divine service and a service to the dead. You will feel this deeply, and notwithstanding many relics of a more playful creativeness, if you walk through any great museum of Egyptian art. Maspero describes how heavily in old Egypt the other-worldly purpose "weighed upon the independence both of art and artist." A very "fatality of utilitarianism," he says, continued to enslave the arts long after the beliefs it rested on were dried and gone. And in his *Cycles of Taste,* a little book far wiser than its title, Frank P. Chambers shows that the Greeks too, even up to the Age of Pericles, "possessed no consciousness of fine art in the modern sense."

"Even subsequent to that time," he says, "this Greek ignorance continued in a manner which has perplexed and disappointed modern students of antiquity. The truth is that Greek art in its earliest and in its finest epoch was completely bound up with the life and religion of the people. . . . The highest panegyric accorded to Phidias by his contemporaries was, not that he had created Art, but that he had enriched the received religion of the State. All his labors for the Athenians were set at nought, once he had been convicted for impiety, and all his genius as an Artist did not protect him from an obscure and shameful death."

The extreme and glib Marxian, of course, will sweep all this up with the remark that religion is but propaganda for the priestly and the kingly caste. It is no doubt true that religion flourishes vastly only in a world conceived in terms of caste. Art in its character of address to the other world often contains an element of this-worldly propaganda ill-concealed even from the mind of the artist; furthermore it rarely or never contains anti-priestly or anti-kingly propaganda. That is to say, it is conditioned by the needs and motives of a dominating class—a thing in turn conditioned by the economic forces and relations. But only a surviving desire to read his own purpose into the evolution of the universe constrains the Marxian to regard that negative conditioning as a positive "determining" of the whole development. To minds unconstrained by such "philosophies of optimism," it must be obvious that men who, like the ancient Egyptian priests and rulers, buried away whole wagon-loads of fabulous riches in rock tombs deep in the sand to be lost to them forever were striving toward occult ends with unalloyed motive and most resolute purpose. To say that sacred art was class propaganda here is almost as remote from concrete fact, as mystical in its sapient way, as were those priests and rulers. Their art was an attempt to achieve utopian objectives in a world conceived in terms of spirit.

5

THE SECULARIZATION OF ART

It is to be hoped that the reader is not conceiving any of these steps in art's development as sharply distinguished. The evolution of human culture is not like a single person going upstairs. Just as there are savages among us now who still believe in magic, so there were skeptics among the earliest tribes. Tomb-robbers must have been almost as numerous as priests in Egypt, and often in cahoots with them. But these hard-headed extraverts are not the ones who influence the early ways of art. Only when the fixed tradition of the supernatural weakens, and the ritual forms of social conduct cease to seem eternal, does art begin to lose its other-worldly sanction.

This process of secularization is completely known to us in the development of Greek drama out of the festivals of Dionysus. Indeed our knowledge goes still farther back to the old springtime magic ritual, the dithyrambic dance performed by the whole village upon the threshing-floor without the help of gods, which preceded that more other-worldly festival. This joyous art of dancing had its sanction in the thought that such high states of consciousness, with acts symbolic and appropriate gestures, must obviously promote the growth of seeds and help on toward the coming harvest. Jane Harrison, whose little book on *Ancient Art and Ritual* is another beacon light in this field, suggests how a more solemn god-invoking ceremony grew up out of this old matter-of-factly magical good time which, as Xenophon laments, "our fathers used to keep in homely jovial fashion."

She makes it seem natural that a generalized recollection of those who led the dancers should gradually turn into the notion of a god who leads them. A temple would be built for him, the threshing-floor become a sacred precinct, and a permanent priesthood gradually take the whole affair in charge.

We need not pretend to know too much about how this earlier change occurred. We know at least that a great part was played in it by the hold these priests professed to have upon the sources of subsistence. And we know that their dominion, and their doctrine of the power of gods, was closely bound up with the dominion of a landed aristocracy. We are not surprised, therefore, to learn that it was under the rebel tyrant, Peisistratus, leader of a revolt of landless peasants and artisans and the city merchant class against the "nobles," that the next great change occurred. The "orchestra," or dancing place, was surrounded with ascending rows of seats described as a "seeing place" or *theatre;* a stage or "scene" appeared, at first a mere tent for the actors to dress in, but soon a good platform encroaching upon the orchestra; and the division thus emphasized between spectators and performers formed the crux of the transition to a secular dramatic art.

The theatre was still, even in the time of Plato and Aristotle, ostensibly a church. It was opened only on the Lord's Day; its sessions were presided over by an image of the deity; its front stalls with their comfortable backs were occupied by the priests of Dionysus and Apollo. The plays too still had much to say—the "choruses" especially, in which the old mass-ritual survived—about the gods. But the "acts" performed in this sacred precinct were no longer addressed by the whole assemblage to the other world. They were presented by a part of the assemblage, the poet and his actors and his dancers, to another part, the spectators, all of them in this world. What had begun as a magic rite performed upon the village threshing-floor, a *dromenon,* or "thing done," and done by the whole community with a thought of some direct effect upon the processes of nature, had of old evolved into a ceremony in propitiation of divine rulers, a plea to them to coerce if possible the processes of nature. And this ceremony had now again transformed itself, shaking off another husk of superstition, and by Plato's time it was in a fair way to become a "thing done" with no pretence at any sanction, but for its own sake and because of the pure desire to have and focus and intensify experience.

6

THE PROBLEM OF ÆSTHETICS

It was at this point that the so-called "science of æsthetics" was born—to be reborn under similar conditions in the eighteenth century. It is a well-nigh universally despised and barren science, and I think the reason is that it does not understand its own origin and nature. The æstheticians do not know, to put it impolitely, what they are talking about. They think that they are asking: "What is art?" But they are really for the most part asking: "What shall art become when mass production and the division of labor have pushed her out of the craftsman's shop, and science and the matter-of-fact technique have shattered the prestige of magic and religion? She cannot die, for she is life itself. But who will give her shelter now? What practical intent or what prudential institution will take charge of this immortal orphan, sanction her and our enjoyment of her with an attribution and a sense of consecrated purpose?" That is the question they were asking in the days of Plato, and they are asking it with no more fruit of answer now.

The dispute began—or so we like to assume—with Plato's sudden announcement that art merely excites people to no end, and ought to be banished out of an ideal state. At least it ought to be kept within the old bounds. "We have of course a natural craving," Plato said, to indulge our feelings, even our tearful feelings, just for their own sake. We keep this in control in our own lives, but when we go to the theatre and observe the imagined experiences of others we think it is all right to indulge it. "We do not often reflect that . . . a feeling of pity which has been nursed and has acquired strength at the sight of the misfortunes of others will come out in our own misfortunes, and cannot easily be controlled. And the same may be said of lust and anger and all the other affections, of desire and pain and pleasure . . . in all of them poetry feeds and waters the passions instead of withering and starving them; she lets them rule instead of ruling them as they ought to be ruled, with a view to the happiness and virtue of mankind. . . .

"We are ready to acknowledge that Homer is the greatest of poets and first of tragedy writers; but we must remain firm in our conviction that hymns to the gods and praises of famous men are the only poetry which ought to be admitted into our State."

This sounds destructive enough, and is indeed close kin to the attitude of the Stalin communists, who have attempted, with their slogan "Bolshevik Creative Line" and "Seizure of Power in Literature," to suppress or scorn out of existence all art that does not celebrate the "essential driving factors," or "idealize the leaders," who are bringing us to socialism with an absolute if not divine necessity. But Plato's austere political moralisms were balanced by a sense of humor and a friendliness toward joy not to be found in these modern scorners of pure poetry. Plato had no sooner issued his decree of banishment than he turned round and offered poetry an apology, laying the blame for his rudeness upon the "course of the argument," which had seemed to demonstrate that she has no "philosophy" in her make-up. And he proposed that she be invited back immediately to sing a song in her own defence.

"Let us assure our sweet friend," he said, "and the sister arts of imitation, that if she will only prove her title to existence in a well-ordered State we shall be delighted to receive her, knowing that we ourselves also are very susceptible of her charms; but we may not on that account betray the truth. I dare say, Glaucon, that you are as much charmed by her as I am, especially when you see her in the garb of Homer?"

"Yes, indeed, I am greatly charmed."

"Shall I propose then, that she be allowed to return from exile, on this condition—that she is to make a defence of herself in lyrical or some other metre?"

"Certainly."

"And I think that we may grant a further privilege to those of her defenders who are lovers of poetry and yet not poets; they shall be allowed to speak in prose on her behalf; let them show not only that she is pleasant but also useful to States and to human life, and we will gladly listen, for if this can be proven we shall surely be the gainers, that is to say if there is a use in poetry as well as a delight?"

It is not generally realized, I think, how direct a reply Aristotle's *Poetics* was to this challenge to those who love poetry and yet are not poets to defend her. Aristotle's theories of art indeed, so far as they differ from Plato's, seem to be nothing but a reply to this challenge. He agrees with his teacher that poetry like all art is imitation, but to the assertion that poetry is not philosophic, and that poetic imitation cannot attain truth, he answers: Although poetry does not tell us what happened, it does tell us "what might have happened." "Hence poetry is more philosophic, and more deserving of attention than history. For poetry speaks more of universals, but history of particulars." And to Plato's warning that if as spectators of tragedy we give way to our feelings of pity at the sight of the misfortunes of others, this feeling "will come out in our own misfortunes and cannot easily be controlled," and that the same is true of other feelings, Aristotle replies: Exactly the contrary, if we relieve ourselves at tragedies of an excess of these feelings, we shall be the better able to control ourselves and behave in real life moderately as befits an Athenian gentleman. Indeed it is the very function of tragedy to "imitate actual deeds . . . and by pity and fear effect a purgation of such emotions." The only other fundamental contribution Aristotle offered was to say that the reason why we pay attention to the artist's imitations in the first place is that we enjoy learning, and that the pleasure in art is the pleasure of "recognizing" what it is that is being imitated—a remark which does credit to Aristotle's love of learning, and proves his unfitness to say another word about poetry or any art whatever.

In spite of this fair warning to posterity, Aristotle's words have gone echoing down through the ages like the words of God, and you can hardly find a book of criticism to-day which does not make its bow either to the purgation theory, or the theory that art consists of teaching general truth by concrete image. It seems to me that the great man was fishing round in a somewhat schoolmasterly anxiety for some respectably practical justification for those too enthusiastically attended performances at that irregular institution called "place of seeing," which had but recently relaxed its pretence at divine worship, and was nevertheless drawing the crowds as never before. He was seeking a substitute for those magical and propitiatory social purposes under whose sanction all such public art had theretofore developed. He was, in short, an earnest bourgeois worried by the revolutionary enjoyment of poetry, but ready to accept it once he had found some way to tell himself that it was useful.

Plato, on the other hand, more aristocratic and more free of mind than Aristotle, more gifted with a smile and a sense of beauty and the future, considerably less worried about being respectable and ethical and having everything just right—Plato saw clearly that people enjoy tragedy for its own sake and merely because they love intense experience. He felt no obligation to pretend that a poet's goings on are true *by definition,* when it is so obvious that they are true or not according to whether the poet has the sense and the intention to make them so. Plato, in short, acknowledged the existence and the charms of the new prodigy of secular or pure art, and with a self-deprecatory humor which is one of his own most artistic charms, and of course a glance of admiration toward Sparta, which was just the last place on earth where he would want to go and live, suggested that the charming child had better be thrown out—or else invited in at once to sing.

I dwell upon this episode in the far-off history of æsthetics, because it contains all the terms of the problem in clear, early and unpretentious guise, just as they arose in the first serious conversations on the subject. One may recognize that art is something which men value for the mere experience of it, and that men value this experience even when it is painful and makes them cry. And having recognized this, one may denounce it and demand that it be subordinated to the uses of the state religion and the state, or one may praise it warmly. Plato did both. One may, on the other hand, refuse to recognize pure art at all, and insist that nothing shall be honored above mere entertainment which cannot be regarded as "improving," whether in the manner of education, or by direct action upon the emotions. Aristotle suggested both these ways of regarding it. If you ignore the attempts of metaphysicians to revive the occult and other-worldly sanctions, and the attempts of shallow "practicals" to win back the viewpoint of the early craftsman for whom "beauty is utility," you will find that these four attitudes comprise about all that the science of æsthetics, with all its great show of "definitions," has had to offer.

7

THE EDUCATIVE SANCTION

It was of course the suggestion of Aristotle that art be sanctioned as an instrument of education which first prevailed. Indeed not Aristotle suggested this, but the very nature of the problem. The growth of reliable knowledge, and a technique based upon it, was what had robbed art of its previous sanctions. What could be more natural than to find new sanctions in the propagation of this knowledge? The artist is all gathered in and focussed with extreme madness upon some particular experience, Aristotle asks us to believe, not because he loves it and wants life and will convey life to others, but because the particular experience is an example of a general truth, and its contemplation will educate others and teach them how to conduct themselves in similar situations. This schoolmaster's view of art became so general and lasted so long throughout Europe, prevailing similarly moreover in the humanistic culture of China, that we may, I think, describe its reign as the next succeeding epoch in the evolution of art's independence. In Europe, to be sure, religious superstition and the faith in sorcery swept back like a black curtain from the east soon after Plato and Aristotle held their immortal conversations. Plato pretty nearly had his wish that only hymns to God survive. What pagan verses did survive were employed at large as incantations. Virgil was renowned for well a thousand years as a magician. But when again men began to think straight about matters of fact, and create science, and develop the technique of life, it was Aristotle's association of art with instruction in the truth that all sober gentlemen seized upon to save art from the imminent disgrace of being once more seen to be entrancing solely of herself.

Sir Philip Sidney answered Gosson's bumptious and contemptuous attack on poetry, not by saying, as he might have, that this man was too enormously composed of gut and stomach, and had too thick a piglike skin, to savor the fine varieties of poetry. He answered by reciting after Aristotle poetry's now well-established justifying function, "to instruct by means of pictures." And that has been the prevailing way of thinking about art, although its authority has dwindled steadily, throughout the whole modern period. It survives in the dictum of the Bolshevik critic, Voronsky, that "art is a knowledge of the world in the form of felt and imaged contemplation of it." It survives also—to prove that we are not dealing with a mere class ideology—in the dictum of the Poet Laureate of England that "The poet apprehends truth by power; the truth which he apprehends cannot be denied save by greater power, and there is no greater power." And it survives in Benedetto Croce's attempt to draw a sharp distinction between two kinds of knowledge, calling that which can be comprised in an act of perception, and so conveyed by the artist's image, "intuition," as though all knowledge did not rest upon this same intuitive act of perception.

Notwithstanding that this view is still held by many who love art in the largest way, it is rapidly passing into history. And this too is a change inherent in the progress of our culture. For knowledge, as it becomes more scientific—more expert, that is, and reliable in action—becomes less and less capable of being conveyed in concrete images. It is indeed almost the essence of the mind's effort in science to depart from the concrete image, the aspect which things wear in experience, and to conceive and describe things, and give names to them, according to the *relations* in which they occur and by knowing which they can be controlled. An increasing gulf between poetic *perception* and practical *conception* of the world, between art and knowledge, poetry and truth, is therefore inherent in the growth of a culture that is scientific. We stand at a high, and in some sense final, point in this growth. Science has not achieved its goal nor ever will, but science has invaded every sphere and laid its hand on every element of human experience. There is no subject-matter in which it is not now possible to distinguish books expressly concerned to conceive things in their relations, from books predominantly concerned to realize them in their qualities. The history of modern literature is a history of this deepening and ever extending distinction between two kinds of books. And what is true in literature is of course more true of all the other arts, for they are closer bound to the concrete image or perception.

This distinction has been obvious in the treatment of external nature for three hundred years, and no one questions it. The poet cannot deal with water—and much less can the landscape artist—in the terms used by the chemist. The term H_2O contains the "truth" of water, in so far as truth consists of *conceiving* a thing in its permanent and practically important relations. But water cannot be *perceived* as H_2O, and if it could, it could not at the same time be perceived as wet. Water which is not wet is of small use to poetry, and this is so obvious that no one dreams of demanding, in the interest of truth, that poets use the language of practical conception.

Our little Willie is laid low;
His face we'll see no more;
What Willie took for H_2O
Was H_2SO_4.

The humor of this small elegy—which rose up from somewhere in our high-school when we studied chemistry—lies, I think, entirely in the opposition, already taken for granted and therefore ridiculous when ignored, between scientific formulæ and the language of poetic feeling. Virgil could teach practical farming in verse and image, but the bulletins of the Department of Agriculture, or the argricultural section of the State Planning Commission, have to be composed in prose. And this is not because the art of poetry is weaker than it was. It is because farming has become too scientific, too dependent upon a correct conception of the relations of things, to revel in their experienced qualities. Here is an example, from Dryden's translation of the first Georgic, of the leisurely manner in which Virgil expounded the early "lore" of agriculture:

"Delve of convenient depth your thrashing floor:
With tempered clay then fill and face it o'er;
And let the mighty roller run the round,
To smooth the surface of the unequal ground . . .
For sundry foes the rural realm surround:
The field-mouse builds her garner under ground
For gathered grain: the blind laborious mole
In winding mazes works her hidden hole:
In hollow caverns vermin make abode,
The hissing serpent and the swelling toad:
The corn devouring weazel here abides,
And the wise ant his wintry store provides."

As old-fashioned poetry this has still a lovely charm; and its leisurely didactic purpose enhances the charm, just as the water-bearing purpose adds a grace of dignity to some antique urn or earthen pitcher never to be lifted to the shoulder and travel to the living spring again. For the purposes of "complete collectivization," however, and getting forward with a "five-year plan in agriculture," this kind of language will not do. We cannot bother with the consideration that a mole is "blind, laborious"—nice reality of moletude though that may be—when we are tensely focussed upon the relation in which he stands to our threshing-floor. Indeed where the five-year plan is prospering we have no longer any threshing-floors. We have a number of large pieces of complicated American machinery that are always getting out of Russian order, and it is hard enough in all conscience to learn to handle these new monsters in straight prose.

The opposition between these two modes of speaking, and the inappropriateness of the poetic mode to science, is less obvious, and less taken for granted, in those sciences which treat of human life and the life of societies. It is still less so in those which study the relations between our body and our mental states. But that is only because knowledge in these spheres is immature and ill defined. In proportion as such knowledge ages and develops, and becomes exact enough to be finely relied upon, its language must diverge—it is diverging—from the language of the poet.

Love cannot come to us in experience as a transference of the mother-image accompanying a heterosexual concentration of the polymorphous perverse sexuality of the infant libido, promoted by pubescent alterations in the equilibrium of the endocrine glands; nor patriotic fervor as a function of the crises of over-production as modified by finance capital and the monopolization of industry; nor Socialism as "the Soviet system plus electrification." And the more definite and dependable these relational concepts, or others like them, become, the less do they suggest the aspect which things wear, and what things therefore are, in actual experience. To seek out a concrete *image* which will convey them when they cannot be concretely *experienced,* becomes an artificial *tour de force* impossible to the vivid life and vigorous abandon of a poet's mind.

8

THE SEARCH FOR NEW SANCTIONS

In this crisis the dupes of practicality, those joyless adults who can never have been children, and would certainly not be so imprudent as to produce a child without first deciding what he is to be used for, have jumped frantically to three desperate conclusions. One is that art is dead or dying rapidly. We owe this thought to Clifford Bax of bourgeois England, who jauntily affirms that "the arts belong to an earlier phase of human society, to a level of mind which is now becoming archaic," and to the Left Front of the Arts in proletarian Russia, whose "program maximum" is to destroy art and replace it with perfected instruments of practical utility. There is no class issue here, but a common bewilderment of those who take art's temporary sanction for the thing art is. Art has survived the death of her first sponsors, magic and religion; she has flourished since her expulsion from the factory; she will find a breathing-space, we may believe, outside the Department of Education.

Another desperate proposal has been to catch this too happy orphan in some net of psychologic theory, and yoke her in under the Department of Public Health. Aristotle himself, you remember, threw out a hint in this direction. Dramatic art, he said, not only teaches truth more true than history, but works upon the passions like a dose of physic. The modern critics of the therapeutic school have not too closely followed Aristotle here, although some psychoanalysts have leaned upon his phrase. They now conceive art rather as a lenitive or analgæsic than a cathartic medicine. Art does not in the first place imitate, they say, but betters nature. It provides an ideal experience in which our passions, noble in themselves but wounded by a crude reality, may find some compensation. This carrying over into healthy life of the view-point of the clinic is so widely popular in our times, that I think we must concede the world is sick. Its doctors, naturally concerned to keep it so, have found some bolstering for their wish-fulfillment theory in the fact that much primitive magic consists in acting out or imagining a thing desired. The difference between a man who creates an image because he believes it will produce the object he desires, and a man who creates an image because he has given up hope of producing the object he desires, does not seem important to these disease-loving doctors. To me it seems so important that I think we may dismiss this valetudinary theory of art as a temporary episode, the most negative and pathetic of all frantic attempts to find ulterior sanctions for man's interest in having conscious life.

A third suggestion how art may be conceived to improve us without pretending to inform our minds comes from the more "normal" branches of psychology. Art, they say, is neither physic nor analgæsic, but is a regulative medicine. It "organizes" our emotions, fixing them in working systems, and directing them to wholesome ends. This theory also arose simultaneously in the Russian proletarian party and the British bourgeoisie. There was no collusion, I am sure, between I. A. Richards of Cambridge University, and Nikolai Bukharin of the Bolshevik Central Committee. Richards was amending the opinion of his forbears in poetics, Philip Sidney, Wordsworth, Shelley, Blake and Matthew Arnold, all following the steps of Aristotle, that poetry is good because it tells the truth in pictures. On the contrary, he declared, poetry is composed of "pseudo-statements" which are good exactly because, without bothering about truth, they organize our emotional attitudes and lead us to a proper mode of action. Bukharin was amending the opinion of his forbears, Byelinsky, Chernishevsky,

Plekhanov—also followers of Aristotle—that poetry is good because it conveys a "knowledge of the world in concrete image." On the contrary, he said, science classifies and arranges men's knowledge, but art "systematizes their feelings."

If you ask these authors who is to tell the poets how and in what direction the feelings of the public are to be organized or systemized, you will uncover a deep difference between them. Richards, skeptical of the reach of scientific knowledge, leaves this to some exalted instinct in the poets themselves—leaves it, that is, to conventional bourgeois morality. Bukharin would have those who do possess knowledge, and supposedly an ultimate scientific knowledge, the leaders of the Marxian party, guide and influence the poets. And some of the more rabid adherents of his view would have the poets work like any other "organizers" under the direct command of the party heads. Otherwise there is no difference, except that Richards has worked out his theory with a more up-to-date set of terms and concepts from the psychological laboratory. They are both seeking with this pseudo-definition to restore to art her lost seat among public utilities.

The word "propaganda" does not introduce a new conception, but merely ignores the argument between the passing educational sanction and the new idea that art organizes the emotions. Art organizes the mind *and* the emotions, according to A. A. Bogdanov, the founder of the Institute of Proletarian Culture in Russia. Art is "both knowledge of the world and instrument for changing it," according to his successors, Stalin's functionary critics, who are primarily responsible for the slogan "art is propaganda." It is a handy slogan, for it keeps a hold upon the education theory, narrowing it to the social field where science is still immature enough to make it plausible, and it catches up the "organization" theory, presenting it also in a limited form, as though one could organize emotions only in two directions, for and against a workers' revolution.

The vogue of these modes of finding art a sanction will. I

think, be brief. There is no clearer line of demarcation among human types than that between the artist and the man of action. Nor is it the "pure" artist, but the artist burning with the full ardor of an action, who makes this line most clear. Pure artists are, indeed, in some sense men of action. They have their aim; they wield all tools and bend all efforts to achieve it. If a man decides to build a picture or a symphony instead of building socialism, that, however you may reprehend it, is a simple act of choice. You rail at him, he growls at you, and there is a certain hostile understanding. But when a man decides to build socialism, and *does not proceed to build it,* but builds instead a work of art portraying and communicating the attributes and circumstances of this great decision, then the man of action is bewildered. Then indeed the depth of difference between an artist and an engineer is evident to all.

9

THE DEFINING FUNCTION

The defining function of the artist is to cherish consciousness. It may be of some action that he wants to make men conscious, yet there is an opposition in the very nature of the brain between the vivid consciousness and the downright fulfillment of an action. It may be an idea that engages him, the understanding upon which some act is based, yet the vivid realization of an idea and the practical communication of it for action's sake are not identical, and they grow less so the more technically the idea is developed. It may be that he wishes to organize emotions, yet he is distinguished from the practical persuader not by the fact that he organizes them, but by the fact that he holds them in a state of equilibrium—he will not let them slide out into action and be lost. So it is with all the so-called "definitions" of art's essence. They point to things that a heightened consciousness may be employed for; they are demands that men or exigencies may present to art and make it useful to some end. But art is not this usefulness.

Even when art is employed as is a modern battle hymn, to consecrate a purpose, giving it a flame of beauty or intensity that may, no longer through the agency of gods or occult potencies but through the paths of our own nervous system, promote the victory—even then the flame is made of the *suspended* purpose. It burns on sabbath days or feast-days or in pauses of the battle. It is the sorcerer and chaplain, not the recruiting sergeant, whose place the artist in an army fills. Men not strong in action will derive from his prayer-like immortalizings of an emotion, its embodiment in some perfect act or object other than the actual victory of the struggle, a sense of something done when nothing has been done. Enemies will drink off the quality of the emotion, not only without action, but without sympathy in thought. And those who do find strength for their life of action in the world of art will find it richest when art *is* that life, its very being brought to consciousness, not its conscious instrument. As to these facts no wise man will deceive himself.

Artists may deceive themselves, but I do not share the opinion that they must. Clive Bell declares that "for an artist to believe that his art is concerned with religion or politics or psychology or scientific truth is well. It keeps him up out of sentimental æstheticism; it keeps to hand a suitable artistic problem. . . . The artist must have something to get into a passion about." This brilliant advocate of the "æsthetic emotion" is indeed as vigorous as any Bolshevik in denouncing "beauty" as an aim of art, and maintaining that "genius-worship is the infallible sign of an uncreative age." It can undoubtedly be proven—at least from the stand-point of the tastes prevailing to-day—that art's heroic ages have been those in which it was not conscious of itself as art at all, but was a devoted service to some great aim. I have observed the same thing in the work of individual artists—in Boardman Robinson, for example, whose political drawings in the old *Masses* and the *Liberator* were as fine as any graphic art in this country, but whose mural paintings, preoccupied with being rhythmic and harmonious, are less compelling even in harmony and rhythm. In the Louvre as you pass out of the galleries of classic Greek sculpture, with their lush complacency in being plump and perfect, and are confronted by that figure of the Egyptian god Horus holding out a vessel toward you in his hands, you experience something that can only be described as an electric shock of life. And a similar change is felt when you pass from the consciously miraculous artistry of the great renaissance painters to the austere and almost scorching presentations of passion in the blinder ages that preceded them.

I think that the generality of this difference, or the absolute superiority of that art which was conceived in superstition, has been somewhat exaggerated by those whose enthusiasm is not so much for ancient art as for a modern fashion. Nevertheless, it is true that up to the present time art has leaned toward lusciousness and empty rhetoric when it has set out consciously to be pure art. It was a sound instinct in the Hebrew story teller to turn Lot's wife into one of those salt pillars over by the Dead Sea, and make Lot's sons-by-incest into the progenitors of the kindred yet hostile tribes of Moab and Ammon. The tale thus besides being a work of art became both a study in geology and a piece of jingo propaganda. Most primitive myths, and many symbolic patterns, carry their significance thus somewhat adventitiously attached to them. The myths and patterns will be found identical in remote tribes and regions with the meanings wholly changed. *Some* meaning, some pointing to another goal, some sanction from the life of action, seemed essential. I said in a previous chapter that the making of pottery upon a potter's wheel is now totally impractical, all but a pure art. And yet in that pure art how much depends upon the ghost of practicality surviving in the forms of these utensils.

It is the artist who most needs that practical sanction, not the enjoyer of his art. And I have no doubt that many artists who read these lines will seize any pretext to reject them. They will accuse me of supporting the art for art's sake people in their wish to cut art off from the full flood of human experience. They will call me counter-revolutionary, and in spite of my precautions accuse me of identifying art with confectionery or confetti. The fact is that I think artists have rarely any greatness except in the depth of their plunge, or copiousness of their grasp of human experience. Aside from many incidental tasks they may fulfill, their major and defining function is to live life and communicate it, and if they live small lives their communications will be small. The revolutionary movement is a boon to art, and art even in its purest forms, for it drags artists out of their studios and opens new ranges of idea, passion and sensation to them. Here is the rarest jewel so far produced by the ferment in America called proletarian poetry, and it is pure art:

"Not to be believed, this blunt savage wind
Blowing in chill empty rooms, this tornado
Surging and bellying across the oily floor
Pushing men out in streams before it;
Not to be believed, this dry fall
Of unseen fog drying the oil
And emptying the jiggling greasecups;
Not to be believed, this unseen hand
Weaving a filmy rust of spiderwebs
Over these turbines and grinding gears,
These snarling chippers and pounding jordans;
These fingers placed to lips saying shshsh;
Keep silent, keep silent, keep silent;
Not to be believed hardly, this clammy silence
Where once feet stamped over the oily floor,
Dinnerpails clattered, voices rose and fell
In laughter, curses, songs. Now the guts
Of this mill have ceased their rumbling, now
The fires are banked, and red changes to black,

Steam is cold water, silence is rust, and quiet
Spells hunger. Look at these men, now,
Standing before the iron gates, mumbling,
'Who could believe it? Who could believe it?'"[1]

Not one suggestion what to do or how to do it, nor one thought or practical meaning accurately so-called, not one hint toward the "organization of class feeling," is contained in this verse. There is not a factory boss in America possessed of sense organs and a feeling heart who could not read it with vital participation. Like Rivera's painting it might well be admired and paid for by the Rockefellers. This is a simple matter of fact. The crux of my position is that I believe in the clear confronting and intelligent understanding of such facts. And I believe in artists. I do not think it is necessary for them to deceive themselves or be deceived. Great art has been and will be created by men possessing great intelligence. It is the sophomoric phase in art's self-consciousness that has produced void rhetoric and exhibitionistic decadence. In completed self-understanding, not in finding a way back with modern slogans into mediæval attitudes, lies the sole way out of this decadence into a great creative future.

This does not mean that art cannot be, in concrete and unmathematical matters, instructive. It does not mean that art cannot be, if the artist is sincerely moved to it, persuasive. It does not mean that art cannot be medicinal, too, and religious, and, if one can strain the term or summon the credulity, possessed of magic influence. It does mean that what gives art all these powers, and is therefore its universal and defining trait, is its evocation of awareness. And it further means that this evocation of awareness has, with the progress of knowledge and technique of action, become an independent profession and of itself a dignified pursuit. To deny this fact, or to define art in less basic or less general terms, is a reactionary anachronism. Whether an artist in this modern world shall combine with his

[1]Joseph Kalar in *We Gather Strength.*

acts of realization the fulfillment of some other wish or purpose is a question which should be dependent upon his natural and spontaneous character, and upon that alone. No intelligent moralist would lay down rules about it. No intelligent political organization would presume to dictate to him. By definition art belongs with life itself, among the ends for which such organizations exist, not among their instruments.

ART AND PROPAGANDA

(Any true general statement of the nature of art is bound to be denounced by the zealots of political propaganda, whether communist or fascist, as an "escapist" theory. These zealots are themselves often only finding an escape in propaganda from the difficulties of creative art. But they think they have a monopoly of reality. For that reason I append here, as a supplement to my theoretical discussion, this brief note that I wrote for *Stage* at the time when Elmer Rice's anti-fascist drama *Judgement Day* was under attack as propaganda and therefore not art.)

ONLY one thing is as stupid as the slogan, "Art is propaganda"; that is the slogan, "Propaganda has no place in art." Not only are both these statements false and ignorant of history and unthinking, but they are both effete and anæmic, both symptoms of a bewildered culture. A man who cannot enjoy a great realization and communication of the stuff of life without kidding himself into believing it is improving his morals, or improving his neighbor's morals, or reforming society, or lifting a new class to power, or in some other ulterior way justifying its right to exist, is a fit representative of a civilization that has lost confidence in its own right to exist. And a man who can get heroically excited about the wrath of Achilles at being cheated out of a Trojan cutie by another coast raider, dead all three of them, if they ever lived, three thousand years ago, but cannot enter in the name of art into the wrath of living German heroes at Hitler's insolent savagery that is cutting down a great people, and whipping them back to barbarism before our eyes, may perhaps have a right to exist but has failed to avail himself of it.

Art is life itself cherished and communicated; it is a heightened consciousness of life. And if life has no intrinsic value, then what is the use bothering with it? What is the use trying to change the conditions in which it is lived? What is the *use* of propaganda?

Art has a value if it merely causes us to pause in our impetuous going nowhere and realize anything. It has another value if it organizes the realization and lifts it into perfection and adds a new eloquence to what life is. It has another value if it imagines something essentially unreal and adds that to the wealth of being. It has still a further value if by making us vividly aware of some situation involving a problem, it impels us toward a noble or intelligent act. But even then the impulsion is not art's essence; its essence is the awareness. No simple and full-blooded person needs to be told these things. They are visible every day in the art galleries, the theatres, the cinemas, the concert halls. They rest on the very obvious proposition that organic life has an interest in living.

A distinguished critic has recently called this a "feminine" view of art. I agree it is feminine; I add that it is also masculine. It is not a view for timid and frigid spinsters of either sex. It is not a view for people who have to hunt around for some moral sanction before they can poke their heads out of the door on a spring morning and take a look at the unreasonable sunrise or a smell of the wantonly fecund earth. It is a view for men and women entirely cured of the Godward inferiority, and bold in the assertion of man's right to live.

Once this view is accepted, and the slogan, "Art is propaganda," rejected as a bureaucratic assault upon the creative rights of man, it is possible to judge and reject with equal force the slogan, "Propaganda has no place in art." If art is primarily a technique of realization and not of action or understanding, it is plain that its power of arousing people to the need of action and understanding is immense. It is equally plain that zealous people who have such a power in their hands are going to use it. Great people, vivid and resolute people, are going to use it.

Therefore great art, and great dramatic art, is going to be, as it very often has been, created by such people. The fact that, after they are long dead and the issues that aroused them dead, the art they created will still be enjoyed for its own sake and without reference to action, is but another proof that art remains in essence realization and not propaganda. It is another tribute to the intrinsic worth of life. It is no valid reason, except to antiquarians and inveterate pedants, for withdrawing from contemporary artists the right, when they are aroused, to paint things in a mood of indignation, admiration, or revolt. It is no reason to pretend that some kind of divine indifference and passive sanctity, and immaculate above-the-battleness, are "greater" in a work of art than vigorous and impassioned choice. The word "great" when so used is a mere glorification of listlessness and leisure-class triviality.

I omit from consideration here the fact that people who demand neutrality in any situation are usually not neutral, but in favor of the *status quo.* I should suspect any man who denounced Elmer Rice's boyish mockery and wholesale Elizabethan destruction of fascists in his recent melodrama, *Judgement Day,* on the ground that art ought not to contain propaganda, of hating the communists more than he loves art. But that is an obvious remark, which will be pressed home far beyond the truth in it by the "Art is propaganda" people.

What they refuse to see is that great art *can* be neutral. Great dramas can be written, and have been, by dramatists seeing a conflict as equal-sided and eternally unresolved. Great art can also be pessimistic, and see the inevitable triumph of the darker force. Spengler's *Decline of the West* is to me a great work of art, a poem, an "epic vision"—to borrow Houston Peterson's expression—which I should not want to miss. It will be enjoyed by those who love epic visions even though it be refuted by the establishment of a scientific economy capable of immortalizing Western culture and joining it with that of the East to produce a culture still more great. To recognize such facts, and so give art its true essence and its true independence of the life of action, and yet also affirm that great art may be a great force, awakening men to the need of action and refreshing in them faith and fighting energy, is not, it seems, an obvious remark. But it is the simple and sole solution of this problem about art and propaganda. It is the solution that will survive the pathological crisis which has raised the problem. Both slogans, "Art is propaganda" and "Propaganda has no place in art," will be dropped hastily in the pail like fouled bandages when humanity, cured of its contemporary illness, takes the road again.

ART AND BIOLOGY

It has always seemed to me that the question about poetry and art is at bottom a biological question, a question as to the nature of life in general. Accordingly, in my *Enjoyment of Poetry,* although I knew then even a little less than I do now about biology, I made bold to assert that the distinction I was drawing between the trance of realization and the impulse to adjustment was to be found in the very origins of life. I developed this idea a little more carefully later in an essay on *The Will to Live,* and Professor C. Judson Herrick has done me the honor—and my present argument the inestimable service—to endorse that essay and quote it in his studies of the nervous system. As I cannot afford to do without this solid and unexpected prop from the laboratories, I am going to reproduce here the passage from my essay which he quotes in his *Neurological Foundations of Animal Behavior.*

"We shall find not only that experience as such is welcome to life, but that life of its own accord goes in search of experience. That 'general motility' which Jennings has to add to the specific reactions, in writing the biography of lower organisms, will, if separately dwelt upon, supply a standpoint from which life can be viewed as fruitfully as from the standpoint of adaptation to stimuli. We are not merely trying to adapt ourselves in order to stay alive, but we are trying even more energetically to live. Everything we do and think is not a reaction; a great deal of it is action. The 'Behaviorist' is not so much to be condemned for his refusal to observe or consider 'states of consciousness,' as for his totally inadequate view of what he does observe and consider. The interaction of organism and environment is for him carefully divided into reflex arcs, all operating in one direction. A stimulus to the end-organ, a commotion in the central-nervous system, then a response in the muscles—that is the whole story of life in his laboratory. But life interflows with reality in full circles. We do things not only because we have a sensation, but also in order to make a sensation. And so do the most elementary organisms. Any rubber ball can react, but it requires life to act. And life does act. It seeks experience."

"Experience," Professor Herrick adds in his own words, "is not something to which the organism is passively subjected. In response to stimulation it reaches out actively to meet the exciting agent; but it does more than this, it is constantly seeking new contacts. . . . The evolutionary factor here is more than self-preservation; it is self-realization and fulfilment."

Whether it is *self*-realization may depend upon a variety and a complexity of things, but that living matter has a tendency toward realization as well as adaptation—a character of striving, without specific ends or narrow discrimination of pain and pleasure, to extend and intensify its experience—seems quite indubitable. To attribute to elementary organisms a "will to live" or an "instinct of self-preservation" in the negative sense of a wish to avoid death is not legitimate, for that "will" or "instinct" is merely a generalization by the scientist of many specific tendencies to behavior in concrete situations. But a will to live in the sense of an affirmative reaching out after life's experience is an actual and concrete action, or tendency to act, of all the instincts; the generalization here is not made by the scientist but by the abounding energies of the organism. I do not see how anybody can stroll through an aquarium after feeding time, or walk down Broadway after dinner, without seeing before his eyes this most elementary fact.

This fact is, indeed, usually conceded incidentally—or implied by some by-remark or footnote or parenthesis—in books which treat of organic life with any thoroughness. William James took a rather mischievous pleasure in reminding his readers that they like the smell of a skunk—until it gets too strong. "Every one," he said, "who has a wound or hurt anywhere, a sore tooth, *e.g.*, will ever and anon press it just to bring out the pain. If we are near a new sort of stink, we must sniff it again just to verify once more how bad it is."

Professor MacDougall, in his *Social Psychology,* says almost the same thing about emotions:

"The intrinsic feeling-tone of the emotions seems to follow the same rule as that of the sensations, namely, that with increase of intensity of the emotion pleasant tends to give way to unpleasant feeling-tone; so that, while at moderate intensities some are pleasant and others unpleasant, at the highest intensity all alike become unpleasant or painful; and, perhaps, at the lowest intensity all are pleasant."

"Thus fear, at low intensity, does but add a pleasurable zest to any pursuit, as we see especially clearly in children, sportsmen, and adventurous spirits generally; whereas at high intensity it is the most horrible of all experiences."

Such is the nature of man. And Margaret Floy Washburn in her book on *The Animal Mind* gives an identical testimony about the amœba. After specifying the causes of his negative reactions, she says: "The significance of the positive reaction is harder to determine. It seems to be given in response not to a special kind of stimulus, but to a mechanical or food stimulus [that is, to any perceptible stimulus] of slight intensity."

These remarks, which I have picked up casually and to which I could easily add others, imply that almost anything which happens along with a quality sharp enough to arouse consciousness is likely to be greeted by a robust organism with the positive reaction. The organism is "interested," that is to say, in experience as such. I suspect that most of what has been entered under the head of "instinct of curiosity" is in no wise a desire to investigate and know, but a desire to taste of and to live through—a "love of trying it," as the Russian word for curiosity more wisely says.

I think one reason why this more affirmative view of life does not prevail among biologists is that the sciences of life are still young enough to imagine that they can explain *why* everything behaves as it does. Chemists and physicists have pretty well ceased to delude themselves about this. They realize more clearly—or they reflect more often—that their explanations merely tell us in highly general terms *how* things behave. When they ask the question *why* in regard to some event, and answer with a learned *because,* all they are doing is showing this event to be a particular example of more general rules already discovered as to *how* things behave.

Now of course if the behavior of living matter could be shown to be but a particular example of rules already discovered as to the behavior of matter in general, the biologists would have a right to use the words *why* and *because* continually in this same sense. And indeed the greatest discovery in biology—the evolution of life and the rôle played by natural selection—did make it seem as though the entire account of living matter might be given in "mechanical" terms. Living organisms have such and such attributes and behave thus and so, according to Darwin's theory, because this makes them fit to survive, and by a simple dying in the struggle of those who were unfit to survive, these traits and behaviors have been perpetuated and developed. Almost all biologists—although refusing to decorate with the word "vitalism" the mere limits of their knowledge—are now ready to concede that this account of the process is inadequate. But nevertheless the habit of assuming that any attribute or mode of behavior is "explained" when it is shown to be useful to some life purpose, and that it cannot be explained otherwise, survives in their minds. It is really a pre-Darwinian habit, a habit of thinking in terms of final causes. So long as the theory of natural selection was believed adequate, it removed final causes from biology—and that was perhaps its greatest service—but now that it is *believed* inadequate and yet *tacitly taken for granted* as an ultimate principle of explanation, it may be said to have given final causes a new lease of life.

If an amœba wiggles, all that is necessary in order to be "scientific" is to insist that the wiggle fulfils a useful purpose of which the amœba knows nothing—that it is directed toward the "universal goal of animal behavior, namely, to dominate more completely the environment." If a puppy gambols or a young lamb skips, to be scientific is to assert that these happy creatures are merely preparing their muscular and nervous coordinations for the future struggle. If a child romps and pries in everywhere, he too is seeking adjustment, is "impelled by his developing needs." If grown-up people throng into side-shows and anatomical museums, they are "resolving complexes" and "compensating for infantile frustrations." If they are to be found at concerts and art-galleries, it is because beauty "reconciles their conflicting impulses," or shows them "a reality that is greater than the real." In short, it rarely occurs to us since Darwin discovered that wonderful theory of natural selection, and performed with it the Herculean labor of cleansing deific mysteries out of the study of evolution, that after all it may still be true and not altogether a naïve remark that

"Dogs delight to bark and bite
For 'tis their nature to."

No doubt it is unfair to attribute the too glib tendency of our times to take practical justification for causal explanation entirely to the prestige of the principle of natural selection. It is a part of the temper of the age. The union of a theological past with a high pressure of business interests and an environment of mechanical contrivances in the present doubtless has something to do with it. When a strong-hearted poet like Conrad Aiken tells us that it "must be because beauty is useful to him, performs some vital function in his life," that this "absurd tickling of the soul" seems important to man, and proposes to mend all our critical confusion with the formula that out of "psychic frustrations . . . we have evolved the universal language of healing which we call art," I think we may fairly conclude that this negative attitude toward life is embedded in the very structure of our overgrown capitalistic civilization. When men are sick, all life itself is but a healing; and I should regard a general acceptance of this criterion in criticism as a proof that the whole world is sick.

My thesis that healthy creatures have an interest in living and not merely in avoiding death, can be supported not only by picking up *obiter dicta* from the general psychologists, but still better by examining the attempts of the more physiological psychologists to decide what the terms pleasant and unpleasant mean, or what conditions in the body correspond to these feelings. One of the most interesting of such attempts is that of Floyd Henry Allport, who suggests that unpleasant feelings arise in consciousness as a result of the discharge of a nerve impulse through the sympathetic division of the autonomic nervous system, which prepares our vital organs for retreat and defense. It is a feeling of the response in those organs to the discharge. Pleasantness is a feeling of the condition in the vital organs enervated by a discharge through the cranio-sacral division, which prepares us for the functions of nutrition and sex. Professor Allport makes this scheme very plausible indeed, but when he gets it all finished, he finds himself obliged to add: "A certain exception must be made to the statement that cranio-sacral impulses underlie pleasant emotional states generally. There are several sources of pleasant affectivity, such as bodily exercise and habit, excitement of games, elation, and mirth, which possess no discoverable relation to the cranio-sacral functions. . . . These pleasant states appear to be due to afferent impulses from reactions carried out by unimpeded cerebro-spinal impulses." Here again *pleasant* is a more general thing than *unpleasant*—a mere matter of being unimpeded in the exercise of life.

In another place Professor Allport says: "Our theory . . . offers a good basis for distinguishing physiologically between pains which are unpleasant and those which are not. It is well known that light pains on the skin are far from unpleasant. Unpleasant pains are severe ones; their efferent impulses are powerful enough to break through into the sympathetic." And here once more the *unpleasantness* of severe pains is explained, but the *far-from-unpleasantness*—that is to say, the *pleasantness*—of mild ones, remains as much a mystery as ever.

It seems to me that Professor Allport could pull his speculation together better by saying that the source of unpleasant feeling may be physiologically identified, and also the source of some feelings that may be described as pleasant in a narrow sense, but over and above that and in a larger sense conscious life itself is pleasant—so long as it is not *too* unpleasant! Such a formula would also resolve a conflict in the statements of James and MacDougall that I quoted above. For according to MacDougall's way of putting it, the painful emotions when enjoyed at a low intensity are *pleasant.* According to James it is the very *unpleasantness* that intrigues us; it is not because it is good, but "to verify how bad it is," that we must forever venture in this way with our senses. The truth in both these views is that beyond good and bad—or not primarily concerned at least to "unperplex bliss from its neighbor pain"—there is that "positive reaction," not to the mechanical or food stimulus, but to stimulus in general.

Professor Herrick sums up his similar opinion in this way: "The simplest view seems to the writer to be that the normal activity of the body within physiological limits is intrinsically pleasurable, so far as it comes to consciousness at all. There is a simple joy of living for its own sake." And again: "The normal discharge, then, of definitely elaborated nervous circuits . . . is pleasurable, in so far as the reaction comes into consciousness at all. . . . Conversely, the impediment to such discharge, no matter what the occasion, results in a stasis in the nerve centres, the summation of stimuli and the development of a situation of unrelieved nervous tension which is unpleasant until the tension is relieved by the appropriate adaptive reaction."

Instead of the word "normal" in this statement I should want to read some word like robust or adequate, for I have known organisms to plunge with alacrity into a large unpleasantness for sheer delight in the fact that, whatever else it may be, it is not normal. But I doubt if Professor Herrick would stick very hard here for any particular idiom. The point is that conscious experience is itself pleasant, and more of it is more pleasant, until or unless some factors enter to make it unpleasant. If this is true, it certainly constitutes the foundation upon which all discussion of æsthetics—if not also of morals, politics and therapeutics—ought to rest.

In fact, in order to pass from Professor Herrick's statement about pleasure to an understanding of art in its elementary and most general character, we need only remark that he has left it entirely to chance whether those precious discharges "come to consciousness at all" or not. Art does not leave that critical matter to chance. Art is a deliberate effort to bring them to consciousness. Professor Herrick, because he is not an artist, but the one opposite thing that is equally alive in these days, a scientist, is content with his remark that the "activity of the body within physiological limits" is pleasurable, and the "discharge" too is O.K., so to speak, and whether it happens to come to consciousness or not, so long as there is no impediment, no stasis in the nerve centres, no tension, and we get the "appropriate adaptive reaction." But the artist has to remember that the very thing, and the only thing, which will bring this "activity of the body" to consciousness, and make it hang there in vivid being, is that same impediment, that stasis in the nerve centres, that condition of tension involving a delay or failure of the appropriate reaction. That is the essential difference between Professor Herrick and an artist. And that is the essential and most general definition of the technique of art. It must arouse a reaction and yet impede it, creating a tension in our nervous system sufficient and rightly calculated to make us completely aware that we are living something.

It seems to me that if all the arts, and not only poetry, were approached by those who wish to judge or understand them with this more affirmative view of life itself, a great deal of solemn and preachy discourse which stands up like a wall between art and the enjoyment of it might be cut down. If we find in some work of art a "reconciliation of our conflicting impulses," then besides being art it is for us a kind of medicine. If we find in it a translation of reality into something greater than the real, then besides being art it is a very charming and dangerous miracle, a thing very much like what magic set out to be. A thousand of these specific values may be found in various works of art, as in poetry, but the value proper to all art is the universal value of an increased consciousness. It is because of this that to all simple minds the antithesis between "fine art" and the practical or "useful" arts is both obvious and very deep. John Dewey would obliterate this distinction. He would resolve the present confusion in æsthetic criticism by getting rid of the "sharp division between means and ends, fruitions and instrumentalities, assumed by current thought." But current thought has arrived at that wisdom by an arduous path of pain and rebellion that it will never retrace. Such a change in criticism is impossible, not only because the artists themselves are in revolt against the tyranny of the practical, or because with religious contemplation fading in our blood they alone can redeem us from that tyranny. It is impossible for a deeper reason—a reason which John Dewey's functional psychology and logic have made so clear—that there is an antithesis in the very nature of things between vivid consciousness and fluent action. This is the very antithesis he is trying to deny. A utensil can only through some ceremonial effort, or when imported from far times or countries, become the source of heightened consciousness, because we flow from a utensil smoothly into the action for which it was designed.

Was it not designed to make that action as nearly as possible unconscious? Who can make lyrics of the handle in his hand? But it is quite otherwise with the picture of a handle, or the picture of a utensil, or the picture of any other thing toward which in its reality we have a prepared response. The picture, like the metaphors of the poets, contains that which excites the response and that also which inhibits it. All fine art is to some extent, and will forever be—and no invention or sophistication can ever quite deliver us from this—an "imitation of nature." But it is an imitation of nature in other material than hers, in a different modality or dimension, deliberately inadequate, and with its inadequacy enhanced by wilful distortions and intrusions of incompleteness. And its purpose is not to divert us when we are tired of real experience with the trick of mimicry, but to enable us at the height of energy to withhold the act and become aware of our experience.

NOTES IN REFUTATION

I. A. RICHARDS' PSYCHOLOGY OF POETRY

I

An eminent place among books on literary criticism of recent years is occupied by those of I. A. Richards of Cambridge University. His books are distinguished by their complete abandonment of the point-of-view of literary truth, their attempt to bring a psychological science to bear upon the problems of the teacher and the critic. He offers, as I do, a definition of poetry, and his statement that "critical remarks are merely a branch of psychological remarks" is obviously akin to the thesis I have advanced. And yet I think his psychology is wrongly based, and that this is greatly retarding the conquest under his leadership of the field he has entered.

Professor Richards' first considerable work, written in collaboration with C. K. Ogden, was an attempt to simplify the logic of science and clarify its language by eliminating all the elements that go to make up what we call the meaning of a word, besides the mere "reference" to a "thing." The book was valuable in showing how many different functions besides that of referring to things are commonly fulfilled by speech—the communication of an attitude toward the thing referred to, toward the person spoken to, the fulfillment of ulterior intentions, etc. What Ogden and Richards attempted was to write a logic for scientists which would enable them to eliminate all attitudes from their use of words except that of simple reference or denotation. But in order to do this they had to ignore the great part played by attitudes in the very constitution of "things." They had to imagine a distinction between the intellectual and the active phases of man's nature far sharper than does, or can possibly, exist. The world is not composed of "things," nor our thoughts of merely "pointing to or reflecting things." It would be as true to say that the world is organized into "things" by our thoughts. And this organization is carried out in the main, especially in its earlier phases, primarily with a view to establishing attitudes and patterns of behavior. It is rather more a classification of responses to what the world presents than of the material presented.

Take even a word like Canada, for example, which has only one single "reference." When I said the other day, on crossing the border, "This is Canada," it was clear to all that I was not so much pointing to a thing as indicating a mode of behavior.[1] Upon reflection it will become clear that that is always true of a word like Canada. The earth presents no such "thing" as Canada. The word would mean nothing at all, and would not exist, if it did not indicate modes of behavior. And this is so in varying degrees with all words. Nature does not make the distinction between a hand and an arm—and neither, by the way, does the Russian language—but we make it. And we distinguish the hand from the fingers, drawing an arbitrary line at the first joints. But we do not distinguish what comes after the second joints. That, although clearly marked off by nature and able—as well at least as Canada—to act independently, has not become a "thing." I am going over old ground, of course, and I offer these casual examples instead of citing authorities because I do not want to identify my criticism of Richards with any particular *kind* of psychology or *system* of logic. It is simply not true, as Richards asserts, that "pointing to or reflecting things is all that thoughts do." And his definition of science as "simply our most elaborate way of *pointing* to things . . . simply the organization of references with a view to the convenience and facilitation of reference," is superficial and misleading. It ignores facts which all psychologists and all logicians, no matter how they may settle with them, are compelled to take into account.

It is significant that while Ogden and Richards were arguing that scientific meaning is a pure pointing to things without attitude or indication of behavior, and saying, "Modern physics is becoming something in connection with which attitudes seem rather *de trop*," an eminent physicist was arguing that attitudes and modes of behavior are the *only and whole* meaning of scientific concepts. "In general," wrote Professor Bridgman of Harvard, "we mean by any concept nothing more than a set of operations; the concept is synonymous with the corresponding set of operations." Professor Bridgman arrived at this operational logic, he tells us, by studying the thought-processes of Einstein. And he asserts that, although Einstein is probably unconscious of it, this "improved understanding of our mental

[1]Written during the reign of Prohibition in the United States.

relations to nature" is the "permanent contribution of relativity." Of course this understanding had been arrived at, starting from a basis in biology and genetic psychology, a good while before Einstein arrived on the scene. John Dewey has pointed that out, and has, in my opinion, far too modestly offered to abandon his more universal word "instrumental" for this higher-scientific term "operational." At any rate according to Professor Bridgman, Einstein's unconscious contribution only confirms that of the higher apes. And with these two strong evidences against it—whatever may lie at the end of the long and arduous dispute entailed—I do not see a ghost of a show for this too easy idea of I. A. Richards that science has nothing to do with attitude and is "simply our most elaborate way of pointing to things."

Having been thus summarily omitted from science, we need not of course be greatly surprised to see attitude and the reference to action reappear in poetry. Indeed, once they had isolated science as a pure pointing to things without attitude and without reference to behavior, it was quite inevitable, I suppose, that Ogden and Richards should turn round and define poetry as a pure evoking of attitudes and organization of behavior *without* pointing to things, and *without* reference to reality.

"A poem . . .," they say, "has no concern with limited and directed reference. It tells us, or should tell us, nothing. It has a different, though an equally important and a far more vital function. . . . What it does, or should do, is to induce a fitting attitude to experience." It is "the supreme form of emotive language. . . . As science frees itself from the emotional outlook, and modern physics is becoming something in connection with which attitudes seem rather *de trop,* so poetry seems about to return to the conditions of its greatness by abandoning the obsession of knowledge. . . . It is not necessary to know what things are in order to take up fitting attitudes towards them. . . ."

This view of poetry, wholly worked out with Mr. Ogden in *The Meaning of Meaning,* is what Mr. Richards has continued to develop, and apply to criticism and teaching, in his three other books. In his *Principles of Literary Criticism* he repeats the theme as follows:

"We may either use words for the sake of the references they promote, or we may use them for the sake of the attitudes and emotions which ensue. . . . Poetry affords the clearest example of this subordination of reference to attitude."

In *Science and Poetry* he divides both the poet and the reader of poetry into two separate streams or branches—the intellectual and the active, the thought and the emotion, the pointing to things and the getting ready to do something about them. Both streams are of course to some extent always present, but in poetry the intellectual stream "is the less important of the two." It "matters only *as a means;* it directs and excites the active stream. It is made up of thoughts . . . which reflect or point to the things the thoughts are 'of.'" But these things pointed to do not have any reality, and the statements made are not true. They are not indeed statements, but "pseudo-statements" and to believe them is "illicit" and a "profanation" of poetry. "A pseudo-statement is a form of words which is justified entirely by its effect in releasing or organizing our impulses and attitudes . . .; a statement, on the other hand, is justified by its truth, *i.e.,* its correspondence, in a highly technical sense, with the fact to which it points." With these pseudo-statements, cut off completely from the function of interpretation and of understanding, the poet regulates the active stream. He uses them "as a means of ordering, controlling and consolidating the whole experience." His "business . . . is to give order and coherence, and so freedom, to a body of experience."

In *Practical Criticism* the same theme is repeated and applied: "The poet makes a statement about something, not in order that the statement may be examined and reflected on, but in order to evoke certain feelings, and when these are evoked the use of the statement is exhausted." But since feelings are the accompaniment of attitudes, and attitudes are "preparations for action," these statements find their real value only when we learn how to use them "as a means of ordering our minds."

Such is, in brief, the device by which I. A. Richards, while accepting the inevitable division of labor between poetry and science, nevertheless proposes to restore poetry to her position of sovereignty. You remember how William Drummond in the days long past described poetry as "the mistress of human life" and the "quintessence of knowledge," and how with the separate development of knowledge she has intermittently but steadily descended from that high place? The *coup d'état* of Ogden and Richards consists of cutting off knowledge from life, and then declaring poetry once more the mistress of life.

II

The problem so valiantly assailed by Ogden and Richards—problem of the relation between the logic of science and the psychology of the thought process—will doubtless be a long time in getting solved. To refute their psychology of poetry, however, it is not necessary to wait until that problem is solved. A psychology of poetry should rest on the psychology, not the logic, of the thought process—the psychology and biology and history of it. Everybody will concede that historically at least "the ruling interest of knowledge," as Clarence I. Lewis says, "is the practical interest of action." Science is an outgrowth of practical effort, and its connection with and dependence upon activity has always been, and is, direct and continual. Poetry was begotten upon magic ritual by day-dreams and play. To identify poetry with the use of words to convey attitudes and prepare for action, and leave to science the rôle of merely pointing to things, is to turn the most obvious history of the matter exactly upside down.

And to pretend, as Richards has to, that the interpretation of experience, the deciding what things are in terms of their relations, is—even in its highest development as pure science—incompatible with the having of emotions about things, is equally false to the most elementary psychology of the matter. The enemy of science is not emotion as such, but premature or inappropriate emotion. And this is not because science is avoiding attitudes, but because it is seeking only those which can on all occasions of a given type be successfully carried forth into complete action. Imagine that you, a poet, are walking in the woods with a zoologist. You are frightened by a rattling in the leaves, and assume an attitude of caution. That is to say, you land approximately ten feet away in the bushes. The scientist laughs at you.

"It's nothing but a garter snake," he says.

"How do you know it isn't a rattler?" you ask.

"Well, for one thing, this isn't their habitat," he replies calmly. And that word *habitat,* which is a large part of what makes his knowledge scientific and not merely practical, relaxes your attitude of caution. So much so that you soon become curiously absorbed in another "Gordian shape" that you find coiled by the pathway. But now your attitude of "disinterested curiosity" is interrupted by a hiss, or shriek from the zoologist: "Look out, that's a copperhead!" And this time it is pure science which is ten feet away in the bushes.

Science involves a severe discipline of unenlightened impulses, and begets a habit of calmness, because it requires a calm procedure, but there is no truth in the notion that the scientific interpretation of a thing fails to evoke the appropriate emotion. It evokes it with a surer force.

III

I believe it can be shown that all Mr. Richards' troubles, all the weaknesses of his books, derive from this fundamental error of trying to cut off the organization and control of practical activity from science and bring it over into poetry. And first among these troubles I should mention the heavy labor it turns out to be, even for those vividly interested in the subject, to read his "Principles of Literary Criticism." Rarely has a man rich in new and important thoughts produced a book so tiring to the mind. We emerge on the last page with a feeling that we have been wading and plunging through a vastly important jungle of ideas, every one so overlaid and entangled with exceptions, interpolations, affiliations, methodological asides, *obiter dictums* and addendums, that no clear impression remains even of those ideas which were—we vaguely remember—brilliantly well stated and defined. We emerge—only to learn in the conclusion, that Mr. Richards spent half of his own labor on the book "in simplifying its structure, in taking out reservations and qualifications"! Well, is not that what always happens when you try to insert a body of facts into a theory which does not fit them —or any other body into any other mismade receptacle? You jam it in on one side and it springs out on the other, and you jump over there and fix it, and then you jump back here and try to get it in again before it gets out again. At last you do get it in, usually, but so much to the detriment of your receptacle that there is no great difference left between in and out.

Not only does Mr. Richards have to tend and tinker his explanation of poetry, plugging and caulking it continually with reservations and qualifications, but he has to admit that, when all's plugged that can be plugged, the thing will not work anyway. It leaves out the main fact that was to be explained. The poet uses certain words, he tells us, "as a means of ordering, controlling and consolidating" an experience. And "to a suitable reader . . . the words will reproduce in his mind a similar play of interests putting him for a while into a similar situation and leading to the same response." But "why this should happen is still somewhat of a mystery. . . ."

Is not this as much as to say, "After all, I have no explanation of poetry"? It is easy enough to see how scientific words order, control and consolidate experience. They do it by pointing to the practically important details of the experience and reminding us that in those details it is the same as certain other experiences, toward which we already know how to behave. X, the unknown quantity, or quality, is another case of the familiar A or B. That is what scientific words tell us. In the last analysis that is all they tell us, but the resulting order, consolidation and control are obvious.

Poetic words also point to details in the given experience, and also remind us that in those details it is the same as some other experience. But the details pointed to are not necessarily of any practical importance, and our mode of behavior toward that other experience would be in the highest degree inept and unsuccessful here. How can such words help us to order, consolidate and control our experience? It remains indeed a mystery. It would be truer to say that their very essence is disorder, disconsolidation and complete loss or abandonment of control.

"Tiger, tiger, burning bright. . . ."

Can anybody control a tiger by confusing him with a camp-fire? Can anybody consolidate the animal kingdom and reduce it to order by designating and classifying its members in this anarchistical fashion? Obviously not. A tiger, if you want order, consolidation and control, is not a small fire but a large cat.

IV

Another of Mr. Richards' serious troubles is that he cannot explain metaphor, and his failure to do so grows more and more distressing with each new book that he writes.

In *The Meaning of Meaning,* he and Mr. Ogden merely offered a brief sweeping of the chaff to be found in the old-time grammars and books of rhetoric on this subject. The function of metaphor, they said, is to provide "new, sudden and striking collocations of references for the sake of the compound effects of contrast, conflict, harmony, inter-animation and equilibrium which may be so attained."

In the *Principles of Literary Criticism* these stock remarks of the scholiasts are happily forgotten, but metaphor appears still less to appertain to the essence of the poetic experience. "Metaphor," we read, "is a semi-surreptitious method by which a greater variety of elements can be wrought into the fabric of the experience. Not that there is any virtue in variety by itself, though the list of critics who seem to have thought so would be lengthy; a page of the dictionary can show more variety than any page of poetry. But what is needed for the wholeness of an experience is not always naturally present, and metaphor supplies an excuse by which what is needed can be smuggled in."

It is amusing to compare this with the statement of Helen Parkhurst:

"Certainly the quintessence of poetry—the pure grain of it that is left when all chaff has been winnowed away, the unalloyed gold that constitutes its substance—is little else than metaphor."

The anti-scientists will find it amusing that one psychologist describes as a surreptitious instrument for smuggling things into poetry, what another takes for little but the defining essence. However, all of Mr. Richards' books may be described as a brilliant effort to smuggle back into poetry its own essence which he has excluded by an initial error.

In his latest book, *Practical Criticism,* he has become aware of some inadequacy in this part of his theory, for he tells us that "A better understanding of metaphor is one of the aims which an imposed curriculum of literary studies might well set before itself." But he does not himself take any steps toward that better understanding. On the contrary he quite relaxes and sinks out of sight in the existing confusion. He now defines metaphor as "a shift, a carrying over of a word from its normal use to a new use"—a definition which has about as much relevance to the general substance of his book as would the leaping of a fish out of its pages. The essential theme and reason-for-being of the book was to distinguish four *different* ways in which words are *normally* used. They are used to make "sense" (the scientific way), to evoke attitude and emotion toward an object (poetry), to express emotion toward the hearer, and to carry out some ulterior intention. What can it mean when an author, professing to offer us an exhaustive analysis in four categories of the ways in which words are used, suddenly forgets all about it, drops back to the crude idea of a "normal" use of words, and defines metaphor as a departure from the "normal"? It means that he has abandoned all hope of ever explaining metaphor in terms of his own categories.

In a weak effort to pull things together, Mr. Richards distinguishes two kinds of departure from what he calls the "normal" use of words—the "sense metaphor" (prosaic or scientific) and the "emotive metaphor" (poetic). "In a sense metaphor," he tells us, "the shift of the word is occasioned and justified by a similarity *between the object* it is usually applied to and the new object. In an emotive metaphor the shift occurs through some similarity *between the feelings* the new situation and the normal situation arouse." And he illustrates this by imagining two situations in which one might call a man a *swine.* "It may be because his features resemble those of a pig, but it may be because you have towards him something of the feeling you conventionally have towards pigs, or because you propose, if possible, to excite those feelings." In the first case, the metaphor belongs to science, according to his scheme, in the second to poetry. Indeed "the poet's task is constantly . . . that of finding ways and means of controlling feeling through metaphor."

See what a complicated tangle Mr. Richards has got himself wound up in, and you will understand why he cries for help from "an imposed curriculum of literary studies." There is first the *normal-scientific* way of naming things, which consists of merely referring to them as they "are." Second there is a *departure from the normal* in science, called metaphor, which consists in not naming things what they *are* but what they *resemble.* Third there is a *normal-poetic* way of naming things, which consists of disregarding what they "are," but giving them a name that will evoke emotions toward them. And fourth there is a *departure* in poetry, which can only consist of not giving them their *normal* emotive name but some other *abnormal* name which evokes the same emotion! All these four situations to be explained, and no explanation whatever is forthcoming. There is not even the hint of a reason why science departs from the "normal" in this childish fashion. And there is no explanation of the poetic departure either—except to say that metaphor is a "ways and means of controlling feeling," and this cannot explain the departure, since it is already the sole explanation of the "normal" poetic use of words.

This inextricable tangle unravels instantly when you recognize that science, or prose, or the practical use of words, does not merely point to things but organizes experience. It does so by showing that one thing *resembles* some other thing or class of things. But the resemblances in which science is interested are those which prove constant, relevant to action and reliable on a large scale. Poetry as such is not interested in organizing experience, but in having it, and therefore poetry transfers the names of things according to resemblances which not only cannot be relied upon in action, but can be relied upon to make action impossible. These poetic transfers of names are all called metaphor, whether they are based on sensation or emotion, and if they appear in practical or scientific talk—except as they may be introduced for mere purposes of expository illustration—then poetry is intermingling in this talk.

Science does not call an object *swine* because it resembles a pig to mere ocular perception, any more than because it resembles a pig in the emotions which its presence evokes. Science has already had its say, when we are informed that the object "is" a man. After that anybody who calls it "swine," *whether because of sensuous or because of emotional resemblance,* is a poet. He may perhaps not be one who will shake the world with his originality, but he is occupied, as poets are, with the immediate qualities of the experience.

V

Not only does Mr. Richards' psychology fail to explain the predominance of metaphor in poetry, but it fails to explain the immemorial association of poetry with metrical or monotonous rhythm. Richards is illuminating in his discussion of the effects which may be created out of the "texture of expectations, satisfactions, disappointments, surprisals, which the sequence of syllables brings about," and the combination of these with similar effects involved in the meanings of the words. He talks more wisely about the musical than the imaginative values in poetry. But the thing to be explained here is not these high and fine values created by the subtle interplay of disappointment and satisfaction, for they belong to free verse and to prose rhythm as well as to poetry. The thing to be explained by a theory of poetry is its original and eternally persisting disposition to imitate the mere sing-song beating of a tom tom. Is there any reason for this persistent effort to be monotonous? That is what we want to know. And according to Richards' theory that poetry is essentially concerned with arousing attitudes and preparations for action, I do not see that there is.

Richards himself reminds us in several places that the fundamental effect of a monotonous metre is to put us into a hypnotic sleep. "We need not boggle," he says, "at the word 'hypnosis.'" Indeed "too simple rhythms, those which are too easily 'seen through,' grow cloying or insipid unless hypnoidal states intervene." Nobody will deny, I think, that in the vast aggregate of human poetry, those simple rhythms which are easily seen through prevail to an overwhelming degree. And if the defining purpose of poetry is to evoke emotional attitudes which are "preparations for action," how shall we explain this almost universal enthusiasm among poets for putting us to sleep? Mr. Richards has made an effort to explain it, and here too the effort goes back to the days of his collaboration with Mr. Ogden:

"Emotionality, exaggeration of belief-feelings, the occulting of the critical faculties . . . all these are characteristics of metrical experiences and fit in well with a hypnosis assumption." So these young authors assured us, and Mr. Richards repeats the theme in his *Principles of Literary Criticism:*

"That certain metres, or rather that a certain handling of metre should produce in a slight degree a hypnoidal state is not surprising. But it does so . . . through the lulling effects more than the awakening. Many of the most characteristic symptoms of incipient hypnosis are present in a slight degree. Among these susceptibility and vivacity of emotion, suggestibility, limitations of the field of attention . . . some degree of hyperæsthesia," etc.

It is noticeable that the emotions—and still more "emotionality" —appear in these quotations in their antique form as a kind of interior liquid, not in their modern form as "signs of attitudes" which are "preparations for action." It would hardly be possible for a logical mind to say—much less an experienced mind to believe—that "more through the lulling than the awakening effects" a metre makes us susceptible to vivacious "attitudes which are preparations for action." Richards is compelled to let his modern view of emotion slip out of his mind here—although his whole doctrine of poetry and criticism rests upon it—because while holding to it he cannot explain why the poets should want to put us to sleep.

I think anybody who has ever been to sleep can testify to the variety of preposterous and outrageous things he has seen happen in that country, and earnestly believed to be happening, without a glimmer of the appropriate emotion or the ghost of an impulse to do anything about it. Anybody who has experimented with hypnosis will as particularly testify that the state of suggestibility, "occulting of the critical faculties," "limitation of the field of attention," "hyperæsthesia"—the openness, in short, to complete and vivid hallucination—is accompanied by the same genius for not getting unnecessarily excited.[1] You can tell a hypnotic subject that there is a lion in the room in such a way as not to produce a flicker of emotion, but if you tell him that he is afraid of the lion you will find him under the bed. It is this disposition to believe and realize to the full any experience which is suggested by the hypnotist, whether it be emotional or not, which distinguishes the hypnotic state. It is this which distinguishes the "hypnoidal" states. And it is in order to produce these states that the poets, even though they wander away at times under pressure from their sophisticated friends in a prosaic world, perpetually recur to a metre that does not conceal or disguise its monotony.

[1]It is hardly necessary to cite authorities in disproof of the assertion that a condition called "emotionality" is increased under hypnosis. It is simpler to ask our brilliant authors to acknowledge that they were yielding to pressure from the hypothesis rather than the facts, when they slipped this abstraction in here. There is a precocious quality in that book, *The Meaning of Meaning,* a slightly too perfect command of thousands of big words and ideas, which makes it possible to say this without denying the value of the book.

They are not interested in evoking attitudes but in conveying imagined experience.

VI

Another of Mr. Richards' troubles which his initial misconception of the mind explains is his trouble with the lovers of art. Soon after he published his *Principles of Literary Criticism,* he was assailed by the English critic of painting Roger Fry for saying that "When we look at a picture, or read a poem, or listen to music, we are not doing something quite unlike what we are doing on our way to the Gallery. . . . Our activity is not of a fundamentally different kind."

Of course it is of a fundamentally different kind, and the more so, the more in haste we are to get there. In that case, every item of our experience is interpreted either as aid or hindrance to that purposive action. When we do get there, the difference is that we are there. The tension towards a specific goal relaxes. We become generically receptive. We are, to recall Professor Herrick, not only reaching out actively "to meet the exicting agent," but "seeking new contacts." It is idle to say that this difference is not fundamental. Everybody knows, because everybody feels, that it is fundamental. Even when we insist upon *interpreting* all the pictures in the gallery, as so many of us pathetically practical mortals have to do in order to convince ourselves that we are there at all, we try to make of the interpretation itself an objective thing, an experience to dwell upon. We enjoy it; we do not merely perform it, as we did the interpretation of the sign on the bus which brought us to the gallery.

The distinction is "fundamental," but it is not absolute, or mysterious or queer. It does not in the least commit us to the rather "arty" position of Mr. Fry, who shows an inclination to put a gold frame round our mood when we are at last solemnly arrived in the gallery, and call it an "æsthetic state" unrelated to all the other states in which we have leisure consciously to enjoy an experience. There is no fundamental difference between our activity in the gallery and on the way there, provided we pause on the way there, seized as it were by the brown twang of a hurdy-gurdy, or the bright orange hues of some display of tropical fruits and vegetables—provided we pause, and pour our energy into the act of perception for its own sake.

All poets and artists know that a child's exuberant excitement about life's experience—either that or a madman's excitement about some particular experience—is what distinguishes them from prosy people. They babble about things more than is prudent or necessary because they are in love with them. When they do not know this, it is merely because they are *too* childlike, or *too* mad, to know anything about themselves. Therefore when Mr. Richards comes along with his solemn attribution to them of a deep zeal for "organizing" their experience, for "ordering, controlling and consolidating" it, working up "preparations for action" upon it—when he accuses poets, in short, of being essentially practical people—they naturally rebel and denounce him for confusing poetry with efficiency, for confusing it with "a perfectly working mental Romeo Steel Cabinet System," to quote T. S. Eliot, or Herbert Read—I have forgotten which. They have both assailed Mr. Richards upon this point, and so I suppose has every reader of his books who has ever known or been a poet. And Mr. Richards has replied with some dudgeon that he does not mean by organization "deliberate planning," and he does not mean by order "tidiness." But that does not make the slightest difference. He is too deeply wrong for any specifications or shifts of emphasis to cure him. He is wrong in his conception of science as merely referring to things and *not interpreting them with a view to action*. And so he is wrong in his conception of poetry as essentially *not* referring to things but *merely interpreting them with a view to action*. He has got the whole thing exactly upside down, and nothing but a revolution can mend him.

VII

Another trouble Mr. Richards gets into by making attitude and preparation for action a part of the definition of poetry. He becomes a painfully austere and moralistic critic. Naturally if the poet is, and the prose thinker is not, concerned with preparations for action, the burden of regulating human conduct, or trying to regulate a little of it, rests entirely upon the poet. And that is no small burden for a sensitive and childlike person to carry. It makes Richards feel compelled to preach to the poets almost as solemnly as a Sunday-school superintendent or Matthew Arnold. In fact he becomes even more melodramatically moral than Arnold in assuring us that with creeds, dogmas, and traditions tumbling and crumbling about us, and the whole human race, so to speak, on the chaos-toboggan, poetry is our only stay.

"It is capable of saving us," he cries. "It is a perfectly possible means of overcoming chaos."

I do not know anything better calculated to strike dumb the singing lips of poets than to have a learned professor step out with this anguished expression on his face, and tell them that science has given up the sponge and the whole world is turning to them in a wild last agony of not very confident hope for salvation. People like to be praised, of course, for whatever virtues they haven't got, but they don't like to be told that everything depends upon their continuing to manifest these virtues.

The poet, Mr. Richards tells us, is "the master of speech because he is the master of experience. . . . The amazing capacity of his for ordering speech is only a part of a more amazing capacity for ordering his experience."

"The poets are failing us," he cries again, "or we them, if after reading them we do not find ourselves changed; not with a temporary change such as luncheon or slumber will produce . . . but with a permanent alteration of our possibilities as responsive individuals in good or bad adjustment to an all but overwhelming concourse of stimulations. . . ."

Imagine talking that way to Sappho—or Catullus, or François Villon, or Bobbie Burns! I do not mean that poets are bad. They are just as good as anybody else. But it is assuredly a little unfortunate to come along in the name of psychological understanding and talk to them in this preachy-preachy tone. It reminds one of St. Francis urging the birds to be good.

Matthew Arnold had this to justify him in his rather heavy hopes of poetry—that he believed true judgment was an intrinsic part of it. He defined poetry not as an arbitrary evocation of emotional attitudes to life,—a preparation for action divorced from any determination of the facts to be acted upon,—but as a "criticism of life." He believed that in poetry "Our race, as time goes on, will find an ever surer and surer stay," because in poetry our race will find true ideas —because "for poetry the idea is everything." This is exactly the opposite of Mr. Richards' opinion, although quoted by him in the title-head of his *Science and Poetry*. For him the idea—or the "intellectual stream," as he calls it—is a "minor branch" of the poetic experience. "It matters only *as a means;* it directs and excites the active stream." And to believe that it gives this direction and excitation by stating any truth or offering any valid criticism of anything, is "illicit" and a "profanation."

Thus his dreadfully moralistic preachment to poets, and his solemn transfer of the whole burden of human salvation to the backs of these rather bewildered minstrels, lacks altogether the plausibility in good sense that Arnold's saintly view of poetry had. The poet is to save us, according to Richards, not by telling us what things are, and so how to take up fitting attitudes towards them. "It is not necessary to know what things are in order to take up fitting attitudes towards them." All that is necessary is to listen to a *line of talk* —for that is the good American equivalent of pseudo-statement— which will leave us in "a strong emotional attitude which feels like belief," although we know quite well that no facts and no true ideas have been adduced or alluded to.

In one place Mr. Richards describes this emotional attitude as one of genuine although "objectless" belief, but his usual position is that "the most important among our attitudes can be aroused and maintained without any belief entering in at all." And to this arousal he looks for salvation against the break-down of belief itself, and the moral and political chaos which he sees ensuing.

"Countless pseudo-statements," he cries in warning,—"about God, about the universe, about human nature, . . . about the soul, its rank and destiny,—pseudo-statements which are pivotal points in the organization of the mind, vital to its well-being, have suddenly become for sincere, honest and informal minds, impossible to believe. . . . This is the contemporary situation. The remedy . . . is to cut our pseudo-statements free from belief, and yet retain them, in this released state, as the main instruments by which we order our attitudes to one another and to the world."

Mr. Richards' nightmare apprehension of an impending chaos seems to me a malady very similar to Joseph Wood Krutch's literary despair. Richards describes the transition from the "Magical View" of the world to the "scientific," not as a discovery that nature is neutral—a rather belated discovery, one would think, since it happens to have been true all along—but as an increasingly "dangerous" process called "Neutralization of Nature." Man "has to face the fact," he cries, "that the edifices of supposed knowledge, with which he has for so long buttressed and supported his attitudes, will no longer stand up, and, at the same time, he has to recognize that pure knowledge is irrelevant to his aims. . . ."

A glance into Russia at the robust composure and good health with which the bulk of the people there have effected the transition from a belief in magic and superstitious religion in its most archaic forms, to modern machine agriculture, atheism and a materialistic philosophy, should be sufficient to explode this hot-house idea of the manner in which man's attitudes are buttressed—and also enough to put to shame the assertion that knowledge is irrelevant to a man's aims. How can knowledge be irrelevant to a man's aims if he has any serious intention of achieving them? It is not the neutralization of nature that is troubling Mr. Richards, but the neutralization of the language in which practical and scientific people talk about nature. It is not the irrelevance of pure knowledge to man's aims, but the inappropriateness of the language of pure knowledge to the *expression* of his aims, which causes this professor to see advancing a "chaos such as man has never before experienced."

And since this is a purely literary chaos, Mr. Richards is naturally satisfied with a purely literary salvation from it. Nobody who seriously foresaw such a disaster descending upon the human race as he delineates could possibly look to poets for deliverance—much less to the universal enthronement of sentimentalism in the form of a definition of poetry. In his *Practical Criticism*—his most empirical and wisest book—Mr. Richards tells us that "A response is sentimental if it is too great for the occasion." And as though this succinct remark were not enough to condemn and wipe out utterly his own doctrine of poetry, he adds: "We cannot, obviously, judge that any response is sentimental in this sense unless we *take careful account of the situation.*" The idea that the race is going to be saved from chaos by the universal propagation of sentimental responses in the form of poetry is so fantastic that it seems a mere act of courtesy to insist that Mr. Richards is not talking about the problem of life in a world of science at all, but about the problem of poetry in a world of scientific terminology.

For Richards is not a sentimentalist, and not a man naturally disposed to delude himself with hollow and fantastic ideas like this. His own ardent labors toward a science of poetry and a scientific attitude in criticism stand there to demonstrate that. He has been led into this untenable position by a deep and admirable love of poetry, and by following out doggedly and with a fertile brain the implications of an error in psychology.

When poetic diction is defined as suggesting the qualities of experience more than practical interpretation demands, we are quite prepared to find the poets in their extreme moments ignoring the practical interpretation altogether, and regaling us with a mere line of talk. We find them more occupied with "what it feels like" to believe something than with whether it is true. In this they are irresponsible rather than sentimental, and we accord them a "poetic license" here as elsewhere, knowing it is not their specialty to conceive things truly but to live them vividly. We slake our own thirst for experience in their poems, and we should be rash to allow a little thing like truth or the meanings of words to stand between us and the fountain of life. Nevertheless we also know, and they know too, that vivid experience must not be confused with good judgment, nor good judgment long ignored or forgotten. Something greater and not less than mere poetry is in progress, when a poet enriches with the living colors of experience an interpretation of it that is true.

JOHN DEWEY'S *ART AS EXPERIENCE*

In his *Art As Experience,* John Dewey does me the honor to declare himself "in close accord" with my account of "the nature of the æsthetic experience." His accord, I take it, concerns my psychology of poetry, and my sociology of it—the wish that poetry should be dissociated from "transcendent ideality" and other connotations that a leisure-class decadence has given the word. We agree that "the æsthetic is no intruder in experience," or as I expressed it that "the poetic in every-day perception should not be separated from the poetic in literature." We agree also, more concretely, that phrases like "heightening of consciousness," "clarification and intensification of an experience," are valid general definitions of art. Mr. Dewey also concedes in one place that some "resistance or inhibition" of action is essential to this heightened consciousness. To that extent, as a psychologist, he concurs in what I say. But as a philosopher—so at least I interpret the difference—he feels compelled to escape from that clear distinction between the æsthetic and the practical which is of the essence of my view. He makes his escape, it seems to me, not by proving the distinction either false or futile, but by ignoring, or forgetting, what an intellectual distinction is.[1]

> "If painter and sculptor [he says] have an experience in which action is not automatic, but emotionally and imaginatively dyed, there is in that one fact proof of the invalidity of the notion that action is *so fluent* as to exclude the elements of resistance and inhibition necessary to heightened consciousness." (Italics mine.)

That is his answer to my assertion of a psychologically profound and historically increasing distinction between art and the life of action. And it is to my mind no answer at all. I take it as quite obvious and a mere starting point that action may be more or less

[1] *Art As Experience,* pp. 261, ff.

fluent, more or less "automatic," more or less "emotionally and imaginatively dyed." Experience does not consist of pure practicalities and pure trances of realization. Almost anything will link in with our purposes, and have or acquire a "meaning in action," if we dwell on it with idle energy. And if things can be said to "mean" when they point only to themselves, as Dewey suggests—and I too after a fashion in my chapter on "The Practical Value of Poetry"—it is indeed difficult to affirm that a purely impractical thing, moment or experience ever was enjoyed. About all this there is no disagreement between us. And as for the painter and sculptor, although their psychology has never been expertly studied, I am prepared to say that if they are true artists, the ability to retain either the reality or the accurate memory of an emotional experience, or be able constantly to recur to it, while doing the practical work and making the practical judgments necessary to its embodiment in an object, is almost their defining trait. It is what distinguishes them from hacks and academics. True artists are rare, but they are not abnormal, and so about that also there is no disagreement between us.

But that is not what we are discussing. We are discussing definitions. And if the æsthetic is to be defined, no matter how roughly, as "heightened consciousness," and if "elements of inhibition" are "necessary to heighten consciousness," then elements of inhibition belong to the definition of the æsthetic. And if elements of inhibition belong to the definition of the æsthetic, then there *is* a psychological, as well as an historic, opposition between art and purposive action. There is in nature itself that "separation of the instrumental and the consummatory," which Dewey is so concerned to evade. For it is certainly not one of the properties of an instrument to provide "elements of resistance and inhibition" when action does tend to become fluent. Art, as I have shown in the example of poetic metaphor, not only tolerates these elements of resistance and inhibition, but seeks them, invents them, *resides in them*. Much as I regret to say so, therefore, it is really impossible for Mr. Dewey to be as a psychologist in "close accord" with my account of the æsthetic experience, and as a philosopher committed to including the instrumental in the *definition* of art.

Mr. Dewey quotes my too extreme statement that "utensils can only, through some ceremonial effort, or when imported from far times or countries, become the source of heightened consciousness because we flow from a utensil smoothly into the action for which it is designed," and he answers:

"As for the producer of utensils, the fact that so many artisans in all times and places have found and taken time to make their products *esthetically pleasing* seems to me a sufficient answer. I do not see how there could be better proof that prevailing social conditions, under which industry is carried on, are the factors that determine the *artistic* or *non-artistic* quality of utensils, rather than anything inherent in the nature of things."

But this seems to me a perfect begging of the question. If something has to be done to a utensil, apart from its utility, in order to make it "æsthetically pleasing," then utility does not belong to the definition of the æsthetic. *Utensils as such, no matter how practical, are not, except incidentally, works of art; prevailing social conditions may permit their producer to incorporate in them an æsthetic quality or they may not.* That is what Mr. Dewey himself is saying. And he continues in the same vein:

"As far as the one who uses the utensil is concerned, I do not see why in drinking tea from a cup he is necessarily stopped from enjoying its shape and the delicacy of its material. Not every one gulps his food and drink in the *shortest possible time* in obedience to some necessary psychological law. . . . There is many a mechanic under present industrial conditions who *stops* to admire the fruit of his labors, *holding it off* to admire its shape and texture, and not merely to examine into its efficiency for practical purposes. . . ."

This, too, as my italics show, is an endorsement of my assertion that the utility and the æsthetic value, although frequently found in the same object, are distinguishable and deeply distinct. It is support to my *definition* of art. It reveals, too, why Mr. Dewey dislikes the definition—namely that he hopes to bring more æsthetic quality into utensils, more æsthetic pleasure both to the producers and the users of them. So do I. But I do not think confusing the definitions is the way to do it. Lewis Mumford in his *Technics and Civilization* has given a very thorough expression to this hope, but I do not see how he could have written his book at all without holding clear the distinction between utility and "æsthetic interest."

In my opinion John Dewey, in his rejection of intellectualism, is sometimes carried to a point where the obliteration of any distinction seems to him a good in itself. In his literary style as in so many of his opinions I sense the perpetual wish to sink back from the lucid audacities of intellection into the flux of fact. William James, as Dewey remarks in this book, perceived the limited validity of intellectual distinctions, especially in psychology. But to James this perception was on the whole intoxicating. He made what distinctions he found useful the more recklessly, trusting to the social dialectic and the good sense of mankind to bevel their sharp edges and prevent his clear talk from doing any harm to truth. In Dewey, so much more burdened as he is with philosophical responsibility, the effect is opposite. While equally sure that his distinctions have no absolute validity, he still wants them to, and so he himself bevels their edges and waters them and spreads them out until they are hardly distinguishable from experience itself, unanalyzed but indubitably valid.

"A definition is good when it is sagacious," he says in this book, "and it is that when it so points the direction in which we can move expeditiously toward having an experience." If that is the criterion, there is certainly no doubt that a definition of poetry which stresses its impractical or "consummatory" character is, especially in and throughout the United States of America, a good one. For if there is one thing that stands between the average American and the enjoyment of poetry, whether in life or literature, it is his attitude of practicality, his inveterate disposition to ask, "What's the use of it?" If you approach poetic literature, and if you approach other art works, with the assumption that a keen or clear experience is worth having for its own sake, many other things, including moral or even political guidance, may at times be added unto you. But if you approach it with the question, "Well, what is the theme here? What can this teach us?" the keen and clear experience will never be yours.

A good definition ought indeed to guide us toward the experience. But it ought also to make a wide, deep and explanatory grasp among the elements of the experience. And it ought to enable us to distinguish the experience from what is commonly regarded as its contrary—for otherwise we are not defining terms but inventing language. Mr. Dewey's definition of poetry, so far as he may be said to make one, fulfills none of these requirements.

"Words serve their poetic purpose," he says, "in the degree in which they summon and evoke into active operation the vital responses that are present whenever we experience qualities."

Now the words which occur to me at this moment as most fitted to evoke vital responses into active operation are: "Get out of the way!" "Look out for the dog!" and "What's that on your collar?" And those words contain none of the characteristic elements of poetry. The notion of evoking vital responses into *active operation* neither grasps those elements nor explains their association together. The notion of evoking vital responses but at the same time *inhibiting* their active operation, in order to make consciousness more keen, does grasp and explain these elements. It explains metaphor—never once mentioned in Dewey's account of poetry—and it explains, as no other theory has, that almost universal association of figurative language with hypnotic metre, which is assuredly the main thing to be explained.

It moreover enables us to distinguish poetry from practical or prose language—not as two absolutes, of course, but as two elements which may stand utterly distinct, as in a cook book at one end and a "pure poem" at the other, or may combine in varying proportions. Mr. Dewey significantly confesses that he is unable to find any "difference that can be exactly defined between prose and poetry." He is compelled to fall back upon such languid and meandering remarks as this:

"One of them realizes the power of words to express what is in heaven and earth and under the seas by means of extension; the other by intension. The prosaic is an affair of description and narration, of details accumulated and relations elaborated. It spreads as it goes like a legal document or catalogue. The poetic reverses the process. It condenses and abbreviates, thus giving words an energy of expansion that is almost explosive. A poem presents material so that it becomes a universe in itself, one which, even when it is a miniature whole, is not embryonic any more than it is labored through argumentation."

Is there no description and narration in poetry, no accumulation of details, no relations elaborated—no allegory, for instance? Is there, on the other hand, no condensation or abbreviation in prose—no epigrams, no telegrams? Do prose essays or novels never present material so that it becomes a universe in itself, and one which is not "labored through argumentation?" Could anybody, in short, seriously maintain that these disorganized and loose remarks "point the direction in which we can move expeditiously toward having an experience" of poetry, or for that matter of good prose?

For my part I can catch no glimpse of a reason, either practical or theoretical, for John Dewey's dodging in the field of æsthetics the obvious implications of his own psychology of thought and action—no reason for his flatly contradicting my account of the æsthetic experience after declaring himself in close accord with it—except a general distaste for distinctions, and the habit of the pragmatist philosopher to regard all serious values as practical and as referred for their real being into the future. If truth is only "the successful working of an idea," we can hardly expect "beauty" to escape a similarly postponed identity. But I do not think this ought to obstruct the development of a clear psychology and a significant history of art.

A WORD WITH LEWIS MUMFORD

In a review of *The Literary Mind* printed in *The New Republic,* February 3, 1932, Lewis Mumford made the following remark about my exposition of the historical divergence between science and poetic literature:

"Setting out to examine the function of literature in a scientific age, he makes the initial mistake of assuming that science and literature were originally one. . . . There is no ground for this belief: Euclid and Menander, Chaucer and Albertus Magnus, Milton and Robert Boyle, were no more and no less separated than James Joyce and Einstein today. . . . In the chapters on *What Poetry Is* and *Art and Biology,* Mr. Eastman happily turns his back upon his original premises and establishes literature as an autonomous function of the personality, seeking to hold and intensify and explore and expand the actualities and the possibilities of experience."

This is one of those glib dismissals by a critic preoccupied with his own thoughts which a writer usually feels constrained to ignore. But it has been quoted in high places, and besides I am interested in the thoughts with which Mr. Mumford is preoccupied. I would ask him to pause and understand that my "original premise" is the psychological and biological distinction between seeking experience and seeking adjustment. Far from saying that science and literature were "originally one," I say that these two impulses, two in the very origins of life, were in early literature neither sharply nor generally distinguished. Poetry and science were written in great part by the same people and appeared in the same books. This is an historic fact, and not a queer idea of mine. Menander, a late poet, was a pure "imitator of life," and Euclid was the author of an unusually mature and abstract science. But almost half the Greek physicists expressed their thoughts in poetry. Empedocles, Doctor of Medicine as well as physicist, was a poet; Parmenides was a poet; Xenophanes was a minstrel of science; Eratosthenes, the great astronomer-mathematician and founder of scientific chronology, was a poet; Solon the Lawgiver was a poet; Homer the historian and, as Plato called him, "educator of Greece," was a poet; and Mr. Bury in *The Early Greek Historians* says: "One of the most serious impediments blocking the way to a scientific examination of early Greece was the orthodox belief in Homer's omniscience and infallibility—a belief which survived the attacks of Ionian philosophers and the irony of Thucydides." Imagine the authority of Longfellow impeding Charles Beard in his scientific study of early America!

If you go back into still more primitive cultures, history becomes more and more metaphorical. The story of Joseph and his brothers is a poet's way of recording the migrations of the tribes of Israel. The mural painting of a bull and tumbling human figure recently unearthed in Crete suggests that the myth of Theseus and the Minotaur is the poem-history of a real situation, that in the period of Cretan domination Athenian youths were actually sacrificed to sacred bulls in a grim precursor of the modern Mediterranean sport. Natural science as well as history, of course, insofar as it rose beyond everyday rules of thumb, was all confused with myth and poetry. Witness the names of the stars. Indeed these facts about early culture are too well known to discuss. Mr. Mumford was simply not letting his mind travel in that direction.

If you travel in the other direction from the early Greeks, you see this process continuing right up to our own time. Euclid was purely scientific; so perhaps was Archimedes. But Lucretius wrote what we should call an "Outline of Science" in poetic form and language. Virgil, as I have said, promoted scientific agriculture in poetry. Virgil was, indeed, for a great period of time regarded, like Homer, as an infallible authority on everything. Does Mr. Mumford not know the position occupied by Virgil in mediæval folklore?

As for Chaucer, he was an astronomer as well as a poet. And Milton—does Mr. Mumford really think it possible to compare Milton's relation to the organized knowledge of his time with that of James Joyce to modern science? Not only was Milton far more like a scientist in his time than Joyce is in ours, but Robert Boyle's science was far more mixed with poetry than Einstein's is. You might as well say that there has been no evolution of knowledge as to say that the understanding of things in their relations has not gradually separated out from the celebration of their experienced qualities.

This is not the miraculous appearance in history of a distinction that did not exist in the organization and operation of the brain and mind. It is the sharpening of a distinction inherent in the nature of mind, and its advancement with the advance of verified knowledge into ever new fields.

As *The Literary Mind* was mainly concerned with the most recent example of this latter process, the *advancement* of science in the form of psychology and sociology into fields heretofore sacred as "the humanities" to poetic literature, it is hard to believe that Mr. Mumford could have made his comment if he had seriously examined my book. Whatever his real disagreements might be, he would find the facts I am describing relevant, and at points extremely important, to his own preoccupations.

GENERAL NOTES AND REFERENCES

GENERAL NOTES AND REFERENCES

[*Page* 5]

In an essay called "The Will to Live," and published in the *Journal of Philosophy, Psychology and Scientific Methods* (Vol. XIV, No. 4), I discussed the scientific basis and implication of the statement that there is in all animal life such an impulse, or "general innate tendency," as I have here described. The substance of that essay will be found in the present volume under the title *Art and Biology.*

[*Page* 8]

The quotation is from Robert Browning's "Saul."

[*Page* 9]

Irving King in *The Psychology of Child Development,* p. 147, records an instance similar to the one I describe. He also, on p. 174, shows very conclusively that what we call in children "the instinct of imitation" is not that, in any intelligible sense, but a desire to enlarge, and intensify (or as he says, because he writes from a purely practical view-point, define) their own experience. To put it in their own words, they are always wanting to "see what it feels like." And this is not merely the instinct of curiosity either, for after they *know* what it feels like, they still want to feel it again. Indeed, the instinct of curiosity itself may, like other feelings, become the object of this desire. "The child is curious," says M. Claparède in his *Psychologie de l'Enfant,* "for the pleasure of being curious; the scholar is curious in order to know." But any work upon the psychology of children will more or less unconsciously bear out the statement that children are more interested in experience for its own sake than adults.

The quotation is from Keats's "Ode to Melancholy."

[*Page* 10]

The quotation is from Wordsworth's sonnet, "The World Is Too Much With Us."

[*Page* 12]

The quotation is from Walt Whitman's "Crossing Brooklyn Ferry."

[*Page* 16]

I have mentioned the three classic theories of the origin of speech. That they should have appeared as opposing theories, and begot volumes, is an example of that puerility of the academic intellect, and the foolishness which infects both science and conversation, of supposing that a single generalization is always possible and is the form of truth. Probably the majority of words never originated in any of these pretty ways. Otto Jespersen in his *Progress in Language* (Chap. IX) has pointed out that simultaneous occurrence, however accidental, is enough to establish a connection between syllables and experiences. Granted, therefore, a savage with excess energy to exhaust in vocal exercises as he goes along, and you have adequate conditions for the birth either of practical or poetic names.

Suppose that he happens to be singing ta-ra-ra-ra boom-de-aye when he is splitting the kindlings this morning; it may well happen that he sings the same syllables at the same time to-morrow morning, and so on, until ta-ra-ra comes to "mean" split-the-kindlings.

[*Page* 16 (2)]

In English a struggle for survival has long raged, and is raging, among these verb-forms. And of late years the battle is not to the strong, but to the handy—the loss of those old forms being one of the poetic sorrows of our tongue, though it would be expeditious and an act of practical good sense, I suppose, to wipe out the whole tribe.

We might examine the character of those strong forms which survived, against those which perished, and see if it were not special poetic strength which determined the issue in many cases, and thus perhaps we could oppose the tendency of scholars nowadays to impute everything that has happened in language to a desire to make it practical.

As examples of that tendency I select these quotations:

"To no other law than that of economy of utterance have any of the phenomena of phonetic change been found traceable (though it is also to be noted that some phenomena have not hitherto been successfully brought under it, and that the way of effecting this is still unclear)."—William Dwight Whitney (Article on "Philology" in the *Encyclopædia Britannica*).

GENERAL NOTES AND REFERENCES

The only test of the merits of languages that is of any value is "the practical interests of the speaking (or talking) community." —OTTO JESPERSEN (*Progress in Language*).

[*Page* 17]

The word rakehell is a poetic "corruption" of the adjective *rakel,* meaning rash. "Train oil," a degeneration from *Thräne* or "tear-like" oil, may serve as an example of a practical corruption.

Corruption in language is often almost as valuable as creation. Out in Colorado there is a winding river which some starving first-settler, a Frenchman, called the *Purgatoire.* But that name has no appropriateness for the prosperous citizens who now dwell along its coils; for them it is the *Picketwire.* The name is still poetic.

Skeat says of *ghastly,* "the *h* has been inserted for no very good reason." But to those who taste the flavors of words it has been inserted, as also in ghost, for the best of all reasons, namely, that it makes the word suggest its object. It is a kind of strange, breathless letter there—essentially unpronounced, unmuscularized, supernatural.

Our ancestors are being scolded by the simplified spelling board for such liberties as this. They took an *h* out of *gossip* and inserted one into ghost! This is highly "irregular," "impractical," and "unscientific," but it shows that they knew in their immediate experience the essential difference between a gossip and a ghost, and they could convey this in the most delicate poetry, and they cared to. Is the lack in them, or in the simplified spelling board?

[*Page* 18]

Bluff, crib, grad, flunk, are slang words of purely practical value.

Swelled head, brass, face, paint the town red, have a bee in your bonnet, down and out, a mossback, a jonah, are poetic, with the usual tincture of humor. *To have a bee in your bonnet* is a metaphor which occurs, if I remember rightly, as the basis of a stanza of one of Burns's poems.

[*Pages* 32, 33]

The quotations are from Keats's early poem, "I Stood Tip-toe Upon a Little Hill," except "The grey fly," which is from Milton's *Lycidas,* and "Million-footed Manhattan," which is from Walt Whitman.

[*Page* 34]

It has been customary to divide comparison, or the association of ideas as it is called, into two kinds—association by resemblance and association by contiguity. That this is not a fundamental difference, but that both kinds of association are instances of the redintegration of a past experience in memory according to the laws of habit, is one of the opinions of Aristotle, rediscovered by modern psychology. In a contribution to the *Journal of Philosophy, Psychology and Scientific Methods,* Vol. VII, No. 6, entitled "To Reconsider the Association of Ideas," I tried to show that this doctrine even as it now stands is not satisfactory and that its terminology needs revising. I do not believe that I reached the bottom of the question in that article, but if any one cares to read it, he will find there some indication of how I came to treat comparison as essentially an interruption, and explain its value to realization in the way I have.

[*Page* 35]

In this section I may appear to give more standing to the purely practical theory of the origin of consciousness, than I wish to. I believe, as I stated in Chapter I and at the beginning of Chapter II, that the impulse toward consciousness for its own sake is fundamental. And I may reconcile what I said then with what I say here, by calling attention to the fact that even though I describe our life in general as blindly practical, I point out that the poets are there, seeking to arouse us. They too must have their explanation. The poetic in each of us must have its explanation. And I believe the only explanation it can have is the placing of it equal with the onward impulse, as an original and arbitrary quality of life.

[*Page* 36]

If "similarity" were the object of attraction in a poetic comparison, we should find pleasure in those pedantic similes in which various points of resemblance are brought forward, and the likeness of two things dwelt upon at length. But this exploitation of similarity itself is a thing which no one with a spark of true poetry in him can tolerate.

[*Page* 39]

I need not explain that this opinion has dominated English minds ever since the days of Elizabeth, and before. The poet makes things, says Philip Sidney, "either better than nature bringeth forth, or, quite a newe, formes such as neuer were in nature." According to Francis Bacon likewise, the great virtue of poetry is that it does not "buckle and bow" the mind to the real facts of experience. Endless quotations are possible to this same effect: that poetry is a means by which too delicate spirits can run away from the terms of existence. It is a parlor idea, and every great poet that ever lived belies it. Milton and Dante, indeed, are supposed to have made supernatural ventures into a realm of unreality, or at least a world of spirit, simply because they *said* that this was where they were going. It is clear enough to the eye of analysis, however, that in proportion as their imaginative passages are great, they are filled with the material colors of the real world. There may be such a thing as pure spirit, but a book of poems is the last place in which it will be found. It will be found in Euclid rather than Dante.

[*Page* 43]

The quotation is from Walt Whitman's "Passage to India."

[*Page* 44]

The Japanese translations are taken, for the most part, from a book by Basil Hall Chamberlain, called *Japanese Poetry.*

[*Page* 48]

The quotations are from Walt Whitman's "The Answerer" and "Salut au Monde."

[*Page* 51]

This definition, and the whole modern treatment of "figures of speech," is perhaps due to a misunderstanding of Aristotle's classifications. "Rhetoric" meant to Aristotle the forensic art, the art of convincing and persuading. This art was a sub-chapter of logic, in which metaphors (for he calls all these things metaphors) have no vital place. They are "ornaments" merely. Aristotle himself recognized, however vaguely, that their position in poetic writing is different, and he never intended his rhetoric for a general Bible.

[*Page* 51 (2)]

This kind of choice is called "metonymy" when some adjunct or pervasive quality of a thing is named, "synecdoche" when a definite part. But if you substitute the word *experience* for *thing* in these definitions, the distinction between metonymy and synecdoche properly disappears.

In defining synecdoche as "naming a part for the whole," it is customary to add "or sometimes the whole for a part." But I think in every example which can be given of the latter, it will be found that the name of *the whole* either offers a more single and somehow apprehensible focus of attention, or stimulates the imagination by the very strangeness of its use, or else is not poetic at all, but merely a less specific way of talking than the reader expected.

Aristotle made the peculiar mistake of including this use of a general term instead of a specific, among his "metaphors." (Poetics, Chap. XXI, 4.) Transferring a name from genus to species, he calls it, and gives as an example from the Odyssey:

"Secure in yonder port my vessel stands."

"For to be moored," he says, "is a species of standing." I do not know what the associative flavors of the words are in Greek, but if the one is really by grammatical definition a species of the other, then there is no transfer of a word "out of its proper signification." There is simply general instead of specific language, as when we say "an animal" instead of "a dog."

Perhaps it is mainly out of a persistent, and generally well-founded, reverence for Aristotle, that this secondary definition of synecdoche survives. There surely are cases when, for accidental reasons either in the word or the thing, it is more vivid to name the whole than the part. "The west warns us," appears to me more poetic than "The sunset warns us." But I think this, and other cases of the kind, are actually (when we substitute *experience* for *thing*) selections of a vivid part.

[*Page* 52]

"Pleonasm" and *"Tautology"* are two other so-called "figures" which find their explanation here. "Saying the same thing over again" is supposed to be a peculiar literary delight upon many occasions. But when this is not exact repetition, it is usually one of the manifestations of poetic choice—an experience being indicated in general first, and then the chosen attribute called forth.

[*Pages* 55 *and* 56]

The quotations are from the Book of Psalms.

[*Page* 58]

Perhaps the intrinsic nature and motive of all poetic utterance is clearest proven in the spontaneous answer of one of these Indians when he was asked, "How do you make your songs?" "When I am herding my sheep," he said, "or away in the fields, and I see something that I like—then I sing about it." Another compiled a commentary upon his song, so that its "inner meaning" might be known to the hearer, and this is what he said: "My song is about butterflies flying over the cornfields and over the beans. One butterfly is running after the other like the hunt, and there are many."

Let us hear the song, for it is one of the few whose poetry is all within the perception of a person who has been civilized.

"Yellow butterflies,
Over the blossoming virgin corn,
With pollen-painted faces,
Chase one another in brilliant throng.

"Blue butterflies,
Over the blossoming virgin beans,
With pollen-painted faces,
Chase one another in brilliant streams.

"Over the blossoming corn,
Over the virgin corn,
Wild bees hum,
Over the blossoming beans,
Over the virgin beans,
Wild bees hum.

"Over your fields of growing corn,
All day shall hang the thunder-cloud;
Over your fields of growing corn,
All day shall come the rushing rain."

All these examples are taken from *The Indians' Book*, by Natalie Curtis.

[*Page* 59]

The pleasure of attributing supremely poetic language to an occult inspiration will set many romantic people, who never wrote poetry, against this description of the poet's mind. But for my part I see no gain, even for intelligent romance, in imputing these qualities to the intuitive or subliminal mind. They are just the same things there, that they are in the deliberate mind. We cannot make a natural thing supernatural by showing that it is not expressly directed at every step by a self-conscious faculty. So while we recognize that these gifts of the poet are often subconscious, we need not therefore hesitate to say that they are what they are. And to this we may add that if biography tells us anything, it tells us that the greatest poets and artists were in a high degree self-conscious and deliberate, as well as exalted, in their creative moments.

[*Page* 60]

The quotation is from Keats's "Endymion."

[*Page* 63]

This twofold function of rhythm can be more technically expressed if we remember that emotions are never *imaged;* they are "real" even when images arouse them. They are of the body. And a poetic rhythm, though its cruder effect is usually to lull us into that state where images grow clear, does also (I would almost say *afterward*) directly intensify the emotions that accompany those images. If this statement is unsatisfactory from a scientific stand-point, that is not, I think, because it idealizes or blurs the facts, but because science has in this direction no dominant hypothesis under which the facts can be arranged.

[*Page* 64]

It is perhaps necessary, in this place, to allude to the fact that the word "poetry" often means "metrical language," regardless of whether any genuine realization is conveyed by such language or not. The opposite of "poetry" in this sense is "straight copy." And since this distinction is valuable in its place, we need not dispute the definition. We are using the word poetry in one of its other senses which is for our purpose, and for the general purposes of life, more important, and we wish to show the historical and scientific relation of metrical language to poetry in this sense.

The dispute over what "poetry" means, as though one word always means and always must mean but one class of things, is so wearisome and (now that we understand the history of words) so full of academic folly, that I insert this note simply to ward off the suggestion of it.

[*Page* 67]

The quotation is from the Book of Genesis.

[*Page* 69]

The quotations of Homer are from Bryant's translation of the "Iliad."

[*Page* 71]

The quotations of Shakespeare are, for the most part, from "Coriolanus" or "King Lear."

[*Page* 72]

As a poet of the world, there is, I think, this failing in Shakespeare —and it is seen by Tolstoy—that he had a too special love of words. Often the experience which his lines convey is an experience of the high wonder of the birth and being of language rather than of things, and it is open only to persons of specialized perception in that direction. I can best show what I mean by calling attention to the entire transparency of the words in this passage from Shelley, how un-Shakespearian it is:

"The rocks are cloven, and through the purple night
I see cars drawn by rainbow-wingéd steeds
Which trample the dim winds: in each there stands
A wild-eyed charioteer urging their flight.
Some look behind, as fiends pursued them there,
And yet I see no shapes but the keen stars:
Others, with burning eyes, lean forth, and drink
With eager lips the wind of their own speed,
As if the thing they loved fled on before,
And now, even now, they clasped it. Their bright locks
Stream like a comet's flashing hair: they all
Sweep onward."

Here is motion, and motion rich with the technique of verbal realization, yet clear in a way that Shakespeare is not often clear, because he loved excessively the feeling of words in his mouth and mind.

"They drink with eager lips the wind of their own speed."

[*Page* 72 (2)]

The term "lyric poetry," as now used, has less than no scientific value. And the word "epic," when it does not express a judgment of value, means simply a long story told in poetry.

[*Page* 74]

The quotations are from Burns's poem "To a Mountain Daisy" and from a song in Tennyson's "Princess," quoted again in Chapter XII.

[*Page* 76]

The expression "word-painting" derives, I believe, from John Ruskin, but the idea that physical vision of imaginary things is the poetic faculty *par excellence* is older than books. "A speaking picture" is Philip Sidney's expression.

The tribute of the eye surpasses that of all the other senses except touch, in giving us the sense of a presence. It is a matter of small moment if we *hear* a lady splashing in the bath at sunrise, but given the least retreating shade of her to our eyesight, and there is a great awakening! It is a topic for myth and song. For such reasons we speak of all mental substance as though it were composed purely of visual memory. "Imagination" and even "idea" are visual words. And the definition of poetry as painting is but a continuation of this way of speaking.

It is in truth a poetic name for poetry. It chooses one, and that an eminent one, of its qualities and compares it upon the basis of that to a material art. But poetry may as truly be compared to sculpture or to any other art that appeals to an external sense. The realizations of other artists are limited to certain of the senses, but the artist of imagination appeals to them all. Therefore, to call the poet "painter" is to speak poetically. Whereas to call the painter a "poet"—a realizer of things through form and color—is almost a scientific generalization.

In Caxton's "Book of Curtesye," I find this appreciation of "Galfreyde Chawcer," which expresses more truly than "word-painting" the characteristic of poetry which we distinguish in this chapter:

"His langage was so fayr and pertynente
It seemeth unto mannys herrynge
Not only the words but verely the Thynge."

GENERAL NOTES AND REFERENCES

[*Page* 79]

The quotation is from the poem called "Walt Whitman."

[*Page* 81]

Even where it appears, as so often in Wordsworth's poems, that exactly the opposite principle has been followed, the commonest of all names being chosen, I think that the poetic effect lies largely in the fact that, for persons who are accustomed to the ways of poetry, that very thing is a surprise. In somewhat the same way, an extreme prose word is often poetic in a passage of continuous poetry.

[*Pages* 81 *and* 82]

The quotations are from a mediæval writer, from Shelley's "Skylark," from the Rig-Veda, and from Robert Burns.

[*Page* 82]

All that we have of Sappho has been collected, with various English translations, by Henry Thornton Wharton, in a book called "Sappho."

[*Pages* 86 *and* 87]

The quotations are a fragment of Shelley's and lines from Shelley's "Adonais."

[*Page* 89]

The quotation is from the "Song of Solomon."

[*Page* 90]

The quotation is from Andrew Lang's translations of Theocritus.

[*Page* 91]

"When Lilacs Last in the Dooryard Bloomed" is Walt Whitman's poem upon the death of Abraham Lincoln.

[*Page* 92]

For any who may read my book studiously, I wish to explain that in this chapter I mean by "abstract ideas," not merely those indicated by terms which are abstract in the logical sense. I mean also those indicated by general terms when they are used, not to denote *some* individual (a dog barked), but to denote *any* individual (a dog is a good friend). The abstraction to which I refer is psychological, not logical. It is the abstraction inherent in any "concept," regarded as a concept, or used for the purpose of exposition—used in any way except to name for the imagination an individual thing. This is what the word abstract signifies in its popular, as well as its psychological use, and, therefore, except for technical purposes, this note is superfluous.

[*Page* 92 (2)]

This way of apprehending poetry appears to be as ancient as any. "Apparent pictures of unapparent natures" is a Zoroastrian definition which sums up all the others.

Aristotle, in contrasting poetry with history, assumes that the *particulars* in poetry are but *instances* of a generalization.

Sidney revives this opinion, and pleases his heart with the idea that the aim of all poetry is to *instruct* by means of pictures.

Emerson shows the same tendency. "I am a poet," he says, "in the sense of a perceiver and dear lover of the harmonies that are in the soul and in matter, and *especially of the correspondences between these and those.*"

It was by this road that I arrived at the present analysis of poetry. I published in the *North American Review* for March, 1908, an article on "The Poet's Mind," which proposed to distinguish poetry from practical language, but did so only in so far as each is employed in the expression of abstract ideas.

Hudson Maxim has written a book in which he defines poetry in much the same way. His book has a grand title, "The Science of Poetry, and the Philosophy of Language," and this, as well as its contents, bears me out a little in my belief that these definitions are, like the others, partial definitions, expressions of taste upon the part of excessively intellectual people. The true generalization does not contradict, but includes them.

[*Pages* 92 *and* 93]

"The butterfly sleeps on the village bell" is a Japanese poem, like those quoted in Chapter VI. The other quotation is from Isaiah.

[*Pages* 93]

The quotation is from Kant's "Critique of Pure Reason."

[*Pages* 94]

"The deep truth is imageless"—Something of this kind must

have been meant by Hegel in his assertion that while poetry is the highest of the arts, "the prose of thought" is one thing higher.

That such a thing as "imageless thought" exists is maintained by very few psychologists to-day. We may say, I think, that, no matter how "pure" one's reason may be, its procedure is dependent in some measure upon fragments of imagery or sensation.

[*Page* 100]

The quotation is from Wordsworth's ode on "Intimations of Immortality."

[*Page* 101]

The quotation is from Emerson.

[*Page* 102]

The quotation is from Fitzgerald's translation of "The Rubáiyát" of Omar Khayyám.

Many of the Japanese Hokku are poems of this kind, there being some idea suggested to the initiated, even though the words appear to us purely pictorial. This is true, I believe, of two or three of those quoted in Chapter VI. But it is not true of all, and is not essential to their being poems.

[*Page* 104]

The quotation is from Tennyson's "Morte d'Arthur."

[*Page* 105]

This decline into a passion for the technique of poetry, as an end in itself, is of course always imminent, when people make a life business of composing it. Browning was almost more infatuated with rhyme, it would appear, than with his very highest imaginations, for he so frequently sacrificed the latter to the former.

A similar, although more intellectual, decadence, is the passion for singularity and similarity as ends in themselves. The aim of a poetic choice or comparison here ceases to be the enhancement of an experience, and it becomes merely an exploitation of intellectual ingenuity.

[*Page* 106]

The quotation is from Tennyson's "The Lotos Eaters."

[*Page* 106 (2)]

Poe has himself given an account of his mood and manner of creating, which supports this judgment. And he too wrote upon the science, or "rationale," of verse, and even made a definition of all poetry as "a pleasurable idea accompanied by music."

The quotation is from Poe's "The Sleeper."

[*Page* 109]

Another reason why it is unfortunate to quote those immemorial lines as examples of poetry is that they are not even illuminating examples of onomatopœia. Their imitation is too obvious and extraordinary. But onomatopœia, in millions of subtle forms, is pervasive in poetry. It is a principle that relates to far other matters than the naming of bees or a buzz-saw. It is the principle of that poetic quality which we found native to all rapid narrative—a similarity in consecutiveness between the words and the events. It is the principle of infinite indescribable appropriateness in language—things that science can but indicate in their variety and leave to unconscious discovery by those whose sensibilities are fine.

That line of Keats, "Lucent syrops tinct with cinnamon," can show that the principle applies to other organs than the ear. *Tinct* is a most delicate imitation of the act of tasting. It is more than that. *Wolfish* again is a poetic word through muscular imitation of a snarl. And *"unflesh your teeth"* is still more so, because it does exactly what it says. But these also are obvious, compared, for instance, to the appropriateness of the dark sound of the word *war* to the thing it conceives, or the thick shock of the word *blood*. It is difficult to distinguish what quality pertains to a word through its previous uses, and what through its purely sensible nature.—*Violet* is so different from *violent!* But certainly some of this quality is purely vocal. Words do have their sensible nature; it is definite; and to those gifted or trained in such perceptions, it may become a strong enhancement of the imagination of things.

If one wished to write a science of these values, he would have to recognize not only similarities in the different senses (sound and sight and motion) involved in word perception, but also similarities between one sense and another (as sound and color in the word *gray*), and between sensations and ideas, or emotions. He would have also to recognize a second principle, besides onomatopœia. For words acquire value through association, not with other things only, but with the names of other things. *Bludgeon,* for instance, is a poetic word because it has blood on it, as well as a good heavy smash of its own. On the other hand, *spectre* and *phantom* and *ghost* are poetic words exactly because they have no associates. They are unique words, naming the unique apparition. Milton speaks of the army of the pigmies as small *infantry,* and the critics accuse him of a pun. But doubtless he chose the word, as he would any other, entirely unconscious of the source of its appropriate flavor. No one has ever studied to classify these sources, but I believe the associative relations among words and syllables themselves would be found almost as important in such a classification as onomatopœia.

[*Page* 109]

The quotation is from that song in Tennyson's "Princess" called "Come Down, O Maid."

[*Page* 112]

The sonnet is by Christina Rossetti.

[*Pages* 112 *and* 113]

The quotation is from Keats' "La Belle Dame Sans Merci."

[*Page* 118]

This will be true about the poetry of books only if one is entirely free from cultural dogmas about what books he "ought to" enjoy, free to make his own arbitrary choices, free to reject all books when the poetry of his own soul is at its highest.

[*Page* 120]

That these intervals are not mathematically equal in the modern reading of poetry has been established by mechanical experiment. An approximation to equality is nevertheless what gives them their rhythmic character, and the act of perception may somehow equalize them in their nervous, as it does in their psychic, effect.

[*Page* 120 (2)]

As a result of this attitude to the line rhythm, at least one so-called "law of prosody" has entirely dominated English poets, and often, I think, to their misfortune. It is the law about left-over syllables at the end, or beginning, of a line in blank verse. Suppose the division between two lines properly falls in the middle of a word, or of an indivisible phrase, as in this example:

"To hím the wáll
That súnders ghósts and shádow-cásting mén
Becáme a crýstal, ánd he sáw them thróugh it."

Prosodists diagnose that contrarious syllable *it,* which properly belongs to the next line, as a sort of abnormal excrescence upon the old line, call this by the terrifying name of acatalectic (or catalectic, or hypercatalectic—one never remembers which) and require that the next line shall begin all fresh with another unaccented syllable. Thus:

"Becáme a crýstal ánd he sáw them thróúgh it
And heárd their vóíces tálk behínd the wáll."

That is, they require that we sacrifice the flow of the accent rhythm, in order to preserve the integrity of the lines upon the page. It is, perhaps, foolish for them to "require" anything, but I think it would be less foolish to require that we cut off the real excrescence, which is the syllable *and,* allowing the syllable *it,* which is the first syllable of the new line, to remain, if it must, upon the end of the old. Thus:

"To hím the wáll
That súnders ghósts and shádow-cásting mén
Becáme a crýstal ánd he sáw them thróúgh it
Heárd their voíces tálk behínd the wáll."

I think so, because the visible rhythm, although more obvious, is not so important as the audible rhythm. I believe that one who composed blank verse in natural freedom from the idea of a printed page—while he might anywhere introduce extra syllables for his pleasure or convenience—would usually overcome this technical difficulty by sacrificing the regularity of both lines rather than by sacrificing the regular recurrence of his accent.

I have taken the example from Tennyson (*Vivien* in "The Idylls of the King"), because he is famous for the studied perfection of his rhythm, but in this matter he follows a pattern which has been accepted, so far as I know, by every English composer of blank verse.

[*Page* 122]

The quotation is from Sidney Lanier's "Song of the Chattahoochee."

[*Page* 122 (2)]

Rhyme is employed in the line, "I hurry amain to reach the plain," to reduplicate the rhythm still again—to bring out, that is, a half-line rhythm within the others.

[*Page* 122 (3)]

The quotations are from Dante Gabriel Rossetti's "Jenny" and Shelley's "To Night."

[*Page* 123]

The quotations are from Burns' "To a Mouse," and "The Banks o' Doon."

[*Page* 123 (2)]

Notice that this regular alternation produces a third reduplication of the wave series. A fourth is produced by separating equal groups of lines into stanzas. Stanzas are usually so long, however, that they can only be perceived in retrospection, and are then not truly rhythmical, but a part of the formal attractiveness of poems.

[*Page* 125]

The alternation of lines of different length is a fifth way of reduplicating the wave series. And the alternation of feet of different length is a sixth. The latter is not common in English poetry, occurring so far as I know only in imitations of ancient unrhymed song, but its effect is both strong and unique. I quote an example from Swinburne's "Sapphics."

"Then the Muses, *stricken at* heart, were silent;
Yea the gods waxed *pale; such a* song was that song.
All reluctant *all with a* fresh repulsion,
*Fled from be*fore her.

"All withdrew long *since, and the* land was barren,
Full of fruitless *women and* music only.
Now perchance, when *winds are* assuaged at sunset,
Lulled at the dewfall,

"By the gray sea-side, unassuaged, unheard of,
Unbeloved, unseen in the ebb of twilight,

Ghosts of outcast women return lamenting,
    Purged not in Lethe.

"Clothed about with flame and with tears, and singing
Songs that move the heart of the shaken heaven,
Songs that break the heart of the earth with pity,
    Hearing, to hear them."

[*Page* 125 (2)]

For the person who sees it on the page, or reads it in a certain way, a similarity of *nature* and *position* remains, even when the length of lines is varied. A broad suggestion of rhythmic recurrence is retained in this way even in Walt Whitman's poetry.

[*Page* 126]

So soon as, and so far as, the poem itself becomes an object of realization, and the elements of writing and utterance are developed in variety for their own sake, much more than this may be said of rhythmical speech. Only it will all be a pointing out of various specific characteristics; it will not be a general theory of poetic rhythm.

An infinite number of good things have already been said upon this subject. But they have not recognized themselves to be a pointing out of new varieties and ways in which verse has attracted a reader; they have taken themselves each to be an exclusively true general theory of English rhythm. And so prosody has been vitiated and rendered ridiculous, just as at some time every science has, by the superstitious assumption that a single, eternal, and futile, and absolute truth exists in answer to every question that may arise.

[*Page* 131]

The quotation is from George Chapman.

[*Page* 131 (2)]

The quotation is from Robert Browning's "Saul."

[*Page* 138]

Herbert Read: *The Form of Modern Poetry,* an essay in *The Symposium,* vol. I, no. 3.

T. S. Eliot: *Homage to John Dryden, Hogarth Essays,* first American edition, p. 210.

Edwin Arlington Robinson: "It seems to me that poetry has two outstanding characteristics. One is that it is indefinable. The other is that it is eventually unmistakable." Quoted by Louis Untermeyer in *The Forms of Poetry.*

[*Page* 139]

"Poetic subject": In one of his prefaces, speaking of the "subordinate character of expression," Arnold says literally that "all depends on the subject." In another he says: "The same tragic stories were handled by all the tragic poets." All the tragic poets were, then, in the essence of the matter identical.

[*Page* 140]

George Santayana: *Poetry and Religion,* p. 251.

Miss Edith Sitwell: The metaphor is from her poem *Aubade,* quoted on p. 73.

Miss Helen Parkhurst: *Beauty, An Interpretation of Art and the Imaginative Life,* p. 208.

[*Page* 142]

John Stuart Mill: *Poetry and Its Varieties,* in *Dissertations and Discussions,* vol. I.

[*Page* 142 (2)]

E. E. Cummings: *is 5,* p. 82.

[*Page* 144]

Miss Edith Sitwell: *Poetry and Criticism.*

[*Page* 145]

Robert Graves: *The Future of the Art of Poetry, Hogarth Essays,* first American edition, p. 185.

Hart Crane: *Letter to Harriet Monroe, Poetry,* October, 1926.

[*Page* 146]

Professor Whitehead: *Science and the Modern World,* p. 125.

Coleridge: *Biographia Literaria,* chapter XIV.

[*Page* 148]

Clarence I. Lewis: *Mind and the World Order,* p. 6.

[*Page* 149]

Professors Greenough and Kittredge: *Words and Their Ways in English Speech.*

Hopkins: *Poems of Gerard Manley Hopkins,* p. 89.

[*Page* 150]

Andrew Lang: *History of English Literature.*

[*Page* 151]

Edward Sapir: *The Musical Foundations of Verse,* in *The Journal of English and Germanic Philology,* vol. XX, no. 2.

Professor Snyder: *Hypnotic Poetry,* p. 20.

[*Page* 153]

Professor MacDougall: I think this statement occurs in his *Outline of Abnormal Psychology.*

[*Page* 155]

"Thrilling point": I borrow this phrase from Edmund Spenser, in whose time the word *thrill,* which is related to *drill,* meant little more than to pierce. It is one of those phrases which have acquired more poetic quality through changes in the language than they originally had.

[*Page* 156]

"Her paps are like fair apples in the prime": The two lines are juxtaposed in a quotation from Greene's *Eclogues* by Taine in his *History of English Literature,* Book II, chapter I, sec. 2, sub-sec. v.

[*Page* 160]

Hugo Münsterberg: *Grundzüge der Psychologie,* I (1900).

Professor Montague: *Consciousness a Form of Energy,* in *Essays Philosophical and Psychological in Honor of William James* (1908).

Professor Margaret Floy Washburn: *Movement and Mental Imagery* (1916).

[*Page* 163]

John Dewey: *The Reflex Arc Concept in Psychology, Psychological Review,* July, 1896.

Jennings: *The Behavior of Lower Organisms,* p. 116.

[*Page* 166]

Sainte-Beuve: *What is a Classic?* in his *Essays,* translated by Elizabeth Lee.

[*Page* 167]

"Society as a whole": I quote the phrase from Edmund Wilson's

Axel's Castle, p. 2. "Romanticism, as every one has heard, was a revolt of the individual. The 'Classicism' against which it was a reaction meant, in the domain of politics and morals, a preoccupation with society as a whole; and, in art, an ideal of objectivity."

Robert Graves: *The Future of the Art of Poetry, Hogarth Essays,* first American edition, p. 172.

[*Page* 168]

Rebecca West: *A Last London Letter, The Bookman,* October, 1930.

Havelock Ellis: *The Dance of Life,* p. 141.

[*Page* 169]

Karl Marx: *Capital,* p. 384 of the English translation by Eden and Cedar Paul.

Drummond of Hawthornden: Quoted by W. P. Ker in *The Art of Poetry,* p. 10.

[*Pages* 169 *and* 170]

Kepler: Quoted by E. A. Burtt in *The Metaphysical Foundations of Modern Physical Science,* p. 48.

Sir William Osler: *The Old Humanities and the New Science,* pp. 5 and 34.

[*Page* 171]

"In 1645": J. Wallis, quoted by Preserved Smith in his *History of Modern Culture,* vol. I, p. 166. I owe much to this excellent book.

Hobbes: *Leviathan,* part I, chapter 5.

[*Page* 172]

Erasmus Darwin: His poem *The Temple of Nature* opens in this way:

> "Say, Muse! how rose from elemental strife
> Organic forms, and kindled into life. . . ."

A somewhat different mode of approach from the voyage of the *Beagle.*

H. G. Wells: *The Science of Life,* written in collaboration with Julian S. Huxley and G. P. Wells, Introduction, p. 3.

GENERAL NOTES AND REFERENCES

[*Page* 173]

Professor Whitehead: *Science and the Modern World,* chapter V, p. 107.

[*Page* 174]

E. E. Kellett: *The Whirligig of Taste* is the title of his book.

Milton: *Reason of Church Government.*

[*Page* 176]

John Dryden: *A Defense of an Essay of Dramatic Poesy,* and *Dramatic Poesy, Epistle Dedicatory to the Right Honorable Charles, Lord Buckhurst.* Dryden was delightfully frank in lowering the standards of literature and elevating its social status. "I confess my chief endeavors are to delight the age in which I live," he says in the same essay, and writing on *The Dramatic Poetry of the Last Age,* he says that the "greatest advantage of our writing" proceeds from conversation, for "in the age wherein those poets lived, there was less of gallantry than in ours; neither did they keep the best company in theirs." In his essay on *The Proper Wit of Poetry,* he said that he had found two military men, a Prince and a General, "incomparably the best subject I ever had, excepting only the Royal Family."

Thomas Hobbes: The Preface, *To the Reader, concerning the Vertues of an Heroique Poem.* I quote from J. E. Spingarn's excellent collection, *Critical Essays of the Seventeenth Century,* vol. II, p. 67.

Sidney: *Defense of Poesie.*

Spenser: Quoted by Edward Dowden in *Spenser, the Poet and Teacher.*

[*Page* 178]

Joseph Glanville: Quoted by Preserved Smith, *History of Modern Culture,* I, p. 168.

[*Page* 179]

Zola: *Le Roman Experimental.*

[*Page* 179]

Footnote: By "prophets of confusion" I mean to suggest such books as Scott Buchanan's *Poetry and Mathematics.*

[*Pages* 180 *and* 181]

Blake: The quotation is from S. Foster Damon's *William Blake, His Philosophy and Symbols,* chapter XIV, p. 89.

Wordsworth: Introduction to the *Lyrical Ballads, Prose Works,* vol. II, p. 79.

Shelley: *Defense of Poetry.*

[*Page* 182]

Keats: The phrase quoted is from a letter reproduced by Clarence D. Thorpe in *The Mind of John Keats,* an interesting book which presents the opposite view from mine.

[*Page* 183]

Matthew Arnold: In *Literature and Science,* for instance, he describes poetry and eloquence as "The criticism of life by gifted men, alive and active with extraordinary power at an unusual number of points."

Hardy: Introduction to *The Dynasts.* In an article in *The English Review* (vol. 38, p. 666) Agnes Stewart ingeniously opposes those who say that Hardy, "having no message, had no will to creation." She says that the message was there, but he didn't know it. It "came from his unconscious which was in advance of his conscious mind." She thus links him up underground with Freud and Einstein, with the advance of knowledge.

[*Page* 184]

Stephen Benét: *John Brown's Body.*

Robert Bridges: As an example we may take these lines about sex, which no one will denounce at least as an erotic poem:

> "First among the lowest types of life we think to find
> no separation of sex: plants in the next degree
> show differentiation at puberty with some signs
> of mutual approachment: next in higher animals
> an early differentiation, and at puberty
> periodic appetite with mutual attraction
> sometimes engaging Beauty. . . ."
>
> —*The Testament of Beauty,* p. 90.

Alfred Noyes: *The Torch-Bearers* is the title of a dramatic trilogy devoted to the lives of great scientists.

John Stuart Mill: *Poetry and Its Varieties,* in *Dissertations and Discussions,* vol. I. "Poetry is feeling confessing itself to itself in moments of solitude, and embodying itself in symbols which are the nearest possible representation of the feeling in the exact shape in which it exists in the poet's mind."

[*Page* 185]

Robert Frost: *Education by Poetry,* in *The Amherst Graduates' Quarterly,* February, 1931.

[*Page* 186]

Archibald MacLeish: *Einstein* and *Ars Poetica,* in *Streets of the Moon.*

[*Page* 187]

Poe: *The Poetic Principle.*

[*Page* 189]

Gautier: Quoted by George Brandes in vol. V of his *Main Currents in Nineteenth Century Literature,* p. 299.

[*Page* 189 (2)]

Axel's Castle: The definition is on pp. 21–22.

[*Page* 190]

Walter Pater: From the Conclusion of *The Renaissance.* This conclusion was omitted from the second edition lest "it might possibly mislead some of those young men into whose hands it might fall," but reprinted in subsequent editions, the young men having presumably all been misled.

Here is the essential passage:

"Not the fruit of experience, but experience itself, is the end. A counted number of pulses only is given to us of a variegated, dramatic life. How may we see in them all that is to be seen in them by the finest senses? How shall we pass most swiftly from point to point, and be present always at the focus where the greatest number of vital forces unite in their purest energy?

"To burn always with this hard, gem-like flame, to maintain this ecstasy, is to succeed in life."

[*Page* 192]

Zola: *Le Roman Experimental.*

[*Page* 192 (2)]

"To know the best": The quotation is from Matthew Arnold, *Literature and Science,* in *Discourses in America.*

[*Page* 196]

Tretiakov's book, *Den-Shi-Hwa, The Bio-Interview of a Chinese Student,* is entitled in the English version, *The Chinese Testament.*

[*Page* 199]

"Feminine or Passive": See Van Wyck Brooks' essay *Max Eastman and Revolution* in his *Sketches in Criticism;* also Joseph Freeman's *Voices of October,* p. 43.

[*Page* 200]

The quotation is from Engels' speech at the grave of Marx.

[*Page* 201]

The quotation in the text is from Engels' Letter to Starkenburg, January 25, 1894.

The quotations in the footnote are from Plekhanov's *Chernishevsky —The Æsthetic Relations of Art to Reality, Fundamental Problems of Marxism* (English translation, p. 61), and *From Idealism to Materialism,* II.

[*Page* 202]

Professor Boas: *Primitive Art,* pp. 25 ff.

[*Page* 203]

Leonardo: Quoted by Clifford Bax in his *Leonardo Da Vinci,* p. 19. A true view of the situation is presented by Thomas Craven in his *Men of Art:* "With the Venetians as a school, but with Titian in particular, painting ceases to be an expression of collective religious interests, and becomes a speculative profession."

[*Page* 204]

Marx: *Die deutsche Ideologie,* p. 236 of the Russian edition.

Boas: *Primitive Art,* pp. 30, 130, 132, 136.

[*Page* 205]

Jane Harrison: *Ancient Art and Ritual,* p. 31.

[*Page* 206]

Yrjö Hirn: *Origins of Art.*

[*Page* 208]

Pausanias: Quoted by Frank P. Chambers in *Cycles of Taste,* p. 15.
Maspero: *Art in Egypt,* pp. 17 and 298.

[*Page* 209]

"Philosophies of optimism": This characterization of the Marxian philosophy is Trotsky's in his *Literature and Revolution.*

[*Page* 212]

Plato: *Republic,* X, 606 ff.

[*Page* 213]

"The Stalin communists": Their essentially religious insistence that art shall celebrate the movement of "Reality" toward socialism, and praise the leaders of this movement, is described in the first chapter of my *Artists in Uniform,* and in a note to page 208.

[*Page* 217]

Sir Philip Sidney: Sidney's *Defense of Poesie* was in some measure a reply to Gosson's *School of Abuse.*

Voronsky: *Art as Knowledge of Life,* in *Krassnaia Nov,* Book V, 1923.

"The Poet Laureate of England": John Masefield, as quoted in the *Bookman,* London, February, 1932.

Benedetto Croce: *Æsthetics.*

[*Page* 220]

Lenin made the statement about Socialism and electrification.

[*Page* 221]

Clifford Bax: *Leonardo Da Vinci,* p. 105.
"Left Front of the Arts": *Left,* No. 1, Moscow, 1923.

[*Page* 222]

I. A. Richards: *Principles of Literary Criticism, Science and Poetry, Practical Criticism.*

The emotive sanction first appeared in Russia in Tolstoy's *What Is Art?* But the artist's function there was evangelical, not revolutionary; to make men brothers in feeling rather than to guide them in act. Plekhanov escaped from this by moving part way back to the educative sanction. Taking for his starting-point Tolstoy's definition: "Art is a human activity consisting in the fact that one man consciously by means of external signs communicates to others feelings experienced by him, and other men are infected by those feelings and live them again," he corrected it as follows: "Art begins when man evokes again within himself feelings *and thoughts* experienced by him under the influence of the environing reality, and gives them a certain expression in image." (Italics mine.) Bukharin again dropped the "thoughts," but gave to art the function not merely of expressing, but of systemizing feelings. "The nature of art is now clear: it is a systematization of feelings in forms; the direct function of art in socializing, transferring, disseminating these feelings, in society, is now also clear." (*Historic Materialism,* English translation, p. 189.)

This shift from the educational to the emotive sanction, and its cause in the increasing technicality of conceptual knowledge, are clearly visible also in Trotsky's theoretic difference from Voronsky. "Art," says Voronsky, "is a knowledge of the world in the form of felt and imaged contemplation of it. Like science art gives objective truth." (*Art as Knowledge of Life,* in *Krassnaia Nov,* Book V, 1923.) Trotsky says: "In the field of poetry we deal with the process of feeling the world in image, and not with the process of knowing the world scientifically." (*Literature and Revolution,* p. 147.)

The sharp opposition of I. A. Richards to Benedetto Croce's æsthetics is an incident in the same process of development. Croce tries to save the educational sanction by drawing a sharp (and non-existent) line between two kinds of knowledge—a position not unlike that of Voronsky—and Richards feels that the day can be saved only by throwing over the knowledge sanction altogether. (Richards' *Principles of Literary Criticism,* p. 255.)

[*Page* 225]

Clive Bell: *Art,* pp. 146 and 150.

[*Page* 235]

The Will to Live: see note to page 5.

[*Page* 236]

Professor Herrick: *Neurological Foundations of Animal Behavior,* pp. 17 and 18.

[*Pages* 236 *and* 237]

William James: *Principles of Psychology.*

Margaret Floy Washburn: *The Animal Mind,* pp. 42–43.

[*Page* 239]

Conrad Aiken: "A Basis for Criticism," *The New Republic,* April 11, 1923.

[*Page* 240]

Floyd Henry Allport: *Social Psychology,* chapter IV.

[*Page* 241]

Professor Herrick: *Introduction to Neurology,* chapter XVIII, pp. 297–298.

[*Page* 243]

John Dewey: *Experience and Nature,* vol I, p. 388. On the same page he says: "The present confusion, deemed chaos by some, in the fine arts and æsthetic criticism seems to be an inevitable consequence of the underlying, even if unavowed, separation of the instrumental and the consummatory."

[*Page* 247]

"Pointing to or reflecting": *Science and Poetry,* pp. 14 and 52, and *Principles of Literary Criticism,* p. 265.

[*Page* 248]

"Modern physics is becoming": *The Meaning of Meaning,* p. 159.

Professor Bridgman: *The Logic of Modern Physics,* pp. 2, 5, 7.

[*Page* 249]

John Dewey: *The Quest for Certainty,* footnote to p. 111.

"Too easy idea": In justice to Ogden and Richards it must be said that they have a sufficiently complicated way of establishing this over-simplification of science. They begin with a quite obvious remark, and one from which a valid psychology of poetry might have flowed almost automatically:

"All experience, using the word in the widest possible sense, is either enjoyed or interpreted (*i.e.,* treated as a sign) or both, and very little of it escapes some degree of interpretation." It was perhaps by accident that the word "enjoyed" dropped in here, as though experiences could not be painful without interpretation. But it puts the authors in the more complete accord with my own thesis, and makes it seem most natural to continue: *Words are used to communicate the enjoyment as well as the interpretation of experience—in poetry the first element predominates, in practical and scientific language the second.* Instead of continuing that way, Ogden and Richards permitted the enjoyment of experience to drop out of sight forever—only to reappear, at least in the austere remark of Richards that "it is not the intensity of the conscious experience, its thrill, its pleasure or its poignancy which gives it value, but the organization of its impulses. . . . There are plenty of ecstatic instants which are valueless." They let all this "valueless" matter drop out of sight, and proceeded to divide the interpretation of experience, or what we call the interpretation of it, into two nearly water-tight compartments: (1) pointing to it, which is real interpretation, or science; and (2) evoking attitudes toward it, which is not interpretation at all, but poetry.

The manner in which Ogden and Richards eliminate from interpretation, and so from science, the element of attitude—or response, or adaptation, or reaction, or anything of that active and profitable kind—is the central mystery of their book on *The Meaning of Meaning*. And although it is wrapped up in an almost impenetrable darkness of language, I believe that if the reader will be patient I can show him at least a fumbling glimpse of what it is. On page 53 the authors are still talking a simple language, the language of biology and psychology. They are explaining the "peculiarity of interpretation" as consisting of the fact that "when a context has affected us in the past the recurrence of merely a part of the context will cause us to *react in the same way* in which we reacted before." The italics are mine, but they are hardly necessary, because the authors are here making no secret of the fact that "reaction" and "adaptation" and "attitude," and indeed action itself, are the essence of the process of interpretation. They illustrate it with the famous dog who came running to the table when he heard the dinner bell, and the famous chicken who did not eat a yellow-and-black caterpillar because having pecked him once before she found him bitter. Interpretation in these cases consisted of *reacting* to a *part* of an experience, the sound of the bell and the colors of the caterpillar, as though the whole experience were there—a meat-bone dropping benignly from the table, a bad caterpillar-taste in the mouth. To the dog, you see, the bell "means" a meat-bone; to the chicken the yellow-and-black "means" a bitter taste. But how can a yellow-and-black color *mean* a bitter taste? We say that it is "directed towards" or "refers to" a bitter taste. But what is this state of being directed towards or referring to a bitter taste? What *is* meaning? This can only be answered by asking how it arose. What caused the sensation of yellow-and-black to mean, or refer to, a bitter taste? Was the cause anything else but a bitter taste? Then why not end all arguments and resolve all mysteries—and most particularly the mystery of how to reconcile psychology with logic—by defining "meaning" as "being caused by"?

Let us go over it once more: A sensation of yellow-and-black which *means* bitter taste is one which has been experienced in the same context with bitter taste in the past. That is the only thing which distinguishes it from sensations of yellow-and-black which mean nothing. A bitter taste is the *cause* of its meaning, and a bitter taste is also *what* it means. Then *meaning* something and *being caused by* something are the same.

If this sounds to you a little topsy-turvy and upside-down, and almost like a kind of ingenious joke, I think you are perfectly right. The bitter taste that a black-and-yellow caterpillar means is not the same bitter taste as the one which caused him to mean it. There are two different experiences involved and the relating them together is an act of the mind. In my opinion, it is only in a world already organized into "things," and classes of things, by the interpretative action of the mind that the act of interpretation could be so inactively conceived.

However, it is not my task to criticize this theory of meaning in detail. I merely wanted to play fair with Ogden and Richards by showing that they have at least a sufficiently arduous, erudite and abstruse manner of effecting the separation of reaction from interpretation, and so negotiating the leap from the psychology of interpretation to a purely denotative logic. The chicken sees a yellow-and-black object and recoils from it in a way that may be described psychologically as the automatic result of a former coincidence of yellow-and-black object with bitter taste. And if the chicken happens to be conscious and to be saying that the black-and-yellow caterpillar *means* bitter taste, that is merely another way of saying that the process is taking place in this way *because of* a bitter taste. The black-and-yellow sensation does not *perform the act of* meaning bitter taste, but the meaning bitter taste is merely the *being a part of* such a process. Thus, although conceding to begin with that the essential thing in interpretation is "reaction," the authors wind up by asserting that "To be an act of interpretation is merely to be a particular member of a psychological context of a certain kind." And they add, "We shall, in what follows, speak of . . . interpretations . . . as references." In this way—or in some such way, for I cannot pretend to have penetrated the darkness completely—reaction is dropped out of interpretation, and attitude or reference to action out of science.

[*Page* 249 (2)]

"A poem, they say . . .": *Meaning of Meaning,* pp. 158–9.
Principles of Literary Criticism: pp. 267, 273.

[*Page* 250]

Science and Poetry: pp. 13, 59, 61, 26, 55.
Practical Criticism: pp. 354 and 349.

[*Page* 251]

Clarence I. Lewis: *Mind and the World Order,* p. 85.

[*Page* 253]

"The poet uses certain words": *Science and Poetry,* pp. 26–7.

[*Page* 254]

The Meaning of Meaning: p. 240.
Principles of Literary Criticism: p. 240.
Helen Parkhurst: *Beauty,* p. 208.
Practical Criticism: pp. 221–223.

[*Page* 256]

"Texture of expectations": *Principles of Literary Criticism,* p. 137.

[*Page* 257]

Hypnotism: *Principles of Literary Criticism,* pp. 138, 144.
"Emotionality": *Meaning of Meaning,* p. 240.
Principles of Literary Criticism: p. 143.

GENERAL NOTES AND REFERENCES

[*Page* 259]

Roger Fry: *Transformations,* p. 2, quoting *Principles of Literary Criticism,* p. 16.

[*Page* 261]

"It is capable of saving us": *Science and Poetry,* p. 82. The quotations immediately following are from pp. 41, 39 and 43.

[*Page* 262]

"It is not necessary to know": *Meaning of Meaning,* p. 159. The quotations immediately following are from *Principles of Literary Criticism,* pp. 279 and 280, and from *Science and Poetry,* pp. 61 and 60.

"Magical View": *Science and poetry,* pp. 47, 52.

[*Page* 263]

"A response is sentimental": *Practical Criticism.* p. 258.

INDEX

INDEX

INDEX

INDEX

INDEX

INDEX

ANTHOLOGY

FOR

ENJOYMENT OF POETRY

ACKNOWLEDGMENTS

For their generosity and coöperation I am grateful to the following publishers and authors who granted permission for the use of the copyrighted material in this anthology, all rights in which are reserved by the holders of the copyrights:

Stephen Vincent Benét and his agents, Brandt & Brandt—for permission to reprint "Litany for Dictatorships" from his *Burning City,* published by Farrar & Rinehart, Inc. (Copyright, 1933, 1935, 1936, by Stephen Vincent Benét).

Kay Boyle and her agent, Ann Watkins—for permission to reprint her poem, "A Funeral in Hungary," which originally appeared in the periodical, *New Directions.*

Coward McCann, Inc.—for permission to reprint "Minnie and Mrs. Hoyne" from *Angel Arms* by Kenneth Fearing (Copyright, 1929).

E. E. Cummings and his agents, Brandt & Brandt—for permission to reprint "If I," "Poem 111," and "Spring" from his *Collected Poems,* published by Harcourt, Brace & Company (Copyright, 1923, 1925, 1931, 1935, 1938, by E. E. Cummings).

The John Day Company, Inc.—for permission to reprint "Country Summer" from *The High Falcon* by Léonie Adams.

Dodd, Mead & Company, Inc.—for permission to reprint "A Ballad of Hell" from *The Last Ballad* by John Davidson; "The Crying of Water" and "Leves Amores" from *Poems* by Arthur Symons.

Doubleday, Doran & Company, Inc.—for permission to reprint "I Dote Upon Myself," "I Think I Could Turn," "Reconciliation" and "When I Heard at Close of Day" from *Leaves of Grass* (Inclusive and Authorized Edition) by Walt Whitman.

Farrar & Rinehart, Inc.—for permission to reprint "Roots Go Down" from *The Red Kite* by Lloyd Frankenberg (Copyright, 1939).

Harcourt, Brace & Company, Inc.—for permission to reprint "Morning at the Window" and "Sweeney Among the Nightingales" from *Collected Poems of T. S. Eliot* (Copyright, 1936); "Baptism" and "My Mother" from *Harlem Shadows* by Claude McKay (Copyright, 1922); "The Flies" and "Just Then the Door" from *The Noise that Time Makes* by Merrill Moore (Copyright, 1929); "Meditation at Kew" from *The Contemplative Quarry* by Anna Wickham (Copyright, 1921).

Harper & Brothers—for permission to reprint "Sapphics" from *Poems and Ballads* by Algernon Charles Swinburne.

Henry Holt & Company, Inc.—for permission to reprint "Silver" and

"Winter Dusk" from *Collected Poems, 1901–1918* by Walter de la Mare; "An Old Man's Winter Night" from *Mountain Interval* by Robert Frost; "From Far" and "Is My Team Plowing?" from *Shropshire Lad* by A. E. Housman; "Fog" and "Graves" from *Chicago Poems* by Carl Sandburg.

Houghton Mifflin Company—for permission to reprint "The End of the World" and "You, Andrew Marvell" from *Poems, 1924–1933* by Archibald MacLeish; "A Prairie Ride" from *Poems and Poetic Dramas* by William Vaughn Moody.

Joseph Kalar—for permission to reprint his "Invocation to the Wind" from *We Gather Strength,* published by Liberal Press, Inc.

Mitchell Kennerley—for permission to reprint "Fate With Devoted Care" from *Sonnets of a Portrait Painter* by Arthur Davison Ficke.

Alfred A. Knopf, Inc.—for permission to reprint "God's Acre" from *Grenstone Poems* by Witter Bynner; "The Runner in the Skies" from *Songs for the New Age* by James Oppenheim; "Star Fear" from *Slow Wall* by Leonora Speyer; "The Snow Man" from *Harmonium* by Wallace Stevens; "Atavism," "August" and "Spring Pastoral" from *Collected Poems* by Elinor Wylie, which are reprinted by permission of, and by special arrangement with, Alfred A. Knopf, Inc.

Little, Brown & Company—for permission to reprint "Don't Put Up My Thread and Needle" and "Lonely House" from *The Poems of Emily Dickinson,* edited by Martha Dickinson Bianchi and Alfred Leete Hampson.

Liveright Publishing Corporation—for permission to reprint "Socratic" from *Selected Poems* by Hilda Doolittle; "The Return" from *Personæ* by Ezra Pound.

The Macmillan Company—for permission to reprint "Farewell to Juliet" and "To a Happy Warrior" from *The Poetical Works of Wilfrid Scawen Blunt;* "In Time of 'The Breaking of Nations'" and "Weather" from *Collected Poems* by Thomas Hardy; "Eve" from *Poems* by Ralph Hodgson; "The Ghost of the Buffaloes" from *Collected Poems* by Vachel Lindsay; "Cargoes" from *Poems* by John Masefield; "Everything" from *Real Property* by Harold Monro; "Critics and Connoisseurs" from *Selected Poems* by Marianne Moore (Copyright by Marianne Moore); "Mr. Flood's Party" from *Collected Poems* by Edwin Arlington Robinson; "The Centaurs," "The Lake" and "Little Things" from *Collected Poems* by James Stephens; "I Shall Not Care" from *Collected Poems* by Sara Teasdale; "An Appointment" and "An Irish Airman Foresees His Death" from *Collected Poems* by William Butler Yeats.

Edna St. Vincent Millay and her agents, Brandt & Brandt—for permission to reprint "Not in a Silver Casket" and "Oh, Sleep Forever in the Latmian Cave" from *Fatal Interview,* published by Harper & Brothers, copyright, 1931, by Edna St. Vincent Millay.

The Nation—for permission to reprint "To Spring," by Virginia Moore, which first appeared in that periodical.

ACKNOWLEDGMENTS

Oxford University Press—for permission to reprint "Epithalamion" and "Pied Beauty" from *Collected Poems* by Gerard Manley Hopkins.

Random House, Inc.—for permission to reprint "November 2 A.M. Conspiracy" from *Darkling Plain* by Sara Bard Field; "Credo" and "Salmon-Fishing" from *The Roan Stallion and Other Poems* by Robinson Jeffers; "The Conflict" from *A Time to Dance* by C. Day Lewis; "Landscape Near an Aerodrome" from *Poems* by Stephen Spender.

Thomas Seltzer—for permission to reprint "The Quiet Woman" and "With Child" from *For Eager Lovers* by Genevieve Taggard.

Charles Scribner's Sons—for permission to reprint "Single Sonnet" from *The Sleeping Fury* by Louise Bogan; "Egrets" and "We Have Been Happy" from *Kinds of Love* by Max Eastman; "Deem Not" and "I Sought on Earth" from *Poems* by George Santayana; "The Letter" and "This Quiet Dust" from *Poems, 1911–1936* by John Hall Wheelock; "October" from *Of Time and the River* by Thomas Wolfe.

The Vanguard Press—for permission to reprint "The Desert" and "Goats" from *The Poet in the Desert* by Charles Erskine Scott Wood.

The Viking Press—for permission to reprint "Woman Without Fear" from *The Flowering Stone* by George Dillon (Copyright, 1931); "On the Beach at Fontana" from *Collected Poems* by James Joyce (Copyright, 1927); "Turkey-Cock" from *Collected Poems* by D. H. Lawrence (Copyright, 1929); "Arms and the Boy," "The Next War" and "The Sentry" from *Poems* by Wilfred Owen.

William Carlos Williams—for permission to reprint "Flowers by the Sea" from his *Collected Poems*, published by The Objectivist Press.

Yale University Press—for permission to reprint "Prayer Against Indifference" from *Letter to a Comrade* by Joy Davidman.

FOREWORD

This anthology is designed to accompany a new and enlarged edition of my *Enjoyment of Poetry*. The announced purpose of that book was "to increase enjoyment," and I meant the phrase as a kind of manifesto of rebellion against textbooks, an invitation to English students in particular to join me in a little game of hookey. The teachers outwitted me—a bewildering number of them—by adopting *Enjoyment of Poetry* as their textbook. In Sioux City, one night after a lecture, a young girl came up and said to me:

"I'm mad at you!"

"Why? What have I done?"

"I had to stay in all afternoon and read your old *Enjoyment of Poetry!"*

One can only bow humbly to the irony of such a fate. So here is a collection of poems to accompany and illustrate my *Introduction to the Psychology of Poetry*. I have adopted the same classification that seemed natural to me there, dividing the poems according as their prevailing values are of sensuous perception, emotion, action or idea—only changing the order for purposes of climax, and adding a section devoted to purely imaginary values. However poetry may arise, and whatever it may at times be used for, these values, desired for their own sake, are what make it poetry to the reader.

There are people in the world, I am forced to conclude, who cannot enjoy the vivid experience of an idea unless they believe in it, who cannot ride along with an action unless it goes toward their chosen ends, nor taste the flavor of a sunset or even a sandwich, unless it is linked by some specious or real wires of connection with what they adhere to or intend to do. Perhaps they have their reward. To me, however, a person unable to participate in a battle song because he is against war, or in a celebration like that described herein by Thomas Dekker because he does not believe in the Second Coming of Christ—a person not dexterous enough to savor the mood of both *Lead Kindly Light* and *I Am the Captain of My Soul*—is afflicted and crippled, not just wisely guided, by his mind. I have not composed this anthology for cripples—nor on the other hand for people who feel required to suspend all connections and retire into a vacuum-tube of ivory in order to "appreciate art."

My classification is founded on those distinctions which seem most obvious to the psychologist, and I do not think it will strike any forthright mind as unnatural. At the same time, of course, and just because it is natural, it is inexact. To some degree, almost every human experience contains all five of the elements I distinguish. I have only asked which one, *for me as I read the poem now,* seems on the whole to prevail. Or rather, I have asked no question at all, but trusted my instinct as the composer of a kind of symphony in these five movements to place each poem where because of its theme and tonal quality it belongs.

You will find, for instance, John Davidson's *Ballad of Hell* among poems of action rather than unreal fancy. This is not because I believe the poem's hell and heaven to be real, but because I think they are not the main content of the experience. I might indeed consider the main content to be an idea, a judgment about life and its moral dogmas, and I dare say there was a time when I should have, but now I feel the poem primarily as a story, the realizing of a great action. T. S. Eliot's *Sweeney Among the Nightingales* I have placed among poems which I call *Vessels of Emotion,* although I once heard Eliot himself, dismissing the idea that it had a meaning, describe it more in the spirit of *Things and Their Colors* as "merely a still life." He added, after a moment of reflection: "I did try to paint the scene in such a way that a certain feeling would hang over it, a feeling of something ominous, some threat, a feeling like that we used to have during the Great War when waiting for an air-raid." With his sudden nightingales and the recollection of Agamemnon, I think he has wonderfully succeeded in doing that. Ezra

Pound's *The Return,* a mysteriously exciting poem to me, I placed among *Vessels of Emotion*—or rather I left it there, even after Mr. Pound informed me that it contains thoughts on "the return of the pagan gods." It seemed to me to be about dogs rather than gods, although they were, I must say, a sort of celestial or star-chasing breed of dogs. Tom Wolfe's *October,* on the other hand, although it is one of the most emotional poems in the book, I have placed among realizations of things. That is because I wanted to make a little tour around the four seasons as a subordinate small symphony within my first movement, showing how differently they can be perceived by different poets, and how poetry thus adds not only vividness and form, but variety, to our experience. This poem (taken from the pages of *Of Time and the River*), together with that other exciting *Autumn* which I translated from Pushkin, forms in my conception a climax to the first movement, after which it subsides again, through the more quiet scenery of winter, arriving in Wordsworth's famous sonnet at a serenely perceptual kind of experience, and concluding in the breathless tranquillity of Sara Bard Field's *November 2 A.M. Conspiracy.*

Here, while we are essentially giving our attention to real things and what they can be like, still an unreal or supernatural something, for the moment believed in, begins to descend into or arise out of them. And that motionless midnight equilibrium between real and unreal, conveyed to us with such exact and exquisite art, forms a transition to the second movement of my symphony where poets give open wing to their fancy, or their belief, and regale us with a world that never was.

In that world, of what Coleridge called "supernatural poetry" —and in which he would be represented, if I had the space, by *Christabel* and not *The Ancient Mariner*—tale-telling tends to prevail over the more spatial realization of things. Therefore in coming back from it to real life we find ourselves, again by a natural transition, among those poems which celebrate action and events with a suspense in time. These again, beginning somewhat placidly, rise toward a climax of feeling in the selection from William Ellery Leonard's *Two Lives,* one of the great dramatic poems of our literature, and in Claude McKay's *My Mother,* a narrative too and yet also, in my opinion, in its simple inevitability, a perfect lyric. This climax, coming at the very end of the third movement, leads into the fourth, which is in a sense the climax of the whole symphony.

I was moved by contemporary events to open this movement with Lord Byron's lament for Israel, and I have closed it with Walt Whitman's most emotional poem, his elegy upon the death of Abraham Lincoln. The intervening pages, I hope, are not too full of sorrow, although the life of man, the inalterable terms of it, are such that any rich passion in a thoughtful mind is apt to dip toward sadness. That is why we tend at last, so many of us, to seek with Plato more sustained adventures in the world of ideas.

I have made the transition to this Platonic world abrupt by placing against Walt Whitman's mystic poem of the heart's sorrow another great elegy in which an audacious mind, accepting the terms of life, and of death too, absolutely, introduces a heroic joy into his grief by thinking. There are one or two other juxtapositions in this last Part, which I hope will not escape the reader. I would like to have him remark how in the sixteenth century Samuel Daniel, describing the "high mind," anticipated the view of war, right, justice, almost of history itself, that we call Marxian, and spoke words pertinent to our own age about "tyrants' threats," the "surly brow of Power," and where to stand

> ". . . . whilst man doth ransack man
> And builds on blood."

It is a great poem of fact-facing and of deliverance through resolute personal elevation; following which Joy Davidman's *Prayer Against Indifference,* also fact-facing and also a great poem, rings like a blacksmith's hammer on a sword. After that glorious burst of warlike thought in music, my symphony subsides once more through Hardy's homely lines and Whitman's sublime recitative, *Reconciliation,* and it concludes in a poem which has seemed more perfect to me every time I have read it throughout my life, and which I sometimes think might ultimately rise above everything else that has been written representative of this era, Matthew Arnold's *Dover Beach.*

Of course my book is not a symphony, and is too long to be so read. But I hope the reader will not mind remembering some of these larger forms that I had in mind when composing it. I have made no extreme effort to be thorough, except to introduce instruments, or tone-qualities, from all the great periods of English poetry. Neither exclusions nor large borrowings necessarily imply a critical judgment upon any poet. I have permitted myself whims. On the question of including something of my own, I consulted Edmund Wilson, who kindly solved the problem by selecting the poems to go in.

In the delicate matter of choosing among my contemporaries, I have tried to have a little respect for current critical opinion, but not very much. To remember at least that my own opinions are a part of it, and not the judgment of posterity, seemed reasonable. And that has given me a regard for some mighty reputations by which I am not personally overwhelmed. On the other hand, I have kept in mind how often in our history both public acclaim and the so-called "advanced taste" were dominated by a shallow fashion that obscured the greater poets. Abraham Cowley in the first half of the seventeenth century is a good example of this.

"A marvel of precocity," says Professor Humphrey Ward, "widely known as a poet at fifteen; the poetical wonder of Cambridge; so famous at thirty that pirates and forgers made free with his name on their title-pages while he was serving the exiled Queen; issuing in self defence, at thirty-eight, a folio of his poems which was destined to pass through eight editions in a generation; accepted by his literary contemporaries, men of cultivated intelligence, as not only the greatest among themselves, but greater than all that had gone before; buried in state at Westminster by the side of Chaucer and Spenser, and ranked by his biographer, a sober critic, as equal not only to them but to 'the authors of that true antiquity, the best of the Greeks and Romans'; in thirty years he had sunk out of notice and his name had become a mere memory."

Another good example is Edmund Waller, of whom Professor Gosse has written:

> During the civil wars he gradually rose to be considered second only to Cowley. After the Restoration, and when that writer was in his grave, Waller found himself still more popular, and when he died, at a very great age, the wits and critics, with Thomas Rymer at their head, exalted him to the first place in the English Parnassus. Until the end of the century it was tacitly admitted that Waller was the greatest English poet. The juster sense of Addison and of Pope curtailed these extravagant honours, while leaving to Waller the praise of unrivalled sweetness. In the hands of Gray, Johnson and Cowper, Waller sank gradually back into the rank and file of poets, while the critics of the beginning of our century went further still, and denied him all lyrical merit. Of late even his historical position has been assailed, and there is perhaps no famous writer at the present moment so little read or considered as Waller.

We all remember the sad struggles of John Keats, not only a great poet but a great intelligence who, had he lived, would perhaps have stood closest to Shakespeare. Even the noble-born Shelley was a subordinate figure throughout his lifetime; and Blake is only now climbing to his place. In America, Poe and Walt Whitman and Emily Dickinson, now so secure among its early gods, lived and wrote their poetry and died without encouragement from either sophisticated critics or the poetry-reading public. We might almost lay it down as a law of criticism that contemporary judgments are eighty per cent dominated by fad.

Our own sophisticates, having but recently discovered, and greatly overpraised, Herman Melville and Emily Dickinson, are highly conscious of this law so far as it relates to the past. But they are prone to imagine their own judgments for that very reason exempt from its operation. It does not occur to them that their overpraise of Melville and Dickinson may itself be a fad, or an effort of the devotees of a fad to find themselves a separate historic tradition.

For my part, I think that poetic criticism is more at sea today, more at the mercy of fashion, more disgeared from enduring human values, than it has usually been in the past. I have advanced some reasons for this in my book, *The Literary Mind*. In chapters called "The Cult of Unintelligibility" and "Poets Talking to Themselves," I have discussed what seems to me the most ignominious capitulation of the critics. They have surrendered almost in a body to the fad of admiring, or pretending to admire, poetry which, whether it has clear values to the writer or not, does not fully communicate them to the reader, and is thus objectively characterized by smears and mental blurs that are undignified, to say the least, and distasteful to an alert and civilized mind. That so many highly placed critics have accepted this return to mumbo jumbo, and even allowed the poets to put it over on them in the name of "intellect," is to me but a part of that general surrender of mental integrity to crude, primitive and unillumined states of passion which is bringing our western civilization to ruin. I think this will seem perfectly obvious, if history survives, to future historians. It is bad enough to live in a world bent on permeating itself with such decay. To make any contribution to the process is intolerable. Therefore in making this anthology I have permitted myself one dogma: there is not a line here of unintelligible poetry.

There are obscure poems, and there should be. Any poet, wrestling honestly to convey a subtle state-of-feeling or a felt conception, has a right to demand that his poem be read, if at all, eight or ten times, and with intense and trustful attention. But if he is to be so trusted, he must be trustworthy. He must himself distinguish obscurity from unintelligibility. As I pointed out in one of those essays, Hart Crane in explaining a poem of his to Harriet Monroe, proved conclusively that without his explanation no human mind could conceivably have grasped any of its essential values.

A minor example of the same thing is seen in the title of a poem by Archibald MacLeish included here. *You, Andrew Marvell.* The poem is a rapt and richly musical realization of the creeping on of darkness round the earth, so appealing to me that in order to get it past my dogma, I wrote to Mr. MacLeish and asked him to solve the riddle of its title. He answered: "I used it because I wanted to hitch the poem on to those lines of Marvell's in his *To His Coy Mistress* in which he hears time's chariot at his back." Now, it is quite obvious that no amount of study would enable any human reader, except by a million-to-one accident, to figure that out. And that is what I mean by unintelligibility. Mr. MacLeish was gracious enough to say: "I suppose it *is* a rather foolish title. I'm sure it is. I've been explaining it for ten years now, which is a bad record for a title to have."

With all admiration to Mr. MacLeish, who is far from addicted to this habit, I think it is not only a foolish title, but an affectation and an insult to the reader's mind—one which our advanced critics, if they had any standards remotely approaching the austere ones that will be applied by "time's chariot" if civilization endures, would long ago have made impossible to so genuine a poet. In a literature regardful of intelligence, and intellectual courtesy, any one wishing to recall the lines of Andrew Marvell would have quoted them under his title.

This affectation, or this vain attempt to sugar-coat poetry for a practical-scientific age by giving it the virtues of a conundrum or a crossword puzzle, I have rigidly excluded from my book. When moved to introduce a poet of the unintelligible cult, I have selected a poem in which through some large special act of condescension, or some slip of the tongue, he has communicated his meaning or experience to my mind.

MAX EASTMAN

August, 1939.

CONTENTS

PART I

THINGS AND THEIR COLORS

CONTENTS

CONTENTS

PART II

BEYOND REALITY

PART III

RIDING WITH TIME AND ACTION

CONTENTS

PART IV

VESSELS OF EMOTION

CONTENTS

PART V

ADVENTURES IN IDEAS

CONTENTS

CONTENTS

CONTENTS

PART I

THINGS AND THEIR COLORS

PIED BEAUTY

GERARD MANLEY HOPKINS

Glory be to God for dappled things—
  For skies of couple-colour as a brinded cow;
    For rose-moles all in stipple upon trout that swim;
Fresh-firecoal chestnut-falls; finches' wings;
  Landscape plotted and pieced—fold, fallow and plough;
    And áll trádes, their gear and tackle and trim.

All things counter, original, spare, strange;
  Whatever is fickle, freckled (who knows how?)
    With swift, slow; sweet, sour; adazzle, dim;
He fathers-forth whose beauty is past change:
            Praise him.

SOCRATIC

H. D.

"They cut it in squares,
sometimes it comes
in little jars—"

"O—?"

"Under the trees—"
"Where?"

"By his *sheep*-pen."

"Whose?"

"The man
who brings eggs:

he put it
in a basket with moss."

"What?"

"Why,
the little jar."

"What for?"

"Why,
to carry it over—"

"Over where?"

"The field to Io's house."

"Then?"

"*Her* mother took it out
of the moss,
opened it—"

"What?"

"The little jar."

"And then?"

"We each *had* some."

"What?"

"Why the thing
in the little jar

they got
from the straw huts."

"What huts?"

"Why,
the little huts
under the apple-trees,
where they live—"

"Who live?"

"Why,
the *bees*."

TO A GARDENER

ROBERT LOUIS STEVENSON

Friend, in my mountain-side demesne,
My plain-beholding, rosy, green
And linnet-haunted garden-ground,
Let still the esculents abound.
Let first the onion flourish there,
Rose among roots, the maiden-fair,
Wine-scented and poetic soul
Of the capacious salad bowl.
Let thyme the mountaineer (to dress
The tinier birds) and wading cress,
The lover of the shallow brook,
From all my plots and borders look.
Nor crisp and ruddy radish, nor
Pease-cods for the child's pinafore
Be lacking; nor of salad clan
The last and least that ever ran

About great nature's garden-beds.
Nor thence be missed the speary heads
Of artichoke; nor thence the bean
That gathered innocent and green
Outsavours the belauded pea.

These tend, I prithee; and for me,
Thy most long-suffering master, bring
In April, when the linnets sing
And the days lengthen more and more,
At sundown to the garden door.
And I, being provided thus,
Shall, with superb asparagus,
A book, a taper, and a cup
Of country wine, divinely sup.

ROOTS GO DOWN

LLOYD FRANKENBERG

Roots go down
not as it is to drown—
falling through green fields of light
    farther and farther,
the green gone blue, gone purple and
    then black,
the black touchless plunging—
but at once under,
at once head-all-shovel lunging against the ground.

Neither is there any sound nor smell
    there. Or what is it
leads the root onward through mazes of
    tryings and twistings?

Touch only? Is it all fingers
come alive in the live dark to be ears, eyes,
nose and the taste and the crying?

As if the hand should open into the night,
flowering upon the darkness all around,
putting its fingers forth to feel out sight
to feel out sound;
to be all tongues for touching and tasting,
knuckle-sinuous and nailsharp against the dark;
to smell out ways;
to hark like hazel
the distant dripping of water wasting through clay.

CARGOES

JOHN MASEFIELD

Quinquireme of Nineveh from distant Ophir,
Rowing home to haven in sunny Palestine,
With a cargo of ivory,
And apes and peacocks,
Sandalwood, cedarwood, and sweet white wine.

Stately Spanish galleon coming from the Isthmus,
Dipping through the Tropics by the palm-green shores,
With a cargo of diamonds,
Emeralds, amethysts,
Topazes, and cinnamon, and gold moidores.

Dirty British coaster with a salt-caked smoke stack,
Butting through the Channel in the mad March days,
With a cargo of Tyne coal,
Road-rails, pig-lead,
Firewood, iron-ware, and cheap tin trays.

GOATS

CHARLES ERSKINE SCOTT WOOD

What I liked best in Sicily
Was not cloud-making Aetna, nor the fanes
Of old Greek gods, silent in majesty
Of death, but the early fresh-milk trains
That come while borage leaves hold dew
And the starry flowers of lapis blue
Are wet with Night: herds of whimsical
Black, brown and spotted grave she-goats,
With stare indifferent and quizzical;
Furry tassels dangling at their throats.
Nonchalantly sauntering to town,
They bite the wayside weed
With dainty, lip-selecting greed,
Skipping lightly to a wall,
Or even a house top, looking down
To mock with wag of beard the herder's call.
Through narrow streets they pass from door to door
And, full of sympathy for motherhood,
Fill frothing bowls for babies of the poor
From bulging udders, soft and round and good.
By the dripping fountain of the public square
Women wait for them, chatting the while
They squirt white jets through bottle-necks; a stair
Of stone one climbs to feed the sick, looking back to smile
A sly satiric grin of goaty guile.
Then all lie down to rest in a shadow place
Against a wall, chewing their sidewise cud
Till, presently, with pretty mincing pace
They seek the mountain and the tumbling flood.

THE FLIES

MERRILL MOORE

Death came to him so quickly that the flies
In the room were unaware that he was dead,
Which is usually not the case.
They avoided his head
Strangely enough and did not light on his eyes
At all as flies are very apt to do
When the blood stops to rest and the brittle ribs stop heaving
And the heat goes off while the last breath is leaving
And the work of the lungs and the brain is finally through.

They continued describing circles in the air
Using the light globe to describe a radius,

But toward dusk this must have become tedious
To them, judging from the deliberate care
With which they took it on themselves to stop
And rest for the night over the mantel-top.

TURKEY-COCK

D. H. LAWRENCE

You ruffled black blossom,
You glossy dark wind.

Your sort of gorgeousness,
Dark and lustrous
And skinny repulsive
And poppy-glossy,
Is the gorgeousness that evokes my most puzzled admiration.

Your aboriginality
Deep, unexplained,
Like a Red Indian darkly unfinished and aloof,
Seems like the black and glossy seeds of countless centuries.

Your wattles are the colour of steel-slag which has been red-hot
And is going cold,
Cooling to a powdery, pale-oxidised sky-blue.

Why do you have wattles, and a naked, wattled head?
Why do you arch your naked-set eye with a more-than-comprehensible arrogance?

The vulture is bald, so is the condor, obscenely,
But only you have thrown this amazing mantilla of oxidised sky-blue
And hot red over you.

This queer dross shawl of blue and vermilion,
Whereas the peacock has a diadem.

I wonder why.
Perhaps it is a sort of uncanny decoration, a veil of loose skin.
Perhaps it is your assertion, in all this ostentation, of raw contradictoriness.
Your wattles drip down like a shawl to your breast
And the point of your mantilla drops across your nose, unpleasantly.

Or perhaps it is something unfinished
A bit of slag still adhering, after your firing in the furnace of creation.

Or perhaps there is something in your wattles of a bull's dewlap
Which slips down like a pendulum to balance the throbbing mass of a generous breast,

The over-drip of a great passion hanging in the balance.
Only yours would be a raw, unsmelted passion, that will not quite fuse from the dross.

You contract yourself,
You arch yourself as an archer's bow
Which quivers indrawn as you clench your spine
Until your veiled head almost touches backward
To the root-rising of your erected tail.
And one intense and backward-curving frisson
Seizes you as you clench yourself together
Like some fierce magnet bringing its poles together.

Burning, pale positive pole of your wattled head!
And from the darkness of that opposite one
The upstart of your round-barred, sun-round tail!

Whilst between the two, along the tense arch of your back
Blows the magnetic current in fierce blasts,
Ruffling black, shining feathers like lifted mail,
Shuddering storm wind, or a water rushing through.
Your brittle, super-sensual arrogance
Tosses the crape of red across your brow and down your breast
As you draw yourself upon yourself in insistence.

It is a declaration of such tension in will
As time has not dared to avouch, nor eternity been able to unbend
Do what it may.
A raw American will, that has never been tempered by life;
You brittle, will-tense bird with a foolish eye.

The peacock lifts his rods of bronze
And struts blue-brilliant out of the far East.
But watch a turkey prancing low on earth

Drumming his vaulted wings, as savages drum
Their rhythms on long-drawn, hollow, sinister drums.
The ponderous, sombre sound of the great drum of Huichilobos
In pyramid Mexico, during sacrifice.

Drum, and the turkey onrush
Sudden, demonic dauntlessness, full abreast,
All the bronze gloss of all his myriad petals
Each one apart and instant.
Delicate frail crescent of the gentle outline of white
At each feather-tip
So delicate:
Yet the bronze wind-bell suddenly clashing
And the eye overweening into madness.

Turkey-cock, turkey-cock,
Are you the bird of the next dawn?

Has the peacock had his day, does he call in vain, screecher, for
    the sun to rise?
The eagle, the dove, and the barnyard rooster, do they call in
    vain, trying to wake the morrow?
And do you await us, wattled father, Westward?
Will your yell do it?

Take up the trail of the vanished American
Where it disappeared at the foot of the crucifix.
Take up the primordial Indian obstinancy,
The more than human, dense insistence of will,
And disdain, and blankness, and onrush, and prise open the
    new day with them?

The East a dead letter, and Europe moribund. . . . Is that so?
And those sombre, dead, feather-lustrous Aztecs, Amerindians,

In all the sinister splendour of their red blood-sacrifices,
Do they stand under the dawn, half-godly, half-demon, awaiting the cry of the turkey-cock?

Or must you go through the fire once more, till you're smelted pure,
Slag-wattled turkey-cock,
Dross-jabot?

LITTLE THINGS

JAMES STEPHENS

Little things, that run, and quail,
And die, in silence and despair!

Little things, that fight, and fail,
And fall, on sea, and earth, and air!

All trapped and frightened little things,
The mouse, the coney, hear our prayer!

As we forgive those done to us,
—The lamb, the linnet, and the hare—

Forgive us all our trespasses,
Little creatures, everywhere!

EPITHALAMION

GERARD MANLEY HOPKINS

Hark, hearer, hear what I do; lend a thought now, make believe
We are leafwhelmed somewhere with the hood
Of some branchy bunchy bushybowered wood,
Southern dene or Lancashire clough or Devon cleave,

That leans along the loins of hills, where a candycoloured, where a gluegold-brown
Marbled river, boisterously beautiful, between
Roots and rocks is danced and dandled, all in froth and water-blowballs, down.
We are there, when we hear a shout
That the hanging honeysuck, the dogeared hazels in the cover
Makes dither, makes hover
And the riot of a rout
Of, it must be, boys from the town
Bathing: it is summer's sovereign good.

By there comes a listless stranger: beckoned by the noise
He drops toward the river: unseen
Sees the bevy of them, how the boys
With dare and with downdolphinry and bellbright bodies huddling out,
Are earthworld, airworld, waterworld thorough hurled, all by turn and turn about.

This garland of their gambols flashes in his breast
Into such a sudden zest
Of summertime joys
That he hies to a pool neighbouring; sees it is the best
There; sweetest, freshest, shadowiest;
Fairyland; silk-beech, scrolled ash, packed sycamore, wild wychelm, hornbeam fretty overstood
By. Rafts and rafts of flake-leaves light, dealt so, painted on the air,
Hang as still as hawk or hawkmoth, as the stars or as the angels there,
Like the thing that never knew the earth, never off roots
Rose. Here he feasts: lovely all is! No more: off with—down he dings
His bleachèd both and woolwoven wear:

Careless these in coloured wisp
All lie tumbled-to; then with loop-locks
Forward falling, forehead frowning, lips crisp
Over finger-teasing task, his twiny boots
Fast he opens, lest he offwrings
Till walk the world he can with bare his feet
And come where lies a coffer, burly all of blocks
Built of chancequarrièd, selfquainèd rocks
And the water warbles over into, filleted with glassy grassy quicksilvery shivès and shoots
And with heavenfallen freshness down from moorland still brims,
Dark or daylight on and on. Here he will then, here he will the fleet
Flinty kindcold element let break across his limbs
Long. Where we leave him, froliclavish while he looks about him, laughs, swims. . . .

EVERY THING

HAROLD MONRO

Since man has been articulate,
Mechanical, improvidently wise
(Servant of Fate),
He has not understood the little cries
And foreign conversations of the small
Delightful creatures that have followed him
Not far behind;
Has failed to hear the sympathetic call
Of Crockery and Cutlery, those kind
Reposeful Teraphim
Of his domestic happiness; the Stool
He sat on, or the Door he entered through:
He has not thanked them, overbearing fool!
What is he coming to?

But you should listen to the talk of these.
Honest they are, and patient they have kept;
Served him without his Thank you or his Please . . .
I often heard
The gentle Bed, a sigh between each word,
Murmuring, before I slept.
The Candle, as I blew it, cried aloud,
Then bowed,
And in a smoky argument
Into the darkness went.

The Kettle puffed a tentacle of breath:—
"Pooh! I have boiled his water, I don't know
Why; and he always says I boil too slow.
He never calls me 'Sukie, dear,' and oh,
I wonder why I squander my desire
Sitting submissive on his kitchen fire."

Now the old Copper Basin suddenly
Rattled and tumbled from the shelf,
Bumping and crying: "I can fall by myself;
Without a woman's hand
To patronize and coax and flatter me,
I understand
The lean and poise of gravitable land."
It gave a raucous and tumultuous shout,
Twisted itself convulsively about,
Rested upon the floor, and, while I stare,
It stares and grins at me.

The old impetuous Gas above my head
Begins irascibly to flare and fret,
Wheezing into its epileptic jet,
Reminding me I ought to go to bed.

EVERY THING

The rafters creak; an Empty-Cupboard door
Swings open; now a wild Plank of the floor
Breaks from its joist, and leaps behind my foot.
Down from the chimney, half a pound of Soot
Tumbles and lies, and shakes itself again.
The Putty cracks against the window-pane.
A piece of Paper in the basket shoves
Another piece, and toward the bottom moves.
My independent Pencil, while I write,
Breaks at the point: the ruminating Clock
Stirs all its body and begins to rock,
Warning the waiting presence of the Night,
Strikes the dead hour, and tumbles to the plain
Ticking of ordinary work again.

You do well to remind me, and I praise
Your strangely individual foreign ways.
You call me from myself to recognize
Companionship in your unselfish eyes.
I want your dear acquaintances, although
I pass you arrogantly over, throw
Your lovely sounds, and squander them along
My busy days. I'll do you no more wrong.

Purr for me, Sukie, like a faithful cat.
You, my well-trampled Boots, and you, my Hat,
Remain my friends: I feel, though I don't speak,
Your touch grow kindlier from week to week.
It well becomes our mutual happiness
To go toward the same end more or less.
There is not much dissimilarity,
Not much to choose, I know it well, in fine,
Between the purposes of you and me,
And your eventual Rubbish Heap, and mine.

THE PASSIONATE SHEPHERD TO HIS LOVE

CHRISTOPHER MARLOWE

Come live with me and be my Love,
And we will all the pleasures prove
That hills and valleys, dales and fields,
Or woods or steepy mountain yields.

And we will sit upon the rocks,
And see the shepherds feed their flocks
By shallow rivers, to whose falls
Melodious birds sing madrigals.

And I will make thee beds of roses
And a thousand fragrant posies;
A cap of flowers, and a kirtle
Embroidered all with leaves of myrtle.

A gown made of the finest wool
Which from our pretty lambs we pull;
Fair-linèd slippers for the cold,
With buckles of the purest gold.

A belt of straw and ivy-buds
With coral clasps and amber studs:
And if these pleasures may thee move,
Come live with me and be my Love.

The shepherd swains shall dance and sing
For thy delight each May morning:
If these delights thy mind may move,
Then live with me and be my Love.

THE BAIT

JOHN DONNE

Come live with me, and be my love,
And we will some new pleasures prove
Of golden sands, and crystal brooks,
With silken lines, and silver hooks.

There will the river whispering run
Warm'd by thy eyes, more than the Sun.
And there th' enamour'd fish will stay,
Begging themselves they may betray.

When thou wilt swim in that live bath,
Each fish, which every channel hath,
Will amourously to thee swim,
Gladder to catch thee, than thou him.

If thou, to be so seen, be'st loth,
By Sun, or Moon, thou dark'nest both,
And if myself have leave to see,
I need not their light, having thee.

Let others freeze with angling reeds,
And cut their legs, with shells and weeds,
Or treacherously poor fish beset,
With strangling snare, or windowy net:

Let coarse bold hands, from slimy nest
The bedded fish in banks out-wrest,
Or curious traitors, sleeve-silk flies
Bewitch poor fishes' wand'ring eyes.

For thee, thou need'st no such deceit,
For thou thyself art thine own bait;
That fish, that is not catch'd thereby,
Alas, is wiser far than I.

TO PHILLIS

ROBERT HERRICK

Live, live with me, and thou shalt see
The pleasures I'll prepare for thee:
What sweets the country can afford
Shall bless thy bed, and bless thy board.
The soft sweet moss shall be thy bed,
With crawling woodbine over-spread:
By which the silver-shedding streams
Shall gently melt thee into dreams.
Thy clothing next, shall be a gown
Made of the fleeces' purest down.
The tongues of kids shall be thy meat;
Their milk thy drink; and thou shalt eat
The paste of filberts for thy bread
With cream of cowslips butteréd:
Thy feasting-table shall be hills
With daisies spread, and daffodils;
Where thou shalt sit, and Red-breast by,
For meat, shall give thee melody.
I'll give thee chains and carcanets
Of primroses and violets.
A bag and bottle thou shalt have,
That richly wrought, and this as brave;
So that as either shall express
The wearer's no mean shepherdess.
At shearing-times, and yearly wakes,
When Themilis his pastime makes,

There thou shalt be; and be the wit,
Nay more, the feast, and grace of it.
On holydays, when virgins meet
To dance the heys with nimble feet,
Thou shalt come forth, and then appear
The Queen of Roses for that year.
And having danced ('bove all the best)
Carry the garland from the rest,
In wicker-baskets maids shall bring
To thee, my dearest shepherdling,
The blushing apple, bashful pear,
And shame-faced plum, all simp'ring there.
Walk in the groves, and thou shalt find
The name of Phillis in the rind
Of every straight and smooth-skin tree;
Where kissing that, I'll twice kiss thee.
To thee a sheep-hook I will send,
Be-prank'd with ribbands, to this end,
This, this alluring hook might be
Less for to catch a sheep, than me.
Thou shalt have possets, wassails fine,
Not made of ale, but spicèd wine;
To make thy maids and self free mirth,
All sitting near the glitt'ring hearth.
Thou shalt have ribbands, roses, rings,
Gloves, garters, stockings, shoes, and strings
Of winning colours, that shall move
Others to lust, but me to love.
—These, nay, and more, thine own shall be
If thou wilt love, and live with me.

COME DOWN, O MAID

ALFRED LORD TENNYSON

"Come down, O maid, from yonder mountain height:
What pleasure lives in height (the shepherd sang),
In height and cold, the splendor of the hills?
But cease to move so near the Heavens, and cease
To glide a sunbeam by the blasted pine,
To sit a star upon the sparkling spire;
And come, for Love is of the valley, come,
For Love is of the valley, come thou down
And find him; by the happy threshold, he,
Or hand in hand with Plenty in the maize,
Or red with spirted purple of the vats,
Or foxlike in the vine; nor cares to walk
With Death and Morning on the Silver Horns,
Nor wilt thou snare him in the white ravine,
Nor find him dropt upon the firths of ice,
That huddling slant in furrow-cloven falls
To roll the torrent out of dusky doors:
But follow; let the torrent dance thee down
To find him in the valley; let the wild
Lean-headed eagles yelp alone, and leave
The monstrous ledges there to slope, and spill
Their thousand wreaths of dangling water-smoke,
That like a broken purpose waste in air:
So waste not thou; but come; for all the vales
Await thee; azure pillars of the hearth
Arise to thee; the children call, and I
Thy shepherd pipe, and sweet is every sound,
Sweeter thy voice, but every sound is sweet;
Myriads of rivulets hurrying thro' the lawn,
The moan of doves in immemorial elms,
And murmuring of innumerable bees."

I BRING TO YOU AS OFFERING TONIGHT

EMILE VERHAEREN

(Translated by Jethro Bithell)

I bring to you as offering tonight
My body boisterous with the wind's delight;
In floods of sunlight I have bathed my skin;
My feet are clean as the grass they waded in;
Soft are my fingers as the flowers they held;
My eyes are brightened by the tears that welled
Within them, when they looked upon the earth
Strong without end and rich with festive mirth;
Space in its living arms has snatched me up,
And whirled me drunk as from the mad wine-cup;
And I have walked I know not where, with pent
Cries that would free my heart's wild wonderment;
I bring to you the life of meadow-lands;
Sweet marjoram and thyme have kissed my hands;
Breathe them upon my body, all the fresh
Air and its light and scents are in my flesh.

EVENING ON THE MOSELLE

AUSONIUS

(Translated by Helen Waddell)

What colour are they now, thy quiet waters?
The evening star has brought the evening light,
And filled the river with the green hillside;
The hill-tops waver in the rippling water,
Trembles the absent vine and swells the grape
In thy clear crystal.

MORNING AT THE WINDOW

T. S. ELIOT

They are rattling breakfast plates in basement kitchens,
And along the trampled edges of the street
I am aware of the damp souls of housemaids
Sprouting despondently at area gates.

The brown waves of fog toss up to me
Twisted faces from the bottom of the street,
And tear from a passer-by with muddy skirts
An aimless smile that hovers in the air
And vanishes along the level of the roofs.

SILVER

WALTER DE LA MARE

Slowly, silently, now the moon
Walks the night in her silver shoon;
This way, and that, she peers, and sees
Silver fruit upon silver trees;
One by one the casements catch
Her beams beneath the silvery thatch;
Couched in his kennel, like a log,
With paws of silver sleeps the dog;
From their shadowy cote the white breasts peep
Of doves in a silver-feathered sleep;
A harvest mouse goes scampering by,
With silver claws and a silver eye;
And moveless fish in the water gleam,
By silver reeds in a silver stream.

FOG

CARL SANDBURG

The fog comes
on little cat feet.
It sits looking
over harbor and city
on silent haunches
and then moves on.

FOG

JOHN REED

Death comes like this, I know—
Snow-soft and gently cold;
Impalpable battalions of thin mist,
Light-quenching and sound-smothering and slow.

Slack as a wind-spilled sail
The spent world flaps in space—
Day's but a grayer night, and the old sun
Up the blind sky goes heavily and pale.

Out of all circumstance
I drift or seem to drift
In a vague vapor-world that clings and veils
Great trees arow like kneeling elephants.

Now Love and all the warm
Pageant of livingness
Trouble my quiet like forgotten dreams
Of ancient thunder on the hills of storm.

THINGS AND THEIR COLORS

How loud, how terribly
Aflame are lights and sounds!
And yet beyond the fog I know there are
But lonely bells across gray wastes of sea.

FLOWERS BY THE SEA

WILLIAM CARLOS WILLIAMS

When over the flowery, sharp pasture's
edge, unseen, the salt ocean

lifts its form—chickory and daisies
tied, released, seem hardly flowers alone

but color and the movement—or the shape
perhaps—of restlessness, whereas

the sea is circled and sways
peacefully upon its plantlike stem

THE DAFFODILS

WILLIAM WORDSWORTH

I wander'd lonely as a cloud
That floats on high o'er vales and hills,
When all at once I saw a crowd,
A host of golden daffodils,
Beside the lake, beneath the trees,
Fluttering and dancing in the breeze.

Continuous as the stars that shine
And twinkle on the milky way,
They stretch'd in never-ending line

Along the margin of a bay:
Ten thousand saw I at a glance
Tossing their heads in sprightly dance.

The waves beside them danced, but they
Out-did the sparkling waves in glee:
A Poet could not but be gay
In such a jocund company!
I gazed–and gazed–but little thought
What wealth the show to me had brought:

For oft, when on my couch I lie
In vacant or in pensive mood,
They flash upon that inward eye
Which is the bliss of solitude;
And then my heart with pleasure fills,
And dances with the daffodils.

THE LANDSCAPE NEAR AN AERODROME

STEPHEN SPENDER

More beautiful and soft than any moth
With burring furred antennae feeling its huge path
Through dusk, the air-liner with shut-off engines
Glides over suburbs and the sleeves set trailing tall
To point the wind. Gently, broadly, she falls
Scarcely disturbing charted currents of air.

Lulled by descent, the travellers across sea
And across feminine land indulging its easy limbs
In miles of softness, now let their eyes trained by watching
Penetrate through dusk the outskirts of this town
Here where industry shows a fraying edge.
Here they may see what is being done.

THINGS AND THEIR COLORS

Beyond the winking masthead light
And the landing-ground, they observe the outposts
Of work: chimneys like lank black fingers
Or figures frightening and mad: and squat buildings
With their strange air behind trees, like women's faces
Shattered by grief. Here where few houses
Moan with faint light behind their blinds
They remark the unhomely sense of complaint, like a dog
Shut out and shivering at the foreign moon.

In the last sweep of love, they pass over fields
Behind the aerodrome, where boys play all day
Hacking dead grass: whose cries, like wild birds,
Settle upon the nearest roofs
But soon are hid under the loud city.

Then, as they land, they hear the tolling bell
Reaching across the landscape of hysteria
To where, larger than all the charcoaled batteries
And imaged towers against that dying sky,
Religion stands, the church blocking the sun.

THE GARDEN

ANDREW MARVELL

How vainly men themselves amaze,
To win the palm, the oak, or bays,
And their incessant labor see
Crown'd from some single herb or tree,
Whose short and narrow-verged shade
Does prudently their toils upbraid,
While all the flowers, and trees, do close,
To weave the garlands of repose!

THE GARDEN

Fair Quiet, have I found thee here,
And Innocence, thy sister dear?
Mistaken long, I sought you then
In busy companies of men.
Your sacred plants, if here below,
Only among the plants will grow;
Society is all but rude,
To this delicious solitude.

No white nor red was ever seen
So amorous as this lovely green.
Fond lovers, cruel as their flame,
Cut in these trees their mistress's name:
Little, alas! they know or heed,
How far these beauties her exceed!
Fair trees! where'er your barks I wound,
No name shall but your own be found.

When we have run our passion's heat,
Love hither makes his best retreat.
The gods, who mortal beauty chase,
Still in a tree did end their race;
Apollo hunted Daphne so,
Only that she might laurel grow;
And Pan did after Syrinx speed,
Not as a nymph, but for a reed.

What wond'rous life is this I lead!
Ripe apples drop about my head;
The luscious clusters of the vine
Upon my mouth do crush their wine;
The nectarine, and curious peach,
Into my hands themselves do reach;
Stumbling on melons, as I pass,
Insnared with flowers, I fall on grass.

Meanwhile the mind, from pleasure less,
Withdraws into its happiness;—
The mind, that ocean where each kind
Does straight its own resemblance find;—
Yet it creates, transcending these,
Far other worlds, and other seas,
Annihilating all that's made
To a green thought in a green shade.

Here at the fountain's sliding foot,
Or at some fruit-tree's mossy root,
Casting the body's vest aside,
My soul into the boughs does glide:
There, like a bird, it sits and sings,
Then whets and claps its silver wings,
And, till prepar'd for longer flight,
Waves in its plumes the various light.

Such was that happy garden-state,
While man there walked without a mate:
After a place so pure and sweet,
What other help could yet be meet!
But 'twas beyond a mortal's share
To wander solitary there:
Two paradises are in one,
To live in paradise alone.

How well the skilful gardener drew
Of flowers, and herbs, this dial new,
Where, from above, the milder sun
Does through a fragrant zodiac run,
And, as it works, the industrious bee
Computes its time as well as we!
How could such sweet and wholesome hours
Be reckoned but with herbs and flowers?

YOU, ANDREW MARVELL

ARCHIBALD MACLEISH

And here face down beneath the sun,
And here upon earth's noonward height,
To feel the always coming on,
The always rising of the night.

To feel creep up the curving east
The earthly chill of dusk and slow
Upon those under lands the vast
And ever-climbing shadow grow,

And strange at Ecbatan the trees
Take leaf by leaf the evening, strange,
The flooding dark about their knees,
The mountains over Persia change,

And now at Kermanshah the gate,
Dark, empty, and the withered grass,
And through the twilight now the late
Few travellers in the westward pass.

And Baghdad darken and the bridge
Across the silent river gone,
And through Arabia the edge
Of evening widen and steal on,

And deepen on Palmyra's street
The wheel rut in the ruined stone,
And Lebanon fade out and Crete
High through the clouds and overblown,

And over Sicily the air
Still flashing with the landward gulls,

And loom and slowly disappear
The sails above the shadowy hulls,

And Spain go under and the shore
Of Africa, the gilded sand,
And evening vanish and no more
The low pale light across that land,

Nor now the long light on the sea—

And here face downward in the sun
To feel how swift, how secretly,
The shadow of the night comes on. . . .

ODE TO EVENING

WILLIAM COLLINS

If aught of oaten stop, or pastoral song,
May hope, chaste eve, to soothe thy modest ear,
  Like thy own solemn springs,
  Thy springs, and dying gales,

O nymph reserved, while now the bright-haired sun
Sits in yon western tent, whose cloudy skirts,
  With brede ethereal wove,
  O'erhang his wavy bed:

Now air is hushed, save where the weak-eyed bat
With short, shrill shriek, flits by on leathern wing;
  Or where the beetle winds
  His small but sullen horn,

As oft he rises 'midst the twilight path,
Against the pilgrim borne in heedless hum:

ODE TO EVENING

Now teach me, maid composed,
To breathe some softened strain,

Whose numbers, stealing through thy darkening vale,
May, not unseemly, with its stillness suit,
As, musing slow, I hail
Thy genial loved return!

For when thy folding star arising shows
His paly circlet, at his warning lamp
The fragrant hours, and elves
Who slept in flowers the day,

And many a nymph who wreathes her brows with sedge,
And sheds the freshening dew, and lovelier still,
The pensive pleasures sweet
Prepare thy shadowy car.

Then lead, calm votaress, where some sheety lake
Cheers the lone heath, or some time-hallowed pile,
Or upland fallows grey
Reflect its last cool gleam.

But when chill blustering winds, or driving rain,
Forbid my willing feet, be mine the hut,
That from the mountain's side,
Views wilds, and swelling floods,

And hamlets brown, and dim-discovered spires;
And hears their simple bell, and marks o'er all
Thy dewy fingers draw
The gradual dusky veil.

While spring shall pour his showers, as oft he wont,
And bathe thy breathing tresses, meekest eve!

While summer loves to sport
Beneath thy lingering light;

While sallow autumn fills thy lap with leaves;
Or winter, yelling through the troublous air,
Affrights thy shrinking train,
And rudely rends thy robes;

So long, sure-found beneath the Sylvan shed,
Shall fancy, friendship, science, rose-lipped health,
Thy gentlest influence own,
And hvmn thy favourite name!

INVOCATION TO SLEEP

FLETCHER

Care-charming Sleep, thou easer of all woes,
Brother to Death, sweetly thyself dispose
On this afflicted prince; fall like a cloud
In gentle showers; give nothing that is loud
Or painful to his slumbers;—easy, sweet,
And as a purling stream, thou son of night,
Pass by his troubled senses; sing his pain
Like hollow murmuring wind or silver rain;
Into this prince gently, oh, gently slide,
And kiss him into slumbers like a bride!

SALMON-FISHING

ROBINSON JEFFERS

The days shorten, the south blows wide for showers now,
The south wind shouts to the rivers,
The rivers open their mouths and the salt salmon

Race up into the freshet.
In Christmas month against the smoulder and menace
Of a long angry sundown
Red ash of the dark solstice, you see the anglers,
Pitiful, cruel, primeval,
Like the priests of the people that built Stonehenge,
Dark silent forms, performing
Remote solemnities in the red shallows
Of the river's mouth at the year's turn,
Drawing landward their live bullion, the bloody mouths
And scales full of the sunset
Twitch on the rocks, no more to wander at will
The wild Pacific pasture nor wanton and spawning
Race up into fresh water.

SONG OF THE CHATTAHOOCHEE

SIDNEY LANIER

Out of the hills of Habersham,
Down the valleys of Hall,
  I hurry amain to reach the plain,
  Run the rapid and leap the fall,
  Split at the rock and together again,
  Accept my bed, or narrow or wide,
  And flee from folly on every side
  With a lover's pain to attain the plain
Far from the hills of Habersham,
Far from the valleys of Hall.

All down the hills of Habersham,
All through the valleys of Hall,
  The rushes cried *Abide, abide,*
  The willful waterweeds held me thrall,
  The laving laurel turned my tide,

The ferns and the fondling grass said *Stay,*
The dewberry dipped for to work delay,
And the little reeds sighed *Abide, abide,*
Here in the hills of Habersham,
Here in the valleys of Hall.

High o'er the hills of Habersham,
Veiling the valleys of Hall,
The hickory told me manifold
Fair tales of shade, the poplar tall
Wrought me her shadowy self to hold,
The chestnut, the oak, the walnut, the pine,
Overleaning, with flickering meaning and sign,
Said, *Pass not, so cold, these manifold*
Deep shades of the hills of Habersham,
These glades in the valleys of Hall.

And oft in the hills of Habersham,
And oft in the valleys of Hall,
The white quartz shone, and the smooth brook-stone
Did bar me of passage with friendly brawl,
And many a luminous jewel lone
—Crystals clear or a-cloud with mist,
Ruby, garnet and amethyst—
Made lures with the lights of streaming stone
In the clefts of the hills of Habersham,
In the beds of the valleys of Hall.

But oh, not the hills of Habersham,
And oh, not the valleys of Hall
Avail: I am fain for to water the plain.
Downward the voices of Duty call—
Downward, to toil and be mixed with the main,
The dry fields burn, and the mills are to turn,
And a myriad flowers mortally yearn,

And the lordly main from beyond the plain
Calls o'er the hills of Habersham,
Calls through the valleys of Hall.

HOME THOUGHTS FROM ABROAD

ROBERT BROWNING

Oh, to be in England now that April's there,
And whoever wakes in England sees, some morning, unaware,
That the lowest boughs and the brushwood sheaf
Round the elm-tree bole are in tiny leaf,
While the chaffinch sings on the orchard bough
In England—now!
And after April, when May follows
And the white-throat builds, and all the swallows!
Hark, where my blossomed pear-tree in the hedge
Leans to the fields and scatters on the clover
Blossoms and dewdrops—at the bent spray's edge—
That's the wise thrush: he sings each song twice over
Lest you should think he never could recapture
The first fine careless rapture!
And, tho' the fields look rough with hoary dew,
All will be gay when noontide wakes anew
The buttercups, the little children's dower
—Far brighter than this gaudy melon-flower!

MY HEART'S IN THE HIGHLANDS

ROBERT BURNS

My heart's in the Highlands, my heart is not here;
My heart's in the Highlands a-chasing the deer;
A-chasing the wild deer, and following the roe,
My heart's in the Highlands wherever I go.

Farewell to the Highlands, farewell to the North,
The birth-place of valor, the country of worth;
Wherever I wander, wherever I rove,
The hills of the Highlands forever I love.

Farewell to the mountains high-cover'd with snow;
Farewell to the straths and green valleys below;
Farewell to the forests and wild-hanging woods;
Farewell to the torrents and loud-pouring floods.
My heart's in the Highlands, my heart is not here;
My heart's in the Highlands a-chasing the deer;
A-chasing the wild deer, and following the roe,
My heart's in the Highlands, wherever I go.

THE OLD MASTERS

EMILE VERHAEREN

(Translated by Jethro Bithell)

In smokey inns whose loft is reached by ladders,
  And with a grimy ceiling splashed by shocks
Of hanging hams, black-puddings, onions, bladders,
  Rosaries of stuffed game, capons, geese, and cocks,
Around a groaning table sit the gluttons
  Before the bleeding viands stuck with forks,
Already loosening their waistcoat buttons,
  With wet mouths when from flagons leap the corks—
Teniers, and Brackenburgh, and Brauwer, shaken
  With listening to Jan Steen's uproarious wit,
Holding their bellies dithering with bacon,
  Wiping their chins, watching the hissing spit.
Their heavy-bodied Hebes, with their curving
  Bosoms in linen white without a stain,
Are going round, and in long jets are serving
  Wine that a sunbeam filters through the pane,

Before it sets on fire the kettles' paunches.
  The Queens of Tippling are these women, whom
Their swearing lovers, greedy of their haunches,
  Belabour as befits their youth in bloom,
With sweating temples, blazing eyes, and lolling
  Tongue that keeps singing songs obscenely gay,
With brandished fists, bodies together rolling,
  Blows fit to bruise their carcases, while they,
With mouth for songs aye ready, throat for bumpers,
  And blood forever level with their skins,
Dance fit to split the floor, they are such jumpers,
  And butt their dancer as around he spins,
And lick his face in kisses endless seeming,
  Then fall with ransacked corsage, wet with heat.
A smell of bacon fat is richly steaming
  From the huge platters charged with juicy meat;
The roasts are passed around, in gravy swimming,
  Under the noses of the guests, and passed
Around again, with fresh relays of trimming.
  And in the kitchen drudges wash up fast
The platters to be sent back to the table;
  The dressers bulge, crowded with crockery;
The cellars hold as much as they are able;
  And round the estrade where is this agape
In glowing red, from pegs hang baskets, ladles,
  Strainers, and saucepans, candlesticks, and flasks.
Two monkeys in a corner show their navels,
  Throning, with glass in hand, on two twin casks;
A mellow light on every angle glimmers,
  Shines on the door-knob, through the great keyhole,
Clings to a pestle, filters through the skimmers,
  Is jewelled on the monster gala bowl,
And slanting on the heated hearthstone sickens,
  Where, o'er the embers, turns to brown the flesh
Of rosy sucking-pigs and fat cock-chickens,

That whet the edge of appetite afresh.
From dawn to eve, from eve to dawn, and after,
The masters with their women revel hold—
Women who play a farce of opulent laughter:
Farce cynical, obscene, with sleeves uprolled,
In corsage ript a flowering gorge not hiding,
Belly that shakes with jollity, bright eyes.
Noises of orgy and of rut are gliding,
Rumbling, and hissing, till they end in cries;
A noise of jammed iron and of vessels banging;
Brauwer and Steen tilt baskets on their crowns;
Brackenburgh is two lids together clanging;
Others with pokers fiddle gridirons, clowns
Are all of them, eager to show their mettle;
They dance round those who lie with feet in air;
They scrape the frying-pan, they scrape the kettle;
And the eldest are the steadiest gluttons there,
Keenest in kisses, and the last to tumble;
With greasy nose they lick the casseroles;
One of them makes a rusty fiddle grumble,
Whose bow exhausts itself in cabrioles;
Some are in corners vomiting, and others
Are snoring with their arms hung round their seats;
Babies are bawling for their sweating mothers
To stuff their little mouths with monster teats.
Men, women, children, all stuffed full to bursting;
Appetites ravening, and instincts rife,
Furies of stomach, and of throats athirsting,
Debauchery, explosion of rich life,
In which these master gluttons, never sated,
Too genuine for insipidities,
Pitching their easels lustily, created
Between two drinking-bouts a masterpiece.

THE DESERT

CHARLES ERSKINE SCOTT WOOD

Never have I found a place, or a season, without beauty.
Neither the sea, where the white stallions champ their bits and
rear against their bridles,
Nor the Desert, bride of the Sun, which sits scornful, apart,
Like an unwooed Princess, careless; indifferent.
She spreads her garments, wonderful beyond estimation,
And embroiders continually her mantle.
She is a queen, seated on a throne of gold
In the Hall of Silence.
She insists upon humility.
She insists upon meditation.
She insists that the soul be free.
She requires an answer.
She demands the final reply to thoughts which cannot be answered.
She lights the Sun for a torch
And sets up the great cliffs as sentinels;
The morning and the evening are curtains before her chambers.
She displays the stars as her coronet.
She is cruel and invites victims,
Restlessly moving her wrists and ankles,
Which are loaded with sapphires.
Her brown breasts flash with opals.
She slays those who fear her,
But runs her hand lovingly over the brow of those who know her,
Soothing with a voluptuous caress.
She is a courtesan, wearing jewels,
Enticing, smiling a bold smile;
Adjusting her brilliant raiment negligently,
Lying brooding upon her floor which is richly carpeted;

Her brown thighs beautiful and naked.
She toys with the dazzlery of her diadems,
Smiling inscrutably.
She is a nun, withdrawing behind her veil;
Gray, subdued, silent, mysterious, meditative; unapproachable.
She is fair as a goddess sitting beneath a flowering peach-tree, beside a clear river.
Her body is tawny with the eagerness of the Sun
And her eyes are like pools which shine in deep canyons.
She is beautiful as a swart woman, with opals at her throat,
Rubies on her wrists and topaz about her ankles.
Her breasts are like the evening and the day stars;
She sits upon her throne of light, proud and silent, indifferent to her wooers.
The Sun is her servitor, the Stars are her attendants; running before her.
She sings a song unto her own ears, solitary, but it is sufficient.
It is the song of her being. O if I may sing the song of my being it will be sufficient.
She is like a jewelled dancer, dancing upon a pavement of gold;
Dazzling, so that the eyes must be shaded.
She wears the stars upon her bosom and braids her hair with the constellations.

THE RUNNER IN THE SKIES

JAMES OPPENHEIM

Who is the runner in the skies
With her blowing scarf of stars,
And our earth and sun hovering like bees about her blossoming heart!
Her feet are on the winds where space is deep;
Her eyes are nebulous and veiled;
She hurries through the night to a far lover.

WEATHERS

THOMAS HARDY

This is the weather the cuckoo likes,
And so do I;
When showers betumble the chestnut spikes,
And nestlings fly;
And the little brown nightingale bills his best,
And they sit outside the "Traveller's Rest,"
And maids come forth sprig-muslin drest,
And citizens dream of the South and West,
And so do I.

This is the weather the shepherd shuns,
And so do I;
When beeches drip in browns and duns,
And thresh, and ply;
And hill-hid tides throb, throe on throe,
And meadow rivulets overflow,
And drops on gate-bars hang in a row,
And rooks in families homeward go,
And so do I.

THE APRIL EARTH

MAX EASTMAN

My peace is broken, my white gentle sleep
So softly drifted on, so cool caressed
By morning's rose and evening's amethyst,
Jarred by the wind's breath, troubled by the sweep
Of the fox's brush, the rabbit's light-foot leap.
On my own rhythms lulled as on a breast,
In habit resting as the heart-beats rest,

From change and danger I lay buried deep.
Had I a shield, a refuge, I might shun
This deed of arson from the distant sun,
This green-clad burning, big with crimson shame,
Big with its own quick death, heavy and hot
And headlong in my nerves. But I can not.
A sky-thrown torch has kindled me to flame.

DESCRIPTION OF SPRING

Wherein each thing renews, save only the Lover

HENRY HOWARD, EARL OF SURRY

The soote season, that bud and bloom forth brings,
With green hath clad the hill and eke the vale:
The nightingale with feathers new she sings;
The turtle to her mate hath told her tale.
Summer is come, for every spray now springs:
The hart hath hung his old head on the pale;
The buck in brake his winter coat he flings;
The fishes flete with new repairèd scale.
The adder all her slough away she slings;
The swift swallow pursueth the flies smale;
The busy bee her honey now she mings;
Winter is worn that was the flowers' bale.

And thus I see among these pleasant things
Each care decays, and yet my sorrow springs.

SPRING'S WELCOME

JOHN LYLY

What bird so sings, yet so does wail?
O 'tis the ravish'd nightingale.
Jug, jug, jug, jug, tereu! she cries,

And still her woes at midnight rise.
Brave prick-song! Who is't now we hear?
None but the lark so shrill and clear;
Now at heaven's gate she claps her wings,
The morn not waking till she sings.
Hark, hark, with what a pretty throat
Poor robin redbreast tunes his note!
Hark how the jolly cuckoos sing
Cuckoo! to welcome in the spring!
Cuckoo! to welcome in the spring!

SPRING

E. E. CUMMINGS

Spring is like a perhaps hand
(which comes carefully
out of Nowhere) arranging
a window, into which people look (while
people stare
arranging and changing placing
carefully there a strange
thing and a known thing here) and

changing everything carefully

spring is like a perhaps
Hand in a window
(carefully to
and fro moving New and
Old things, while
people stare carefully
moving a perhaps
fraction of flower here placing
an inch of air there) and

without breaking anything.

TO SPRING

VIRGINIA MOORE

Unsullied Spring, O just-about-to-begin:
Fresh river-flags, cold crocuses, low bed
Of deep-dyed violets where snows have been;
Tulips as pale as butter or as red
As Aphrodite's bosom where it bled;
Sweetpeas crowded together, dappled with dew
(Pink, pale, color of salmon, lavender almost blue),
Pushing the fence—and over all the spell
Of a rich, rank, germinating smell
Out of the earth, an odor green and brown—
Bushes of rainy lilacs weighted down.

O Spring, O light of limb, O lovely stepping one,
Brushing the speared grass, leading the warm sun;
O leafy glade, unspoiled, unspotted, cool,
Dipping your matted roots into the rain's pool:
Mortal am I, mortal and twisted with pain,
But I would begin too—I would begin again.

SPRING PASTORAL

ELINOR WYLIE

Liza, go steep your long white hands
In the cool waters of that spring
Which bubbles up through shiny sands
The colour of a wild-dove's wing.

Dabble your hands, and steep them well
Until those nails are pearly white
Now rosier than a laurel bell;
Then come to me at candlelight.

COUNTRY SUMMER

Lay your cold hands across my brows,
And I shall sleep, and I shall dream
Of silver-pointed willow boughs
Dipping their fingers in a stream.

COUNTRY SUMMER

LEONIE ADAMS

Now the rich cherry whose sleek wood
And top with silver petals traced,
Like a strict box its gems encased,
Has spilt from out that cunning lid,
All in an innocent green round,
Those melting rubies which it hid;
With moss ripe-strawberry-encrusted,
So birds get half, and minds lapse merry
To taste that deep-red lark's-bite berry,
And blackcap-bloom is yellow-dusted.

The wren that thieved it in the eaves
A trailer of the rose could catch
To her poor droopy sloven thatch,
And side by side with the wren's brood,—
O lovely time of beggars' luck—
Opens the quaint and hairy bud.
And full and golden is the yield
Of cows that never have to house,
But all night nibble under boughs
Or cool their sides in the moist field.

Into the rooms flow meadow airs,
The warm farm-baking smell blows round;
Inside and out and sky and ground
Are much the same; the wishing star,
Hesperus, kind and early-born,

Is risen only finger-far.
All stars stand close in summer air,
And tremble, and look mild as amber;
When wicks are lighted in the chamber
You might say stars were settling there.

Now straightening from the flowery hay,
Down the still light the mowers look;
Or turn, because their dreaming shook,
And they waked half to other days,
When left alone in yellow-stubble,
The rusty-coated mare would graze.
Yet thick the lazy dreams are born;
Another thought can come to mind,
But like the shivering of the wind,
Morning and evening in the corn.

AUGUST

ELINOR WYLIE

Why should this Negro insolently stride
Down the red noonday on such noiseless feet?
Piled in his barrow, tawnier than wheat,
Lie heaps of smouldering daisies, sombre-eyed,
Their copper petals shrivelled up with pride,
Hot with a superfluity of heat,
Like a great brazier borne along the street
By captive leopards, black and burning pied.

Are there no water-lilies, smooth as cream,
With long stems dripping crystals? Are there none
Like those white lilies, luminous and cool,
Plucked from some hemlock-darkened northern stream
By fair-haired swimmers, diving where the sun
Scarce warms the surface of the deepest pool?

TO AUTUMN

JOHN KEATS

Season of mists and mellow fruitfulness,
    Close bosom-friend of the maturing sun;
Conspiring with him how to load and bless
    With fruit the vines that round the thatch-eves run;
To bend with apples the moss'd cottage-trees,
    And fill all fruit with ripeness to the core;
        To swell the gourd, and plump the hazel shells
With a sweet kernel; to set budding more,
    And still more, later flowers for the bees,
    Until they think warm days will never cease,
        For Summer has o'er-brimm'd their clammy cells.

Who hath not seen thee oft amid thy store?
    Sometimes whoever seeks abroad may find
Thee sitting careless on a granary floor,
    Thy hair soft-lifted by the winnowing wind;
Or on a half-reap'd furrow sound asleep,
    Drows'd with the fume of poppies, while thy hook
        Spares the next swath and all its twined flowers:
And sometimes like a gleaner thou dost keep
    Steady thy laden head across a brook;
    Or by a cyder-press, with patient look,
        Thou watchest the last oozings hours by hours.

Where are the songs of Spring? Ay, where are they?
    Think not of them, thou hast thy music too,—
While barred clouds bloom the soft-dying day,
    And touch the stubble-plains with rosy hue;
Then in a wailful choir the small gnats mourn
    Among the river sallows, borne aloft
        Or sinking as the light wind lives or dies;

And full-grown lambs loud bleat from hilly bourn;
Hedge-crickets sing; and now with treble soft
The red-breast whistles from a garden-croft;
And gathering swallows twitter in the skies.

AUTUMN

ALEXANDER PUSHKIN

(Translated by Max Eastman)

October at last has come! The thicket has shaken
The last leaf lingering down from the naked branch.
Autumn is breathing cold, the road is frozen—
The brook still runs with a murmur behind the mill,
But the pond is still. My neighbor is up and away
With a hunt, away to the farthest dreaming field,
Where the winter wheat will suffer from his mad sport,
And the bark of dogs will startle the forest oaks.

It is my time now! I never could love the spring,
The dragging thaw, the mud, the stink—I am sick
In spring: my blood's astray, my mind is oppressed
With a yearning pain. Winter is better for me.
I love the serious snow fields under the moon!
How the light run of the sled is swift and free,
And the hand of a girl down under the sables warm . . .

And Oh the fun to be shod with the sharpest steel
And glide on the glassy face of the standing river!
The bright alarm of a winter holiday!
But still there's a limit to things. A half year's snow—
Even at last to the old cave-dweller, the bear,
It is long enough. You can not for ever and ever
Slide in a sled with a beautiful young Armida,
Or sulk behind double glass by a friendly stove!

AUTUMN

They commonly scold the last days of Autumn. To me,
My reader and friend, they are dear. Their beauty is quiet,
Their modesty brilliant; they draw me to them like a child
Whom the family does not love. I will tell you frankly:
Of all the seasons of time I have loved but one.
I find in her—I am not a vainglorious lover,
Though wilful of fancy—I find in my love much good.

How shall I tell you? She ravishes me
As a dying virgin perhaps might ravish you.
Condemned and bending meekly and murmuring not,
Not angry—a smile on the fading lips—
She does not perceive the abysmal opening mouth
Of the tomb. The purplish light on her features plays.
Today she is here—she lives—and tomorrow not.

Sweet mournful days, charm of the dreaming eyes,
Your beauty is dear to me that says farewell!
I love the sumptuous decline of Nature's life—
The tents of the forest adorned with purple and gold,
And loud with the sound of the faster breath of the wind,
A billowy curtain of fog concealing the sky,
And the sun's rare beam, and the early frost,
And the threat of the gray-head winter standing off!

With every Autumn that comes I bloom again.
It is good for my health, it is good, this Russian cold.
I fall afresh in love with the habit of being;
Sleep flies early and hunger is in his place,
The blood romps joyfully through my heart,
Desire seethes up, I laugh again, I am young,
I am living life—such is my organism
(If you will excuse me please the prosaism).

So saddle my horse, and into the plentiful open
With fluttering mane he will carry me flying, and under
His body his glittering hoofs will ring like a tune

Through the frozen valley, will crackle and crash on the ice—
Till the brief day dies! And then the forgotten chimney
Will waken again with flame—will pour sharp light
Or dimly glow, while I sit reading long,
And nourishing the long thoughts in my soul. . . .

OCTOBER

THOMAS WOLFE

October is the richest of the seasons: the fields are cut, the granaries are full, the bins are loaded to the brim with fatness, and from the cider-press the rich brown oozings of the York Imperials run. The bee bores to the belly of the yellowed grape, the fly gets old and fat and blue, he buzzes loud, crawls slow, creeps heavily to death on sill and ceiling, the sun goes down in blood and pollen across the bronzed and mown fields of old October.

The corn is shocked: it sticks out in hard yellow rows upon dried ears, fit now for the great red barns in Pennsylvania, and the big stained teeth of crunching horses. The indolent hooves kick swiftly at the boards, the barn is sweet with hay and leather, wood and apples—this, and the clean dry crunching of the teeth is all: the sweat, the labor and the plow is over. The late pears mellow on a sunny shelf; smoked hams hang to the warped barn rafters; the pantry shelves are loaded with 300 jars of fruit. Meanwhile the leaves are turning, turning up in Maine, the chestnut burrs plop thickly to the earth in gusts of wind, and in Virginia the chinkapins are falling.

There is a smell of burning in the small towns in afternoon, and men with buckles on their arms are raking leaves in yards as boys come by, the straps slung back across their shoulders. The oak leaves, big and brown, are bedded deep in yard and gutter: they make deep wadings to the knee for children in the streets. The fire will snap and crackle like a whip, sharp acrid smoke will sting the eyes, in mown fields the little vipers of the flame eat past the black coarse edges of burned stubble like a line of locusts. Fire drives a thorn of memory in the heart.

The bladed grass, a forest of small spears of ice, is thawed by noon: summer is over but the sun is warm again, and there are days throughout the land of gold and russet. But summer is dead and gone, the earth is waiting, suspense and ecstasy are gnawing at the hearts of men, the brooding prescience of frost is there. The sun flames red and bloody as it sets, there are old red glintings on the battered pails, the great barn gets the ancient light as the boy slops homeward with the warm foaming milk. Great shadows lengthen in the fields, the old redlight dies swiftly, and the sunset barking of the hounds is faint and far and full of frost: there are shrewd whistles to the dogs, and frost and silence—that is all. Wind stirs and scuffs and rattles up the old brown leaves, and through the night the great oak leaves keep falling.

Trains cross the continent in a swirl of dust and thunder, the leaves fly down the tracks behind them: the great trains cleave through gulch and gully, they rumble with spoked thunder on the bridges over the powerful brown wash of mighty rivers, they toil through hills, they skirt the rough brown stubble of shorn fields, they whip past empty stations in the little towns and their giant stride pounds its every pulse across America. Field and hill and lift and gulch and hollow, mountain and plain and river, a wilderness with fallen trees across it, a thicket of bedded brown and twisted undergrowth, a plain, a desert, and a plantation, a mighty landscape with no fenced niceness, an immensity of fold and convolution that can never be remembered, that can never be forgotten, that has never been described —weary with harvest, potent with every fruit and ore, the immeasurable richness embrowned with autumn, rank, crude, unharnessed, careless of scars or beauty, everlasting and magnificent, a cry, a space, an ecstasy!—American earth in old October.

And the great winds howl and swoop across the land: they

make a distant roaring in great trees, and boys in bed will stir in ecstasy, thinking of demons and vast swoopings through the earth. All through the night there is the clean, the bitter rain of acorns, and the chestnut burrs are plopping to the ground.

And often in the night there is only the living silence, the distant frosty barking of a dog, the small clumsy stir and feathery stumble of the chickens on limed roosts, and the moon, the low and heavy moon of autumn, now barred behind the leafless poles of pines, now at the pinewoods' brooding edge and summit, now falling with the ghost's dawn of milky light upon rimed clods of fields and on frosty scurf on pumpkins, now whiter, smaller, brighter, hanging against the steeple's slope, hanging the same way in a million streets, steeping all the earth in frost and silence.

Then a chime of frost-cold bells may peal out on the brooding air and people lying in their beds will listen. They will not speak or stir, silence will gnaw the darkness like a rat, but will whisper in their hearts:

"Summer has come and gone, has come and gone. And now—?" But they will say no more, they will have no more to say: they will wait listening, silent and brooding as the frost, to time, strange ticking time, dark time that haunts us with the briefness of our days. They will think of men long dead, of men now buried in the earth, of frost and silence long ago, of a forgotten face and moment of lost time, and they will think of things they have no words to utter.

TO WINTER

WILLIAM BLAKE

"O Winter! bar thine adamantine doors:
The north is thine; there hast thou built thy dark
Deep-founded habitation. Shake not thy roofs,
Nor bend thy pillars with thine iron car."

He hears me not, but o'er the yawning deep
Rides heavy; his storms are unchain'd, sheathed
In ribbed steel; I dare not lift mine eyes,
For he hath rear'd his sceptre o'er the world.

Lo! now the direful monster, whose skin clings
To his strong bones, strides o'er the groaning rocks:
He withers all in silence, and in his hand
Unclothes the earth, and freezes up frail life.

He takes his seat upon the cliffs,—the mariner
Cries in vain. Poor little wretch, that deal'st
With storms!—till heaven smiles, and the monster
Is driv'n yelling to his caves beneath Mount Hecla.

IN THE GREENWOOD

WILLIAM SHAKESPEARE

Under the greenwood tree
Who loves to lie with me,
And turn his merry note
Unto the sweet bird's throat,
Come hither, come hither, come hither:
Here shall he see
No enemy
But winter and rough weather.

Who doth ambition shun
And loves to live i' the sun,
Seeking the food he eats
And pleased with what he gets
Come hither, come hither, come hither:
Here shall he see
No enemy
But winter and rough weather.

DECEMBER FUGITIVE

HENRY MORTON ROBINSON

Were I the red-brushed fox, I should go warier
  In dawns like this (when shrivelled leaves cry riot
To the beagle's ear) than when the tufted wood
  Lay ankle-deep in quiet.

Were I the whirring grouse, I should fly cunninger
  On noons like this (when barren boughs uncover
Plumes to the marksman's eye) than when the bush
  With fruit was berried over.

Were I the fugitive heart, I should run wearier
  On nights like this (when cheeks are nipped by sleet)
Than ever I ran when summer was my hunter
  And loneliness more fleet.

THE SNOW MAN

WALLACE STEVENS

One must have a mind of winter
To regard the frost and the boughs
Of the pine-trees crusted with snow;

And have been cold a long time
To behold the junipers shagged with ice,
The spruces rough in the distant glitter

Of the January sun; and not to think
Of any misery in the sound of the wind,
In the sound of a few leaves,

Which is the sound of the land
Full of the same wind
That is blowing in the same bare place

For the listener, who listens in the snow,
And, nothing himself, beholds
Nothing that is not there and the nothing that is.

AN OLD MAN'S WINTER NIGHT

ROBERT FROST

All out of doors looked darkly in at him
Through the thin frost, almost in separate stars,
That gathers on the pane in empty rooms.
What kept his eyes from giving back the gaze
Was the lamp tilted near them in his hand.
What kept him from remembering what it was
That brought him to that creaking room was age.
He stood with barrels round him—at a loss.
And having scared the cellar under him
In clomping there, he scared it once again
In clomping off;—and scared the outer night,
Which has its sounds, familiar, like the roar
Of trees and crack of branches, common things,
But nothing so like beating on a box.
A light he was to no one but himself
Where now he sat, concerned with he knew what,
A quiet light, and then not even that.
He consigned to the moon, such as she was,
So late-arising, to the broken moon
As better than the sun in any case
For such a charge, his snow upon the roof,
His icicles along the wall to keep;
And slept. The log that shifted with a jolt

Once in the stove, disturbed him and he shifted,
And eased his heavy breathing, but still slept.
One aged man—one man—can't keep a house,
A farm, a countryside, or if he can,
It's thus he does it of a winter night.

COMPOSED UPON WESTMINSTER BRIDGE SEPT. 3, 1802

WILLIAM WORDSWORTH

Earth has not anything to show more fair:
Dull would he be of soul who could pass by
A sight so touching in its majesty:
This City now doth, like a garment, wear
The beauty of the morning; silent, bare,
Ships, towers, domes, theatres, and temples lie
Open unto the fields, and to the sky;
All bright and glittering in the smokeless air.
Never did sun more beautifully steep
In his first splendour, valley, rock, or hill;
Ne'er saw I, never felt, a calm so deep!
The river glideth at his own sweet will:
Dear God! the very houses seem asleep;
And all that mighty heart is lying still!

NOVEMBER 2 A.M. CONSPIRACY

SARA BARD FIELD

Cold, strange, withdrawn our friendly court and still—
Still, though in motion under full moon flood.
Acknowledging the wind's official will
Compliant heads on every stem-end nod.
His occult whisper passes among all

NOVEMBER 2 A.M. CONSPIRACY

Some secret countersign, some dark command,
Some final word of Sivaistic Fall
Plant, stone and air alike appear to understand.
Grape leaves on dry, curled edges scud
Along the pavement toward an angled wall
And gather there in milling rebel knot.
Even the distant moon that laves the land
With so detached, impersonal a hand
Lies on the wind's wish, listens with full stare
And all her shadows with her. Now late-leaved,
Sky-flung cherry boughs (by day aloof
From groundling dreams frustrated or achieved)
Shudder with passionate consent. What plot
Have I, a wakeful sleeper, chanced upon?
What proof
Of machinations vast no mortal ear
Was meant by these conspirators to hear?
What sinister design is now conceived
By these unhuman allies to my fear?
The murmurous agreement tightly binds
Wind, moonlight, shadows, leaves and tree,
The patio stones and even part of me
Beyond my active wish or willing act
Into the fateful, unknown, ominous pact
Too formidable for this ear and eye
Behind the window. Pale, I draw the blinds
Lest I, discovered, perish as a spy.

PART II

BEYOND REALITY

WINTER DUSK

WALTER DE LA MARE

Dark frost was in the air without,
The dusk was still with cold and gloom,
When less than even a shadow came
  And stood within the room.

But of the three around the fire,
None turned a questioning head to look,
Still read a clear voice, on and on,
  Still stooped they o'er their book.

The children watched their mother's eyes
Moving on softly line to line;
It seemed to listen too—that shade,
  Yet made no outward sign.

The fire-flames crooned a tiny song,
No cold wind moved the wintry tree;
The children both in Faerie dreamed
  Beside their mother's knee.

And nearer yet that spirit drew
Above that heedless one, intent
Only on what the simple words
  Of her small story meant.

No voiceless sorrow grieved her mind,
No memory her bosom stirred,
Nor dreamed she, as she read to two,
  'Twas surely three who heard.

Yet when, the story done, she smiled
From face to face, serene and clear,
A love, half dead, sprang up, as she
  Leaned close and drew them near.

A SEA DIRGE

WILLIAM SHAKESPEARE

Full fathom five thy father lies;
  Of his bones are coral made;
Those are pearls that were his eyes:
  Nothing of him that doth fade
But doth suffer a sea-change
Into something rich and strange.
Sea-nymphs hourly ring his knell:
Ding-dong.
Hark! now I hear them,—Ding-dong, bell.

ARIEL'S SONG

WILLIAM SHAKESPEARE

Where the bee sucks, there suck I.
In a cowslip's bell I lie:
There I couch when owls do cry
On the bat's back I do fly
After summer merrily.
Merrily, merrily, shall I live now
Under the blossom that hangs on the bough.

THE CENTAURS

JAMES STEPHENS

Playing upon the hill three centaurs were!
They lifted each a hoof! They stared at me
And stamped the dust!

They stamped the dust! They snuffed upon the air!
And all their movements had the fierce glee
Of power, and pride, and lust!

Of power and pride and lust! Then, with a shout,
They tossed their heads, and wheeled, and galloped round,
In furious brotherhood!

In furious brotherhood! Around, about,
They charged, they swerved, they leaped! Then, bound on bound,
They raced into the wood!

JUST THEN THE DOOR

MERRILL MOORE

Just then the door decided to close itself.
In walked One, in walked Two, in walked Three.

With the door shut it was impossible for that to be,
You say, but they walked right in through the door.

And One sat down cross-legged on the floor
And the second propped himself against the wall
And Three, chiefly because he was so tall,
Sat down on and let his legs dangle from the shelf.

Then they all spoke, first one, then another,
Every one of them distinctly calling me "brother"

And every one smiling in his ghastly way
As if his eyes contradicted what his mouth would say,

And each one disappeared like whirling smoke
Just about the time the morning broke.

THE SATYR IN THE PERIWIG

EDITH SITWELL

The Satyr Scarabombardon
Pulled periwig and breeches on:
"Grown old and stiff, this modern dress
Adds monstrously to my distress.
The gout within a hoofen heel
Is very hard to bear; I feel
When crushed into a buckled shoe
The twinge will be redoubled, too;
And when I walk in gardens green
And, weeping, think on what has been,
Then wipe one eye,—the other sees
The plums and cherries on the trees.
Small bird-quick women pass me by
With sleeves that flutter airily,
And baskets blazing like a fire
With laughing fruits of my desire:
Plums sunburnt as the King of Spain,
Gold-cheeked as any Nubian,
With strawberries all goldy-freckled,
Pears fat as thrushes and as speckled.
Pursue them? . . . Yes, and squeeze a tear:
'Please spare poor Satyr one, my dear!'

'Be off, sir! Go and steal your own!'
—Alas, poor Scarabombardon,
Trees rend his ruffles, stretch a twig,
Tear off a satyr's periwig!"

THE FAIRIES

WILLIAM ALLINGHAM

Up the airy mountain,
  Down the rushy glen,
We daren't go a-hunting
  For fear of little men;
Wee folk, good folk,
  Trooping all together;
Green jacket, red cap,
  And white owl's feather!

Down along the rocky shore
  Some make their home,
They live on crispy pancakes
  Of yellow tide-foam;
Some in the reeds
  Of the black mountain lake,
With frogs for their watch-dogs,
  All night awake.

High on the hill-top
  The old King sits;
He is now so old and gray
  He's nigh lost his wits.
With a bridge of white mist
  Columbkill he crosses,
On his stately journeys
  From Slieveleague to Rosses;

Or going up with music
  On cold starry nights
To sup with the Queen
  Of the gay Northern Lights.

They stole little Bridget
  For seven years long;
When she came down again
  Her friends were all gone.
They took her lightly back,
  Between the night and morrow,
They thought that she was fast asleep,
  But she was dead with sorrow.
They have kept her ever since
  Deep within the lake,
On a bed of flag-leaves,
  Watching till she wake.

By the craggy hill-side,
  Through the mosses bare,
They have planted thorn-trees
  For pleasure here and there.
If any man so daring
  As dig them up in spite,
He shall find their sharpest thorns
  In his bed at night.

Up the airy mountain,
  Down the rushy glen,
We daren't go a-hunting
  For fear of little men;
Wee folk, good folk,
  Trooping all together;
Green jacket, red cap,
  And white owl's feather!

THE GHOST OF THE BUFFALOES

VACHEL LINDSAY

Last night at black midnight I woke with a cry,
The windows were shaking, there was thunder on high,
The floor was atremble, the door was ajar,
White fires, crimson fires, shone from afar.
I rushed to the dooryard. The city was gone.
My home was a hut without orchard or lawn.
It was mud-smear and logs near a whispering stream,
Nothing else built by man could I see in my dream . . .
Then . . .
Ghost-kings came headlong, row upon row,
Gods of the Indians, torches aglow.

They mounted the bear and the elk and the deer,
And eagles gigantic, aged and sere,
They rode long-horn cattle, they cried "A-la-la."
They lifted the knife, the bow, and the spear,
They lifted ghost-torches from dead fires below,
The midnight made grand with the cry "A-la-la."
The midnight made grand with a red-god charge,
A red-god show,
A red-god show,
"A-la-la, a-la-la, a-la-la, a-la-la."

With bodies like bronze, and terrible eyes
Came the rank and the file, with catamount cries,
Gibbering, yipping, with hollow-skull clacks,
Riding white bronchos with skeleton backs,
Scalp-hunters, beaded and spangled and bad,
Naked and lustful and foaming and mad,
Flashing primeval demoniac scorn,
Blood-thirst and pomp amid darkness reborn.

Power and glory that sleep in the grass
While the winds and the snows and the great rains pass.
They crossed the gray river, thousands abreast,
They rode in infinite lines to the west,
Tide upon tide of strange fury and foam,
Spirits and wraiths, the blue was their home,
The sky was their goal where the star-flags were furled,
And on past those far golden splendors they whirled.
They burned to dim meteors, lost in the deep.
And I turned in dazed wonder, thinking of sleep.
And the wind crept by
Alone, unkempt, unsatisfied,
The wind cried and cried—
Muttered of massacres long past,
Buffaloes in shambles vast . . .
An owl said: "Hark, what is a-wing?"
I heard a cricket carolling,
I heard a cricket carolling,
I heard a cricket carolling.

Then . . .
Snuffing the lightning that crashed from on high
Rose royal old buffaloes, row upon row.
The lords of the prairie came galloping by.
And I cried in my heart "A-la-la, a-la-la,
A red-god show,
A red-god show,
A-la-la, a-la-la, a-la-la, a-la-la."

Buffaloes, buffaloes, thousands abreast,
A scourge and amazement, they swept to the west.
With black bobbing noses, with red rolling tongues,
Coughing forth steam from their leather-wrapped lungs,
Cows with their calves, bulls big and vain,
Goring the laggards, shaking the mane,

Stamping flint feet, flashing moon eyes,
Pompous and owlish, shaggy and wise.
Like sea-cliffs and caves resounded their ranks
With shoulders like waves, and undulant flanks.
Tide upon tide of strange fury and foam,
Spirits and wraiths, the blue was their home,
The sky was their goal where the star-flags are furled,
And on past those far golden splendors they whirled.
They burned to dim meteors, lost in the deep,
And I turned in dazed wonder, thinking of sleep.

I heard a cricket's cymbals play,
A scarecrow lightly flapped his rags,
And a pan that hung by his shoulder rang,
Rattled and thumped in a listless way,
And now the wind in the chimney sang,
The wind in the chimney,
The wind in the chimney,
The wind in the chimney,
  Seemed to say:—
"Dream, boy, dream,
If you anywise can.
To dream is the work
Of beast or man.
Life is the west-going dream-storms' breath,
Life is a dream, the sigh of the skies,
The breath of the stars, that nod on their pillows
With their golden hair mussed over their eyes."
The locust played on his musical wing,
Sang to his mate of love's delight.
I heard the whippoorwill's soft fret.
I heard a cricket carolling,
I heard a cricket carolling,
I heard a cricket say: "Good-night, good-night,
Good-night, good-night, . . . good-night."

CHRIST'S COMING TO JUDGMENT

THOMAS DEKKER

As in a royal army, led by a king,
After the cannons' sulphurous thundering;
Horror on all sides roaring; wings here flying
At wings, like armed eagles; here, troops dying;
A butcherous execution through the field,
Bellowing with fiend-like threats, where yet none yield;
Though death stalks up and down, ghastly and pale,
The victor's wreath lying in a doubtful scale;—
The king himself, safeguarded on a hill,
Seeing this black day, yet stirring not until
He finds fit time to strike; then down, amain,
Worrying he comes—a glorious, dreadful train
Of high heroic spirit circling him round,
Who with swift vengeance do their foes confound,
And, slave-like, drag them at proud chariot-wheels,
Whilst miseries worse than death tread on their heels:—
So, but with greater terror, state, and wonder,
Heaven's Supreme Monarch—one hand gripping thunder;
The other, storms of hail, whirlwinds and fire—
(Ensigns of his hot-burning, quenchless ire,)
When the world's buildings smothered lay in smoke,
With sparkling eyes majestically broke
Out of his palace, ne'er set ope before,
And stood like a triumphant conqueror,
Trampling on Death and Hell. About him round,
Like petty viceroys, spirits, methought, all crown'd,
Show'd as if none but kings had been his guard;
Whole hierarchies of saints were then preferred,
With principalities, powers, and dominations,
Thrones, angels, and archangels, all at once
Filling the presence; then, like heaven-born twins,

Flew fiery cherubins and seraphins;
Whilst the old patriarchs, clothed all in white,
Were rapt with joy, to see beams far more bright,
About the prophets and the apostles run,
Than those whose flames were kindled at the sun.
Martyrs, methought, with self-same lustre shined
As gold which seven times was by fire refined;
Virgins, whose souls in life from lust liv'd clear,
Had silver robes, and on their heads did wear
Coronets of diamonds . . .
God's heir-apparent (here, once, made away)
Triumphed in this, his coronation-day,
In which heaven was his kingdom, mercy his throne,
Justice his sceptre, a communion
Of sanctified souls the courtly peers,
And his star-chamber lords; who now had years
Which never turned them grey by time's rough weather:
Greatness was now no more called fortune's feather,
Nor honour held a fruitless, golden dream,
Nor riches a bewitching swallowing stream,
Nor learning laughed at, as the beggar's dower,
Nor beauty's painted cheek a summer flower;
No, no: life endless was, yet without loathing,
Honour and greatness were immortal clothing,
Riches were subject to no base consuming,
Learning burnt bright without contentious fuming,
Beauty no painting bought, but still renew'd:
Each one had here his full beatitude.
  That face, whose picture might have ransomed kings,
Yet put up spittings, bafflings, buffetings,—
That head, which could a crown of stars have worn,
Yet spitefully was wrenched with wreaths of thorn,—
Those hands and feet, where purest stamps were set,
Yet nail'd up like to pieces counterfeit,—
Those lips, which, though they had command o'er all,

Being thirsty, vinegar had to drink, and gall,—
That body, scourged and torn with many a wound,
That his dear blood, like balm, might leave us sound,—
The well of life, which with a spear being tried,
Two streams mysterious gushed out from his side;—
Messias, great Jehovah, God on high,
Yet hail'd King of the Jews in mockery,—
The manger-cradled babe, the beggar born,
The poorest worm on earth, the height of scorn;—
That Lord, by his own subjects crucified,
Lo, at this grand assize, comes glorified,
With troops of angels, who his officers are,
To call by sound of trump his foes to a bar.
Thus stood he armed—justice his breastplate was,
Judgment his helmet, stronger far than brass;
On his right arm truth's shield he did advance:
And turned his sharpened wrath into a lance;
Out of his mouth a two-edged sword did fly,
To wound body and soul eternally:
Armed cap-à-pie thus, who 'gainst him durst fight?
There was no ground for strength nor yet for flight.
  At this, methought, all graves that ever held
Dead corses, yawn'd wide open, and compell'd
The bones of dead men up, with flesh, to rise;
Yea, those on whom the seas did tyrannize,
And drown'd in wrecks, and which were piece-meal eaten,
With lively bodies to the shores were beaten;
Whom sword or fire, gibbets or wheels had torn,
Had their own limbs again, and new were born;
From the first man God made to the last that died,
The names of all were here exemplified:
Emperors and kings, patriarchs, and tribes forgotten,
The conquerors of the world—moulder'd and rotten—
Lords, beggars, men and women, young and old,

Up, at a bar set forth, their hands did hold.
The Judge being set, in open court were laid
Huge books, at sight of which all were dismay'd,
Would fain have shrunk back, and fell down with fear;
In sheets of brass all stories written were
(Which those great volumes held) charactered deep
With pens of steel, eternal files to keep
Of every nation since the world began,
And every deed, word, thought, of every man.
Sins hatched in caves, or such whose bawd was night,
The minutes of the act, were here set right;
Great men, whose secret, damn'd sins vizards wore
So close, that none upon their brows could score
The least black line—because none durst—had here
A bill of items in particular,
What their souls owed for sin to death and hell;
Or, if it happened that they e'er did well,
In these true journals it at large was found,
And with rich promise of reward was crown'd.

LUCIFER IN STARLIGHT

GEORGE MEREDITH

On a starred night Prince Lucifer uprose.
Tired of his dark dominion swung the fiend
Above the rolling ball in cloud part screened,
Where sinners hugged their spectre of repose.
Poor prey to his hot fit of pride were those.
And now upon his western wing he leaned,
Now his huge bulk o'er Afric's sands careened,
Now the black planet shadowed Arctic snows.
Soaring through wider zones that pricked his scars
With memory of the old revolt from Awe,

He reached a middle height, and at the stars,
Which are the brain of heaven, he looked, and sank.
Around the ancient track marched, rank on rank,
The army of unalterable law.

MORTE D'ARTHUR

TENNYSON

So all day long the noise of battle roll'd
Among the mountains by the winter sea,
Until King Arthur's table, man by man,
Had fallen in Lyonness about their lord,
King Arthur; then, because his wound was deep,
The bold Sir Bedivere uplifted him,
Sir Bedivere, the last of all his knights,
And bore him to a chapel nigh the field,
A broken chancel with a broken cross,
That stood on a dark strait of barren land.
On one side lay the ocean, and on one
Lay a great water, and the moon was full.
  Then spake King Arthur to Sir Bedivere:
"The sequel of today unsolders all
The goodliest fellowship of famous knights
Whereof this world holds record. Such a sleep
They sleep—the men I loved. I think that we
Shall never more, at any future time,
Delight our souls with talk of knightly deeds,
Walking about the gardens and the halls
Of Camelot, as in the days that were.
I perish by this people which I made,—
Tho' Merlin sware that I should come again
To rule once more—but let what will be be,
I am so deeply smitten thro' the helm
That without help I cannot last till morn.

Thou therefore take my brand Excalibur,
Which was my pride; for thou rememberest how
In those old days, one summer noon, an arm
Rose up from out the bosom of the lake,
Clothed in white samite, mystic, wonderful,
Holding the sword—and how I row'd across
And took it, and have worn it, like a king;
And, wheresoever I am sung or told
In aftertime, this also shall be known.
But now delay not; take Excalibur,
And fling him far into the middle mere;
Watch what thou seest, and lightly bring me word."
  To him replied the bold Sir Bedivere:
"It is not meet, Sir King, to leave thee thus,
Aidless, alone, and smitten thro' the helm.
A little thing may harm a wounded man.
Yet I thy hest will all perform at full,
Watch what I see, and lightly bring thee word."
  So saying, from the ruin'd shrine he stept
And in the moon athwart the place of tombs,
Where lay the mighty bones of ancient men,
Old knights, and over them the sea-wind sang
Shrill, chill, with flakes of foam. He, stepping down
By zigzag paths and juts of pointed rock,
Came on the shining levels of the lake.
  There drew he forth the brand Excalibur,
And o'er him, drawing it, the winter moon,
Brightening the skirts of a long cloud, ran forth
And sparkled keen with frost against the hilt;
For all the haft twinkled with diamond sparks,
Myriads of topaz-lights, and jacinth-work
Of sublest jewellery. He gazed so long
That both his eyes were dazzled, as he stood,
This way and that dividing the swift mind,
In act to throw; but at the last it seem'd

Better to leave Excalibur conceal'd
There in the many-knotted water-flags,
That whistled stiff and dry about the marge.
So strode he back slow to the wounded king.
  Then spake King Arthur to Sir Bedivere:
"Hast thou perform'd my mission which I gave?
What is it thou hast seen, or what hast heard?"
  And answer made the bold Sir Bedivere:
"I heard the ripple washing in the reeds,
And the wild water lapping on the crag."
  To whom replied King Arthur, faint and pale:
"Thou hast betray'd thy nature and thy name,
Not rendering true answer, as beseem'd
Thy fealty, nor like a noble knight;
For surer sign had follow'd, either hand,
Or voice, or else a motion of the mere.
This is a shameful thing for men to lie.
Yet now, I charge thee, quickly go again
As thou art lief and dear, and do the thing
I bade thee, watch, and lightly bring me word."
  Then went Sir Bedivere the second time
Across the ridge, and paced beside the mere,
Counting the dewy pebbles, fix'd in thought;
But when he saw the wonder of the hilt,
How curiously and strangely chased, he smote
His palms together, and he cried aloud:
  "And if indeed I cast the brand away,
Surely a precious thing, one worthy note,
Should thus be lost forever from the earth,
Which might have pleased the eyes of many men.
What good should follow this, if this were done?
What harm, undone? deep harm to disobey,
Seeing obedience is the bond of rule.
Were it well to obey then, if a king demand
An act unprofitable, against himself?

The king is sick, and knows not what he does.
What record, or what relic of my lord
Should be to aftertime, but empty breath
And rumors of a doubt? but were this kept,
Stored in some treasure-house of mighty kings,
Some one might show it at a joust of arms,
Saying, 'King Arthur's sword, Excalibur,
Wrought by the lonely maiden of the lake;
Nine years she wrought it, sitting in the deeps
Upon the hidden bases of the hills.'
So might some old man speak in the aftertime
To all the people, winning reverence;
But now much honor and much fame were lost."
  So spake he, clouded with his own conceit,
And hid Excalibur the second time,
And so strode back slow to the wounded king.
  Then spoke King Arthur, breathing heavily:
"What is it thou hast seen, or what hast heard?"
  And answer made the bold Sir Bedivere:
"I heard the water lapping on the crag,
And the long ripple washing in the reeds."
  To whom replied King Arthur, much in wrath:
"Ah, miserable and unkind, untrue,
Unknightly, traitor-hearted! Woe is me!
Authority forgets a dying king,
Laid widow'd of the power in his eye
That bow'd the will. I see thee what thou art,
For thou, the latest-left of all my knights,
In whom should meet the offices of all,
Thou wouldst betray me for the precious hilt;
Either from lust of gold, or like a girl
Valuing the giddy pleasure of the eyes.
Yet, for a man may fail in duty twice,
And the third time may prosper, get thee hence;
But, if thou spare to fling Excalibur,

I will arise and slay thee with my hands."
  Then quickly rose Sir Bedivere, and ran,
And, leaping down the ridges lightly, plunged
Among the bulrush-beds, and clutch'd the sword,
And strongly wheel'd and threw it. The great brand
Made lightnings in the splendor of the moon,
And flashing round and round, and whirl'd in an arch,
Shot like a streamer of the northern morn,
Seen where the moving isles of winter shock
By night, with noises of the northern sea.
So flash'd and fell the brand Excalibur;
But ere he dipt the surface, rose an arm
Cloth'd in white samite, mystic, wonderful,
And caught him by the hilt, and brandish'd him
Three times, and drew him under in the mere.
And lightly went the other to the king.
  Then spake King Arthur, drawing thicker breath:
"Now see I by thine eyes that this is done.
Speak out; what is it thou hast heard, or seen?"
  And answer made the bold Sir Bedivere:
"Sir King, I closed mine eyelids, lest the gems
Should blind my purpose, for I never saw,
Nor shall see, here or elsewhere, till I die,
Not tho' I live three lives of mortal men,
So great a miracle as yonder hilt.
Then with both hands I flung him, wheeling him;
But when I look'd again, behold an arm,
Clothed in white samite, mystic, wonderful,
That caught him by the hilt, and brandish'd him
Three times, and drew him under in the mere."
  And answer made King Arthur, breathing hard:
"My end draws nigh; 'tis time that I were gone.
Make broad thy shoulders to receive my weight,
And bear me to the margin; yet I fear
My wound hath taken cold, and I shall die."

So saying, from the pavement he half rose,
Slowly, with pain, reclining on his arm,
And looking wistfully with wide blue eyes
As in a picture. Him Sir Bedivere
Remorsefully regarded thro' his tears,
And would have spoken, but he found not words,
Then took with care, and kneeling on one knee,
O'er both his shoulders drew the languid hands,
And rising bore him thro' the place of tombs.
But, as he walk'd, King Arthur panted hard,
Like one that feels a nightmare on his bed
When all the house is mute. So sigh'd the king,
Muttering and murmuring at his ear,
"Quick, quick!
I fear it is too late, and I shall die."
But the other swiftly strode from ridge to ridge,
Clothed with his breath, and looking, as he walk'd,
Larger than human on the frozen hills.
He heard the deep behind him, and a cry
Before. His own thought drove him like a goad.
Dry clash'd his harness in the icy caves
And barren chasms, and all to left and right
The bare black cliff clang'd round him, as he based
His feet on juts of slippery crag that rang
Sharp-smitten with the dint of armed heels—
And on a sudden, lo! the level lake,
And the long glories of the winter moon.
Then saw they how there hove a dusky barge,
Dark as a funeral scarf from stem to stern,
Beneath them; and descending they were ware
That all the decks were dense with stately forms
Black-stoled, black-hooded, like a dream—by these
Three queens with crowns of gold—and from them rose
A cry that shiver'd to the tingling stars,
And, as it were one voice, an agony

Of lamentation, like a wind that shrills
All night in a waste land, where no one comes,
Or hath come, since the making of the world.
  Then murmur'd Arthur, "Place me in the barge,"
And to the barge they came. There those three queens
Put forth their hands, and took the king, and wept.
But she that rose the tallest of them all
And fairest laid his head upon her lap,
And loosed the shatter'd casque, and chafed his hands,
And called him by his name, complaining loud,
And dropping bitter tears against his brow
Striped with dark blood; for all his face was white
And colorless, and like the wither'd moon
Smote by the fresh beam of the springing east;
And all his greaves and cuisses dash'd with drops
Of onset; and the light and lustrous curls—
That made his forehead like a rising sun
High from the dais-throne—were parch'd with dust;
Or, clotted into points and hanging loose,
Mix'd with the knightly growth that fringed his lips.
So like a shatter'd column lay the king;
Not like that Arthur who, with lance in rest,
From spur to plume a star of tournament,
Shot thro' the lists at Camelot, and charged
Before the eyes of ladies and of kings.
  Then loudly cried the bold Sir Bedivere:
"Ah! my Lord Arthur, whither shall I go?
Where shall I hide my forehead and my eyes?
For now I see the true old times are dead,
When every morning brought a noble chance,
And every chance brought out a noble knight.
Such times have been not since the light that led
The holy Elders with the gift of myrrh.
But now the whole Round Table is dissolved
Which was an image of the mighty world;

And I, the last, go forth companionless,
And the days darken round me, and the years,
Among new men, strange faces, other minds."
  And slowly answer'd Arthur from the barge:
"The old order changeth, yielding place to new,
And God fulfills himself in many ways,
Lest one good custom should corrupt the world.
Comfort thyself: what comfort is in me?
I have lived my life, and that which I have done
May He within himself make pure! but thou,
If thou shouldst never see my face again,
Pray for my soul. More things are wrought by prayer
Than this world dreams of. Wherefore, let thy voice
Rise like a fountain for me night and day.
For what are men better than sheep or goats
That nourish a blind life within the brain,
If, knowing God, they lift not hands of prayer
Both for themselves and those who call them friend?
For so the whole round earth is every way
Bound by gold chains about the feet of God.
But now farewell. I am going a long way
With these thou seest—if indeed I go—
For all my mind is clouded with a doubt—
To the island-valley of Avilion;
Where falls not hail, or rain, or any snow,
Nor ever wind blows loudly, but it lies
Deep-meadow'd, happy, fair with orchard lawns
And bowery hollows crown'd with summer sea,
Where I will heal me of my grievous wound."
  So said he, and the barge with oar and sail
Moved from the brink, like some full-breasted swan
That, fluting a wild carol ere her death,
Ruffles her pure cold plume, and takes the flood
With swarthy webs. Long stood Sir Bedivere
Revolving many memories, till the hull

Look'd one black dot against the verge of dawn,
And on the mere the wailing died away.

SATURN FALLEN

JOHN KEATS

Deep in the shady sadness of a vale
Far sunken from the healthy breath of morn,
Far from the fiery noon, and eve's one star,
Sat gray-hair'd Saturn, quiet as a stone,
Still as the silence round about his lair;
Forest on forest hung about his head
Like cloud on cloud. No stir of air was there,
Not so much life as on a summer's day
Robs not one light seed from the feather'd grass,
But where the dead leaf fell, there did it rest.
A stream went voiceless by, still deadened more
By reason of his fallen divinity
Spreading a shade: the Naiad 'mid her reeds
Press'd her cold finger closer to her lips.

Along the margin-sand large foot-marks went,
No further than to where his feet had stray'd,
And slept there since. Upon the sodden ground
His old right hand lay nerveless, listless, dead,
Unsceptred; and his realmless eyes were closed;
While his bow'd head seem'd list'ning to the Earth,
His ancient mother, for some comfort yet.
It seem'd no force could wake him from his place;
But there came one, who with a kindred hand
Touch'd his wide shoulders, after bending low
With reverence, though to one who knew it not.
She was a Goddess of the infant world;
By her in stature the tall Amazon

Had stood a pigmy's height: she would have ta'en
Achilles by the hair and bent his neck;
Or with a finger stay'd Ixion's wheel.
Her face was large as that of Memphian sphinx,
Pedestal'd haply in a palace court,
When sages look'd to Egypt for their lore.
But oh! how unlike marble was that face:
How beautiful, if sorrow had not made
Sorrow more beautiful than Beauty's self.
There was a listening fear in her regard,
As if calamity had but begun;
As if the vanward clouds of evil days
Had spent their malice, and the sullen rear
Was with its stored thunder labouring up.
One hand she press'd upon that aching spot
Where beats the human heart, as if just there,
Though an immortal, she felt cruel pain:
The other upon Saturn's bended neck
She laid, and to the level of his ear
Leaning with parted lips, some words she spake
In solemn tenour and deep organ tone:
Some mourning words, which in our feeble tongue
Would come in these like accents; O how frail
To that large utterance of the early Gods!
"Saturn, look up!—though wherefore, poor old King?
"I have no comfort for thee, no not one:
"I cannot say, 'O wherefore sleepest thou?'
"For heaven is parted from thee, and the earth
"Knows thee not, thus afflicted, for a God;
"And ocean too, with all its solemn noise,
"Has from thy sceptre pass'd; and all the air
"Is emptied of thine hoary majesty.
"Thy thunder, conscious of the new command,
"Rumbles reluctant o'er our fallen house;
"And thy sharp lightning in unpractised hands

"Scorches and burns our once serene domain.
"O aching time! O moments big as years!
"All as ye pass swell out the monstrous truth,
"And press it so upon our weary griefs
"That unbelief has not a space to breathe.
"Saturn, sleep on:—O thoughtless, why did I
"Thus violate thy slumbrous solitude?
"Why should I ope thy melancholy eyes?
"Saturn, sleep on! while at thy feet I weep." . . .

ENDYMION

EDNA ST. VINCENT MILLAY

Oh, sleep forever in the Latmian cave,
Mortal Endymion, darling of the Moon!
Her silver garments by the senseless wave
Shouldered and dropped and on the shingle strewn,
Her fluttering hand against her forehead pressed,
Her scattered looks that trouble all the sky,
Her rapid footsteps running down the west—
Of all her altered state oblivious lie!
Whom earthen you, by faultless lips adored,
Wild-eyed and stammering to the grasses thrust,
And deep into her crystal body poured
The hot and sorrowful sweetness of the dust:
Whereof she wanders mad, being all unfit
For mortal love, that might not die of it.

ARTEMIS PROLOGIZES

ROBERT BROWNING

I am a goddess of the ambrosial courts,
And save by Here, Queen of Pride, surpassed
By none whose temples whiten this the world.

Thro' heaven I roll my lucid moon along;
I shed in hell o'er my pale people peace;
On earth I, caring for the creatures, guard
Each pregnant yellow wolf and fox-bitch sleek,
And every feathered mother's callow brood,
And all that love green haunts and loneliness.
Of men, the chaste adore me, hanging crowns
Of poppies red to blackness, bell and stem,
Upon my image at Athenai here;
And this dead youth, Asclepios bends above,
Was dearest to me. He, my buskined step
To follow thro' the wild-wood leafy ways,
And chase the panting stag, or swift with darts
Stop the swift ounce, or lay the leopard low,
Neglected homage to another god:
Whence Aphrodite, by no midnight smoke
Of tapers lulled, in jealousy despatched
A noisome lust that, as the gadbee stings,
Possessed his stepdame Phaidra for himself
The son of Theseus her great absent spouse.
Hippolutos exclaiming in his rage
Against the fury of the Queen, she judged
Life insupportable; and, pricked at heart
An Amazonian stranger's race should dare
To scorn her, perished by the murderous cord:
Yet, ere she perished, blasted in a scroll
The fame of him her swerving made not swerve.
And Theseus read, returning, and believed,
And exiled, in the blindness of his wrath,
The man without a crime who, last as first,
Loyal, divulged not to his sire the truth.
Now Theseus from Poseidon had obtained
That of his wishes should be granted three,
And one he imprecated straight—"Alive
May ne'er Hippolutos reach other lands!"

Poseidon heard, ai ai! And scarce the prince
Had stepped into the fixed boots of the car
That give the feet stay against the strength
Of the Henetian horses, and around
His body flung the rein, and urged their speed
Along the rocks and shingles of the shore,
When from the gaping wave a monster flung
His obscene body in the coursers' path.
These, mad with terror, as the sea-bull sprawled
Wallowing about their feet, lost care of him
That reared them; and the master-chariot-pole
Snapping beneath their plunges like a reed,
Hippolutos, whose feet were trammeled fast,
Was yet dragged forward by the circling rein
Which either hand directed; nor they quenched
The frenzy of their flight before each trace,
Wheel-spoke and splinter of the woeful car,
Each boulder-stone, sharp stub and spiny shell,
Huge fish-bone wrecked and wreathed amid the sands
On that detested beach, was bright with blood
And morsels of his flesh: then fell the steeds
Head-foremost, crashing in their moonèd fronts,
Shivering with sweat, each white eye horror-fixed.
His people, who had witnessed all afar,
Bore back the ruins of Hippolutos.
But when his sire, too swoln with pride, rejoiced
(Indomitable as a man foredoomed)
That vast Poseidon had fulfilled his prayer,
I, in a flood of glory visible,
Stood o'er my dying votary and, deed
By deed, revealed, as all took place, the truth.
Then Theseus lay the woefullest of men,
And worthily; but ere the death-veils hid
His face, the murdered prince full pardon breathed
To his rash sire. Whereat Athenai wails.

So I, who ne'er forsake my votaries,
Lest in the cross-way none the honey-cake
Should tender, nor pour out the dog's hot life;
Lest at my fane the priest disconsolate
Should dress my image with some faded poor
Few crowns, made favours of, nor dare object
Such slackness to my worshipers who turn
Elsewhere the trusting heart and loaded hand,
As they had climbed Olumpos to report
Of Artemis and nowhere found her throne—
I interposed: and, this eventful night,—
(While round the funeral pyre the populace
Stood with fierce light on their black robes which bound
Each sobbing head, while yet their hair they clipped
O'er the dead body of their withered prince,
And, in his palace, Theseus prostrated
On the cold hearth, his brow cold as the slab
'Twas bruised on, groaned away the heavy grief—
As the pyre fell, and down the cross-logs crashed
Sending a crowd of sparkles thro' the night,
And the gay fire, elate with mastery,
Towered like a serpent o'er the clotted jars
Of wine, dissolving oils and frankincense,
And splendid gums like gold),—my potency
Conveyed the perished man to my retreat
In the thrice-venerable forest here.
And this white-bearded sage who squeezes now
The berried plant, is Phoibos' son of fame,
Asclepios, whom my radiant brother taught
The doctrine of each herb and flower and root,
To know their secret'st virtue and express
The saving soul of all: who so has soothed
With lavers the torn brow and murdered cheeks,
Composed the hair and brought its gloss again,
And called the red bloom to the pale skin back,

And laid the strips and jagged ends of flesh
Even once more, and slacked the sinew's knot
Of every tortured limb—that now he lies
As if mere sleep possessed him underneath
These interwoven oaks and pines. Oh cheer,
Divine presenter of the healing rod,
Thy snake, with ardent throat and lulling eye,
Twines his lithe spires around! I say, much cheer!
Proceed thou with thy wisest pharmacies!
And ye, white crowd of woodland sister-nymphs,
Ply as the sage directs, these buds and leaves
That strew the turf around the twain! While I
Await, in fitting silence, the event.

SAPPHICS

ALGERNON CHARLES SWINBURNE

All the night sleep came not upon my eyelids,
Shed not dew, nor shook nor unclosed a feather,
Yet with lips shut close and with eyes of iron
  Stood and beheld me.

Then to me so lying awake a vision
Came without sleep over the seas and touched me,
Softly touched mine eyelids and lips; and I too,
  Full of the vision,

Saw the white implacable Aphrodite,
Saw the hair unbound and the feet unsandalled
Shine as fire of sunset on western waters;
  Saw the reluctant

Feet, the straining plumes of the doves that drew her,
Looking always, looking with necks reverted,
Back to Lesbos, back to the hills whereunder
  Shone Mitylene;

SAPPHICS

Heard the flying feet of the Loves behind her
Make a sudden thunder upon the waters,
As the thunder flung from the strong unclosing
  Wings of a great wind.

So the goddess fled from her place, with awful
Sound of feet and thunder of wings around her;
While behind a clamor of singing women
  Severed the twilight.

Ah the singing, ah the delight, the passion!
All the Loves wept, listening; sick with anguish,
Stood the crowned nine Muses about Apollo;
  Fear was upon them,

While the tenth sang wonderful things they knew not.
Ah the tenth, the Lesbian! the nine were silent,
None endured the sound of her song for weeping;
  Laurel by laurel,

Faded all their crowns; but about her forehead,
Round her woven tresses and ashen temples
White as dead snow, paler than grass in summer,
  Ravaged with kisses,

Shown a light of fire as a crown forever.
Yea, almost the implacable Aphrodite
Paused, and almost wept; such a song was that song,
  Yea, by her name too,

Called her, saying, "Turn to me, O my Sappho";
Yet she turned her face from the Loves, she saw not
Tears for laughter darken immortal eyelids,
  Heard not about her

Fearful fitful wings of the doves departing,
Saw not how the bosom of Aphrodite
Shook with weeping, saw not her shaken raiment,
  Saw not her hands wrung;

Saw the Lesbians kissing across their smitten
Lutes with lips more sweet than the sound of lute-strings,
Mouth to mouth and hand upon hand, her chosen
  Fairer than all men;

Only saw the beautiful lips and fingers,
Full of songs and kisses and little whispers,
Full of music; only beheld among them
  Soar, as a bird soars

Newly fledged, her visible song, a marvel,
Made of perfect sound and exceeding passion,
Sweetly shapen, terrible, full of thunders,
  Clothed with the wind's wings.

Then rejoiced she, laughing with love, and scattered
Roses, awful roses of holy blossom;
Then the Loves thronged sadly with hidden faces
  Round Aphrodite,

Then the Muses, stricken at heart, were silent;
Yea, the gods waxed pale; such a song was that song.
All reluctant, all with a fresh repulsion,
  Fled from before her.

All withdrew long since, and the land was barren,
Full of fruitless women and music only.
Now perchance, when winds are assuaged at sunset,
  Lulled at the dewfall,

By the gray sea-side, unassuaged, unheard of,
Unbeloved, unseen in the ebb of twilight,
Ghosts of outcast women return lamenting,
  Purged not in Lethe,

Clothed about with flame and with tears, and singing
Songs that move the heart of the shaken heaven,
Songs that break the heart of the earth with pity,
  Hearing, to hear them.

THE CITY IN THE SEA

EDGAR ALLAN POE

Lo! Death has reared himself a throne
In a strange city lying alone
Far down within the dim West,
Where the good and the bad and the worst and the best
Have gone to their eternal rest.
There shrines and palaces and towers
(Time-eaten towers that tremble not!)
Resemble nothing that is ours.
Around, by lifting winds forgot,
Resignedly beneath the sky
The melancholy waters lie.

No rays from the holy heaven come down
On the long night-time of that town;
But light from out the lurid sea
Streams up the turrets silently—
Gleams up the pinnacles far and free—
Up domes—up spires—up kingly halls—
Up fanes—up Babylon-like walls—
Up shadowy long-forgotten bowers
Of sculptured ivy and stone flowers—

Up many and many a marvellous shrine
Whose wreathed friezes intertwine
The viol, the violet, and the vine.
Resignedly beneath the sky
The melancholy waters lie.
So blend the turrets and shadows there
That all seem pendulous in air,
While from a proud tower in the town
Death looks gigantically down.

There open fanes and gaping graves
Yawn level with the luminous waves
But not the riches there that lie
In each idol's diamond eye—
Not the gaily-jewelled dead
Tempt the waters from their bed;
For no ripples curl, alas!
Along that wilderness of glass—
No swellings tell that winds may be
Upon some far-off happier sea—
No heavings hint that winds have been
On seas less hideously serene.

But lo, a stir is in the air!
The wave—there is a movement there!
As if the towers had thrust aside,
In slightly sinking, the dull tide—
As if their tops had feebly given
A void within the filmy Heaven.
The waves have now a redder glow—
The hours are breathing faint and low—
And when, amid no earthly moans,
Down, down that town shall settle hence,
Hell, rising from a thousand thrones,
Shall do it reverence.

THE HAUNTED HOUSE

THOMAS HOOD

(Condensed version)

PART I

Some dreams we have are nothing else but dreams,
Unnatural, and full of contradictions;
Yet others of our most romantic schemes
Are something more than fictions.

It might be only on enchanted ground;
It might be merely by a thought's expansion;
But in the spirit, or the flesh, I found
An old deserted Mansion.

A residence for women, child, and man,
A dwelling-place,—and yet no habitation;
A House,—but under some prodigious ban
Of excommunication.

No dog was at the threshold, great or small;
No pigeon on the roof—no household creature—
No cat demurely dozing on the wall—
Not one domestic feature.

No human figure stirr'd, to go or come,
No face look'd forth from shut or open casement;
No chimney smoked—there was no sign of Home
From parapet to basement.

O'er all there hung a shadow and a fear;
A sense of mystery the spirit daunted,
And said, as plain as whisper in the ear,
The place is Haunted!

The wren had built within the Porch, she found
Its quiet loneliness so sure and thorough;
And on the lawn,—within its turfy mound,—
The rabbit made its burrow.

The rabbit wild and gray, that flitted thro'
The shrubby clumps, and frisk'd, and sat, and vanish'd,
But leisurely and bold, as if he knew
His enemy was banish'd.

No sound was heard except, from far away,
The ringing of the Whitwall's shrilly laughter,
Or, now and then, the chatter of the jay,
That Echo murmur'd after.

But Echo never mock'd the human tongue;
Some weighty crime, that Heaven could not pardon,
A secret curse on that old Building hung,
And its deserted Garden.

The vine unprun'd, and the neglected peach,
Droop'd from the wall with which they used to grapple;
And on the canker'd tree, in easy reach,
Rotted the golden apple.

But awfully the truant shunn'd the ground,
The vagrant kept aloof, and daring Poacher,
In spite of gaps that thro' the fences round
Invited the encroacher.

For over all there hung a cloud of fear,
A sense of mystery the spirit daunted,
And said, as plain as whisper in the ear,
The place is Haunted!

The pear and quince lay squander'd on the grass;
The mould was purple with unheeded showers
Of bloomy plums—a Wilderness it was
Of fruits, and weeds, and flowers!

The bear-bine with the lilac interlaced,
The sturdy bur-dock choked its slender neighbour,
The spicy pink. All tokens were effac'd
Of human care and labour.

The Fountain was a-dry—neglect and time
Had marr'd the work of artisan and mason,
And efts and croaking frogs, begot of slime,
Sprawled in the ruin'd bason.

The Statue, fallen from its marble base,
Amidst the refuse leaves, and herbage rotten,
Lay like the Idol of some bygone race,
Its names and rites forgotten.

On ev'ry side the aspect was the same,
All ruin'd, desolate, forlorn, and savage:
No hand or foot within the precinct came
To rectify or ravage.

For over all there hung a cloud of fear,
A sense of mystery the spirit daunted,
And said as plain as whisper in the ear,
The place is Haunted!

PART II

O, very gloomy is the House of Woe,
Where tears are falling while the bell is knelling,
With all the dark solemnities which show
That Death is in the dwelling!

O very, very dreary is the room
Where Love, domestic Love, no longer nestles,
But smitten by the common stroke of doom,
The Corpse lies on the trestles!

But House of Woe, and hearse, and sable pall,
The narrow home of the departed mortal,
Ne'er look'd so gloomy as that Ghostly Hall,
With its deserted portal!

Howbeit, the door I pushed—or so I dream'd—
Which slowly, slowly gaped,—the hinges creaking
With such a rusty eloquence, it seem'd
That Time himself was speaking.

But Time was dumb within that Mansion old,
Or left his tale to the heraldic banners,
That hung from the corroded walls, and told
Of former men and manners:—

The startled bats flew out—bird after bird—
The screech-owl overhead began to flutter,
And seem'd to mock the cry that she had heard
Some dying victim utter!

A shriek that echo'd from the joisted roof,
And up the stair, and further still and further,
Till in some ringing chamber far aloof
It ceased its tale of murther!

The window jingled in its crumbled frame,
And thro' its many gaps of destitution
Dolorous moans and hollow sighings came,
Like those of dissolution.

THE HAUNTED HOUSE

The wood-louse dropped and rolled into a ball,
Touch'd by some impulse occult or mechanic;
And nameless beetles ran along the wall
In universal panic.

The subtle spider, that from overhead
Hung like a spy on human guilt and error,
Suddenly turn'd, and up its slender thread
Ran with a nimble terror.

The very stains and fractures on the wall
Assuming features solemn and terrific,
Hinted some tragedy of that old Hall,
Lock'd up in Hieroglyphic.

Some tale that might, perchance, have solved the doubt,
Wherefore amongst those flags so dull and livid,
The banner of the Bloody Hand shone out
So ominously vivid.

Some key to that inscrutable appeal,
Which made the very frame of Nature quiver;
And every thrilling nerve and fibre feel
So ague-like a shiver.

For over all there hung a cloud of fear,
A sense of mystery the spirit daunted,
And said, as plain as whisper in the ear,
The place is Haunted!

If but a rat had lingered in the house,
To lure the thought into a social channel!
But not a rat remain'd, or tiny mouse,
To squeak behind the panel.

Huge drops roll'd down the walls, as if they wept;
And where the cricket used to chirp so shrilly,
The toad was squatting, and the lizard crept
On that damp hearth and chilly.

No mark of leathern jack or metal can,
No cup—no horn—no hospitable token—
All social ties between that board and Man
Had long ago been broken.

There was so foul a rumour in the air,
The shadow of a Presence so atrocious;
No human creature could have feasted there,
Even the most ferocious.

For over all there hung a cloud of fear,
A sense of mystery the spirit daunted,
And said, as plain as whisper in the ear,
The place is Haunted!

PART III

'Tis hard for human actions to account,
Whether from reason or from impulse only—
But some internal prompting bade me mount
The gloomy stairs and lonely.

Those gloomy stairs, so dark, and damp, and cold
With odours as from bones and relics carnal,
Deprived of rite, and consecrated mould,
The chapel vault, or charnel.

The air was thick—and in the upper gloom
The bat—or something in its shape—was winging,
And on the wall, as chilly as a tomb,
The Death's Head moth was clinging.

That mystic moth, which, with a sense profound
Of all unholy presence, augurs truly;
And with a grim significance flits round
The taper burning bluely.

Such omens in the place there seem'd to be,
At ev'ry crooked turn, or on the landing,
The straining eyeball was prepared to see
Some Apparition standing.

For over all there hung a cloud of fear,
A sense of mystery the spirit daunted,
And said, as plain as whisper in the ear,
The place is Haunted.

Yet no portentous Shape the sight amaz'd;
Each object plain, and tangible, and valid;
But from their tarnish'd frames dark Figures gaz'd,
And Faces spectre-pallid.

Not merely with the mimic life that lies
Within the compass of Art's simulation;
Their souls were looking thro' their painted eyes
With awful speculation.

On every lip a speechless horror dwelt;
On ev'ry brow the burthen of affliction;
The old Ancestral Spirits knew and felt
The House's malediction.

No other sound or stir of life was there,
Except my steps in solitary clamber,
From flight to flight, from humid stair to stair,
From chamber into chamber.

Deserted rooms of luxury and state,
That old magnificence had richly furnish'd
With pictures, cabinets of ancient date,
And carvings gilt and burnish'd.

Rich hangings, storied by the needle's art,
With scripture history, or classic fable;
But all had faded, save one ragged part,
Where Cain was slaying Abel.

The silent waste of mildew and the moth
Had marr'd the tissue with a partial ravage;
But undecaying frown'd upon the cloth
Each feature stern and savage.

The sky was pale; the cloud a thing of doubt;
Some hues were fresh, and some decay'd and duller;
But still the Bloody Hand shone strangely out
With vehemence of colour!

The Bloody Hand that with a lurid stain
Shone on the dusty floor, a dismal token,
Projected from the casement's painted pane,
Where all beside was broken.

The Bloody Hand significant of crime,
That glaring on the old heraldic banner,
Had kept its crimson unimpair'd by time,
In such a wondrous manner!

O'er all there hung the shadow of a fear,
A sense of mystery the spirit daunted,
And said, as plain as whisper in the ear,
The place is Haunted!

THE HAUNTED HOUSE

The Death watch tick'd behind the panel'd oak,
Inexplicable tremors shook the arras,
And echoes strange and mystical awoke,
The fancy to embarrass.

Prophetic hints that filled the soul with dread,
But thro' one gloomy entrance pointing mostly,
The while some secret inspiration said
That Chamber is the Ghostly!

Across the door no gossamer festoon
Swung pendulous—no web—no dusty fringes,
No silky chrysalis or white cocoon
About its nooks and hinges.

The spider shunn'd the interdicted room,
The moth, the beetle, and the fly were banish'd,
And where the sunbeam fell athwart the gloom,
The very midge had vanish'd.

One lonely ray that glanc'd upon a Bed,
As if with awful aim direct and certain,
To show the Bloody Hand in burning red
Embroider'd on the curtain.

And yet no gory stain was on the quilt—
The pillow in its place had slowly rotted;
The floor alone retain'd the trace of guilt,
Those boards obscurely spotted.

Obscurely spotted to the door, and thence
With mazy doubles to the grated casement—
Oh what a tale they told of fear intense,
Of horror and amazement!

What human creature in the dead of night
Had coursed like hunted hare that cruel distance?
Had sought the door, the window in his flight,
Striving for dear existence?

What shrieking Spirit in that bloody room
Its mortal frame had violently quitted?—
Across the sunbeam, with a sudden gloom,
A ghostly Shadow flitted.

Across the sunbeam, and along the wall,
But painted on the air so very dimly,
It hardly veil'd the tapestry at all,
Or portrait frowning grimly.

O'er all there hung the shadow of a fear,
A sense of mystery the spirit daunted,
And said, as plain as whisper in the ear,
The place is Haunted!

ATAVISM

ELINOR WYLIE

I always was afraid of Somes's Pond:
Not the little pond, by which the willow stands,
Where laughing boys catch alewives in their hands
In brown, bright shallows; but the one beyond.
There, when the frost makes all the birches burn
Yellow as cow-lilies, and the pale sky shines
Like a polished shell between black spruce and pines,
Some strange thing tracks us, turning where we turn.

You'll say I dream it, being the true daughter
Of those who in old times endured this dread.

EVE

Look! Where the lily-stems are showing red
A silent paddle moves below the water,
A sliding shape has stirred them like a breath;
Tall plumes surmount a painted mask of death.

EVE

RALPH HODGSON

Eve, with her basket, was
Deep in the bells and grass,
Wading in bells and grass
Up to her knees,
Picking a dish of sweet
Berries and plums to eat,
Down in the bells and grass
Under the trees.

Mute as a mouse in a
Corner the cobra lay,
Curled round a bough of the
Cinnamon tall . . .
Now to get even and
Humble proud heaven and
Now was the moment or
Never at all.

"Eva!" Each syllable
Light as a flower fell,
"Eva!" he whispered the
Wondering maid,
Soft as a bubble sung
Out of a linnet's lung,
Soft and most silverly
"Eva!" he said.

BEYOND REALITY

Picture that orchard sprite,
Eve, with her body white,
Supple and smooth to her
Slim finger tips,
Wondering, listening,
Listening, wondering,
Eve with a berry
Half-way to her lips.

Oh had our simple Eve
Seen through the make-believe!
Had she but known the
Pretender he was!
Out of the boughs he came,
Whispering still her name,
Tumbling in twenty rings
Into the grass.

Here was the strangest pair
In the world anywhere,
Eve in the bells and grass
Kneeling, and he
Telling his story low . . .
Singing birds saw them go
Down the dark path to
The Blasphemous Tree.

Oh what a clatter when
Titmouse and Jenny Wren
Saw him successful and
Taking his leave!
How the birds rated him,
How they all hated him!
How they all pitied
Poor motherless Eve!

EVE

Picture her crying
Outside in the lane,
Eve, with no dish of sweet
Berries and plums to eat,
Haunting the gate of the
Orchard in vain . . .
Picture the lewd delight
Under the hill to-night—
"Eva!" the toast goes round,
"Eva!" again.

PART III

RIDING WITH TIME AND ACTION

A BALLAD OF HELL

JOHN DAVIDSON

"A letter from my love today!
  Oh, unexpected, dear appeal!"
She struck a happy tear away,
  And broke the crimson seal.

"My love, there is no help on earth,
  No help in heaven; the dead-man's bell
Must toll our wedding; our first hearth
  Must be the well-paved floor of hell."

The color died from out her face,
  Her eyes like ghostly candles shone;
She cast dread looks about the place,
  Then clenched her teeth and read right on

"I may not pass the prison door;
  Here must I rot from day to day,
Unless I wed whom I abhor,
  My cousin, Blanche of Valencay.

"At midnight with my dagger keen,
  I'll take my life; it must be so.
Meet me in hell tonight, my queen,
  For weal and woe."

She laughed, although her face was wan,
  She girded on her golden belt,
She took her jewelled ivory fan,
  And at her glowing missal knelt.

Then rose, "And am I mad?" she said:
She broke her fan, her belt untied;

With leather girt herself instead,
  And stuck a dagger at her side.

She waited, shuddering in her room,
  Till sleep had fallen on all the house.
She never flinched; she faced her doom:
  They two must sin to keep their vows.

Then out into the night she went,
  And, stooping, crept by hedge and tree;
Her rose-bush flung a snare of scent,
  And caught a happy memory.

She fell, and lay a minute's space;
  She tore the sward in her distress;
The dewy grass refreshed her face;
  She rose and ran with lifted dress.

She started like a morn-caught ghost
  Once when the moon came out and stood
To watch; the naked road she crossed,
  And dived into the murmuring wood.

The branches snatched her streaming cloak;
  A live thing shrieked; she made no stay!
She hurried to the trysting-oak—
  Right well she knew the way.

Without a pause she bared her breast,
  And dived into the murmuring wood.
And lay like one that takes her rest,
  And died and wakened up in hell.

She bathed her spirit in the flame,
  And near the center took her post;

A BALLAD OF HELL

From all sides to her ears there came
  The dreary anguish of the lost.

The devil started at her side,
  Comely, and tall, and black as jet.
"I am young Malespina's bride;
  Has he come hither yet?"

"My poppet, welcome to your bed."
  "Is Malespina here?"
"Not he! Tomorrow he must wed
  His cousin Blanche, my dear!"

"You lie, he died with me tonight."
  "Not he! it was a plot" . . . "You lie."
"My dear, I never lie outright."
  "We died at midnight, he and I."

The devil went. Without a groan
  She, gathered up in one fierce prayer,
Took root in hell's midst all alone,
  And waited for him there.

She dared to make herself at home
  Amidst the wail, the uneasy stir.
The blood-stained flame that filled the dome,
  Scentless and silent, shrouded her.

How long she stayed I cannot tell;
  But when she felt his perfidy,
She marched across the floor of hell;
  And all the damned stood up to see.

The devil stopped her at the brink:
  She shook him off; she cried, "Away!"

"My dear, you have gone mad, I think."
  "I was betrayed: I will not stay."

Across the weltering deep she ran;
  A stranger thing was never seen:
The damned stood silent to a man;
  They saw the great gulf set between.

To her it seemed a meadow fair;
  And flowers sprang up about her feet.
She entered heaven; she climbed the stair
  And knelt down at the mercy-seat.

Seraphs and saints with one great voice
  Welcomed that soul that knew not fear.
Amazed to find it could rejoice,
  Hell raised a hoarse, half-human cheer.

THE EXECUTION OF KING CHARLES

ANDREW MARVELL

  While round the armed bands
  Did clap their bloody hands:
He nothing common did, or mean,
Upon that memorable scene,
  But with his keener eye
  The axe's edge did try;
Nor called the gods with vulgar spite
To vindicate his helpless right,
  But bowed his comely head
  Down, as upon a bed.

A PRAIRIE RIDE

WILLIAM VAUGHN MOODY

I

When I look back and say, of all our hours
This one or that was best,
Straightway, from north and south, from east and west,
With banners strange and tributary powers
The others camp against me. Thus,
Now for many nights and days,
The hills of memory are mutinous,
Hearing me raise
Above all other praise
That autumn morn
When league on league between ripe fields of corn,
Galloping neck and neck or loitering hand in hand,
We rode across the prairie land
Where I was born.

II

I never knew how good
Were those fields and happy farms,
Till, leaning from her horse, she stretched her arms
To greet and to receive them; nor for all
My knowing, did I know her womanhood
Until I saw the gesture understood,
And answer made, and amity begun.
On the proud fields and on her proud bent head
The sunlight like a covenant did fall;
Then with a gesture rich and liberal
She raised her hands with laughter to the sun,—
And it was done,
Never in life or death to be gainsaid!

And I, till then,
Home-come yet alien,
Held by some thwart and skeptic mind aloof
From nature's dear behoof,
Knelt down in heart and kissed the kindly earth,
And, having swept on wings of mirth
The big horizon round, I swiftly clomb,
And from the utter dome
Of most high morning laughed, and sang my loved one home!
Meanwhile, within the rings our laughter made,
Bending like a water-arum
Where impetuous waters meet,
Rhythmic to the strong alarum,
Of her horse's rushing feet,
Before me and beside me and on before me swayed
Her body like a water-arum blade,
Like a slanted gull for motion,
And the blown corn like an ocean
For its billows and their rumor, and the tassels snapping free
As whittled foam and brine-scud of the sea.
Thanks to God,
No ocean, but the rife and homely sod,
And golden corn to feed
A universe at need!
Land of mine, my mother's country!
My heritage!—But through her loosening hair
She has tossed me back the dare.
Drunken-hearted! shall it be a race indeed?
Then drink again, and drink again, to reeling drink the winy
speed!

III

Ye on the jealous hills,
Ye shall not have your wills
For many a dreaming day

And haunted night.
To that high morning, walled and domed with light,
I am given away;
And often here, above the weary feet
That pour along this fierce and jaded street,
As from a taintless source
Of power and grace,
Anxious and shrill and sweet
I hear her strong unblemished horse
Neigh to the pastured mothers of the race.

DANNY

J. M. SYNGE

One night a score of Erris men,
A score I'm told and nine,
Said, "We'll get shut of Danny's noise
Of girls and widows dyin'.

"There's not his like from Binghamstown
To Boyle and Ballycroy,
At playing hell on decent girls,
At beating man and boy.

"He's left two pairs of female twins
Beyond in Killacreest,
And twice in Crossmolina fair
He's struck the parish priest.

"But we'll come round him in the night
A mile beyond the Mullet;
Ten will quench his bloody eyes,
And ten will choke his gullet."

It wasn't long till Danny came,
From Bangor making way,
And he was damning moon and stars
And whistling grand and gay.

Till in a gap of hazel glen—
And not a hare in sight—
Out lepped the nine-and-twenty lads
Along his left and right.

Then Danny smashed the nose on Byrne,
He split the lips on three,
And bit across the right hand thumb
On one Red Shawn Magee.

But seven tripped him up behind,
And seven kicked before,
And seven squeezed around his throat
Till Danny kicked no more.

Then some destroyed him with their heels,
Some tramped him in the mud,
Some stole his purse and timber pipe,
And some washed off the blood.

. . . .

And when you're walking out the way
From Bangor to Belmulet,
You'll see a flat cross on a stone
Where men choked Danny's gullet.

LONELY HOUSE

EMILY DICKINSON

I know some lonely houses off the road
A robber'd like the look of,—

LONELY HOUSE

Wooden barred,
And windows hanging low,
Inviting to
A portico,

Where two could creep:
One hand the tools,
The other peep
To make sure all's asleep.
Old-fashioned eyes,
Not easy to surprise!

How orderly the kitchen'd look by night,
With just a clock,—
But they could gag the tick,
And mice won't bark;
And so the walls don't tell,
None will.

A pair of spectacles ajar just stir—
An almanac's aware.
Was it the mat winked,
Or a nervous star?
The moon slides down the stair
To see who's there.

There's plunder,—where?
Tankard, or spoon,
Earring, or stone,
A watch, some ancient brooch
To match the grandmamma,
Staid sleeping there.

Day rattles, too,
Stealth's slow;

The sun has got as far
As the third sycamore.
Screams chanticleer,
"Who's there?"

And echoes, trains away,
Sneer—"Where?"
While the old couple, just astir,
Think that the sunrise left the door ajar!

IS MY TEAM PLOWING?

A. E. HOUSMAN

"Is my team ploughing,
  That I was used to drive
And hear the harness jingle
  When I was man alive?"

Ay, the horses trample,
  The harness jingles now;
No change though you lie under
  The land you used to plough.

"Is football playing
  Along the river shore,
With lads to chase the leather,
  Now I stand up no more?"

Ay, the ball is flying,
  The lads play heart and soul;
The goal stands up, the keeper,
  Stands up to keep the goal.

"Is my girl happy,
  That I thought hard to leave,

And has she tired of weeping
  As she lies down at eve?"

Ay, she lies down lightly,
  She lies not down to weep:
Your girl is well contented.
  Be still, my lad, and sleep.

"Is my friend hearty,
  Now I am thin and pine,
And has he found to sleep in
  A better bed than mine?"

Yes, lad, I lie easy,
  I lie as lads would choose;
I cheer a dead man's sweetheart,
  Never ask me whose.

THE REVENGE OF HAMISH

SIDNEY LANIER

It was three slim does and a ten-tined buck in the bracken lay;
  And all of a sudden the sinister smell of a man,
  Awaft on a wind-shift, wavered and ran
Down the hill-side and sifted along through the bracken and passed that way.

Then Nan got a-tremble at nostril; she was the daintiest doe;
  In the print of her velvet flank on the velvet fern
  She reared, and rounded her ears in turn.
Then the buck leapt up, and his head as a king's to a crown did go

Full high in the breeze, and he stood as if Death had the form of a deer;

And the two slim does long lazily stretching arose,
For their day-dream slowlier came to a close,
Till they woke and were still, breath-bound with waiting and wonder and fear.

Then Alan the huntsman sprang over the hillock, the hounds shot by,
The does and the ten-tined buck made a marvellous bound,
The hounds swept after with never a sound,
But Alan loud winded his horn in sign that the quarry was nigh.

For at dawn of that day proud Maclean of Lochbuy to the hunt had waxed wild,
And he cursed at old Alan till Alan fared off with the hounds
For to drive him the deer to the lower glen-grounds:
"I will kill a red deer," quoth Maclean, "in the sight of the wife and the child."

So gayly he paced with the wife and the child to his chosen stand;
But he hurried tall Hamish the henchman ahead: "Go turn,"—
Cried Maclean—"if the deer seek to cross to the burn,
Do thou turn them to me: nor fail, lest thy back be as red as thy hand."

Now hard-fortuned Hamish, half blown of his breath with the height of the hill,
Was white in the face when the ten-tined buck and the does
Drew leaping to burn-ward; huskily rose
His shouts, and his nether lip twitched, and his legs were o'er-weak for his will.

So the deer darted lightly by Hamish and bounded away to the burn.

But Maclean never bating his watch tarried waiting below;
Still Hamish hung heavy with fear for to go
All the space of an hour; then he went, and his face was greenish and stern,

And his eye sat back in the socket, and shrunken the eye-balls shone,
As withdrawn from a vision of deeds it were shame to see.
"Now, now, grim henchman, what is't with thee?"
Brake Maclean, and his wrath rose red as a beacon the wind hath upblown.

"Three does and a ten-tined buck made out," spoke Hamish, full mild,
"And I ran for to turn, but my breath it was blown, and they passed;
I was weak, for ye called ere I broke me my fast."
Cried Maclean: "Now a ten-tined buck in the sight of the wife and the child

I had killed if the gluttonous kern had not wrought me a snail's own wrong!"
Then he sounded, and down came kinsmen and clansmen all:
"Ten blows, for ten tine, on his back let fall,
And reckon no stroke if the blood follow not at the bite of the thong!"

So Hamish made bare, and took him his strokes; at the last he smiled.
"Now I'll to the burn," quoth Maclean, "for it still may be,
If a slimmer-paunched henchman will hurry with me,
I shall kill me the ten-tined buck for a gift to the wife and the child!"

Then the clansmen departed, by this path and that; and over the hill

Sped Maclean with an outward wrath for an inward shame;
And that place of the lashing full quiet became;
And the wife and the child stood sad; and bloody-backed Hamish sat still.

But look! red Hamish has risen; quick about and about turns he.
"There is none betwixt me and the crag-top!" he screams under breath.
Then, livid as Lazarus lately from death,
He snatches the child from the mother, and clambers the crag toward the sea.

Now the mother drops breath; she is dumb, and her heart goes dead for a space,
Till the motherhood, mistress of death, shrieks, shrieks through the glen,
And that place of the lashing is live with men,
And Maclean, and the gillie that told him, dash up in a desperate race.

Not a breath's time for asking; an eye-glance reveals all the tale untold.
They follow mad Hamish afar up the crag toward the sea,
And the lady cries: "Clansmen, run for a fee!—
Yon castle and lands to the two first hands that shall hook him and hold

Fast Hamish back from the brink!"—and ever she flies up the steep,
And the clansmen pant, and they sweat, and they jostle and strain.
But, mother, 'tis vain; but, father, 'tis vain;
Stern Hamish stands bold on the brink, and dangles the child o'er the deep.

Now a faintness falls on the men that run, and they all stand still.
And the wife prays Hamish as if he were God, on her knees,
Crying: "Hamish! O Hamish! but please, but please
For to spare him!" and Hamish still dangles the child, with a wavering will.

On a sudden he turns; with a sea-hawk scream, and a gibe, and a song,
Cries: "So; I will spare ye the child if, in sight of ye all,
Ten blows on Maclean's bare back shall fall,
And ye reckon no stroke if the blood follows not at the bite of the thong!"

Then Maclean he set hardly his tooth to his lip that his tooth was red
Breathed short for a space, said: "Nay, but it never shall be!
Let me hurl off the damnable hound in the sea!"
But the wife: "Can Hamish go fish us the child from the sea, if dead?

Say yea!—Let them lash *me,* Hamish?"—"Nay!"—"Husband, the lashing will heal;
But, oh, who will heal me the bonny sweet bairn in his grave?
Could ye cure me my heart with the death of a knave?
Quick Love! I will bare thee—so—kneel!" Then Maclean 'gan slowly to kneel

With never a word, till presently downward he jerked to the earth.
Then the henchman—he that smote Hamish—would tremble and lag;
"Strike hard!" quoth Hamish, full stern, from the crag;
Then he struck him, and "One!" sang Hamish, and danced with the child in his mirth.

And no man spake beside Hamish; he counted each stroke with a song.
When the last stroke fell, then he moved him a pace down the height,
And he held forth the child in the heartaching sight
Of the mother, and looked all pitiful grave, as repenting a wrong.

And there as the motherly arms stretched out with the thanksgiving prayer—
And there as the mother crept up with a fearful swift pace,
Till her finger nigh felt of the bairnie's face—
In a flash fierce Hamish turned round and lifted the child in the air,

And sprang with the child in his arms from the horrible height in the sea,
Still screeching, "Revenge!" in the wind-rush; and pallid Maclean,
Age-feeble with anger and impotent pain,
Crawled up on the crag, and lay flat, and locked hold of dead roots of a tree—

And gazed hungrily o'er, and the blood from his back drip-dripped in the brine,
And a sea-hawk flung down a skeleton fish as he flew,
And the mother stared white on the waste of blue,
And the wind drove a cloud to seaward, and the sun began to shine.

THE CHERRY-TREE CAROL

UNKNOWN

Joseph was an old man,
And an old man was he,

When he wedded Mary
  In the land of Galilee.

Joseph and Mary walk'd
  Through an orchard good,
Where was cherries and berries
  So red as any blood.

Joseph and Mary walk'd
  Through an orchard green,
Where was berries and cherries
  As thick as might be seen.

O then bespoke Mary,
  So meek and so mild,
"Pluck me one cherry, Joseph,
  For I am with child."

O then bespoke Joseph
  With words so unkind,
"Let him pluck thee a cherry
  That brought thee with child."

O then bespoke the babe
  Within his mother's womb,
"Bow down then the tallest tree
  For my mother to have some."

Then bow'd down the highest tree
  Unto his mother's hand:
Then she cried, "See, Joseph,
  I have cherries at command!"

O then bespake Joseph—
  "I have done Mary wrong;

But cheer up, my dearest,
  And be not cast down.

"O eat your cherries, Mary,
  O eat your cherries now;
O eat your cherries, Mary,
  That grow upon the bough."

Then Mary pluck'd a cherry
  As red as the blood;
Then Mary went home
  With her heavy load.

JOLY WAT

UNKNOWN

Can I not sing but "Hoy,"
Whan the joly shepard made so much joy?

I

The shepard upon a hill he sat;
He had on him his tabard and his hat,
His tarbox, his pipe, and his flagat;
His name was callèd Joly Joly Wat,
  For he was a gud herdés boy.
      Ut hoy!
  For in his pipe he made so much joy.

II

The shepard upon a hill was laid;
His dog unto his girdell was taid;
He had not slept but a litill braid,
But "Gloria in excelsis" was to him said.
      Ut hoy!
  For in his pipe he made so much joy.

---

tabard—short coat; *flagat*—flask; *taid*—tied; *braid*—time.

III

The shepard on a hill he stode;
Round about him his shepe they yode;
He put his hond under his hode,
He saw a star as rede as blode.
Ut hoy!
For in his pipe he made so much joy.

IV

The shepard said anon right,
"I will go see yon ferly sight,
Whereas the angel singeth on hight,
And the star that shineth so bright."
Ut hoy!
For in his pipe he made so much joy.

V

"Now farewell, Mall, and also Will!
For my love go ye all still
Unto I cum again you till,
And evermore, Will, ring well thy bell."
Ut hoy!
For in his pipe he made so much joy.

VI

"Now must I go there Crist was born;
Farewell! I cum again to-morn.
Dog, kepe well my shepe fro the corn,
And warn well 'Warroke' when I blow my horn!"
Ut hoy!
For in his pipe he made so much joy.

---

yode—went; *hode*—hood; *ferly*—marvellous.

VII

Whan Wat to Bedlem cumen was,
He swet, he had gone faster than a pace;
He found Jesu in a simpell place,
Between an ox but and an asse.
Ut hoy!
For in his pipe he made so much joy.

VIII

"Jesu, I offer to thee here my pipe,
My skirt, my tar box, and my scrip;
Home to my felowes now will I skip,
And also look unto my shepe."
Ut hoy!
For in his pipe he made so much joy.

IX

"Now farewell, mine owne herdesman Wat!"—
"Yea, for God, lady, even so I hat;
Lull well Jesu in thy lap,
And farewell, Joseph, with thy round cap!"
Ut hoy!
For in his pipe he made so much joy.

X

"Now may I well both hope and sing,
For I have bene at Cristes bering;
Home to my felowes now will I fling.
Crist of heven to his bliss us bring!"
Ut hoy!
For in his pipe he made so much joy.

hat—am hight, called.

MR. FLOOD'S PARTY

EDWIN ARLINGTON ROBINSON

Old Eben Flood, climbing alone one night
Over the hill between the town below
And the forsaken upland hermitage
That held as much as he should ever know
On earth again of home, paused warily.
The road was his with not a native near;
And Eben, having leisure, said aloud,
For no man else in Tilbury Town to hear:

"Well, Mr. Flood, we have the harvest moon
Again, and we may not have many more;
The bird is on the wing, the poet says,
And you and I have said it here before.
Drink to the bird." He raised up to the light
The jug that he had gone so far to fill,
And answered huskily: "Well, Mr. Flood,
Since you propose it, I believe I will."

Alone, as if enduring to the end
A valiant armor of scarred hopes outworn,
He stood there in the middle of the road
Like Roland's ghost winding a silent horn.
Below him, in the town among the trees,
Where friends of other days had honored him,
A phantom salutation of the dead
Rang thinly till old Eben's eyes were dim.

Then, as a mother lays her sleeping child
Down tenderly, fearing it may awake,
He set the jug down slowly at his feet

With trembling care, knowing that most things break;
And only when assured that on firm earth
It stood, as the uncertain lives of men
Assuredly did not, he paced away,
And with his hand extended paused again:

"Well, Mr. Flood, we have not met like this
In a long time; and many a change has come
To both of us, I fear, since last it was
We had a drop together. Welcome home!"
Convivially returning with himself,
Again he raised the jug up to the light;
And with an acquiescent quaver said:
"Well, Mr. Flood, if you insist, I might.

"Only a very little, Mr. Flood—
For auld lang syne. No more, sir; that will do."
So, for the time, apparently it did,
And Eben evidently thought so too;
For soon amid the silver loneliness
Of night he lifted up his voice and sang,
Secure, with only two moons listening,
Until the whole harmonious landscape rang—

"For auld lang syne." The weary throat gave out,
The last word wavered, and the song was done.
He raised again the jug regretfully
And shook his head, and was again alone.
There was not much that was ahead of him,
And there was nothing in the town below—
Where strangers would have shut the many doors
That many friends had opened long ago.

MAUD MULLER

JOHN GREENLEAF WHITTIER

Maud Muller on a summer's day,
Raked the meadow sweet with hay.

Beneath her torn hat glowed the wealth
Of simple beauty and rustic health.

Singing, she wrought, and her merry glee
The mock-bird echoed from his tree.

But when she glanced to the far-off town,
White from its hill-slope looking down,

The sweet song died, and a vague unrest
And a nameless longing filled her breast,—

A wish that she hardly dared to own,
For something better than she had known.

The Judge rode slowly down the lane,
Smoothing his horse's chestnut mane.

He drew his bridle in the shade
Of the apple-trees, to greet the maid,

And asked a draught from the spring that flowed
Through the meadow across the road.

She stooped where the cool spring bubbled up,
And filled for him her small tin cup,

And blushed as she gave it, looking down
On her feet so bare, and her tattered gown.

"Thanks!" said the Judge; "a sweeter draught
From a fairer hand was never quaffed."

He spoke of the grass and flowers and trees,
Of the singing birds and the humming bees;

Then talked of the haying, and wondered whether
The cloud in the west would bring foul weather.

And Maud forgot her brier-torn gown,
And her graceful ankles bare and brown;

And listened, while a pleased surprise
Looked from her long-lashed hazel eyes.

At last, like one who for delay
Seeks a vain excuse, he rode away.

Maud Muller looked and sighed: "Ah me!
That I the Judge's bride might be!

"He would dress me up in silks so fine,
And praise and toast me at his wine.

"My father should wear a broadcloth coat;
My brother should sail a painted boat.

"I'd dress my mother so grand and gay,
And the baby should have a new toy each day.

"And I'd feed the hungry and clothe the poor,
And all should bless me who left our door."

The Judge looked back as he climbed the hill,
And saw Maud Muller standing still.

MAUD MULLER

"A form more fair, a face more sweet,
Ne'er hath it been my lot to meet.

"And her modest answer and graceful air
Show her wise and good as she is fair.

"Would she were mine, and I to-day,
Like her, a harvester of hay;

"No doubtful balance of rights and wrongs,
Nor weary lawyers with endless tongues,

"But low of cattle and song of birds,
And health and quiet and loving words."

But he thought of his sisters, proud and cold,
And his mother, vain of her rank and gold.

So, closing his heart, the Judge rode on,
And Maud was left in the field alone.

But the lawyers smiled that afternoon,
When he hummed in court an old love-tune;

And the young girl mused beside the well
Till the rain on the unraked clover fell.

He wedded a wife of richest dower,
Who lived for fashion, as he for power.

Yet oft, in his marble hearth's bright glow,
He watched a picture come and go;

And sweet Maud Muller's hazel eyes
Looked out in their innocent surprise.

Oft, when the wine in his glass was red,
He longed for the wayside well instead;

And closed his eyes on his garnished rooms
To dream of meadows and clover-blooms.

And the proud man sighed, with a secret pain,
"Ah, that I were free again!

"Free as when I rode that day,
Where the barefoot maiden raked her hay."

She wedded a man unlearned and poor,
And many children played round her door.

But care and sorrow, and childbirth pain,
Left their traces on heart and brain.

And oft, when the summer sun shone hot
On the new-mown hay in the meadow lot,

And she heard the little spring brook fall
Over the roadside, through the wall,

In the shade of the apple-tree again
She saw a rider draw his rein;

And, gazing down with timid grace,
She felt his pleased eyes read her face.

Sometimes her narrow kitchen walls
Stretched away into stately halls;

The weary wheel to a spinnet turned,
The tallow candle an astral burned,

And for him who sat by the chimney lug,
Dozing and grumbling o'er pipe and mug,

A manly form at her side she saw,
And joy was duty and love was law.

Then she took up her burden of life again,
Saying only, "It might have been."

Alas for maiden, alas for Judge,
For rich repiner and household drudge!

God pity them both! and pity us all,
Who vainly the dreams of youth recall.

For of all sad words of tongue or pen,
The saddest are these: "It might have been!"

Ah, well! for us all some sweet hope lies
Deeply buried from human eyes;

And, in the hereafter, angels may
Roll the stone from its grave away!

HEATHER ALE

ROBERT LOUIS STEVENSON

From the bonny bells of heather
  They brewed a drink long-syne,
Was sweeter far than honey,
  Was stronger far than wine.
They brewed it and they drank it,
  And lay in a blessed swound

For days and days together
  In their dwellings underground.

There rose a king in Scotland,
  A fell man to his foes,
He smote the Picts in battle,
  He hunted them like roes.
Over miles of the red mountain
  He hunted as they fled,
And strewed the dwarfish bodies
  Of the dying and the dead.

Summer came in the country,
  Red was the heather bell;
But the manner of the brewing
  Was none alive to tell.
In graves that were like children's
  On many a mountain head,
The Brewsters of the Heather
  Lay numbered with the dead.

The king in the red moorland
  Rode on a summer's day;
And the bees hummed, and the curlews
  Cried beside the way.
The king rode, and was angry,
  Black was his brow and pale,
To rule in a land of heather
  And lack the Heather Ale.

It fortuned that his vassals,
  Riding free on the heath,
Came on a stone that was fallen
  And vermin hid beneath.
Rudely plucked from their hiding,

Never a word they spoke:
A son and his aged father—
Last of the dwarfish folk.

The king sat high on his charger,
He looked on the little men;
And the dwarfish and swarthy couple
Looked at the king again.
Down by the shore he had them;
And there on the giddy brink—
"I will give you life, ye vermin,
For the secret of the drink."

There stood the son and father
And they looked high and low;
The heather was red around them,
The sea rumbled below.
And up and spoke the father,
Shrill was his voice to hear:
"I have a word in private,
A word for the royal ear.

"Life is dear to the aged,
And honour a little thing;
I would gladly sell the secret,"
Quoth the Pict to the king.
His voice was small as a sparrow's,
And shrill and wonderful clear:
"I would gladly sell my secret,
Only my son I fear.

"For life is a little matter,
And death is nought to the young;
And I dare not sell my honour
Under the eye of my son.

Take *him,* O king, and bind him,
  And cast him far in the deep;
And it's I will tell the secret
  That I have sworn to keep."

They took the son and bound him,
  Neck and heels in a thong,
And a lad took him and swung him,
  And flung him far and strong,
And the sea swallowed his body,
  Like that of a child of ten;—
And there on the cliff stood the father,
  Last of the dwarfish men.

"True was the word I told you:
  Only my son I feared;
For I doubt the sapling courage
  That goes without the beard.
But now in vain is the torture,
  Fire shall never avail:
Here dies in my bosom
  The secret of Heather Ale."

THE HAYSTACK IN THE FLOODS

WILLIAM MORRIS

Had she come all the way for this,
To part at last without a kiss?
Yea, had she borne the dirt and rain
That her own eyes might see him slain
Beside the haystack in the floods?

Along the dripping leafless woods,
The stirrup touching either shoe,
She rode astride as troopers do;

With kirtle kilted to her knee,
To which the mud splashed wretchedly;
And the wet dripp'd from every tree
Upon her head and heavy hair,
And on her eyelids broad and fair;
The tears and rain ran down her face.
By fits and starts they rode apace,
And very often was his place
Far off from her; he had to ride
Ahead to see what might betide
When the roads cross'd; and sometimes, when
There rose a murmuring from his men,
Had to turn back with promises;
Ah me! she had but little ease;

And often for pure doubt and dread
She sobb'd, made giddy in the head
By the swift riding; while, for cold,
Her slender fingers scarce could hold
The wet reins; yea, and scarcely, too,
She felt the foot within her shoe
Against the stirrup: all for this,
To part at last without a kiss
Beside the haystack in the floods.

For when they near'd that old soak'd hay,
They saw across the only way
That Judas, Godmar, and the three
Red running lions dismally
Grinn'd from his pennon, under which,
In one straight line along the ditch,
They counted thirty heads.

So then,
While Robert turn'd round to his men,

She saw at once the wretched end,
And, stooping down, tried hard to rend
Her coif the wrong way from her head,
And hid her eyes; while Robert said:
"Nay, love, 'tis scarcely two to one,
At Poictiers where we made them run
So fast—why, sweet my love, good cheer.
The Gascon frontier is so near,
Nought after this."

But, "O," she said,
"My God! my God! I have to tread
The long way back without you; then
The court at Paris; those six men;
The gratings of the Chatelet;
The swift Seine on some rainy day
Like this, and people standing by,
And laughing, while my weak hands try
To recollect how strong men swim.
All this, or else a life with him,
For which I should be damned at last.
Would God that this next hour were past!"

He answer'd not, but cried his cry,
"St. George for Marny!" cheerily;
And laid his hand upon her rein.
Alas! no man of all his train
Gave back that cheery cry again;
And, while for rage his thumb beat fast
Upon his sword-hilts, some one cast
About his neck a kerchief long,
And bound him.

Then they went along
To Godmar; who said: "Now, Jehane,

Your lover's life is on the wane
So fast, that, if this very hour
You yield not as my paramour,
He will not see the rain leave off—
Nay, keep your tongue from gibe and scoff,
Sir Robert, or I slay you now."

She laid her hand upon her brow,
Then gazed upon the palm, as though
She thought her forehead bled, and—"No,"
She said, and turn'd her head away,
As there were nothing else to say,
And everything were settled: red
Grew Godmar's face from chin to head:
"Jehane, on yonder hill there stands
My castle, guarding well my lands:
What hinders me from taking you
And doing that I list to do
To your fair wilful body, while
Your knight lies dead?"

A wicked smile
Wrinkled her face, her lips grew thin,
A long way out she thrust her chin:
"You know that I should strangle you
While you were sleeping; or bite through
Your throat, by God's help—ah!" she said,
"Lord Jesus, pity your poor maid!

For in such wise they hem me in,
I cannot choose but sin and sin,
Whatever happens: yet I think
They could not make me eat or drink
And so should I just reach my rest."
"Nay, if you do not my behest,

O Jehane! though I love you well,"
Said Godmar, "would I fail to tell
All that I know?" "Foul lies," she said.
"Eh? lies, my Jehane? by God's head,
At Paris folks would deem them true!
Do you know, Jehane, they cry for you,
'Jehane the brown! Jehane the brown!
Give us Jehane to burn or drown!'—
Eh—gag me Robert!—sweet my friend,
This were indeed a piteous end
For those long fingers, and long feet,
And long neck, and smooth shoulders sweet;
An end that few men would forget
That saw it— So, an hour yet:
Consider, Jehane, which to take
Of life or death!"

So, scarce awake,
Dismounting, did she leave that place,
And totter some yards: with her face
Turn'd upward to the sky she lay,
Her head on a wet heap of hay,
And fell asleep: and while she slept,
And did not dream, the minutes crept
Round to the twelve again; but she,
Being waked at last, sigh'd quietly,
And strangely childlike came, and said:
"I will not." Straightway Godmar's head,
As though it hung on strong wires, turn'd
Most sharply round, and his face burn'd.

For Robert—both his eyes were dry,
He could not weep, but gloomily
He seem'd to watch the rain; yea, too,

His lips were firm; he tried once more
To touch her lips; she reach'd out, sore
And vain desire so tortured them,
The poor grey lips, and now the hem
Of his sleeve brush'd them.

With a start
Up Godmar rose, thrust them apart;
From Robert's throat he loosed the bands
Of silk and mail; with empty hands
Held out, she stood and gazed and saw
The long bright blade without a flaw
Glide out from Godmar's sheath, his hand
In Robert's hair; she saw him bend
Back Robert's head; she saw him send

The thin steel down; the blow told well,
Right backward the knight Robert fell,
And moan'd as dogs do, being half dead,
Unwitting, as I deem: so then
Godmar turn'd grinning to his men,
Who ran, some five or six, and beat
His head to pieces at their feet.

Then Godmar turn'd again and said:
"So, Jehane, the first fitte is read!
Take note, my lady, that your way
Lies backward to the Chatelet!"
She shook her head and gazed awhile
At her cold hands with a rueful smile,
As though this thing had made her mad.

This was the parting that they had
Beside the haystack in the floods.

THE SENTRY

WILFRED OWEN

We'd found an old Boche dug-out, and he knew,
And gave us hell, for shell on frantic shell
Hammered on top, but never quite burst through.
Rain, guttering down in waterfalls of slime
Kept slush waist-high that, rising hour by hour
Choked up the steps too thick with clay to climb.
What murk of air remained stank old, and sour
With fumes of whizz-bangs, and the smell of men
Who'd lived there years, and left their curse in the den,
If not their corpses. . . .
There we herded from the blast
Of whizz-bangs, but one found our door at last,—
Buffeting eyes and breath, snuffing the candles.
And thud! flump! thud! down the steep steps came thumping
And splashing in the flood, deluging muck—
The sentry's body; then, his rifle, handles
Of old Boche bombs, and mud in ruck on ruck.
We dredged him up, for killed, until he whined
"O sir, my eyes—I'm blind—I'm blind, I'm blind!"
Coaxing, I held a flame against his lids
And said if he could see the least blurred light
He was not blind; in time he'd get all right.
"I can't," he sobbed. Eyeballs, huge-bulged like squids',
Watch my dreams still; but I forgot him there
In posting next for duty, and sending a scout
To beg a stretcher somewhere, and floundering about
To other posts under the shrieking air.

. . . .

Those other wretches, how they bled and spewed,
And one who would have drowned himself for good,—

FROM TWO LIVES

I try not to remember these things now.
Let dread hark back for one word only: how
Half listening to that sentry's moans and jumps,
And the wild chattering of his broken teeth,
Renewed most horribly whenever crumps
Pummelled the roof and slogged the air beneath—
Through the dense din, I say, we heard him shout
"I see your lights!" But ours had long died out.

FROM TWO LIVES

WILLIAM ELLERY LEONARD

Lo, had begun again for her the time,
The cyclic time (through Nature's fixed decree),
That woman in her large fecundity
Shares with the barren moon in every clime:
Ten times in the revolving year plus three,
As often as the moon moves round the earth,
Whether a savage, queen or peasant she,
Then must she pause amid her toil or mirth;
And, as a priestess under holy law,
Pour the Great Mother, pour with reeling brain,
Pour, often with the mystic rites of pain,
Libations of the purple blood of awe,
Blood of no sheep with fillets girdled thrice—
From her own body is the sacrifice.

The Cosmic Rhythms have old right of way,
And roll through man as though the heaving sea:
Should the moon stop above us just for me,
Because I neared the Valley of Death that day?
Should the Great Mother mercifully delay,—
As satiate with ten million women's pine,—
Delay her workings on this one of mine,

Because my wife in grief, in madness lay,
Already stricken?—Onward still and on
The Cosmic Rhythms roll; I've felt, I've thought,
And I have mated man and star and sun
As of one pulse, one breath, one being wrought,
With gain and loss alike for sun, man, star—
Because ('tis all we know), because they are.

She dressed in white that morning and she passed
So slow, so aimless (*was* she without aim,
Without some purpose that she dared not name?)
From room to room; and now and then she cast
Such piteous love upon me here and there.
I rang my Colleague on the phone to say
"Write on the board, 'my class won't meet to-day' ";
And strove to still my terror and despair
That I might conquer hers.—All, all was vain,
And turned to dead-sea apples, ashes all,
Or rather into quick-lime in her brain,—
All that I did or said. She heard my call
Upon the phone . . . "My work was more than she,"
She thought (and brooded still . . . to set me free).

She heard me say: "Now round the corner, dear,
I'll run an instant to the shop, and you
Must sit and guess what 'tis I'm after, dear,
Or better take this little book-in-blue"
(Shelley's *The West Wind,* the one book I'd bought her
On her one birthday as a wife), "and learn"
(I spoke as to a little child or daughter)
"At least one stanza well, ere I return" . . .
When I appeared with package in pink tissue
(The playful husband I, with broken heart):
"And now recite, recite before I kiss you
Or open this" . . . "I've only learned a part,"

She answered tremblingly. "Let's have it, dear"—
" '*Destroyer and preserver,* hear, O hear!' "

"This is the red rose, dear, and this the white,
The white rose this, beloved, this the red,"
As I unpinned the paper, thus I said;
"Love's passion and Love's purity—ere night
You'll laugh with their green stems amid your hair."
She set in slender vase of blue and gold
(I never saw them after), with slow stare
Put hands upon my shoulders (as of old?—
Not quite), and gazed long and unspeakably. . . .
"These flowers I wore upon my wedding dress." . . .
A pause. . . . "O my poor husband . . . must it be?"
Then clung so close, as in a wilderness. . . .
And then would dart away. . . . "You mustn't go—
Come back; come, sing the cheeriest song you know."

And she obeyed . . . lapsing into the child,
The docile child again . . . upon the stool
Before the music . . . where the mother smiled . . .
To do my bidding like a girl in school.—
And sang the melody of bride and wife,
Thinking of other thoughts she could not speak,—
"Freut euch des Lebens—take ye joy of life,"
One stanza only,—and so weak, so weak. . . .
Put hands again on shoulders . . . gazed at me . . .
"I'll sing it only in my wedding dress." . . .
Kissed me. . . . "O my poor husband . . . must it be?"
Then clung again as in a wilderness. . . .
Then glided swiftly out and up the stair—
Whilst I sank hopeless in the nearest chair.

An instant—leapt—leapt—followed.—In the hall
I heard the click of key on upper floor—

Strength left my knees—I could but crawl and crawl—
And trembled groping to her chamber door—
I heard the rattling of a box—a knife?—
Razor at throat?—the panel—shall I break?—
Perhaps it's nothing—I grip the knob,—"My wife!
O open! Open for your husband's sake!"
She opened . . . with a vision on her face,
And hands uplifted to immortal things,
And past me flew . . . upon her toilet case
An emptied glass with foam in awful rings,
And a green bottle labelled with the red
Letters that shrieked upon me, *"She is dead!"*

But in the bathroom, struggling to undo
Her horrible fate, thinking again of sky
And flower and bird, too young, too young to die,
She gulped the antidote my science knew,—
Gulped (as I clapped it in my palm to lip)
In voiceless frenzy—hand on head and hip—
Whilst I repeated: "Tell me, tell me, tell,
You love me, love me, love me!" . . . Then she fell. . . .
The neighbors and the doctors and the maid
Were soon at work beside me. . . . "Is there hope?"
"Perhaps . . . one day will show." . . . My business now,
What was it?—In bridal chamber, undismayed
And swift with desperation, there to cope
With love's convulsive hands and sweating brow,

Whilst I undressed her, as she groaned; detail,
The critics tell us, makes reality;
But should I chronicle each look and wail,
Each garment, as I rent it horribly
With twitch and twist of fingers, clutch of hands,
Each ridge in face of me, you'd say I were

(Though doing the waiting doctor's fierce commands)
O not the husband, but the ravisher. . . .
I saw her never after. The next day
The nurse reported from the room above:
"I gave the flowers; she sends her dearest love." . . .
And the next night she heard across the way
My tip-toe in the hall, and wailed my name—
I was forbid to answer: and I came

From out of the darkness not. . . . They led her forth
That morning; I was told she must not see
Her husband now, lest both should blasted be.
They led her to the City west of north—
Across the lake. . . . To die among the mad
Alone, all, all alone . . . next day . . . my wife. . . .
"I'll never see this house again in life,"
She said (I'm told) with the last look she had
Of porch and lilacs, entering the car
With nurse and doctor . . . entering, to die
Alone, all, all alone (and yet not far!)
Among the mad and with no last good-bye,
Entering the auto, murmuring "Where is he?—
Be good to my poor husband." . . . If ye be,

Ye that do hear my story, wroth with me
Or puzzled, hear how 'twas they took her there:
That orderly Physician debonair
Was poorly read in poisons, I divine;
Nor knew how slow their cunning Chemistry
Sometimes may burn before it eats the heart;
Knew not to spell in blood and eye, the sign
That yet it burned in her, despite his art;—
And as for me who sleepless stepped and passed,
None counselled aught with me—intruder wan,

Questioning (with scant replies) from dawn to dawn. . . .
Man blundered with her being to the last. . . .
Alone . . . among the mad . . . and . . . "Where is he?--
Be good to my poor husband." . . . If ye be,

Ye that do read these verses, friends with me,
Or friends with Sorrow, as the moment nears,
Now sit with me, without all sobs or tears,
Awaiting, as beside the infinite sea,
On the front steps of that deserted manse,
The ultimatum of the Eternal Deep,
Quiet before the House of Evil Chance,
Whilst she is sinking quietly to sleep. . . .
Hush . . . hush . . . start not . . . again the phone it rings—
One tiptoes swiftly back into the hall:
"Hello? . . . At five? . . . yes . . . so?" . . . Hangs up . . .
    and brings
The word: "She's passed away." And that is all. . . .
Save his good hand upon my shoulder. . . . "Dead? . . .
I think I'll walk around a bit," I said. . . .

MY MOTHER

CLAUDE MCKAY

I

Reg wished me to go with him to the field,
I paused because I did not want to go;
But in her quiet way she made me yield
Reluctantly, for she was breathing low.
Her hand she slowly lifted from her lap
And, smiling sadly in the old sweet way,
She pointed to the nail where hung my cap.
Her eyes said: I shall last another day.
But scarcely had we reached the distant place,

When o'er the hills we heard a faint bell ringing;
A boy came running up with frightened face;
We knew the fatal news that he was bringing.
I heard him listlessly, without a moan,
Although the only one I loved was gone.

II

The dawn departs, the morning is begun,
The trades come whispering from off the seas,
The fields of corn are golden in the sun,
The dark-brown tassels fluttering in the breeze;
The bell is sounding and the children pass,
Frog-leaping, skipping, shouting, laughing shrill,
Down the red road, over the pasture-grass,
Up to the school-house crumbling on the hill.
The older folk are at their peaceful toil,
Some pulling up the weeds, some plucking corn,
And others breaking up the sun-baked soil.
Float, faintly-scented breeze, at early morn
Over the earth where mortals sow and reap—
Beneath its breast my mother lies asleep.

PART IV

VESSELS OF EMOTION

OH! WEEP FOR THOSE

LORD BYRON

Oh! weep for those that wept by Babel's stream,
Whose shrines are desolate, whose land a dream;
Weep for the harp of Judah's broken shell;
Mourn—where their God hath dwelt, the godless dwell!

And where shall Israel lave her bleeding feet?
And when shall Zion's songs again seem sweet?
And Judah's melody once more rejoice
The hearts that leap'd before its heavenly voice?

Tribes of the wandering foot and weary breast,
How shall ye flee away and be at rest!
The wild-dove hath her nest, the fox his cave,
Mankind their country—Israel but the grave!

CYNARA

ERNEST DOWSON

Last night, ah, yesternight, betwixt her lips and mine
There fell thy shadow, Cynara! thy breath was shed
Upon my soul between the kisses and the wine;
And I was desolate and sick of an old passion,
  Yea, I was desolate and bowed my head:
I have been faithful to thee, Cynara! in my fashion.

All night upon mine heart I felt her warm heart beat,
Night-long within mine arms in love and sleep she lay;
Surely the kisses of her bought red mouth were sweet;

But I was desolate and sick of an old passion,
  When I awoke and found the dawn was gray:
I have been faithful to thee, Cynara! in my fashion.

I have forgot much, Cynara! gone with the wind,
Flung roses, roses riotously with the throng,
Dancing, to put thy pale, lost lilies out of mind;
But I was desolate and sick of an old passion,
  Yea, all the time, because the dance was long:
I have been faithful to thee, Cynara! in my fashion.

I cried for madder music and for stronger wine,
But when the feast is finished and the lamps expire,
Then falls thy shadow, Cynara! the night is thine;
And I am desolate and sick of an old passion,
  Yea, hungry for the lips of my desire:
I have been faithful to thee, Cynara! in my fashion.

THE SOLITARY REAPER

WILLIAM WORDSWORTH

Behold her, single in the field,
Yon solitary Highland Lass!
Reaping and singing by herself;
Stop here, or gently pass!
Alone she cuts and binds the grain,
And sings a melancholy strain;
O listen! for the vale profound
Is overflowing with the sound.

No nightingale did ever chaunt
More welcome notes to weary bands
Of travellers in some shady haunt,
Among Arabian sands:
A voice so thrilling ne'er was heard

In spring-time from the cuckoo-bird,
Breaking the silence of the seas
Among the farthest Hebrides.

Will no one tell me what she sings?
Perhaps the plaintive numbers flow
For old, unhappy, far-off things,
And battles long ago:
Or is it some more humble lay,
Familiar matter of today?
Some natural sorrow, loss, or pain,
That has been, and may be again?

Whate'er the theme, the maiden sang
As if her song could have no ending;
I saw her singing at her work,
And o'er the sickle bending;—
I listen'd motionless and still;
And, as I mounted up the hill
The music in my heart I bore,
Long after it was heard no more.

I DOTE UPON MYSELF

WALT WHITMAN

I dote on myself, there is that lot of me and all so luscious,
Each moment and whatever happens thrills me with joy,
I cannot tell how my ankles bend, nor whence the cause of my faintest wish,
Nor the cause of the friendship I emit, nor the cause of the friendship I take again.

That I walk up my stoop, I pause to consider if it really be,
A morning-glory at my window satisfies me more than the metaphysics of books.

BY THIS HE KNEW

GEORGE MEREDITH

By this he knew she wept with waking eyes:
That, at his hand's light quiver by her head,
The strange low sobs that shook their common bed
Were called into her with a sharp surprise,
And strangled mute, like little gaping snakes,
Dreadfully venomous to him. She lay
Stone-still, and the long darkness flowed away
With muffled pulses. Then, as midnight makes
Her giant heart of Memory and Tears
Drink the pale drug of silence, and so beat
Sleep's heavy measure, they from head to feet
Were moveless, looking through their dead black years,
By vain regret scrawled over the blank wall.
Like sculptured effigies they might be seen
Upon their marriage-tomb, the sword between;
Each wishing for the sword that severs all.

NOT IN A SILVER CASKET

EDNA ST. VINCENT MILLAY

Not in a silver casket cool with pearls
Or rich with red corundum or with blue,
Locked, and the key withheld, as other girls
Have given their loves, I give my love to you;
Not in a lovers'-knot, not in a ring
Worked in such fashion, and the legend plain—
Semper fidelis, where a secret spring
Kennels a drop of mischief for the brain:
Love in the open hand, no thing but that,
Ungemmed, unhidden, wishing not to hurt,

As one should bring you cowslips in a hat
Swung from the hand, or apples in her skirt,
I bring you, calling out as children do:
"Look what I have!—And these are all for you."

THE QUIET WOMAN

GENEVIEVE TAGGARD

I will defy you down until my death
With cold body, indrawn breath;
Terrible and cruel I will move with you
Like a surly tiger. If you knew
Why I am shaken, if fond you could see
All the caged arrogance in me,
You would not lean so boyishly, so bold,
To kiss my body, quivering and cold.

SINGLE SONNET

LOUISE BOGAN

Now, you great stanza, you heroic mould,
Bend to my will, for I must give you love:
The weight in the heart that breathes, but cannot move,
Which to endure flesh only makes so bold.

Take up, take up, as it were lead or gold
The burden; test the dreadful mass thereof.
No stone, slate, metal under or above
Earth, is so ponderous, so dull, so cold.

Too long as ocean bed bears up the ocean,
As earth's core bears the earth, have I borne this;

Too long have lovers, bending for their kiss
Felt bitter force cohering without motion.

Staunch meter, great song, it is yours, at length,
To prove how stronger you are than my strength.

REMEMBER

CHRISTINA ROSSETTI

Remember me when I am gone away,
Gone far away into the silent land;
When you can no more hold me by the hand,
Nor I half turn to go, yet turning stay.
Remember me when no more, day by day,
You tell me of our future that you planned:
Only remember me; you understand
It will be late to counsel then or pray.
Yet if you should forget me for a while
And afterwards remember, do not grieve:
For if the darkness and corruption leave
A vestige of the thoughts that once I had,
Better by far you should forget and smile
Than that you should remember and be sad.

STAR-FEAR

LEONORA SPEYER

What thing insistent urges me away
Out of the garden, the smooth, familiar paths
I walk unswervingly, as were it day?

Here it is home. Each blossom in its bed
Is known to me by name, by drowsy scent;
Each bough, the one where I must bend my head,

Is known, the nested bird within—I hear
A fledgling-robin murmur, half-awake—
Why do I turn? What is it that I fear?

It is these stars, immutable and wise,
Flaunting their fateful chart and peering, moving
As I do, I in my garden, they in their skies.

Intent and cold they watch, until I run
Back to the shadowy house, to bolt the door,
Shut windows swinging wide, and one by one,
Draw heavy curtains closer, make more light,
Saying, "The stars are beautiful tonight!"

I SHALL NOT CARE

SARA TEASDALE

When I am dead and over me bright April
  Shakes out her rain-drenched hair,
Though you should lean above me broken-hearted,
  I shall not care.

I shall have peace, as leafy trees are peaceful
  When rain bends down the bough;
And I shall be more silent and cold-hearted
  Than you are now.

ULALUME

EDGAR ALLAN POE

The skies they were ashen and sober;
  The leaves they were crispèd and sere—
  The leaves they were withering and sere;
It was night in the lonesome October
  Of my most immemorial year;

It was hard by the dim lake of Auber,
  In the misty mid region of Weir—
It was down by the dank tarn of Auber,
  In the ghoul-haunted woodland of Weir.

Here once, through an alley Titanic,
  Of cypress, I roamed with my Soul—
  Of cypress, with Psyche, my Soul.
Those were days when my heart was volcanic
  As the scoriac rivers that roll—
  As the lavas that restlessly roll
Their sulphurous currents down Yaanek
  In the ultimate climes of the pole—
That groan as they roll down Mount Yaanek
  In the realms of the boreal pole.

Our talk had been serious and sober,
  But our thoughts they were palsied and sere—
  Our memories were treacherous and sere—
For we knew not the month was October,
  And we marked not the night of the year—
  (Ah, night of all nights in the year!)
We noted not the dim lake of Auber—
  (Though once we had journeyed down here)—
Remembered not the dank tarn of Auber
  Nor the ghoul-haunted woodland of Weir.

And now, as the night was senescent
  And star-dials pointed to morn—
  As the star-dials hinted of morn—
At the end of our path a liquescent
  And nebulous lustre was born,
Out of which a miraculous crescent
  Arose with a duplicate horn—
Astarte's bediamonded crescent
  Distinct with its duplicate horn.

And I said—"She is warmer than Dian:
  She rolls through an ether of sighs—
  She revels in a region of sighs:
She has seen that the tears are not dry on
  These cheeks, where the worm never dies,
And has come past the stars of the Lion
  To point us the path to the skies—
  To the Lethean peace of the skies—
Come up, in despite of the Lion,
  To shine on us with her bright eyes—
Come up through the lair of the Lion,
  With love in her luminous eyes."

But Psyche, uplifting her finger,
  Said—"Sadly this star I mistrust—
  Her pallor I strangely mistrust:—
Oh, hasten!—oh, let us not linger!
  O fly!—let us fly!—for we must."
In terror she spoke, letting sink her
  Wings until they trailed in the dust—
In agony sobbed, letting sink her
  Plumes till they trailed in the dust—
  Till they sorrowfully trailed in the dust.

I replied—"This is nothing but dreaming:
  Let us on by this tremulous light!
  Let us bathe in this crystalline light!
Its Sybillic splendor is beaming
  With Hope and in Beauty tonight:—
  See!—it flickers up the sky through the night!
Ah, we safely may trust to its gleaming,
  And be sure it will lead us aright—
We safely may trust to a gleaming
  That cannot but guide us aright,
  Since it flickers up to Heaven through the night."

Thus I pacified Psyche and kissed her,
  And tempted her out of her gloom—
  And conquered her scruples and gloom;
And we passed to the end of the vista,
  But were stopped by the door of a tomb—
  By the door of a legended tomb;
And I said—"What is written, sweet sister,
  On the door of this legended tomb?"
  She replied—"Ulalume—Ulalume—
  'Tis the vault of thy lost Ulalume!"

Then my heart it grew ashen and sober
  As the leaves that were crispèd and sere—
  As the leaves that were withering and sere,
And I cried—"It was surely October
  On this very night of last year
  That I journeyed—I journeyed down here—
  That I brought a dread burden down here—
  On this night of all nights in the year,
  Ah! what demon has tempted me here?
Well I know, now, this dim lake of Auber,
  This misty mid region of Weir—
Well I know, now, this dank tarn of Auber,
  This ghoul-haunted woodland of Weir."

DEJECTION: AN ODE

SAMUEL TAYLOR COLERIDGE

Late, late yestreen I saw the new Moon, 11-12-19
With the old Moon in her arms;
And I fear, I fear, my Master dear!
We shall have a deadly storm.
Ballad of Sir Patrick Spence.

DEJECTION: AN ODE

I

Well! If the Bard was weather-wise, who made
The grand old ballad of Sir Patrick Spence,
This night, so tranquil now, will not go hence
Unroused by winds, that ply a busier trade
Than those which mould yon cloud in lazy flakes,
Or the dull sobbing draft, that moans and rakes
Upon the strings of this Æolian lute,
Which better far were mute.
For lo! the New-moon winter-bright!
And overspread with phantom light,
(With swimming phantom light o'erspread
But rimmed and circled by a silver thread)
I see the old Moon in her lap, foretelling
The coming-on of rain and squally blast.
And oh! that even now the gust were swelling,
And the slant night-shower driving loud and fast!
Those sounds which oft have raised me, whilst they awed,
And sent my soul abroad,
Might now perhaps their wonted impulse give,
Might startle this dull pain, and make it move and live!

II

A grief without a pang, void, dark, and drear,
A stifled, drowsy, unimpassioned grief,
Which finds no natural outlet, no relief,
In word, or sigh, or tear—
O Lady! in this wan and heartless mood,
To other thoughts by yonder throstle woo'd,
All this long eve, so balmy and serene,
Have I been gazing on the western sky,
And its peculiar tint of yellow green:
And still I gaze—and with how blank an eye!
And those thin clouds above, in flakes and bars,

That give away their motion to the stars;
Those stars, that glide behind them or between,
Now sparkling, now bedimmed, but always seen:
Yon crescent Moon, as fixed as if it grew
In its own cloudless, starless lake of blue;
I see them all so excellently fair,
I see, not feel, how beautiful they are!

III

My genial spirits fail;
And what can these avail
To lift the smothering weight from off my breast?
It were a vain endeavour,
Though I should gaze for ever
On that green light that lingers in the west:
I may not hope from outward forms to win
The passion and the life, whose fountains are within.

IV

O Lady! we receive but what we give,
And in our life alone does Nature live:
Ours is her wedding garment, ours her shroud!
And would we aught behold, of higher worth,
Than that inanimate cold world allowed
To the poor loveless ever-anxious crowd,
Ah! from the soul itself must issue forth
A light, a glory, a fair luminous cloud
Enveloping the Earth—
And from the soul itself must there be sent
A sweet and potent voice, of its own birth,
Of all sweet sounds the life and element!

V

O pure of heart! thou need'st not ask of me
What this strong music in the soul may be!

What, and wherein it doth exist,
This light, this glory, this fair luminous mist,
This beautiful and beauty-making power.
  Joy, virtuous Lady! Joy that ne'er was given,
Save to the pure, and in their purest hour,
Life, and Life's effluence, cloud at once and shower,
Joy, Lady! is the spirit and the power,
Which wedding Nature to us gives in dower
  A new Earth and new Heaven,
Undreamt of by the sensual and the proud—
Joy is the sweet voice, Joy the luminous cloud—
  We in ourselves rejoice!
And thence flows all that charms or ear or sight,
  All melodies the echoes of that voice,
All colours a suffusion from that light.

VI

There was a time when, though my path was rough,
  This joy within me dallied with distress,
And all misfortunes were but as the stuff
  Whence Fancy made me dreams of happiness:
For hope grew round me, like the twining vine,
And fruits, and foliage, not my own, seemed mine.
But now afflictions bow me down to earth:
Nor care I that they rob me of my mirth;
  But oh! each visitation
Suspends what nature gave me at my birth,
  My shaping spirit of Imagination.
For not to think of what I needs must feel,
  But to be still and patient, all I can;
And haply by abstruse research to steal
  From my own nature all the natural man—
  This was my sole resource, my only plan:
Till that which suits a part infects the whole,
And now is almost grown the habit of my soul.

VII

Hence, viper thoughts, that coil around my mind,
  Reality's dark dream!
I turn from you, and listen to the wind,
  Which long has raved unnoticed. What a scream
Of agony by torture lengthened out
That lute sent forth! Thou Wind, that rav'st without,
  Bare crag, or mountain-tairn, or blasted tree,
Or pine-grove whither woodman never clomb,
Or lonely house, long held the witches' home,
  Methinks were fitter instruments for thee,
Mad Lutanist! who in this month of showers,
Of dark-brown gardens, and of peeping flowers,
Mak'st Devils' yule, with worse than wintry song,
The blossoms, buds, and timorous leaves among.
  Thou Actor, perfect in all tragic sounds!
Thou mighty Poet, e'en to frenzy bold!
  What tell'st thou now about?
  'Tis of the rushing of an host in rout,
With groans, of trampled men, with smarting wounds—
At once they groan with pain, and shudder with the cold!
But hush! there is a pause of deepest silence!
  And all that noise, as of a rushing crowd,
With groans, and tremulous shudderings—all is over—
  It tells another tale, with sounds less deep and loud!
  A tale of less affright,
  And tempered with delight,
As Otway's self had framed the tender lay,—
  'Tis of a little child
  Upon a lonesome wild,
Not far from home, but she hath lost her way:
And now moans low in bitter grief and fear,
And now screams loud, and hopes to make her mother hear.

VIII

'Tis midnight, but small thoughts have I of sleep:
Full seldom may my friend such vigils keep!
Visit her, gentle Sleep! with wings of healing,
  And may this storm be but a mountain-birth,
May all the stars hang bright above her dwelling,
  Silent as though they watched the sleeping Earth!
  With light heart may she rise,
  Gay fancy, cheerful eyes,
  Joy lift her spirit, joy attune her voice;
To her may all things live, from pole to pole,
Their life the eddying of her living soul!
  O simple spirit, guided from above,
Dear Lady! friend devoutest of my choice,
Thus mayest thou ever, evermore rejoice.

MELANCHOLIA

JAMES THOMSON

(From "The City of Dreadful Night")

Anear the center of that northern crest
  Stands out a level upland bleak and bare,
From which the city east and south and west
  Sinks gentle in long waves; and throned there
An Image sits, stupendous, superhuman,
The bronze colossus of a winged woman,
  Upon a graded granite base foursquare.

Low-seated she leans forward massively,
  With cheek on clenched left hand, the forearm's might
Erect, its elbow on her rounded knee;
  Across a clasped book in her lap the right

Upholds a pair of compasses; she gazes
With full set eyes but wandering in thick mazes
  Of somber thought beholds no outward sight.

Words cannot picture her; but all men know
  That solemn sketch the pure sad artist wrought
Three centuries and three score years ago,
  With phantasies of his peculiar thought:
The instruments of carpentry and science
Scattered about her feet, in strange alliance
  With the keen wolf-hound sleeping undistraught;

Scales, hour-glass, bell, and magic-square above;
  The grave and solid infant perched beside,
With open winglets that might bear a dove,
  Intent upon its tablets, heavy-eyed;
Her folded wings as of a mighty eagle,
But all too impotent to lift the regal
  Robustness of her earth-born strength and pride;

And with those wings, and that light wreath which seems
  To mock her grand head and the knotted frown
Of forehead charged with baleful thoughts and dreams,
  The household bunch of keys, the housewife's gown
Voluminous, indented, and yet rigid
As if a shell of burnished metal frigid,
  The feet thick shod to tread all weakness down;

The comet hanging o'er the waste dark seas,
  The massy rainbow curved in front of it,
Beyond the village with the masts and trees;
  The snaky-imp, dog-headed, from the Pit,
Bearing upon its batlike leathern pinions
Her name unfolded in the sun's dominions,
  The "Melancholia" that transcends all wit.

Thus has the artist copied her, and thus
  Surrounded to expound her form sublime,
Her fate heroic and calamitous;
  Fronting the dreadful mysteries of Time,
Unvanquished in defeat and desolation,
Undaunted in the hopeless conflagration
  Of the day setting on her baffled prime.

THEY FLEE FROM ME

SIR THOMAS WYATT

They flee from me that sometime did me seek,
With naked foot stalking within my chamber:
  Once have I seen them gentle, tame, and meek,
    That now are wild, and do not once remember
    That sometime they have put themselves in danger
To take bread at my hand; and now they range,
Busily seeking in continual change.

Thanked be fortune, it hath been otherwise
Twenty times better; but once especial—
  In thin array: after a pleasant guise,
    When her loose gown did from her shoulders fall,
    And she me caught in her arms long and small,
And therewithal so sweetly did me kiss,
And softly said, "Dear heart, how like you this?"

It was no dream; for I lay broad awaking:
But all is turn'd now, through my gentleness,
  Into a bitter fashion of forsaking;
    And I have leave to go of her goodness;
    And she also to use new-fangleness.
But since that I unkindly so am servèd,
"How like you this?"—what hath she now deservèd?

WITH CHILD

GENEVIEVE TAGGARD

Now I am slow and placid, fond of sun,
Like a sleek beast, or a worn one:
No slim and languid girl—not glad
With the windy trip I once had,
But velvet-footed, musing of my own,
Torpid, mellow, stupid as a stone.

You cleft me with your beauty's pulse, and now
Your pulse has taken body. Care not how
The old grace goes, how heavy I am grown,
Big with this loneliness, how you alone
Ponder our love. Touch my feet and feel
How earth tingles, teeming at my heel!
Earth's urge, not mine—my little death, not hers;
And the pure beauty yearns and stirs.

It does not heed our ecstasies, it turns
With secrets of its own, its own concerns,
Toward a windy world of its own, toward stark
And solitary places. In the dark,
Defiant even now, it tugs and moans
To be untangled from these mother's bones.

SWEENEY AMONG THE NIGHTINGALES

T. S. ELIOT

Apeneck Sweeney spreads his knees
Letting his arms hang down to laugh,
The zebra stripes along his jaw
Swelling to maculate giraffe.

SWEENEY AMONG THE NIGHTINGALES

The circles of the stormy moon
Slide westward toward the River Plate,
Death and the Raven drift above
And Sweeney guards the hornèd gate.

Gloomy Orion and the Dog
Are veiled; and hushed the shrunken seas;
The person in the Spanish cape
Tries to sit on Sweeney's knees

Slips and pulls the table cloth
Overturns a coffee-cup,
Reorganized upon the floor
She yawns and draws a stocking up;

The silent man in mocha brown
Sprawls at the window-sill and gapes;
The waiter brings in oranges
Bananas figs and hothouse grapes;

The silent vertebrate in brown
Contracts and concentrates, withdraws;
Rachel née Rabinovitch
Tears at the grapes with murderous paws;

She and the lady in the cape
Are suspect, thought to be in league;
Therefore the man with heavy eyes
Declines the gambit, shows fatigue,

Leaves the room and reappears
Outside the window, leaning in,
Branches of wistaria
Circumscribe a golden grin;

VESSELS OF EMOTION

The host with someone indistinct
Converses at the door apart,
The nightingales are singing near
The Convent of the Sacred Heart,

And sang within the bloody wood
When Agamemnon cried aloud,
And let their liquid siftings fall
To stain the stiff dishonoured shroud.

THE RETURN

EZRA POUND

See, they return; ah, see the tentative
Movements, and the slow feet,
The trouble in the pace and the uncertain
Wavering!

See, they return, one, and by one,
With fear, as half-awakened;
As if the snow should hesitate
And murmur in the wind,
        and half turned back;
These were the "Wing'd-with-Awe,"
        inviolable.

Gods of the wingèd shoe!
With them the silver hounds,
        sniffing the trace of air!

Haie! Haie!
  These were the swift to harry;
These the keen-scented;
These were the souls of blood.

Slow on the leash,
        pallid the leash-men!

HYMN TO THE NIGHT

HENRY WADSWORTH LONGFELLOW

I heard the trailing garments of the Night
Sweep through her marble halls;
I saw her sable skirts all fringed with light
From the celestial walls.

I felt her presence, by its spell of might,
Stoop o'er me from above—
The calm, majestic presence of the Night,
As of the one I love.

I heard the sounds of sorrow and delight,
The manifold, soft chimes,
That fill the haunted chambers of the Night,
Like some old poet's rhymes.

From the cool cisterns of the midnight air
My spirit drank repose;
The fountain of perpetual peace flows there,
From those deep cisterns flows.

O holy Night! from thee I learn to bear
What man has borne before;
Thou layest thy finger on the lips of Care,
And they complain no more.

Peace! Peace! Orestes-like I breathe this prayer;
Descend with broad-winged flight,
The welcome, the thrice-prayed for, the most fair,
The best-beloved Night!

EPISTLE TO AUGUSTA

LORD BYRON

My sister! my sweet sister! if a name
Dearer and purer were, it should be thine.
Mountains and seas divide us, but I claim
No tears, but tenderness to answer mine:
Go where I will, to me thou art the same—
A loved regret which I would not resign.
There yet are two things in my destiny,—
A world to roam through, and a home with thee.

The first were nothing—had I still the last,
It were the haven of my happiness;
But other claims and other ties thou hast,
And mine is not the wish to make them less.
A strange doom is thy father's son's, and past
Recalling, as it lies beyond redress;
Reversed for him our grandsire's fate of yore,—
He had no rest at sea, nor I on shore.

If my inheritance of storms hath been
In other elements, and on the rocks
Of perils, overlook'd or unforseen,
I have sustain'd my share of worldly shocks,
The fault was mine; nor do I seek to screen
My errors with defensive paradox;
I have been cunning in mine overthrow,
The careful pilot of my proper woe.

Mine were my faults, and mine be their reward.
My whole life was a contest, since the day
That gave me being, gave me that which marr'd
The gift,—a fate, or will, that walk'd astray;

And I at times have found the struggle hard,
And thought of shaking off my bonds of clay:
But now I fain would for a time survive,
If but to see what next can well arrive.

Kingdoms and empires in my little day
I have outlived, and yet I am not old;
And when I look on this, the petty spray
Of my own years of trouble, which have roll'd
Like a wild bay of breakers, melts away:
Something—I know not what—does still uphold
A spirit of slight patience;—not in vain,
Even for its own sake, do we purchase pain.

Perhaps the workings of defiance stir
Within me,—or perhaps a cold despair,
Brought on when ills habitually recur,
Perhaps a kinder clime, or purer air
(For even to this may change of soul refer,
And with light armour we may learn to bear),
Have taught me a strange quiet, which was not
The chief companion of a calmer lot.

I feel almost at times as I have felt
In happy childhood; trees, and flowers, and brooks,
Which do remember me of where I dwelt
Ere my young mind was sacrificed to books,
Come as of yore upon me, and can melt
My heart with recognition of their looks;
And even at moments I could think I see
Some living thing to love—but none like thee.

Here are the Alpine landscapes which create
A fund for contemplation;—to admire
Is a brief feeling of a trivial date;

But something worthier do such scenes inspire:
Here to be lonely is not desolate,
For much I view which I could most desire,
And, above all, a lake I can behold
Lovelier, not dearer, than our own of old.

Oh that thou wert but with me!—but I grow
The fool of my own wishes, and forget
The solitude, which I have vaunted so,
Has lost its praise in this but one regret;
There may be others which I less may show;—
I am not of the plaintive mood, and yet
I feel an ebb in my philosophy,
And the tide rising in my alter'd eye.

I did remind thee of our own dear Lake,
By the old Hall which may be mine no more.
Leman's is fair; but think not I forsake
The sweet remembrance of a dearer shore:
Sad havoc Time must with my memory make
Ere *that* or *thou* can fade these eyes before;
Though, like all things which I have loved, they are
Resign'd for ever, or divided far.

The world is all before me; I but ask
Of Nature that with which she will comply—
It is but in her summer's sun to bask,
To mingle with the quiet of her sky,
To see her gentle face without a mask,
And never gaze on it with apathy.
She was my early friend, and now shall be
My sister—till I look again on thee.

I can reduce all feelings but this one,
And that I would not;—for at length I see

Such scenes as those wherein my life begun,
The earliest—even the only paths for me:
Had I but sooner learnt the crowd to shun,
I had been better than I now can be;
The passions which have torn me would have slept;
I had not suffer'd, and *thou* hadst not wept.

With false Ambition what had I to do?
Little with Love, and least of all with Fame;
And yet they came unsought, and with me grew,
And made me all which they can make—a name.
Yet this was not the end I did pursue;
Surely I once beheld a nobler aim.
But all is over—I am one the more
To baffled millions which have gone before.

And for the future, this world's future may
From me demand but little of my care;
I have outlived myself by many a day;
Having survived so many things that were;
My years have been no slumber, but the prey
Of ceaseless vigils; for I had the share
Of life which might have fill'd a century,
Before its fourth in time had pass'd me by.

And for the remnant which may be to come,
I am content; and for the past I feel
Not thankless,—for within the crowded sum
Of struggles, happiness at times would steal;
And for the present, I would not benumb
My feelings farther.—Nor shall I conceal
That with all this I still can look around,
And worship Nature with a thought profound.

For thee, my own sweet sister, in thy heart
I know myself secure, as thou in mine;

We were and are—I am, even as thou art—
Beings who ne'er each other can resign;
It is the same, together or apart,
From life's commencement to its slow decline
We are entwined—let death come slow or fast,
The tie which bound the first endures the last!

LEVES AMORES

ARTHUR SYMONS

Your kisses, and the way you curl,
Delicious and distracting girl,
Into one's arms, and round about,
Inextricably in and out
Twining luxuriously, as twine
The clasping tangles of the vine;
So loving to be loved, so gay
And greedy for our holiday;
Strong to embrace and long to kiss,
And strenuous for the sharper bliss,
A little tossing sea of sighs,
Till the slow calm seal up your eyes.
And then how prettily you sleep!
You nestle close and let me keep
My straying fingers in the nest
Of your warm comfortable breast;
And as I dream, lying awake,
Of sleep well wasted for your sake,
I feel the very pulse and heat
Of your young life-blood beat, and beat
With mine; and you are mine, my sweet!

THERE'S A REGRET

WILLIAM ERNEST HENLEY

There's a regret
So grinding, so immitigably sad,
Remorse thereby feels tolerant, even glad. . . .
Do you not know it yet?

For deeds undone
Rankle and snarl and hunger for their due,
Till there seems naught so despicable as you
In all the grin o' the sun.

Like an old shoe
The sea spurns and the land abhors, you lie
About the beach of Time, till by and by
Death, that derides you too—

Death, as he goes
His ragman's round, espies you, where you stray,
With half-an-eye, and kicks you out of his way
And then—and then, who knows

But the kind Grave
Turns on you, and you feel the convict Worm,
In that black bridewell working out his term,
Hanker and grope and crave?

"Poor fool that might—
That might, yet would not, dared not, let this be,
Think of it, here and thus made over to me
In the implacable night!"

And writhing, fain
And like a triumphing lover, he shall take
His fill where no high memory lives to make
His obscene victory vain.

A SONNET

CONRAD AIKEN

Think, when a starry night of bitter frost
Is ended, and the small pale winter sun
Shines on the garden trellis, ice-embossed,
And the stiff frozen flower-stalks, every one,
And turns their fine embroideries of ice
Into a loosening silver, skein by skein,
Warming cold sticks and stones, till, in a trice,
The garden sighs, and smiles, and breathes again:
And further think how the poor frozen snail
Creeps out with trembling horn to feel that heat,
And thaws the snowy mildew from his mail,
Stretching with all his length from his retreat:
Will he not praise, with his whole heart, the sun?
Then think at last I too am such an one.

THE LETTER

JOHN HALL WHEELOCK

The night is measureless, no voice, no cry,
  Pierces the dark in which the planet swings—
  It is the shadow of her bulk that flings
So deep a gloom on the enormous sky;
This timorous dust, this phantom that is I,
  Cowers in shelter, while the evening brings
  A sense of mystery and how all things
Waver like water and are gliding by.

Now, while the stars in heaven like blowing sand
  Drift to their darkness, while oblivion
  Hushes the fire of some fading sun,

I turn the page again—and there they stand,
Traced by love's fleeting but victorious hand,
The words: "My darling, my belovèd one."

111

E. E. CUMMINGS

perhaps it is to feel strike
the silver fish of her nakedness
with fins sharply pleasant, my

youth has travelled toward her these years

or to snare the timid like
of her mind to my mind that i

am come by little countries to the yes

of her youth.
And if somebody hears
what i say—let him be pitiful:
because i've travelled all alone
through the forest of wonderful,
and that my feet have surely known
the furious ways and the peaceful,

and because she is beautiful

LOVE IN THE VALLEY

GEORGE MEREDITH

Under yonder beech-tree single on the green-sward,
Couched with her arms behind her golden head,
Knees and tresses folded to slip and ripple idly,
Lies my young love sleeping in the shade.

Had I the heart to slide an arm beneath her,
  Press her parting lips as her waist I gather slow,
Waking in amazement she could not but embrace me:
  Then would she hold me and never let me go?

. . . . . .

Shy as the squirrel and wayward as the swallow,
  Swift as the swallow along the river's light
Circleting the surface to meet his mirrored winglets,
  Fleeter she seems in her stay than in her flight.
Shy as the squirrel that leaps among the pine-tops,
Wayward as the swallow overhead at set of sun,
She whom I love is hard to catch and conquer,
  Hard, but O the glory of the winning were she won!

When her mother tends her before the laughing mirror,
  Tying up her laces, looping up her hair,
Often she thinks, were this wild thing wedded,
  More love should I have, and much less care.
When her mother tends her before the lighted mirror,
  Loosening her laces, combing down her curls,
Often she thinks, were this wild thing wedded,
  I should miss but one for many boys and girls.

. . . . . .

Heartless she is as the shadow in the meadows
  Flying to the hills on a blue and breezy noon.
No, she is athirst and drinking up her wonder:
  Earth to her is young as the slip of the new moon.
Deals she an unkindness, 'tis but her rapid measure,
  Even as in a dance; and her smile can heal no less:
Like the swinging May-cloud that pelts the flowers with hail-
    stones
  Off a sunny border, she was made to bruise and bless.

Lovely are the curves of the white owl sweeping
  Wavy in the dusk lit by one large star.

LOVE IN THE VALLEY

Lone on the fir-branch, his rattle-note unvaried,
  Brooding o'er the gloom, spins the brown evejar.
Darker grows the valley, more and more forgetting:
  So were it with me if forgetting could be willed.
Tell the grassy hollow that holds the bubbling well-spring,
  Tell it to forget the source that keeps it filled.

. . . . . .

Stepping down the hill with her fair companions,
  Arm in arm, all against the raying West,
Boldly she sings, to the merry tune she marches,
  Brave is her shape, and sweeter unpossessed.
Sweeter, for she is what my heart first awaking
  Whispered the world was; morning light is she.
Love that so desires would fain keep her changeless;
  Fain would fling the net, and fain have her free.

Happy happy time, when the white star hovers
  Low over dim fields fresh with bloomy dew,
Near the face of dawn, that draws athwart the darkness,
  Threading it with colour, like yewberries the yew.
Thicker crowd the shades as the grave East deepens
  Glowing, and with crimson a long cloud swells.
Maiden still the morn is; and strange she is, and secret;
  Strange her eyes; her cheeks are cold as cold sea-shells.

. . . . . .

Sunrays, leaning on our southern hills and lighting
  Wild cloud-mountains that drag the hills along,
Oft ends the day of your shifting brilliant laughter
  Chill as a dull face frowning on a song.
Ay, but shows the South-West a ripple-feathered bosom
  Blown to silver while the clouds are shaken and ascend
Scaling the mid-heavens as they stream, there comes a sunset
  Rich, deep like love in beauty without end.

When at dawn she sighs, and like an infant to the window

Turns grave eyes craving light, released from dreams,
Beautiful she looks, like a white water-lily
Bursting out of bud in havens of the streams.
When from bed she rises clothed from neck to ankle
In her long nightgown sweet as boughs of May,
Beautiful she looks, like a tall garden lily
Pure from the night, and splendid for the day.

. . . . . .

Mother of the dews, dark eye-lashed twilight,
Low-lidded twilight, o'er the valley's brim,
Rounding on thy breast sings the dew-delighted skylark,
Clear as though the dewdrops had their voice in him.
Hidden where the rose-flush drinks the rayless planet,
Fountain-full he pours the spraying fountain-showers.
Let me hear her laughter, I would have her ever
Cool as dew in twilight, the lark above the flowers.

All the girls are out with their baskets for the primrose;
Up lanes, woods through, they troop in joyful bands.
My sweet leads: she knows not why, but now she loiters,
Eyes the bent anemones, and hangs her hands.
Such a look will tell that the violets are peeping,
Coming the rose: and unaware a cry
Springs in her bosom for odours and for colour,
Covert and the nightingale; she knows not why.

. . . . . .

Kerchiefed head and chin she darts between her tulips,
Streaming like a willow grey in arrowy rain:
Some bend beaten cheek to gravel, and their angel
She will be; she lifts them, and on she speeds again.
Black the driving raincloud breasts the iron gateway:
She is forth to cheer a neighbour lacking mirth.
So when sky and grass met rolling dumb for thunder
Saw I once a white dove, sole light of earth.

Prim little scholars are the flowers of her garden,
  Trained to stand in rows, and asking if they please.
I might love them well but for loving more the wild ones:
  O my wild ones! they tell me more than these.
You, my wild one, you tell of honied field-rose,
  Violet, blushing eglantine in life; and even as they,
They by the wayside are earnest of your goodness,
  You are of life's, on the banks that line the way.

. . . . . .

Peering at her chamber the white crowns the red rose,
  Jasmine winds the porch with stars two and three.
Parted is the window; she sleeps; the starry jasmine
  Breathes a falling breath that carries thoughts of me.
Sweeter unpossessed, have I said of her my sweetest?
  Not while she sleeps: while she sleeps the jasmine breathes,
Luring her to love; she sleeps; the starry jasmine
  Bears me to her pillow under white rose-wreaths.

Yellow with birdfoot-trefoil are the grass-glades;
  Yellow with cinquefoil of the dew-grey leaf;
Yellow with stonecrop; the moss-mounds are yellow;
  Blue-necked the wheat sways, yellowing to the sheaf.
Green-yellow bursts from the copse the laughing yaffle;
  Sharp as a sickle is the edge of shade and shine:
Earth in her heart laughs looking at the heavens,
  Thinking of the harvest: I look and think of mine.

. . . . . .

This I may know: her dressing and undressing
  Such a change of light shows as when the skies in sport
Shift from cloud to moonlight; or edging over thunder
  Slips a ray of sun; or sweeping into port
White sails furl; or on the ocean borders
  White sails lean along the waves leaping green.

Visions of her shower before me, but from eyesight
  Guarded she would be like the sun were she seen.

Front door and back of the mossed old farmhouse
  Open with the morn, and in a breezy link
Freshly sparkles garden to stripe-shadowed orchard,
  Green across the rill where on sand the minnows wink.
Busy in the grass the early sun of summer
  Swarms, and the blackbird's mellow fluting notes
Call my darling up with round and roguish challenge:
  Quaintest, richest carol of all the singing throats!

. . . . . .

Cool was the woodside; cool as her white dairy
  Keeping sweet the cream-pan; and there the boys from school,
Cricketing below, rushed brown and red with sunshine;
  O the dark translucence of the deep-eyed cool!
Spying from the farm, herself she fetched a pitcher
  Full of milk, and tilted for each in turn the beak.
Then a little fellow, mouth up and on tiptoe,
  Said, "I will kiss you": she laughed and leaned her cheek.

Doves of the fir-wood walling high our red roof
  Through the long noon coo, crooning through the coo.
Loose droop the leaves, and down the sleepy roadway
  Sometimes pipes a chaffinch; loose droops the blue.
Cows flap a slow tail knee-deep in the river,
  Breathless, given up to sun and gnat and fly.
Nowhere is she seen; and if I see her nowhere,
  Lightning may come, straight rains and tiger sky.

. . . . . .

O the golden sheaf, the rustling treasure-armful!
  O the nutbrown tresses nodding interlaced!
O the treasure-tresses one another over
  Nodding! O the girdle slack about the waist!

Slain are the poppies that shot their random scarlet
  Quick amid the wheatears: wound about the waist,
Gathered, see these brides of Earth one blush of ripeness.
  O the nutbrown tresses nodding interlaced!

Large and smoky red the sun's cold disk drops,
  Clipped by naked hills, on violet shaded snow:
Eastward large and still lights up a bower of moonrise,
  Whence at her leisure steps the moon aglow.
Nightlong on black print-branches our beech-tree
  Gazes in this whiteness: nightlong could I.
Here may life on death or death on life be painted.
  Let me clasp her soul to know she cannot die!

. . . . . .

Gossips count her faults; they scour a narrow chamber
  Where there is no window, read not heaven or her.
"When she was a tiny," one aged woman quavers,
  Plucks at my heart and leads me by the ear.
Faults she had once as she learnt to run and tumbled:
  Faults of feature some see, beauty not complete.
Yet, good gossips, beauty that makes holy
  Earth and air, may have faults from head to feet.

Hither she comes; she comes to me; she lingers,
  Deepens her brown eyebrows, while in new surprise
High rise the lashes in wonder of a stranger;
  Yet am I the light and living of her eyes.
Something friends have told her fills her heart to brimming,
  Nets her in her blushes, and wounds her, and tames.—
Sure of her haven, O like a dove alighting,
  Arms up, she dropped: our souls were in our names.

. . . . . .

Soon will she lie like a white frost sunrise.
  Yellow oats and brown wheat, barley pale as rye,

Long since your sheaves have yielded to the thresher,
  Felt the girdle loosened, seen the tresses fly.
Soon wiii she lie like a blood-red sunset.
  Swift with the to-morrow, green-winged Spring!
Sing from the South-West, bring her back the truants,
  Nightingale and swallow, song and dipping wing.

Soft new beech-leaves, up to beamy April
  Spreading bough on bough a primrose mountain, you
Lucid in the moon, raise lilies to the skyfields,
  Youngest green transfused in silver shining through:
Fairer than the lily, than the wild white cherry:
  Fair as in image my seraph love appears
Borne to me by dreams when dawn is at my eyelids:
  Fair as in the flesh she swims to me on tears.

. . . . . .

Could I find a place to be alone with heaven,
  I would speak my heart out: heaven is my need.
Every woodland tree is flushing like the dogwood,
  Flashing like the whitebeam, swaying like the reed.
Flushing like the dogwood crimson in October;
  Streaming like the flag-reed South-West blown;
Flashing as in gusts the sudden-lighted whitebeam:
  All seem to know what is for heaven alone.

ON THE BEACH AT FONTANA

JAMES JOYCE

Wind whines and whines the shingle,
The crazy pierstakes groan;
A senile sea numbers each single
Slimesilvered stone.

From whining wind and colder
Grey sea I wrap him warm

And touch his trembling fineboned shoulder
And boyish arm.

Around us fear, descending
Darkness of fear above
And in my heart how deep unending
Ache of love!

WITH HOW SAD STEPS

SIR PHILIP SIDNEY

With how sad steps, O Moon, thou climb'st the skies,
How silently, and with how wan a face!
What, may it be that even in heav'nly place
That busy archer his sharp arrows tries?
Sure, if that long-with-love-acquainted eyes
Can judge of love, thou feel'st a lover's case,
I read it in thy looks; thy languisht grace,
To me, that feel the like, thy state descries.
Then, ev'n of fellowship, O Moon, tell me,
Is constant love deem'd there but want of wit?
Are beauties there as proud as here they be?
Do they above love to be lov'd, and yet
Those lovers scorn whom that love doth possess?
Do they call virtue there ungratefulness?

ON DANTE'S DIVINE COMEDY

HENRY WADSWORTH LONGFELLOW

Oft have I seen at some cathedral door
A laborer, pausing in the dust and heat,
Lay down his burden, and with reverent feet
Enter, and cross himself, and on the floor

Kneel to repeat his paternoster o'er;
Far off the noises of the world retreat;
The loud vociferations of the street
Become an undistinguishable roar.
So, as I enter here from day to day,
And leave my burden at this minster gate,
Kneeling in prayer, and not ashamed to pray,
The tumult of the time disconsolate
To inarticulate murmurs dies away,
While the eternal ages watch and wait.

HOLY SONNETS

JOHN DONNE

Thou hast made me, and shall Thy work decay?
Repair me now, for now mine end doth haste,
I run to death, and death meets me as fast,
And all my pleasures are like yesterday;
I dare not move my dim eyes any way,
Despair behind, and death before doth cast
Such terror, and my feeble flesh doth waste
By sin in it, which it towards hell doth weigh;
Only Thou art above, and when towards Thee
By Thy leave I can look, I rise again;
But our old subtle foe so tempteth me,
That not one hour myself I can sustain;
Thy Grace may wing me to prevent his art,
And thou like Adamant draw mine iron heart.

O might those sighs and tears return again
Into my breast and eyes, which I have spent,
That I might in this holy discontent
Mourn with some fruit, as I have mourn'd in vain;

In mine Idolatry what showers of rain
Mine eyes did waste? what griefs my heart did rent?
That sufferance was my sin; now I repent;
'Cause I did suffer I must suffer pain.
Th' hydroptic drunkard, and night-scouting thief,
The itchy Lecher, and self-tickling proud
Have the remembrance of past joys, for relief
Of coming ills. To poor me is allow'd
No ease; for, long, yet vehement grief hath been
Th' effect and cause, the punishment and sin.

This is my play's last scene, here heavens appoint
My pilgrimage's last mile; and my race
Idly, yet quickly run, hath this last pace,
My span's last inch, my minute's latest point,
And gluttonous death, will instantly unjoint
My body, and soul, and I shall sleep a space,
But my ever-waking part shall see that face,
Whose fear already shakes my every joint:
Then, as my soul, to heaven her first seat, takes flight,
And earth-born body, in the earth shall dwell,
So, fall my sins, that all may have their right,
To where they're bred, and would press me, to hell.
Impute me righteous, thus purg'd of evil,
For thus I leave the world, the flesh, the devil.

At the round earth's imagin'd corners, blow
Your trumpets, Angels, and arise, arise
From death, you numberless infinities
Of souls, and to your scatter'd bodies go,
All whom the flood did, and fire shall o'erthrow,
All whom war, dearth, age, agues, tyrannies,
Despair, law, chance, hath slain, and you whose eyes,
Shall behold God, and never taste death's woe.

But let them sleep, Lord, and me mourn a space,
For, if above all these, my sins abound,
'Tis late to ask abundance of Thy grace,
When we are there, here on this lowly ground,
Teach me how to repent; for that's as good
As if Thou hadst seal'd my pardon, with Thy blood.

If poisonous minerals, and if that tree,
Whose fruit threw death on else immortal us,
If lecherous goats, if serpents envious
Cannot be damn'd; alas! why should I be?
Why should intent or reason, born in me,
Make sins, else equal, in me more heinous?
And mercy being easy, and glorious
To God; in His stern wrath, why threatens He?
But who am I, that dare dispute with Thee
O God? Oh! of thine only worthy blood,
And my tears, make a heavenly Lethean flood,
And drown in it my sin's black memory;
That Thou remember them, some claim as debt,
I think it mercy, if Thou wilt forget.

Death be not proud, though some have called thee
Mighty and dreadful, for, thou art not so,
For, those, whom thou think'st, thou dost overthrow,
Die not, poor death, nor yet canst thou kill me.
From rest and sleep, which but thy pictures be,
Much pleasure, then from thee, much more must flow,
And soonest our best men with thee do go,
Rest of their bones, and soul's delivery.
Thou art slave to Fate, Chance, kings, and desperate men,
And dost with poison, war, and sickness dwell,
And poppy, or charms can make us sleep as well,
And better than thy stroke; why swell'st thou then?

One short sleep past, we wake eternally,
And death shall be no more; death, thou shalt die.

Batter my heart, three-person'd God; for, you
As yet but knock, breathe, shine, and seek to mend;
That I may rise, and stand, o'erthrow me, and bend
Your force, to break, blow, burn and make me new.
I, like an usurp'd town, to another due,
Labour to admit you, but Oh, to no end,
Reason your viceroy in me, me should defend,
But is captiv'd, and proves weak or untrue.
Yet dearly I love you, and would be loved fain,
But am betroth'd unto your enemy:
Divorce me, unite, or break that knot again,
Take me to you, imprison me, for I
Except you enthral me, never shall be free,
Nor ever chaste, except you ravish me.

THE LARK NOW LEAVES HIS WAT'RY NEST

SIR WILLIAM DAVENANT

The lark now leaves his wat'ry nest,
  And climbing, shakes his dewy wings,
He takes your window for the east,
  And to implore your light, he sings;
Awake, awake, the morn will never rise
Till she can dress her beauty at your eyes.

The merchant bows unto the seaman's star,
  The ploughman from the sun his season takes;
But still the lover wonders what they are,
  Who look for day before his mistress wakes.
Awake, awake, break through your veils of lawn,
Then draw your curtains, and begin the dawn.

A PARTING

MICHAEL DRAYTON

Since there's no help, come let us kiss and part:
  Nay, I have done, you get no more of me;
And I am glad, yea, glad with all my heart,
  That thus so clearly I myself can free.
Shake hands for ever, cancel all our vows,
  And, when we meet at any time again,
Be it not seen in either of our brows
  That we one jot of former love retain.

Now, at the last gasp of Love's latest breath,
  When, his pulse failing, Passion speechless lies,
When Faith is kneeling by his bed of death,
  And Innocence is closing up his eyes;
Now, if thou wouldst, when all have given him over,
From death to life thou mightst him yet recover.

FAREWELL TO JULIET

WILFRID SCAWEN BLUNT

Juliet, farewell. I would not be forgiven
Even if I forgave. These words must be
The last between us two in Earth or Heaven,
The last and bitterest. You are henceforth free
For ever from my bitter words and me.
You shall not at my hand be further vexed
With either love, reproach or jealousy
(So help me Heaven), in this world or the next.
Our souls are single for all time to come
And for eternity, and this farewell

Is as the trumpet note, the crack of doom,
Which heralds an eternal silence. Hell
Has no more fixed and absolute decree.
And Heaven and Hell may meet,—yet never we.

A MORNING SONG FOR IMOGEN

WILLIAM SHAKESPEARE

Hark! hark! the lark at heaven's gate sings,
  And Phœbus 'gins arise,
His steeds to water at those springs
  On chalic'd flowers that lies;
And winking Mary-buds begin
  To ope their golden eyes:
With everything that pretty is,
  My lady sweet arise:
      Arise, arise.

ECHO'S LAMENT OF NARCISSUS

BEN JONSON

Slow, slow, fresh fount, keep time with my salt tears;
  Yet slower, yet; O faintly, gentle springs:
List to the heavy part the music bears,
  Woe weeps out her division, when she sings.
    Droop herbs and flowers,
    Fall grief in showers,
    Our beauties are not ours;
      O, I could still,
Like melting snow upon some craggy hill,
    Drop, drop, drop, drop,
Since nature's pride is now a withered daffodil.

THE CRYING OF WATER

ARTHUR SYMONS

O water, voice of my heart, crying in the sand,
All night long crying with a mournful cry,
As I lie and listen, and cannot understand
The voice of my heart in my side or the voice of the sea,
O water crying for rest, is it I, is it I?
All night long the water is crying to me.

Unresting water, there shall never be rest
Till the last moon drop and the last tide fail,
And the fire of the end begin to burn in the west;
And the heart shall be weary and wonder and cry like the sea,
All life long crying without avail,
As the water all night long is crying to me.

ODE TO THE WEST WIND

PERCY BYSSHE SHELLEY

O Wild West Wind, thou breath of Autumn's being,
Thou, from whose unseen presence the leaves dead
Are driven, like ghosts from an enchanter fleeing,
Yellow, and black, and pale, and hectic red,
Pestilence-stricken multitudes: O thou,
Who chariotest to their dark wintry bed
The wingèd seeds, where they lie cold and low,
Each like a corpse within its grave, until
Thine azure sister of the spring shall blow
Her clarion o'er the dreaming earth, and fill
(Driving sweet buds like flocks to feed in air)
With living hues and odors plain and hill:
Wild Spirit, which art moving everywhere;
Destroyer and preserver; hear, O hear!

ODE TO THE WEST WIND

Thou on whose stream, mid the steep sky's commotion,
Loose clouds like earth's decaying leaves are shed,
Shook from the tangled boughs of Heaven and Ocean,
Angels of rain and lightning: there are spread
On the blue surface of thine airy surge,
Like the bright hair uplifted from the head
Of some fierce Maenad, even from the dim verge
Of the horizon to the zenith's height
The locks of the approaching storm. Thou dirge
Of the dying year, to which this closing night
Will be the dome of a vast sepulchre,
Vaulted with all thy congregated might
Of vapors, from whose solid atmosphere
Black rain, and fire, and hail will burst: Oh hear!

Thou who didst waken from his summer dreams
The blue Mediterranean, where he lay,
Lulled by the coil of his crystalline streams,
Beside a pumice isle in Baiæ's bay,
And saw in sleep old palaces and towers
Quivering within the wave's intenser day,
All overgrown with azure moss and flowers
So sweet, the sense faints picturing them! Thou
For whose path the Atlantic's level powers
Cleave themselves into chasms, while far below
The sea-blooms and the oozy woods which wear
The sapless foliage of the ocean, know
Thy voice, and suddenly grow gray with fear,
And tremble and despoil themselves. Oh hear!

If I were a dead leaf thou mightest bear;
If I were a swift cloud to fly with thee;
A wave to pant beneath thy power, and share
The impulse of thy strength, only less free
Than thou, O uncontrollable! If even

I were as in my boyhood, and could be
The comrade of thy wanderings over heaven,
As then, when to outstrip thy skyey speed
Scarce seemed a vision; I would ne'er have striven
As thus with thee in prayer in my sore need.
Oh lift me as a wave, a leaf, a cloud!
I fall upon the thorns of life! I bleed!
A heavy weight of hours has chained and bowed
One too like thee: tameless, and swift, and proud.

Make me thy lyre, even as the forest is:
What if my leaves are falling like its own!
The tumult of thy mighty harmonies
Will take from both a deep autumnal tone,
Sweet tho' in sadness. Be thou, spirit fierce,
My spirit! Be thou me, impetuous one!
Drive my dead thoughts over the universe
Like withered leaves to quicken a new birth!
And, by the incantation of this verse,
Scatter, as from an unextinguisht hearth
Ashes and sparks, my words among mankind!
Be thro' my lips to unawakened earth
The trumpet of a prophecy! O, wind,
If Winter comes, can Spring be far behind?

LINES

PERCY BYSSHE SHELLEY

The cold earth slept below,
  Above the cold sky shone;
And all around, with a chilling sound,
  From caves of ice and fields of snow,
  The breath of night like death did flow
  Beneath the sinking moon.

THE LAKE

The wintry hedge was black,
  The green grass was not seen,
The birds did rest on the bare thorn's breast,
  Whose roots, beside the pathway track,
  Had bound their folds o'er many a crack,
  Which the frost had made between.

Thine eyes glowed in the glare
  Of the moon's dying light;
As a fen-fire's beam on a sluggish stream,
  Gleams dimly, so the moon shone there,
  And it yellowed the strings of thy raven hair,
  That shook in the wind of night.

The moon made thy lips pale, beloved—
  The wind made thy bosom chill—
The night did shed on thy dear head
  Its frozen dew, and thou didst lie
  Where the bitter breath of the naked sky
  Might visit thee at will.

THE LAKE

JAMES STEPHENS

He could see the little lake
Cuddled on a mountain's arm,
And the rushes were a'shake,
On the margin of the lake.

And the gloom of evening threw
On the surface of the lake,
Just a shadow on the blue
Where the night came creeping through.

There was silence all around,
Not a whisper stirred the lake,
And the trees made not a sound
Standing silent in the ground.

Then a moon of beauty swept
One slim finger on the lake,
And the glory of it crept
Past the lilies where they slept,

And just where a lily flung
Its broad flag upon the lake
Was a dead face pale and young
And the wet hair spread and swung;

And the moon beamed mild and dim
On that dead face in the lake,
Then it grew fierce, wide and grim,
And a mad moon glared at Him.

ODE TO A NIGHTINGALE

JOHN KEATS

My heart aches, and a drowsy numbness pains
  My sense, as though of hemlock I had drunk,
Or emptied some dull opiate to the drains
  One minute past, and Lethe-wards had sunk:
'Tis not through envy of thy happy lot,
  But being too happy in thine happiness,—
    That thou, light-winged Dryad of the trees,
        In some melodious plot
Of beechen green, and shadows numberless,
  Singest of summer in full-throated ease.

ODE TO A NIGHTINGALE

O, for a draught of vintage! that hath been
  Cool'd a long age in the deep-delved earth,
Tasting of Flora and the country green,
  Dance, and Provençal song, and sunburnt mirth!
O for a beaker full of the warm South,
  Full of the true, the blushful Hippocrene,
    With beaded bubbles winking at the brim,
        And purple-stained mouth;
  That I might drink, and leave the world unseen,
    And with thee fade into the forest dim:

Fade far away, dissolve, and quite forget
  What thou among the leaves hast never known,
The weariness, the fever, and the fret
  Here, where men sit and hear each other groan;
Where palsy shakes a few, sad, last gray hairs,
  Where youth grows pale, and spectre-thin, and dies;
    Where but to think is to be full of sorrow
        And leaden-eyed despairs,
  Where Beauty cannot keep her lustrous eyes,
    Or new Love pine at them beyond to-morrow.

Away! away! for I will fly to thee,
  Not charioted by Bacchus and his pards,
But on the viewless wings of Poesy,
  Though the dull brain perplexes and retards:
Already with thee! tender is the night,
  And haply the Queen-Moon is on her throne,
    Cluster'd around by all her starry Fays;
        But here there is no light,
  Save what from heaven is with the breezes blown
    Through verdurous glooms and winding mossy ways.

I cannot see what flowers are at my feet,
  Nor what soft incense hangs upon the boughs,

But, in embalmed darkness, guess each sweet
  Wherewith the seasonable month endows
The grass, the thicket, and the fruit-tree wild;
  White hawthorn, and the pastoral eglantine;
    Fast fading violets cover'd up in leaves;
        And mid-May's eldest child,
  The coming musk-rose, full of dewy wine,
    The murmurous haunt of flies on summer eaves.

Darkling I listen; and, for many a time
  I have been half in love with easeful Death,
Call'd him soft names in many a mused rhyme,
  To take into the air my quiet breath;
Now more than ever seems it rich to die,
  To cease upon the midnight with no pain,
    While thou art pouring forth thy soul abroad
        In such an ecstasy!
  Still wouldst thou sing, and I have ears in vain—
    To thy high requiem become a sod.

Thou wast not born for death, immortal Bird!
  No hungry generations tread thee down;
The voice I hear this passing night was heard
  In ancient days by emperor and clown:
Perhaps the self-same song that found a path
  Through the sad heart of Ruth, when, sick for home,
    She stood in tears amid the alien corn;
        The same that oft-times hath
  Charm'd magic casements, opening on the foam
    Of perilous seas, in faery lands forlorn.

Forlorn! the very word is like a bell
  To toll me back from thee to my sole self!
Adieu! the fancy cannot cheat so well
  As she is fam'd to do, deceiving elf.

Adieu! adieu! thy plaintive anthem fades
Past the near meadows, over the still stream,
Up the hill-side; and now 'tis buried deep
In the next valley-glades:
Was it a vision, or a waking dream?
Fled is that music:—Do I wake or sleep?

SONNET

JOHN KEATS

Bright star! would I were steadfast as thou art—
Not in lone splendour hung aloft the night,
And watching, with eternal lids apart,
Like Nature's patient sleepless Eremite,
The moving waters at their priestlike task
Of pure ablution round earth's human shores,
Or gazing on the new soft fallen mask
Of snow upon the mountains and the moors—
No—yet still steadfast, still unchangeable,
Pillow'd upon my fair love's ripening breast,
To feel for ever its soft fall and swell,
Awake for ever in a sweet unrest,
Still, still to hear her tender-taken breath
Half passionless, and so swoon on to death.

ON THE SALE BY AUCTION OF KEATS' LOVE LETTERS

OSCAR WILDE

These are the letters which Endymion wrote
To one he loved in secret, and apart.
And now the brawlers of the auction mart
Bargain and bid for each poor blotted note,

Ay! for each separate pulse of passion quote
The merchant's price. I think they love not art
Who break the crystal of a poet's heart
That small and sickly eyes may glare and gloat.

Is it not said that many years ago,
In a far Eastern town, some soldiers ran
With torches through the midnight, and began
To wrangle for mean raiment, and to throw
Dice for the garments of a wretched man,
Not knowing the God's wonder, or His woe?

DAISY

FRANCIS THOMPSON

Where the thistle lifts a purple crown
Six foot out of the turf,
And the harebell shakes on the windy hill—
O breath of the distant surf!—

The hills look over on the South,
And southward dreams the sea;
And with the sea-breeze hand in hand
Came innocence and she.

Where 'mid the gorse the raspberry
Red for the gatherer springs;
Two children did we stray and talk
Wise, idle, childish things.

She listened with big-lipped surprise,
Breast-deep 'mid flower and spine:
Her skin was like a grape whose veins
Run snow instead of wine.

DAISY

She knew not those sweet words she spake,
  Nor knew her own sweet way;
But there's never a bird, so sweet a song
  Thronged in whose throat all day.

Oh, there were flowers in Storrington
  On the turf and on the spray;
But the sweetest flower on Sussex hills
  Was the Daisy-flower that day!

Her beauty smoothed earth's furrowed face.
  She gave me tokens three:—
A look, a word of her winsome mouth,
  And a wild raspberry.

A berry red, a guileless look,
  A still word,—strings of sand!
And yet they made my wild, wild heart
  Fly down to her little hand.

For standing artless as the air
  And candid as the skies,
She took the berries with her hand
  And the love with her sweet eyes.

The fairest things have fleetest end,
  Their scent survives their close:
But the rose's scent is bitterness
  To him that loved the rose.

She looked a little wistfully,
  Then went her sunshine way:—
The sea's eye had a mist on it,
  And the leaves fell from the day.

She went her unremembering way,
She went and left in me
The pang of all the partings gone,
And partings yet to be.

She left me marveling why my soul
Was sad that she was glad;
At all the sadness in the sweet,
The sweetness in the sad.

Still, still I seemed to see her, still
Look up with soft replies,
And take the berries with her hand,
And the love with her lovely eyes.

Nothing begins, and nothing ends,
That is not paid with moan,
For we are born in other's pain,
And perish in our own.

WE HAVE BEEN HAPPY

MAX EASTMAN

We have been happy in this little straight-up square house on the rolling moors.
It is like a child's drawing of a house on crumpled yellow paper.
If all the sheep that used to live in this house when it was a barn
Came trotting and huddling in a great woolly crowd over the hill,
Shouting baa baa, and each ringing a little resurrection bell under his throat,
That would not sound so happy as we have been all summer long under the sheep's roof.

The wind can not blow so happy, though he sounds a high note like bright fire through the screened window beside our beds.
The great sea can not say it with his blue swinging and hushed thunderous murmur along the low still shore.
The mist that blows in from the sea and sweeps over the moors like a murmur,
Tells nothing, though coming so near with his farness away.
And the little pine grove that will not grow high because it is bound to be strong and green,
And the huge birds that fly over that grove like thoughts over a Chinese poem but never go in—
They have not noticed how the flower of our joy grew here and blossomed all summer without any more reason than the sky has.
And nothing they could do with their solemnly far wandering wings,
Or the kingbirds with their tiny wings that quiver like sunbeams,
Or the humming-birds whose wings are invisible and sing,
Or I, a poet, with rhythm and meaning upon my tongue, would tell forth our happiness.
And so I have only spoken these words, and I will save them for you like a child's drawing on a piece of paper.

WHEN I HEARD AT THE CLOSE OF THE DAY

WALT WHITMAN

When I heard at the close of the day how my name had been receiv'd with plaudits in the capitol, still it was not a happy night for me that follow'd;
And else, when I carous'd, or when my plans were accomplish'd, still I was not happy;

But the day when I rose at dawn from the bed of perfect health, refresh'd, singing, inhaling the ripe breath of autumn,
When I saw the full moon in the west grow pale and disappear in the morning light,
When I wander'd alone over the beach, and undressing, bathed, laughing with the cool waters, and saw the sun rise,
And when I thought how my dear friend, my lover, was on his way coming, O then I was happy;
O then each breath tasted sweeter—and all that day my food nourish'd me more—and the beautiful day pass'd well,
And the next came with equal joy—and with the next, at evening, came my friend;
And that night, while all was still, I heard the waters roll slowly continually up the shores,
I heard the hissing rustle of the liquid and sands, as directed to me, whispering, to congratulate me,
For the one I love most lay sleeping by me under the same cover in the cool night,
In the stillness, in the autumn moonbeams, his face was inclined toward me,
And his arm lay lightly around my breast—and that night I was happy.

TO A MOUNTAIN DAISY

On Turning One Down with the Plough in April, 1786

ROBERT BURNS

Wee, modest, crimson-tippèd flow'r,
Thou's met me in an evil hour;
For I maun crush amang the stoure
Thy slender stem.
To spare thee now is past my pow'r,
Thou bonny gem.

TO A MOUNTAIN DAISY

Alas! it's no thy neebor sweet,
The bonny Lark, companion meet!
Bending thee 'mang the dewy weet!
        Wi' speckl'd breast,
When upward-springing, blythe, to greet
        The purpling east.

Cauld blew the bitter-biting north
Upon thy early, humble birth;
Yet cheerfully thou glinted forth
        Amid the storm,
Scarce rear'd above the parent-earth
        Thy tender form.

The flaunting flow'rs our gardens yield,
High shelt'ring woods and wa's maun shield,
But thou, beneath the random bield
        O' clod or stane,
Adorns the histie stibble-field,
        Unseen, alane.

There, in thy scanty mantle clad,
Thy snawie bosom sun-ward spread,
Thou lifts thy unassuming head
        In humble guise;
But now the share uptears thy bed,
        And low thou lies!

Such is the fate of artless Maid,
Sweet flow'ret of the rural shade!
By love's simplicity betray'd,
        And guileless trust,
Till she, like thee, all soil'd, is laid
        Low i' the dust.

Such is the fate of simple Bard,
On life's rough ocean luckless starr'd!

Unskilful he to note the card
Of prudent lore,
Till billows rage, and gales blow hard,
And whelm him o'er!

Such fate to suffering worth is giv'n,
Who long with wants and woes has striv'n,
By human pride or cunning driv'n
To mis'ry's brink,
Till wrench'd of ev'ry stay but Heav'n,
He, ruin'd, sink!

Ev'n thou who mourn'st the Daisy's fate,
That fate is thine—no distant date;
Stern Ruin's ploughshare drives, elate,
Full on thy bloom,
Till crush'd beneath the furrow's weight,
Shall be thy doom!

TO A MOUSE

On Turning Her Up in Her Nest with the Plough
November, 1785

ROBERT BURNS

Wee, sleekit, cowrin', tim'rous beastie,
O, what a panic's in thy breastie!
Thou need na start awa sae hasty,
Wi' bick'ring brattle!
I wad be laith to rin an' chase thee,
Wi' murd'ring pattle!

I'm truly sorry man's dominion
Has broken Nature's social union,

An' justifies that ill opinion,
Which mak's thee startle,
At me, thy poor, earth-born companion,
An' fellow-mortal!

I doubt na, whyles, but thou may thieve;
What then? poor beastie, thou maun live!
A daimen-icker in a thrave
'S a sma' request:
I'll get a blessin' wi' the lave,
And never miss't!

Thy wee bit housie, too, in ruin!
Its silly wa's the win's are strewin'!
An' naething, now, to big a new ane,
O' foggage green!
An' bleak December's winds ensuin',
Baith snell an' keen!

Thou saw the fields laid bare and waste,
An' weary winter comin' fast,
An' cozie here, beneath the blast,
Thou thought to dwell,
Till crash! the cruel coulter past,
Out thro' thy cell.

That wee bit heap o' leaves an' stibble,
Has cost thee mony a weary nibble!
Now thou's turn'd out, for a' thy trouble,
But house or hauld,
To thole the winter's sleety dribble,
An' cranreuch cauld!

But Mousie, thou are no thy lane,
In proving foresight may be vain:

The best laid schemes o' mice an' men
Gang aft a-gley,
An' lea'e us nought but grief an' pain,
For promised joy.

Still thou are blest, compar'd wi' me!
The present only toucheth thee:
But, och! I backward cast my e'e
On prospects drear!
An' forward tho' I canna see,
I guess an' fear!

A SLUMBER DID MY SPIRIT SEAL

WILLIAM WORDSWORTH

A slumber did my spirit seal;
I had no human fears:
She seemed a thing that could not feel
The touch of earthly years.

No motion has she now, no force;
She neither hears nor sees;
Rolled round in earth's diurnal course,
With rocks, and stones, and trees.

BESIDE THE BED

CHARLOTTE MEW

Someone has shut the shining eyes, straightened and folded
The wandering hands quietly covering the unquiet breast:
So, smoothed and silenced you lie, like a child, not again to be questioned or scolded:
But, for you, not one of us believes that this is rest.

Not so to close the windows down can cloud and deaden

The blue beyond: or to screen the wavering flame subdue its breath:
Why, if I lay my cheek to your cheek, your gray lips, like dawn, would quiver and redden,
Breaking into the old, odd smile at this fraud of death.

Because all night you have not turned to us or spoken
It is time for you to wake; your dreams were never very deep:
I, for one, have seen the thin bright, twisted threads of them dimmed suddenly and broken.
This is only a most piteous pretense of sleep!

TO A TRAVELER

LIONEL JOHNSON

The mountains, and the lonely death at last
Upon the lonely mountains: O strong friend!
The wandering over, and the labor passed,
Thou art indeed at rest:
Earth gave thee of her best,
That labor and this end.

Earth was thy mother, and her true son thou:
Earth called thee to a knowledge of her ways,
Upon the great hills, up the great streams: now:
Upon earth's kindly breast
Thou art indeed at rest:
Thou, and thine arduous days.

Fare thee well, O strong heart! The tranquil night
Looks calmly on thee: and the sun pours down
His glory over thee, O heart of might!
Earth gives thee perfect rest:
Earth, whom thy swift feet pressed:
Earth, whom the vast stars crown.

LYCIDAS

JOHN MILTON

Yet once more, O ye laurels, and once more,
Ye myrtles brown, with ivy never sere,
I come to pluck your berries harsh and crude,
And with forced fingers rude
Shatter your leaves before the mellowing year.
Bitter constraint and sad occasion dear
Compels me to disturb your season due;
For Lycidas is dead, dead ere his prime,
Young Lycidas, and hath not left his peer.
Who would not sing for Lycidas? he knew
Himself to sing, and build the lofty rhyme.
He must not float upon his watery bier
Unwept, and welter to the parching wind,
Without the meed of some melodious tear.
  Begin, then, Sisters of the sacred well
That from beneath the seat of Jove doth spring;
Begin, and somewhat loudly sweep the string.
Hence with denial vain and coy excuse:
So may some gentle Muse
With lucky words favour my destined urn,
And as he passes turn,
And bid fair peace be to my sable shroud!
  For we were nursed upon the self-same hill,
Fed the same flock, by fountain, shade, and rill;
Together both, ere the high lawns appeared
Under the opening eyelids of the Morn,
We drove a-field, and both together heard
What time the grey-fly winds her sultry horn,
Battening our flocks with the fresh dews of night,
Oft till the star that rose at evening bright
Toward heaven's descent had sloped his westering wheel.

Meanwhile the rural ditties were not mute;
Tempered to the oaten flute
Rough Satyrs danced, and Fauns with cloven heel
From the glad sound would not be absent long;
And old Damœtas loved to hear our song.
  But, oh! the heavy change, now thou art gone,
Now thou art gone and never must return!
Thee, Shepherd, thee the woods and desert caves,
With wild thyme and the gadding vine o'ergrown,
And all their echoes, mourn.
The willows, and the hazel copses green,
Shall now no more be seen
Fanning their joyous leaves to thy soft lays.
As killing as the canker to the rose,
Or taint-worm to the weanling herds that graze,
Or frost to flowers, that their gay wardrobe wear,
When first the white-thorn blows;
Such, Lycidas, thy loss to shepherd's ear.
  Where were ye, Nymphs, when the remorseless deep
Closed o'er the head of your loved Lycidas?
For neither were ye playing on the steep
Where your old bards, the famous Druids, lie,
Nor on the shaggy top of Mona high,
Nor yet where Deva spreads her wizard stream.
Ay me! I fondly dream
"Had ye been there," . . . for what could that have done?
What could the Muse herself that Orpheus bore,
The Muse herself, for her enchanting son,
Whom universal nature did lament,
When, by the rout that made the hideous roar,
His gory visage down the stream was sent,
Down the swift Hebrus to the Lesbian shore?
  Alas! what boots it with uncessant care
To tend the homely, slighted, shepherd's trade,
And strictly meditate the thankless Muse?

Were it not better done, as others use,
To sport with Amaryllis in the shade,
Or with the tangles of Neaera's hair?
Fame is the spur that the clear spirit doth raise
(That last infirmity of noble mind)
To scorn delights and live laborious days;
But the fair guerdon when we hope to find,
And think to burst out into sudden blaze,
Comes the blind Fury with the abhorrèd shears,
And slits the thin-spun life. "But not the praise,"
Phœbus replied, and touched my trembling ears:
"Fame is no plant that grows on mortal soil,
Nor in the glistering foil
Set off to the world, nor in broad rumour lies,
But lives and spreads aloft by those pure eyes
And perfect witness of all-judging Jove;
As he pronounces lastly on each deed,
Of so much fame in heaven expect thy meed."
  O fountain Arethuse, and thou honoured flood,
Smooth-sliding Mincius, crowned with vocal reeds,
That strain I heard was of a higher mood.
But now my oat proceeds,
And listens to the Herald of the Sea,
That came in Neptune's plea.
He asked the waves, and asked the felon winds,
What hard mishap hath doomed this gentle swain?
And questioned every gust of rugged wings
That blows from off each beakèd promontory.
They knew not of his story;
And sage Hippotades their answer brings,
That not a blast was from his dungeon strayed:
The air was calm, and on the level brine
Sleek Panope with all her sisters played.
It was that fatal and perfidious bark,
Built in the eclipse, and rigged with curses dark,

That sunk so low that sacred head of thine.
  Next, Camus, reverend sire, went footing slow,
His mantle hairy, and his bonnet sedge,
Inwrought with figures dim, and on the edge
Like to that sanguine flower inscribed with woe.
"Ah! who hath reft," quoth he, "my dearest pledge?"
Last came, and last did go,
The Pilot of the Galilean Lake;
Two massy keys he bore of metals twain
(The golden opes, the iron shuts amain).
He shook his mitred locks, and stern bespake:—
"How well could I have spared for thee, young swain,
Enow of such as, for their bellies' sake,
Creep, and intrude, and climb into the fold!
Of other care they little reckoning make
Than how to scramble at the shearers' feast,
And shove away the worthy bidden guest.
Blind mouths! that scarce themselves know how to hold
A sheep-hook, or have learnt aught else the least
That to the faithful herdsman's art belongs!
What recks it them? What need they? They are sped;
And, when they list, their lean and flashy songs
Grate on their scrannel pipes of wretched straw;
The hungry sheep look up, and are not fed,
But, swoln with wind and the rank mist they draw,
Rot inwardly, and foul contagion spread;
Besides what the grim wolf with privy paw
Daily devours apace, and nothing said.
But that two-handed engine at the door
Stands ready to smite once, and smite no more."
  Return, Alpheus; the dread voice is past
That shrunk thy streams; return, Sicilian Muse,
And call the vales, and bid them hither cast
Their bells and flowerets of a thousand hues.
Ye valleys low, where the mild whispers use

Of shades, and wanton winds, and gushing brooks,
On whose fresh lap the swart star sparely looks,
Throw hither all your quaint enamelled eyes,
That on the green turf suck the honeyed showers,
And purple all the ground with vernal flowers.
Bring the rathe primrose that forsaken dies,
The tufted crow-toe, and pale jessamine,
The white pink, and the pansy freaked with jet,
The glowing violet,
The musk-rose, and the well-attired woodbine,
With cowslips wan that hang the pensive head,
And every flower that sad embroidery wears;
Bid amaranthus all his beauty shed,
And daffadillies fill their cups with tears,
To strew the laureate hearse where Lysid lies.
For so, to interpose a little ease,
Let our frail thoughts dally with false surmise.
Ay me! whilst thee the shores and sounding seas
Wash far away, where'er thy bones are hurled;
Whether beyond the stormy Hebrides,
Where thou perhaps under the whelming tide
Visit'st the bottom of the monstrous world;
Or whether thou, to our moist vows denied,
Sleep'st by the fable of Bellerus old,
Where the great Vision of the guarded mount
Looks toward Namancos and Bayona's hold.
Look homeward, Angel, now, and melt with ruth:
And, O ye dolphins, waft the hapless youth.
  Weep no more, woeful shepherds, weep no more,
For Lycidas, your sorrow, is not dead,
Sunk though he be beneath the watery floor.
So sinks the day-star in the ocean bed,
And yet anon repairs his drooping head,
And tricks his beams, and with new-spangled ore
Flames in the forehead of the morning sky:

So Lycidas sunk low, but mounted high,
Through the dear might of Him that walked the waves,
Where, other groves and other streams along,
With nectar pure his oozy locks he laves,
And hears the unexpressive nuptial song,
In the blest kingdoms meek of joy and love.
There entertain him all the Saints above,
In solemn troops, and sweet societies,
That sing, and singing in their glory move,
And wipe the tears for ever from his eyes.
Now, Lycidas, the shepherds weep no more;
Henceforth thou art the Genius of the shore,
In thy large recompense, and shalt be good
To all that wander in that perilous flood.

Thus sang the uncouth swain to the oaks and rills,
While the still morn went out with sandals grey:
He touched the tender stops of various quills,
With eager thought warbling his Doric lay:
And now the sun had stretched out all the hills,
And now was dropt into the western bay.
At last he rose, and twitched his mantle blue:
To-morrow to fresh woods, and pastures new.

WHEN LILACS LAST IN THE DOORYARD BLOOM'D

WALT WHITMAN

When lilacs last in the dooryard bloom'd,
And the great star early droop'd in the western sky in the night,
I mourn'd, and yet shall mourn with ever-returning spring.

Ever-returning spring, trinity sure to me you bring,
Lilac blooming perennial and drooping star in the west,
And thought of him I love.

2

O powerful western fallen star!
O shades of night—O moody, tearful night!
O great star disappear'd—O the black murk that hides the star!
O cruel hands that hold me powerless—O helpless soul of me!
O harsh surrounding cloud that will not free my soul.

3

In the dooryard fronting an old farm-house near the white-wash'd palings,
Stands the lilac-bush tall-growing with heart-shaped leaves of rich green,
With many a pointed blossom rising delicate, with the perfume strong I love,
With every leaf a miracle—and from this bush in the dooryard,
With delicate-color'd blossoms and heart-shaped leaves of rich green,
A sprig with its flower I break.

4

In the swamp in secluded recesses,
A shy and hidden bird is warbling a song.

Solitary the thrush,
The hermit withdrawn to himself, avoiding the settlements,
Sings by himself a song.

Song of the bleeding throat,
Death's outlet song of life (for well dear brother I know,
If thou wast not granted to sing thou would'st surely die).

5

Over the breast of the spring, the land, amid cities,
Amid lanes and through old woods, where lately the violets peep'd from the ground, spotting the gray debris,

Amid the grass in the fields each side of the lanes, passing the endless grass,
Passing the yellow-spear'd wheat, every grain from its shroud in the dark-brown fields uprisen,
Passing the apple-tree blows of white and pink in the orchards,
Carrying a corpse to where it shall rest in the grave,
Night and day journeys a coffin.

6

Coffin that passes through lanes and streets,
Through day and night with the great cloud darkening the land,
With the pomp of the inloop'd flags with the cities draped in black,
With the show of the States themselves as of crape-veil'd women standing,
With processions long and winding and the flambeaus of the night,
With the countless torches lit, with the silent sea of faces and the unbared heads,
With the waiting depot, the arriving coffin, and the sombre faces,
With dirges through the night, with the thousand voices rising strong and solemn,
With all the mournful voices of the dirges pour'd around the coffin,
The dim-lit churches and the shuddering organs—where amid these you journey,
With the tolling tolling bells' perpetual clang,
Here, coffin that slowly passes,
I give you my sprig of lilac.

7

(Nor for you, for one alone,
Blossoms and branches green to coffins all I bring,

For fresh as the morning, thus would I chant a song for you O
sane and sacred death.

All over bouquets of roses,
O death, I cover you over with roses and early lilies,
But mostly and now the lilac that blooms the first,
Copious I break, I break the sprigs from the bushes,
With loaded arms I come, pouring for you,
For you and the coffins all of you O death.)

8

O western orb sailing the heaven,
Now I know what you must have meant as a month since I
walk'd,
As I walk'd in silence the transparent shadowy night,
As I saw you had something to tell as you bent to me night after
night,
As you droop'd from the sky low down as if to my side (while
the other stars all look'd on),
As we wander'd together the solemn night (for something I
know not what kept me from sleep),
As the night advanced, and I saw on the rim of the west how
full you were of woe,
As I stood on the rising ground in the breeze in the cool trans-
parent night,
As I watch'd where you pass'd and was lost in the netherward
black of the night,
As my soul in its trouble dissatisfied sank, as where you sad orb,
Concluded, dropt in the night, and was gone.

9

Sing on there in the swamp,
O singer bashful and tender, I hear your notes, I hear your call,
I hear, I come presently, I understand you,
But a moment I linger, for the lustrous star has detain'd me,
The star my departing comrade holds and detains me.

10

O how shall I warble myself for the dead one there I loved?
And how shall I deck my song for the large sweet soul that has gone?
And what shall my perfume be for the grave of him I love?

Sea-winds blown from east and west,
Blown from the Eastern sea and blown from the Western sea, till there on the prairies meeting,
These and with these and the breath of my chant,
I'll perfume the grave of him I love.

11

O what shall I hang on the chamber walls?
And what shall the pictures be that I hang on the walls,
To adorn the burial-house of him I love?

Pictures of growing spring and farms and homes,
With the Fourth-month eve at sundown, and the gray smoke lucid and bright,
With floods of the yellow gold of the gorgeous, indolent, sinking sun, burning, expanding the air,
With the fresh sweet herbage under foot, and the pale green leaves of the trees prolific,
In the distance the flowing glaze, the breast of the river, with a wind-dapple here and there,
With ranging hills on the banks, with many a line against the sky, and shadows,
And the city at hand with dwellings so dense, and stacks of chimneys,
And all the scenes of life and the workshops, and the workmen homeward returning.

12

Lo, body and soul—this land,
My own Manhattan with spires, and the sparkling and hurrying tides, and the ships,

The varied and ample land, the South and the North in the light, Ohio's shores and flashing Missouri,
And ever the far-spreading prairies cover'd with grass and corn.

Lo, the most excellent sun so calm and haughty,
The violet and purple morn with just-felt breezes,
The gentle soft-born measureless light,
The miracle spreading bathing all, the fulfill'd noon,
The coming eve delicious, the welcome night and the stars,
Over my cities shining all, enveloping man and land.

13

Sing on, sing on you gray-brown bird,
Sing from the swamps, the recesses, pour your chant from the bushes,
Limitless out of the dusk, out of the cedars and pines.

Sing on dearest brother, warble your reedy song,
Loud human song, with voice of uttermost woe.

O liquid and free and tender!
O wild and loose to my soul—O wondrous singer!
You only I hear—yet the star holds me (but will soon depart),
Yet the lilac with mastering odor holds me.

14

Now while I sat in the day and look'd forth,
In the close of the day with its light and the fields of spring, and the farmers preparing their crops,
In the large unconscious scenery of my land with its lakes and forests,
In the heavenly aerial beauty (after the perturb'd winds and the storms),
Under the arching heavens of the afternoon swift passing, and the voices of children and women,

The many-moving sea-tides, and I saw the ships how they sail'd,
And the summer approaching with richness, and the fields all busy with labor,
And the infinite separate houses, how they all went on, each with its meals and minutia of daily usages,
And the streets how their throbbings throbb'd, and the cities pent—lo, then and there,
Falling upon them all and among them all, enveloping me with the rest,
Appear'd the cloud, appear'd the long black trail,
And I knew death, its thought, and the sacred knowledge of death.

Then with the knowledge of death as walking one side of me,
And the thought of death close-walking the other side of me,
And I in the middle as with companions, and as holding the hands of companions,
I fled forth to the hiding receiving night that talks not,
Down to the shores of the water, the path by the swamp in the dimness,
To the solmen shadowy cedars and ghostly pines so still.

And the singer so shy to the rest receiv'd me,
The gray-brown bird I know receiv'd us comrades three,
And he sang the carol of death, and a verse for him I love.

From deep secluded recesses,
From the fragrant cedars and the ghostly pines so still,
Came the carol of the bird.

And the charm of the carol rapt me,
As I held as if by their hands my comrades in the night,
And the voice of my spirit tallied the song of the bird.

Come lovely and soothing death,
Undulate round the world, serenely arriving, arriving,

In the day, in the night, to all, to each,
Sooner or later delicate death.

Prais'd be the fathomless universe,
For life and joy, and for objects and knowledge curious,
And for love, sweet love—but praise! praise! praise!
For the sure-enwinding arms of cool-enfolding death.

Dark mother always gliding near with soft feet,
Have none chanted for thee a chant of fullest welcome?
Then I chant it for thee, I glorify thee above all,
I bring thee a song that when thou must indeed come, come unfalteringly.

Approach strong deliveress,
When it is so, when thou hast taken them I joyously sing the dead,
Lost in the loving floating ocean of thee,
Laved in the flood of thy bliss O death.

From me to thee glad serenades,
Dances for thee I propose saluting thee, adornments and feastings for thee,
And the sights of the open landscape and the high-spread sky are fitting,
And life and the fields, and the huge and thoughtful night.

The night in silence under many a star,
The ocean shore and the husky whispering wave whose voice I know,
And the soul turning to thee O vast and well-veil'd death,
And the body gratefully nestling close to thee.

Over the tree-tops I float thee a song,
Over the rising and sinking waves, over the myriad fields and the prairies wide,

Over the dense-pack'd cities all and the teeming wharves and ways,
I float this carol with joy, with joy to thee O death.

15

To the tally of my soul,
Loud and strong kept up the gray-brown bird,
With pure deliberate notes spreading filling the night.

Loud in the pines and cedars dim,
Clear in the freshness moist and the swamp-perfume,
And I with my comrades there in the night.

While my sight that was bound in my eyes unclosed,
As to long panoramas of visions.

And I saw askant the armies,
I saw as in noiseless dreams hundreds of battle-flags,
Borne through the smoke of the battles and pierc'd with missiles I saw them,
And carried hither and yon through the smoke, and torn and bloody,
And at last but a few shreds left on the staffs (and all in silence),
And the staffs all splinter'd and broken.

I saw battle-corpses, myriads of them,
And the white skeletons of young men, I saw them,
I saw the debris and debris of all the slain soldiers of the war,
But I saw they were not as was thought,
They themselves were fully at rest, they suffer'd not,
The living remain'd and suffer'd, the mother suffer'd,
And the wife and the child and the musing comrade suffer'd,
And the armies that remain'd suffer'd.

16

Passing the visions, passing the night,
Passing, unloosing the hold of my comrades' hands

Passing the song of the hermit bird and the tallying song of my soul,
Victorious song, death's outlet song, yet varying ever-altering song,
As low and wailing, yet clear the notes, rising and falling, flooding the night,
Sadly sinking and fainting, as warning and warning, and yet again bursting with joy,
Covering the earth and filling the spread of the heaven,
As that powerful psalm in the night I heard from recesses,
Passing, I leave thee lilac with heart-shaped leaves,
I leave thee there in the door-yard, blooming, returning with spring.

I cease from my song for thee,
From my gaze on thee in the west, fronting the west, communing with thee,
O comrade lustrous with silver face in the night.

Yet each to keep and all, retrievements out of the night,
The song, the wondrous chant of the gray-brown bird,
And the tallying chant, the echo arous'd in my soul,
With the lustrous and drooping star with the countenance full of woe,
With the holders holding my hand nearing the call of the bird,
Comrades mine and I in the midst, and their memory ever to keep, for the dead I loved so well,
For the sweetest, wisest soul of all my days and lands—and this for his dear sake,
Lilac and star and bird twined with the chant of my soul,
There in the fragrant pines and the cedars dusk and dim.

PART V

ADVENTURES IN IDEAS

TO A HAPPY WARRIOR

(George Wyndham)

WILFRID SCAWEN BLUNT

Glory to God who made a man like this!
To God be praise who in the empty heaven
Set Earth's gay globe
With its green vesture given
And nuptial robe
To be the home enthroned of happiness!
Who from the silences
Of the dumb Universe,
For listening ears,
Constructed song
And fashioned the first note
Of the first linnet's throat,
His audible whisper the deep woods among!
Who, with His dance-masters,
The dappled deer
And their fleet fawns,
With rhythmic beat
Of their light feet
Upon the thyme-sweet lawns,
Framed the free gamut of the wakening year
And gave command to mirth His minister
That all things young and glad
And mad,
In this fair world's expanse
Should dance!
Praise be! and most for these,
The lyric ecstasies
Sublime in each least lot,

The passionate plot
Subtly contrived to propagate their kind
By beast and bird and in Man's livelier mind
To make of life new life,
Of joy new joy, in corporal bliss
Entwined,
Man's who is man and wife,
Though neither he have thought
Nor she, in their love blind,
Of that child's smile
Half hers half his
Unborn, the while
They clasp and kiss!
These are the vastnesses
That bid us give God glory for his depths of guile.

And he? The ultimate man,
The heir of their delight,
Whose keener sight
Grasped the full vision of Time's master-plan,
And who, because he knew,
Found power to do
What the rest dared not and was thus the priest
Of the divine high feast
Of Love on Earth? Poet, whose prosody
Embraced heaven's infinite blue
And the white light of stars,
The moon's proud chastity
And the sea beating on its prison bars;
Whose ritual
Was the procession of the months and days
In ordered praise
Of ceremonial flowers, Earth's virginal
Patchwork of shredded colours in the grass;
Whose incense was

The mist of morning, and whose sacrifice
The sun in splendour by whose light all live?
How shall we give
To one thus wise
Our homage who so loved him and alas
Now weep for him with unavailing eyes?

For what is wisdom more than this one thought,
To harvest happiness? Time has its wheat,
Its rule of life discreet,
By scholars taught,
For daily bread; and its weeds too,
Its wild crop of the woods which is not bought,
Its way that fools call folly,
Choke-pear, crab, holly,
All the riot
Of the bird's diet,
For maid and boy,
Their winter-pick of joy,
If they but knew!
And these to learn and gather in their prime
Is youth's sublime.

Here lay his victory. Not flowers alone
Nor fruits were his,
But the world's sadnesses
He gathered also, its loves lost and gone,
The tragic things that are
As the maple leaves
Of the fast dying year,
Crowning its funeral car,
The glory of its passing set on fire
In the late hedges,
The wreathed bryony
Black with the Autumn saltings of the Sea,

And those lone sedges at the lake's edges
Which winter winds have whitened on the mere.
These, as the symbols of his Soul's romance
In antique lands,
He bound into the sheaves
Of his desire,
A wreath,
Nobler for death.
Of these he fashioned a new chivalry
For days to be,
Incorporate with the glories of all Time,
The immortal rhyme
Of Roland and the paladins of France,
Of Charlemagne,
The Cid Bivar of Spain,
And those proud questers of the Holy Grail
Who rode with Arthur *cap à pie* in mail,
Till in his hands
It seemed the actual lance
Of Lancelot trembled and took edge and shook
Defiance at his foes in Lyonnesse,
No less than those
Of whom it is written in the old French book
That he pursued and slew and scattering rent
Their ranks in fear,
While the Earth trembled his glad shout to hear.
So he in his high rage in Parliament.

Anon, too, at the feasts
Where with the knights and ladies crowned he sat,
Their laureate
Of that famed Table Round, its pleasure's lord,
His was the tongue
To celebrate their praise,
Theirs the adored,

With virile minstrelsy and mirth and song,
And generous wine
Outpoured
In draughts divine from flagons
Rich with the mellow fruitage of the vine;
His was the tongue
To tell of valorous deeds
Done for high honour's needs
On pestilent dragons in dank forest places
Vanquished and slain, and felon knights laid low,
For fair loved faces
In days long ago;
Amorous sad tales of dolorous mistakes
At hands that sought to save;
Ancient heart-aches,
Each laid to rest in its forgotten grave.
And with them griefs, which venturing found their hour,
Fruitage and flower,
And were fulfilled of joy;—and chiefly hers,
Royal sad Guinevere's,
Noblest of all among the tragic dead.
Of her he loved to tell.
And he did well;
For she, the lady of his dreams, one night,
As it is said,
In Glastonbury,
Hearing his young steps hurry
As to a goal,
To kneel at her dead feet,
Where as she lay with her sleep-folded palms
In the long calms
Of a passed soul,
Did from her cerements white
Awake,
And feel her passionate heart beat

To his desire,
And in new bride's attire
Arise and live a woman for his sake,
A woman and no dream.
These were the rhapsodies of life to him,
The things that his heart's zeal
Made real.

And who shall wonder if to-day we weep
Our Prince of happiness,
Our warrior dead?
If we, who saw
These wonders beyond law,
And his proud soul's essay
To live the great life of the Fellowship
In our late day,
Should mourn him fled,
Yet, none the less,
Give praise
To God, with chastened but undoubting lip,
For this exemplar of His works and ways?
Since that we know that in His scheme of bliss
No permanent anguish is,
But beauty only and high ruth and truth,
And that Life's law is this:
Pleasure is duty, duty pleasure
In equal measure;
And Time's happiness
God's all-sufficient reason with the wise,
As with this man
Who sleeps in Paradise.

GRAVES

CARL SANDBURG

I dreamed one man stood against a thousand,
One man damned as a wrongheaded fool.
One year and another he walked the streets,
And a thousand shrugs and hoots
Met him in the shoulders and mouths he passed.

He died alone
And only the undertaker came to his funeral.

Flowers grow over his grave anod in the wind,
And over the graves of the thousand, too,
The flowers grow anod in the wind.

Flowers and the wind,
Flowers anod over the graves of the dead,
Petals of red, leaves of yellow, streaks of white,
Masses of purple sagging . . .
I love you and your great way of forgetting.

GOD'S ACRE

WITTER BYNNER

Because we felt there could not be
A mowing in reality
So white and feathery-blown and gay,
With blossoms of wild caraway,
I said to Celia, "Let us trace
The secret of this pleasant place!"
We knew some deeper beauty lay
Beneath the blooms of caraway;

And when we brushed these blooms aside
We came to paupers who had died:
Rough wooden shingles row on row,
And God's name written there—"John Doe."

ELEGY WRITTEN IN A COUNTRY CHURCHYARD

THOMAS GRAY

The curfew tolls the knell of parting day,
  The lowing herd wind slowly o'er the lea,
The ploughman homeward plods his weary way,
  And leaves the world to darkness and to me.

Now fades the glimmering landscape on the sight,
  And all the air a solemn stillness holds,
Save where the beetle wheels his droning flight,
  And drowsy tinklings lull the distant folds;

Save that from yonder ivy-mantled tower
  The moping owl does to the moon complain
Of such as, wand'ring near her secret bower,
  Molest her ancient solitary reign.

Beneath those rugged elms, that yew-tree's shade,
  Where heaves the turf in many a mould'ring heap,
Each in his narrow cell for ever laid,
  The rude Forefathers of the hamlet sleep.

The breezy call of incense-breathing Morn,
  The swallow twitt'ring from the straw-built shed,
The cock's shrill clarion, or the echoing horn,
  No more shall rouse them from their lowly bed.

IN A COUNTRY CHURCHYARD

For them no more the blazing hearth shall burn,
  Or busy housewife ply her evening care;
No children run to lisp their sire's return,
  Or climb his knees the envied kiss to share.

Oft did the harvest to their sickle yield,
  Their furrow oft the stubborn glebe has broke;
How jocund did they drive their team afield!
  How bowed the woods beneath their sturdy stroke!

Let not Ambition mock their useful toil,
  Their homely joys, and destiny obscure;
Nor Grandeur hear, with a disdainful smile,
  The short and simple annals of the poor.

The boast of heraldry, the pomp of power,
  And all that beauty, all that wealth e'er gave,
Await alike th' inevitable hour.
  The paths of glory lead but to the grave.

Nor you, ye Proud, impute to these the fault,
  If Mem'ry o'er their tomb no trophies raise,
Where thro' the long-drawn aisle and fretted vault
  The pealing anthem swells the note of praise.

Can storied urn or animated bust
  Back to its mansion call the fleeting breath?
Can Honour's voice provoke the silent dust,
  Or Flatt'ry soothe the dull cold ear of Death?

Perhaps in this neglected spot is laid
  Some heart once pregnant with celestial fire;
Hands, that the rod of empire might have swayed,
  Or waked to ecstasy the living lyre.

But Knowledge to their eyes her ample page
  Rich with the spoils of time did ne'er unroll;
Chill Penury repressed their noble rage,
  And froze the genial current of the soul.

Full many a gem, of purest ray serene,
  The dark unfathomed caves of ocean bear;
Full many a flower is born to blush unseen,
  And waste its sweetness on the desert air.

Some village-Hampden, that with dauntless breast
  The little tyrant of his fields withstood;
Some mute inglorious Milton here may rest,
  Some Cromwell guiltless of his country's blood.

Th' applause of list'ning senates to command,
  The threats of pain and ruin to despise,
To scatter plenty o'er a smiling land,
  And read their history in a nation's eyes,

Their lot forbad; nor circumscribed alone
  Their growing virtues, but their crimes confined:
Forbad to wade through slaughter to a throne,
  And shut the gates of mercy on mankind,

The struggling pangs of conscious truth to hide.
  To quench the blushes of ingenuous shame.
Or heap the shrine of Luxury and Pride
  With incense kindled at the Muse's flame.

Far from the madding crowd's ignoble strife,
  Their sober wishes never learned to stray;
Along the cool sequestered vale of life
  They kept the noiseless tenor of their way.

Yet ev'n these bones from insult to protect
 Some frail memorial still erected nigh,
With uncouth rhymes and shapeless sculpture decked,
 Implores the passing tribute of a sigh.

Their name, their years, spelt by th' unlettered Muse,
 The place of fame and elegy supply;
And many a holy text around she strews,
 That teach the rustic moralist to die.

For who, to dumb Forgetfulness a prey,
 This pleasing anxious being e'er resigned,
Left the warm precincts of the cheerful day,
 Nor cast one longing ling'ring look behind?

On some fond breast the parting soul relies,
 Some pious drops the closing eye requires;
Ev'n from the tomb the voice of Nature cries,
 Ev'n in our ashes live their wonted fires.

For thee, who mindful of th' unhonoured Dead
 Dost in these lines their artless tale relate
If chance, by lonely contemplation led,
 Some kindred spirit shall inquire thy fate,

Haply some hoary-headed swain may say,
 "Oft have we seen him at the peep of dawn
"Brushing with hasty steps the dews away
 "To meet the sun upon the upland lawn.

"There at the foot of yonder nodding beech,
 "That wreathes its old fantastic roots so high,
"His listless length at noontide would he stretch,
 "And pore upon the brook that babbles by.

"Hard by yon wood, now smiling as in scorn,
  "Mutt'ring his wayward fancies he would rove,
"Now drooping, woeful wan, like one forlorn,
  "Or crazed with care, or crossed in hopeless love.

"One morn I missed him on the customed hill,
  "Along the heath and near his fav'rite tree;
"Another came; nor yet beside the rill,
  "Nor up the lawn, nor at the wood was he;

"The next with dirges due in sad array
  "Slow thro' the church-way path we saw him borne.
"Approach and read (for thou can'st read) the lay,
  "Graved on the stone beneath yon aged thorn."

The Epitaph

Here rests his head upon the lap of Earth
  A Youth to Fortune and to Fame unknown.
Fair Science frowned not on his humble birth,
  And Melancholy marked him for her own.

Large was his bounty, and his soul sincere,
  Heav'n did a recompence as largely send;
He gave to Misery all he had, a tear,
  He gained from Heav'n ('twas all he wished) a friend.

No farther seek his merits to disclose,
  Or draw his frailties from their dread abode
(There they alike in trembling hope repose),
  The bosom of his Father and his God.

FUNERAL IN HUNGARY

KAY BOYLE

Rakob is dead, what is left of him travels
The ruts and the road puddles granite with frost.
He is dead and his Sunday suit on him, and the look of the dead
Like a wreath on his mouth for a while.

Six white oxen with black ribbons entwined
In their horns draw his hearse. He is lighter than pig-root,
Not so heavy as dung to them. Their collars are timber,
Their mouths slobber sweet with the morning.

Around his corpse roam the gypsy musicians
Singing wild high nostalgic, their gut strings bewailing
That Rakob is dead. Behind come the cattle
Yoked two by two, their tails hanging clean as silk tassels,
The weight moving slow as a heart's beat from split hoof to
split hoof.

Behind, drawn by four pie-bald oxen, the family of Rakob
Wears clothes that are festive, the horns of the oxen
Are twisted with flowers. The music that stamps on foot by
their wheels
Is foreign to grief; the jigs and the reels of the country dances
Danced with the flute and accordion playing.

Rakob wrote down the way these things should be,
Leaving his cattle and lands, his fortune and words
Set down in his last will and testament, saying:
"My cattle were my peaceful friends. Let them follow close to
me when I go towards the grave.
Because of their innocence I have taken them into my heart

As if they were little children who came to me.
None of my people feel for them the gratitude they have earned
So I have put aside for them a portion of my wealth that they may die in peace,
Not of abuse, while laboring in the fields as they have always done.
I bid my relatives to follow me with music playing, wearing
Their dance dresses and colored waistcoats. My death will bring them ease
And so they must rejoice. I ask them not to allow the temptations of the city
To seduce them. Only a knowledge of the seasons can bring dignity to man.
But let an orchestra of gypsies wander beside me grieving
Who have cause to grieve now that their horses may no longer
Roam at night grazing in my pastures, now that they may no longer in the darkness
Gather my pine-brush and light fires unmolested underneath my trees."

ODE ON A GRECIAN URN

JOHN KEATS

Thou still unravish'd bride of quietness,
  Thou foster-child of silence and slow time,
Sylvan historian, who canst thus express
  A flowery tale more sweetly than our rhyme:
What leaf-fring'd legend haunts about thy shape
  Of deities or mortals, or of both,
    In Tempe or the dales of Arcady?
  What men or gods are these? What maidens loth?
What mad pursuit? What struggle to escape?
  What pipes and timbrels? What wild ecstasy?

2

Heard melodies are sweet, but those unheard
  Are sweeter; therefore, ye soft pipes, play on;
Not to the sensual ear, but, more endear'd,
  Pipe to the spirit ditties of no tone:
Fair youth, beneath the trees, thou canst not leave
  Thy song, nor ever can those trees be bare;
    Bold Lover, never, never canst thou kiss,
Though winning near the goal—yet, do not grieve;
  She cannot fade, though thou hast not thy bliss,
    For ever wilt thou love, and she be fair!

3

Ah, happy, happy boughs! that cannot shed
  Your leaves, nor ever bid the Spring adieu;
And, happy melodist, unwearied,
  For ever piping songs for ever new;
More happy love! more happy, happy love!
  For ever warm and still to be enjoy'd,
    For ever panting, and for ever young;
All breathing human passion far above,
  That leaves a heart high-sorrowful and cloy'd,
    A burning forehead, and a parching tongue.

4

Who are these coming to the sacrifice?
  To what green altar, O mysterious priest,
Lead'st thou that heifer lowing at the skies,
  And all her silken flanks with garlands drest?
What little town by river or sea shore,
  Or mountain-built with peaceful citadel,
    Is emptied of this folk, this pious morn?
And, little town, thy streets for evermore
  Will silent be; and not a soul to tell
    Why thou art desolate, can e'er return.

5

O Attic shape! Fair attitude! with brede
  Of marble men and maidens overwrought,
With forest branches and the trodden weed;
  Thou, silent form, dost tease us out of thought
As doth eternity: Cold Pastoral!
  When old age shall this generation waste,
    Thou shalt remain, in midst of other woe
Than ours, a friend to man, to whom thou say'st,
  "Beauty is truth, truth beauty,"—that is all
    Ye know on earth, and all ye need to know.

THE TRUE KNIGHT

STEPHEN HAWES

(Died 1523)

For knighthood is not in the feats of warre,
  As for to fight in quarrel right or wrong,
But in a cause which truth can not defarre:
  He ought himself for to make sure and strong,
  Justice to keep mixt with mercy among:
  And no quarrell a knight ought to take
  But for a truth, or for the common's sake.

EQUALITY

JAMES SHIRLEY

The glories of our blood and state
  Are shadows, not substantial things;
There is no armour against fate;
  Death lays his icy hand on kings:
    Scepter and crown
    Must tumble down,

And in the dust be equal made
With the poor crooked scythe and spade.

Some men with swords may reap the field,
   And plant fresh laurels where they kill;
But their strong nerves at last must yield;
   They tame but one another still:
      Early or late
      They stoop to fate,
And must give up their murmuring breath
While they, pale captives, creep to death.

The garlands wither on your brow;
   Then boast no more your mighty deeds:
Upon Death's purple altar now
   See where the victor-victim bleeds!
      Your heads must come
      To the cold tomb:
Only actions of the just
Smell sweet, and blossom in their dust.

I THINK I COULD TURN

WALT WHITMAN

I think I could turn and live with animals, they are so placid
   and self-contain'd;
I stand and look at them long and long.
They do not sweat and whine about their condition;
They do not lie awake in the dark and weep for their sins;
They do not make me sick discussing their duty to God;
Not one is dissatisfied—not one is demented with the mania of
   owning things;
Not one kneels to another, nor to his kind that lived thousands
   of years ago;
Not one is respectable or industrious over the whole earth.

TO CYRIACK SKINNER

JOHN MILTON

Cyriack, this three years' day these eyes, though clear,
To outward view, of blemish or of spot,
Bereft of light, their seeing have forgot;
Nor to their idle orbs doth sight appear
Of sun, or moon, or star, throughout the year,
Or man, or woman. Yet I argue not
Against Heaven's hand or will, nor bate a jot
Of heart or hope, but still bear up and steer
Right onward. What supports me, dost thou ask?
The conscience, friend, to have lost them overplied
In Liberty's defence, my noble task,
Of which all Europe rings from side to side.
This thought might lead me through the world's vain mask
Content, though blind, had I no better guide.

TO THE LORD GENERAL CROMWELL, MAY, 1652

JOHN MILTON

Cromwell, our chief of men, who through a cloud
Not of war only, but detractions rude,
Guided by faith and matchless fortitude,
To peace and truth thy glorious way hast plough'd,
And on the neck of crowned Fortune proud
Hast rear'd God's trophies, and his work pursued,
While Darwen stream, with blood of Scots imbrued,
And Dunbar field, resounds thy praises loud,
And Worcester's laureate wreath: yet much remains
To conquer still; peace hath her victories

No less renowned than war: new foes arise,
Threatening to bind our souls with secular chains.
Help us to save free conscience from the paw
Of hireling wolves, whose gospel is their maw.

SONNET ON CHILLON

LORD BYRON

Eternal Spirit of the chainless Mind!
Brightest in dungeons, Liberty! thou art,
For there thy habitation is the heart—
The heart which love of thee alone can bind;
And when thy sons to fetters are consign'd—
To fetters, and the damp vault's dayless gloom,
Their country conquers with their martyrdom,
And Freedom's fame finds wings on every wind.
Chillon! thy prison is a holy place,
And thy sad floor an altar; for 'twas trod,
Until his very steps have left a trace
Worn, as if thy cold pavement were a sod,
By Bonnivard!—May none those marks efface!
For they appeal from tyranny to God.

TO TOUSSAINT L'OUVERTURE

WILLIAM WORDSWORTH

Toussaint, the most unhappy man of men!
Whether the whistling Rustic tend his plough
Within thy hearing, or thy head be now
Pillowed in some deep dungeon's earless den;—
O miserable Chieftain! where and when
Wilt thou find patience? Yet die not; do thou
Wear rather in thy bonds a cheerful brow:

Though fallen thyself, never to rise again,
Live, and take comfort. Thou hast left behind
Powers that will work for thee; air, earth, and skies;
There's not a breathing of the common wind
That will forget thee; thou hast great allies;
Thy friends are exultations, agonies,
And love, and man's unconquerable mind.

FEELINGS OF A REPUBLICAN ON THE FALL OF BONAPARTE

PERCY BYSSHE SHELLEY

I hated thee, fallen tyrant! I did groan
To think that a most unambitious slave,
Like thou, shouldst dance and revel on the grave
Of Liberty. Thou mightst have built thy throne
Where it had stood even now: thou didst prefer
A frail and bloody pomp which time has swept
In fragments towards oblivion. Massacre,
For this I prayed, would on thy sleep have crept,
Treason and Slavery, Rapine, Fear, and Lust,
And stifled thee, their minister. I know
Too late, since thou and France are in the dust,
That virtue owns a more eternal foe
Than force or fraud: old Custom, legal Crime,
And bloody Faith the foulest birth of time.

TO RONGE

JOHN GREENLEAF WHITTIER

(This was written after reading the powerful and manly protest of Johannes Ronge against the "pious fraud" of the Bishop of Treves. The bold movement of the young Catholic priest of Prussian Silesia seemed to me full of promise to the cause of political as well as religious liberty in Europe. That it failed was due partly to the faults of the reformer, but mainly to the disagreement of the Liberals of Germany upon a matter of dogma, which prevented them from unity of action.)

Strike home, strong-hearted man! Down to the root
Of old oppression sink the Saxon steel.
Thy work is to hew down. In God's name then
Put nerve into thy task. Let other men
Plant, as they may, that better tree whose fruit
The wounded bosom of the Church shall heal.
Be thou the image-breaker. Let thy blows
Fall heavy as the Suabian's iron hand,
On crown or crosier, which shall interpose
Between thee and the weal of Fatherland.
Leave creeds to closet idlers. First of all,
Shake thou all German dream-land with the fall
Of that accursed tree, whose evil trunk
Was spared of old by Erfurt's stalwart Monk.
Fight not with ghosts and shadows. Let us hear
The snap of chain-links. Let our gladdened ear
Catch the pale prisoner's welcome, as the light
Follows thy axe-stroke, through his cell of night.
Be faithful to both worlds; nor think to feed
Earth's starving millions with the husks of creed.
Servant of Him whose mission high and holy
Was to the wronged, the sorrowing, and the lowly,
Thrust not His Eden promise from our sphere,
Distant and dim beyond the blue sky's span;
Like him of Patmos, see it, now and here,
The New Jerusalem comes down to man!
Be warned by Luther's error. Nor like him,
When the roused Teuton dashes from his limb
The rusted chain of ages, help to bind
His hands for whom thou claim'st the freedom of the mind!

LITANY FOR DICTATORSHIPS

STEPHEN VINCENT BENÉT

For all those beaten, for the broken heads,
The fosterless, the simple, the oppressed,
The ghosts in the burning city of our time . . .

For those taken in rapid cars to the house and beaten
By the skilful boys, the boys with the rubber fists,
—Held down and beaten, the table cutting their loins,
Or kicked in the groin and left, with the muscles jerking
Like a headless hen's on the floor of the slaughter-house
While they brought the next man in with his white eyes staring.
For those who still said "Red Front!" or "God Save the Crown!"
And for those who were not courageous
But were beaten nevertheless.
For those who spit out the bloody stumps of their teeth
Quietly in the hall,
Sleep well on stone or iron, watch for the time
And kill the guard in the privy before they die,
Those with the deep-socketed eyes and the lamp burning.

For those who carry the scars, who walk lame—for those
Whose nameless graves are made in the prison-yard
And the earth smoothed back before morning and the lime scattered.

For those slain at once. For those living through months and years
Enduring, watching, hoping, going each day
To the work or the queue for meat or the secret club,
Living meanwhile, begetting children, smuggling guns,
And found and killed at the end like rats in a drain.

LITANY FOR DICTATORSHIPS

For those escaping
Incredibly into exile and wandering there.
For those who live in the small rooms of foreign cities
And who yet think of the country, the long green grass,
The childhood voices, the language, the way wind smelt then,
The shape of rooms, the coffee drunk at the table,
The talk of friends, the loved city, the waiter's face,
The gravestones, with the name, where they will not lie
Nor in any of that earth. Their children are strangers.

For those who planned and were leaders and were beaten
And for those, humble and stupid, who had no plan
But were denounced, but grew angry, but told a joke,
But could not explain, but were sent away to the camp,
But had their bodies shipped back in the sealed coffins,
"Died of pneumonia." "Died trying to escape."

For those growers of wheat who were shot by their own wheat-
stacks,
For those growers of bread who were sent to the ice-locked
wastes,
And their flesh remembers their fields.

For those denounced by their smug, horrible children
For a peppermint-star and the praise of the Perfect State,
For all those strangled or gelded or merely starved
To make perfect states; for the priest hanged in his cassock,
The Jew with his chest crushed in and his eyes dying,
The revolutionist lynched by the private guards
To make perfect states, in the names of the perfect states.

For those betrayed by the neighbors they shook hands with
And for the traitors, sitting in the hard chair
With the loose sweat crawling their hair and their fingers
restless
As they tell the street and the house and the man's name.

And for those sitting at table in the house
With the lamp lit and the plates and the smell of food,
Talking so quietly; when they hear the cars
And the knock at the door, and they look at each other quickly
And the woman goes to the door with a stiff face,
Smoothing her dress.
"We are all good citizens here.
We believe in the Perfect State."
And that was the last
Time Tony or Karl or Shorty came to the house
And the family was liquidated later.
It was the last time.

We heard the shots in the night
But nobody knew next day what the trouble was
And a man must go to his work. So I didn't see him
For three days, then, and me near out of my mind
And all the patrols on the streets with their dirty guns
And when he came back, he looked drunk, and the blood was on him.

For the women who mourn their dead in the secret night,
For the children taught to keep quiet, the old children,
The children spat-on at school.
For the wrecked laboratory,
The gutted house, the dunged picture, the pissed-in well,
The naked corpse of Knowledge flung in the square
And no man lifting a hand and no man speaking.

For the cold of the pistol-butt and the bullet's heat,
For the rope that chokes, the manacles that bind,
The huge voice, metal, that lies from a thousand tubes
And the stuttering machine-gun that answers all.

For the man crucified on the crossed machine-guns
Without name, without resurrection, without stars,

His dark head heavy with death and his flesh long sour
With the smell of his many prisons—John Smith, John Doe,
John Nobody—oh, crack your mind for his name!
Faceless as water, naked as the dust,
Dishonored as the earth the gas-shells poison
And barbarous with portent.
                                        This is he.
This is the man they ate at the green table
Putting their gloves on ere they touched the meat.
This is the fruit of war, the fruit of peace,
The ripeness of invention, the new lamb,
The answer to the wisdom of the wise.
And still he hangs, and still he will not die,
And still, on the steel city of our years
The light fails and the terrible blood streams down.

We thought we were done with these things but we were
    wrong.
We thought, because we had power, we had wisdom.
We thought the long train would run to the end of Time.
We thought the light would increase.
Now the long train stands derailed and the bandits loot it.
Now the boar and the asp have power in our time.
Now the night rolls back on the West and the night is solid.
Our fathers and ourselves sowed dragon's teeth.
Our children know and suffer the armed men.

MINNIE AND MRS. HOYNE

KENNETH FEARING

She could die laughing,
  On Sunday noon, back of the pawn-shop, under the smoke-
      stack, with Mrs. Hoyne.
  She could hide her face in rags and die laughing on the street.

She could snicker in the broom closet. In the dark of the movies. In bed.
Die, at the way some people talk.
The things they talk about and believe and do.
She and Mrs. Hoyne could sit together and laugh.
Minnie could nicker in the dark alone.
Jesus, what do they mean?
Girls trying to be in love.
People worried about other people. About the world. Do they own it?
People that don't believe a street is what it looks like. They think there's more.
There isn't any more, the coo-coos.
She could die laughing.
Free milk for babies, Mrs. Hoyne!
Crazy liars, all of them, and what next?
Minnie will be a millionaire.
Mrs. Hoyne will fly a balloon.
Give my regards to the Queen of France when you get there.
Ask her if she remembers me: "Say, Queen,
Have you got any old bloomers you don't want, for Minnie Spohr?"
She could die, grinning among the buckets at midnight,
Snicker, staring down the elevator shaft,
Minnie doesn't care. Get the money!
She could die laughing some time
Alone in the broom closet on the forty-third floor.

ON PASSING THE NEW MENIN GATE

SIEGFRIED SASSOON

Who will remember, passing through this Gate,
The unheroic Dead who fed the guns?
Who shall absolve the foulness of their fate,—

Those doomed, conscripted, unvictorious ones?
  Crudely renewed, the Salient holds its own.
  Paid are its dim defenders by this pomp;
  Paid, with a pile of peace-complacent stone,
  The armies who endured that sullen swamp.

Here was the world's worst wound. And here with pride
"Their name liveth for ever," the Gateway claims.
Was ever an immolation so belied
As these intolerably nameless names?
Well might the Dead who struggled in the slime
Rise and deride this sepulchre of crime.

THE NEXT WAR

WILFRED OWEN

Out there, we've walked quite friendly up to Death;
  Sat down and eaten with him, cool and bland,—
  Pardoned his spilling mess-tins in our hand.
We've sniffed the green thick odour of his breath,—
Our eyes wept, but our courage didn't writhe.
  He's spat at us with bullets and he's coughed
  Shrapnel. We chorussed when he sang aloft;
We whistled while he shaved us with his scythe.

Oh, Death was never enemy of ours!
  We laughed at him, we leagued with him, old chum.
No soldier's paid to kick against his powers.
  We laughed, knowing that better men would come,
And greater wars; when each proud fighter brags
He wars on Death—for Life; not men—for flags.

ARMS AND THE BOY

WILFRED OWEN

Let the boy try along this bayonet-blade
How cold steel is, and keen with hunger of blood;
Blue with all malice, like a madman's flash;
And thinly drawn with famishing for flesh.

Lend him to stroke these blind, blunt bullet-heads
Which long to nuzzle in the hearts of lads,
Or give him cartridges of fine zinc teeth,
Sharp with the sharpness of grief and death.

For his teeth seem for laughing round an apple.
There lurk no claws behind his fingers supple;
And god will grow no talons at his heels,
Nor antlers through the thickness of his curls.

THE CONFLICT

C. DAY LEWIS

I sang as one
Who on a tilting deck sings
To keep their courage up, though the wave hangs
That shall cut off their sun.

As storm-cocks sing,
Flinging their natural answer in the wind's teeth,
And care not if it is waste of breath
Or birth-carol of spring.

As ocean-flyer clings
To height, to the last drop of spirit driving on
While yet ahead is land to be won
And work for wings.

INVOCATION TO THE WIND

Singing I was at peace,
Above the clouds, outside the ring:
For sorrow finds a swift release in song
And pride its poise.

Yet living here,
As one between two massing powers I live
Whom neutrality cannot save
Nor occupation cheer.

None such shall be left alive:
The innocent wing is soon shot down,
And private stars fade in the blood-red dawn
Where two worlds strive.

The red advance of life
Contracts pride, calls out the common blood,
Beats song into a single blade,
Makes a depth-charge of grief.

Move then with new desires,
For where we used to build and love
Is no man's land, and only ghosts can live
Between two fires.

INVOCATION TO THE WIND

JOSEPH KALAR

O sprinting of the wind over land
like a colt galloping swift
pounding over grass, neighing
to the sun, snorting howdoyoudo
to the clouds, with a flying mane—
O wind coming over the lean land
like a fatness of green in spring

or flowers blooming in Mojave
blow, blow into all dusty corners,
reach cool fingers beyond cobwebs
festooning this dark room where
throats are choked with dust and
beauty shrivels like mushrooms
in dry cellars—blow, blow, blow
into factories with windows of dust
and a shuffling of feet tired
in silk stockings, and fingers
red at the tips—blow, blow into
jail, come like a draught of spring
water to faces hungering against
steel bars—blow, blow into slums,
cleave the darkness festering
in mines, coal and iron, glide over
pale children bowing in beetfields—
blow wind, sprint over the land
like a colt pounding over grass—
rattle the shutters of this dark room
where beauty whimpers softly like a child—
O surely someday we'll fill the fields
with our dancing and laughing and singing,
O wind coming over the lean brown land
or flowers creeping over Mojave!

PROCRASTINATION

DOCTOR EDWARD YOUNG

Be wise to-day; 'tis madness to defer:
Next day the fatal precedent will plead,
Thus on, till wisdom is pushed out of life.
Procrastination is the thief of time;
Year after year it steals, till all are fled,

And to the mercies of a moment leaves
The vast concerns of an eternal scene.
If not so frequent, would not this be strange?
That 'tis so frequent, this is stranger still.
  Of man's miraculous mistakes this bears
The palm, "That all men are about to live,"
For ever on the brink of being born:
All pay themselves the compliment to think
They one day shall not drivel, and their pride
On this reversion takes up ready praise;
At least their own; their future selves applauds,
How excellent that life they ne'er will lead!
Time lodged in their own hands is Folly's vails;
That lodged in Fate's to wisdom they consign;
The thing they can't but purpose, they postpone.
'Tis not in folly not to scorn a fool,
And scarce in human wisdom to do more.
All promise is poor dilatory man,
And that through every stage. When young, indeed,
In full content we sometimes nobly rest,
Unanxious for ourselves, and only wish,
As duteous sons, our fathers were more wise.
At thirty man suspects himself a fool;
Knows it at forty, and reforms his plan;
At fifty chides his infamous delay,
Pushes his prudent purpose to resolve;
In all the magnanimity of thought
Resolves, and re-resolves; then dies the same.
  And why? because he thinks himself immortal,
All men think all men mortal but themselves;
Themselves, when some alarming shock of Fate
Strikes through their wounded hearts the sudden dread:
But their hearts wounded, like the wounded air,
Soon close; where past the shaft no trace is found.
As from the wing no scar the sky retains,

The parted wave no furrow from the keel,
So dies in human hearts the thought of death:
Even with the tender tear which Nature sheds
O'er those we love, we drop it in their grave.

TO DAFFODILS

ROBERT HERRICK

Fair Daffodils, we weep to see
You haste away so soon:
As yet the early-rising sun
Has not attain'd his noon.
Stay, stay,
Until the hasting day
Has run
But to the even-song;
And, having pray'd together, we
Will go with you along.

We have short time to stay, as you;
We have as short a spring;
As quick a growth to meet decay,
As you, or any thing.
We die
As your hours do, and dry
Away,
Like to the summer's rain;
Or as the pearls of morning's dew,
Ne'er to be found again.

GHOUL CARE

RALPH HODGSON

Sour fiend, go home and tell the Pit
For once you met your master,—
A man who carried in his soul
Three charms against disaster,
The Devil and disaster.

Away, away, and tell the tale
And start your whelps a-whining,
Say "In the greenwood of his soul
A lizard's eye was shining,
A little eye kept shining."

Away, away, and salve your sores,
And set your hags a-groaning,
Say "In the greenwood of his soul
A drowsy bee was droning,
A dreamy bee was droning."

Prodigious Bat! Go start the walls
Of Hell with horror ringing,
Say "In the greenwood of his soul
There was a goldfinch singing,
A pretty goldfinch singing."

And then come back, come, if you please,
A fiercer ghoul and ghaster,
With all the glooms and smuts of Hell
Behind you, I'm your master!
You know I'm still your master.

MAN

HENRY VAUGHAN

Weighing the stedfastness and state
  Of some mean things which here below reside,
Where birds like watchful Clocks the noiseless date
  And Intercourse of times divide,
Where Bees at night get home and hive, and flowrs
    Early, as well as late,
Rise with the Sun, and set in the same bowrs;

I would (said I) my God would give
The staidness of these things to man! for these
To his divine appointments ever cleve,
  And no new business breaks their peace;
The birds nor sow, nor reap, yet sup and dine,
    The flowers without clothes live,
Yet Solomon was never drest so fine.

  Man hath stil either toyes, or Care,
He hath no root, nor to one place is ty'd,
But ever restless and Irregular
  About this Earth doth run and ride,
He knows he hath a home, but scarce knows where,
    He sayes it is so far
That he hath quite forgot how to go there.

  He knocks at all doors, strays and roams,
Nay hath not so much wit as some stones have
Which in the darkest nights point to their homes,
  By some hid sense their Maker gave;
Man is the shuttle, to whose winding quest
    And passage through these looms
God order'd motion, but ordain'd no rest.

FROM FAR

A. E. HOUSMAN

From far, from eve and morning
  And yon twelve-winded sky,
The stuff of life to knit me
  Blew hither: here am I.

Now—for a breath I tarry
  Nor yet disperse apart—
Take my hand quick and tell me,
  What have you in your heart.

Speak now, and I will answer;
  How shall I help you, say;
Ere to the wind's twelve quarters
  I take my endless way.

ON HIS SEVENTY-FIFTH BIRTHDAY

WALTER SAVAGE LANDOR

I strove with none; for none was worth my strife,
  Nature I loved, and next to Nature, Art;
I warmed both hands before the fire of life,
  It sinks, and I am ready to depart.

EPIGRAM

WILLIAM WATSON

Momentous to himself as I to me
  Hath each man been that ever woman bore;
Once, in a lightning-flash of sympathy,
  I *felt* this truth, an instant, and no more.

CREDO

ROBINSON JEFFERS

My friend from Asia has powers and magic, he plucks a blue leaf from the young blue-gum
And gazing upon it, gathering and quieting
The God in his mind, creates an ocean more real than the ocean, the salt, the actual
Appalling presence, the power of the waters.
He believes that nothing is real except as we make it. I humbler have found in my blood
Bred west of Caucasus a harder mysticism.
Multitude stands in my mind but I think that the ocean in the bone vault is only
The bone vault's ocean: out there is the ocean's;
The water is the water, the cliff is the rock, come shocks and flashes of reality. The mind
Passes, the eye closes, the spirit is a passage;
The beauty of things was born before eyes and sufficient to itself; the heart-breaking beauty
Will remain when there is no heart to break for it.

THIS QUIET DUST

JOHN HALL WHEELOCK

Here in my curving hands I cup
This quiet dust; I lift it up.
Here is the mother of all thought;
Of this the shining heavens are wrought,
The laughing lips, the feet that rove,
The face, the body, that you love:
Mere dust, no more, yet nothing less,

And this has suffered consciousness,
Passion, and terror, this again
Shall suffer passion, death, and pain.

For, as all flesh must die, so all,
Now dust, shall live. 'Tis natural;
Yet hardly do I understand—
Here in the hollow of my hand
A bit of God Himself I keep,
Between two vigils fallen asleep.

TO HIM THAT WAS CRUCIFIED

WALT WHITMAN

My spirit to yours, dear brother;
Do not mind because many, sounding your name, do not understand you;
I do not sound your name, but I understand you (there are others also);
I specify you with joy, O my comrade, to salute you, and to salute those who are with you, before and since—and those to come also,
That we all labor together, transmitting the same charge and succession;
We few, equals, indifferent of lands, indifferent of times;
We, enclosers of all continents, all castes—allowers of all theologies,
Compassionaters, perceivers, rapport of men,
We walk silent among disputes and assertions, but reject not the disputers, nor any thing that is asserted;
We hear the bawling and din—as are reach'd at by divisions, jealousies, recriminations on every side,
They close peremptorily upon us, to surround us, my comrade,

Yet we walk unheld, free, the whole earth over, journeying up and down, till we make our ineffaceable mark upon time and the diverse eras,

Till we saturate time and eras, that the men and women of races, ages to come, may prove brethren and lovers, as we are.

DEEM NOT

GEORGE SANTAYANA

Deem not, because you see me in the press
Of this world's children run my fated race,
That I blaspheme against a proffered grace,
Or leave unlearned the love of holiness.
I honour not that sanctity the less
Whose aureole illumines not my face,
But dare not tread the secret, holy place
To which the priest and prophet have access.
For some are born to be beatified
By anguish, and by grievous penance done;
And some, to furnish forth the age's pride,
And to be praised of men beneath the sun;
And some are born to stand perplexed aside
From so much sorrow—of whom I am one.

I SOUGHT ON EARTH

GEORGE SANTAYANA

I sought on earth a garden of delight,
Or island altar to the Sea and Air,
Where gentle music were accounted prayer,
And reason, veiled, performed the happy rite.
My sad youth worshipped at the piteous height
Where God vouchsafed the death of man to share;

His love made mortal sorrow light to bear,
But his deep wounds put joy to shamèd flight.
And though his arms, outstretched upon the tree,
Were beautiful, and pleaded my embrace,
My sins were loth to look upon his face.
So came I down from Golgotha to thee,
Eternal Mother; let the sun and sea
Heal me, and keep me in thy dwelling-place.

BAPTISM

CLAUDE MCKAY

Into the furnace let me go alone;
Stay you without in terror of the heat.
I will go naked in—for thus 'tis sweet—
Into the weird depths of the hottest zone.
I will not quiver in the frailest bone,
You will not note one flicker of defeat;
My heart shall tremble not its fate to meet,
Nor mouth give utterance to any moan.
The yawning oven spits forth fiery spears;
Red aspish tongues shout wordlessly my name.
Desire destroys, consumes my mortal fears,
Transforming me into a shape of flame.
I will come out, back to your world of tears,
A stronger soul within a finer frame.

O EARTH!

RICHARD REALF

O Earth! thou hast not any wind that blows
Which is not music: every weed of thine
Pressed rightly flows in aromatic wine;

And every humble hedgerow flower that grows;
And every little brown bird that doth sing;
Hath something greater than itself, and bears
A living Word to every living thing,
Albeit it hold the Message unawares.
All shapes and sounds have something which is not
Of them: A Spirit broods amid the grass;
Vague outlines of the Everlasting Thought
Lie in the melting shadows as they pass;
The touch of an Eternal Presence thrills
The fringes of the sunset and the hills.

LIFE AND FAME

ABRAHAM COWLEY

Oh Life, thou Nothing's younger brother!
  So like, that one might take one for the other.
  What's somebody, or nobody?
In all the cobwebs of the schoolmen's trade,
We no such nice distinction woven see,
  As 'tis to be, or not to be.
Dream of a shadow! A reflection made
From the false glories of the gay reflected bow,
  Is a more solid thing than thou.
Vain weak-built isthmus, which dost proudly rise
  Up betwixt two eternities;
  Yet canst nor wave nor wind sustain,
But broken and o'erwhelm'd, the endless oceans meet again.

And with what rare inventions do we strive,
  Ourselves then to survive?
Wise, subtle arts, and such as well befit
  That nothing man's no wit.
Some with vast costly tombs would purchase it,

And by the proofs of Death pretend to live.
Here lies the Great—False marble, where?
Nothing but small, and sordid dust lies there.
Some build enormous mountain-palaces,
  The fools and architects to please:
A lasting life in well-hewn stone they rear:
  So he who on th' Egyptian shore,
Was slain so many hundred years before,
  Lives still (Oh life most happy and most dear!
  Oh life that epicures envy to hear!)
Lives in the dropping ruins of his amphitheatre.

His father-in-law an higher place does claim
In the seraphic entity of fame.
  He since that toy his death,
Does fill all mouths, and breathes in all men's breath.
'Tis true, the two immortal syllables remain,
  But, oh ye learned men explain,
  What essence, what existence this,
What substance, what subsistence, what hypostasis
  In six poor letters is?
In those alone does the great Cæsar live,
  'Tis all the conquer'd world could give.
  We poets madder yet than all,
With a refin'd fantastic vanity,
Think we not only have, but give eternity.
  Fain would I see that prodigal,
  Who his to-morrow would bestow,
For all old Homer's life e'er since he died till now.

306

E. E. CUMMINGS

if i

or anybody don't
know where it her his

my next meal's coming from
i say to hell with that
that doesn't matter (and if

he she it or everybody gets a
bellyful without
lifting my finger i say to hell
with that i

say that doesn't matter) but
if somebody
or you are beautiful or
deep or generous what
i say is

whistle that
sing that yell that spell
that out big (bigger than cosmic
rays war earthquakes famine or the ex

prince of whoses diving into
a whatses to rescue miss nobody's
probably handbag) because i say that's not

swell (get me) babe not (understand me) lousy
kid that's something else my sweet (i feel that's

true)

CHAUCER'S ENVOY TO THE STORY OF PATIENT GRISELDA

GEOFFREY CHAUCER

(Done into modern English by Walter William Skeat)

Griseld is dead, and eke her patience,
And both alike are buried, cold and pale;
And hence I cry, in open audience,
No wedded man should boldly thus assail
His spouse's patience, in the hope to find
Griselda's; for he certainly will fail.

O noble wives, well blessed with providence,
Bid no humility your tongue to nail;
Let never clerk have cause or diligence
To write of you so marvellous a tale
As of Griselda, patient, mild and kind,
Lest "Lean-Cow" swallow you in her entrail!

Like Echo, keep no silent diffidence,
But, always answering back, be prompt to rail;
Be ne'er deluded by your innocence,
But sharply let your tyranny prevail.
Imprint full well this lesson in your mind,
For profit, such as may your hearts regale.

Ye arch-wives, stand upon your own defence,
Since ye are strong as is a mighty whale;
Nor suffer men to do the least offence.
And slender wives, that in the fight are frail,
Be eager as a tiger is in Ind,
And clatter like a mill-wheel or a flail.

Ne'er stand in dread, nor show them reverence;
For though thy husband should be armed in mail,
The arrows of thy bitter eloquence
Shall through his breast or helmet work him bale;
In jealousy endeavour him to bind,
And thou shalt make him cower as doth a quail.

If thou be fair, be well in evidence;
Display thy visage, and thy garments trail;
If ugly, spare not to incur expense,
And get thee friends by bidding men "all hail!"
Be light of mien as linden-leaves in wind,
And let him weep, and wring his hands, and wail!

THE GARLAND

HENRY VAUGHAN

Thou, who dost flow and flourish here below,
  To whom a falling star and nine days' glory,
Or some frail beauty makes the bravest show,
  Hark, and make use of this ensuing story.

When first my youthful, sinful age
  Grew master of my ways,
Appointing Error for my Page,
  And Darkness for my days;
I flung away, and with full cry
  Of wild affections, rid
In post for pleasures, bent to try
  All gamesters that would bid.
I play'd with fire, did counsel spurn,
  Made life my common stake;
But never thought that fire would burn,
  Or that a soul could ache.

Glorious deceptions, gilded mists,
  False joys, fantastic flights,
Pieces of sackcloth with silk lists,
  These were my prime delights.
I sought choice bowers, haunted the spring,
  Cull'd flowers and made me posies;
Gave my fond humours their full wing,
  And crown'd my head with roses.
But at the height of this career
  I met with a dead man,
Who, noting well my vain abear,
  Thus unto me began:
Desist, fond fool, be not undone;
  What thou hast cut to-day
Will fade at night, and with this sun
  Quite vanish and decay.

Flowers gather'd in this world, die here; if thou
Wouldst have a wreath that fades not, let them grow,
And grow for thee. Who spares them here, shall find
A garland, where comes neither rain, nor wind.

GATHER YE ROSE-BUDS

ROBERT HERRICK

Gather ye rose-buds while ye may,
  Old Time is still a-flying:
And this same flower that smiles to-day,
  To-morrow will be dying.

The glorious Lamp of Heaven, the Sun,
  The higher he's a-getting
The sooner will his race be run,
  And nearer he's to setting.

That age is best which is the first,
  When youth and blood are warmer:
But being spent, the worse, and worst
  Times will succeed the former.

Then be not coy, but use your time;
  And while ye may, go marry:
For having lost but once your prime,
  You may forever tarry.

CONSTANCY

SIR JOHN SUCKLING

Out upon it, I have loved
  Three whole days together;
And am like to love three more,
  If it prove fair weather.

Time shall moult away his wings,
  Ere he shall discover
In the whole wide world again
  Such a constant lover.

But the spite on't is, no praise
  Is due at all to me:
Love with me had made no stays,
  Had it any been but she.

Had it any been but she,
  And that very face,
There had been at least ere this
  A dozen dozen in her place.

EPITAPHIUM CITHARISTRIÆ

VICTOR PLARR

Stand not uttering sedately
  Trite oblivious praise above her!
Rather say you saw her lately
  Lightly kissing her last lover.

Whisper not, "There is a reason
  Why we bring her no white blossom":
Since the snowy bloom's in season,
  Strow it on her sleeping bosom:

Oh, for it would be a pity
  To o'erpraise her or to flout her:
She was wild, and sweet, and witty—
  Let's not say dull things about her.

SONG

BEN JONSON

Still to be neat, still to be drest,
As you were going to a feast;
Still to be powdered, still perfumed:
Lady, it is to be presumed,
Though art's hid causes are not found,
All is not sweet, all is not sound.

Give me a look, give me a face,
That makes simplicity a grace;
Robes loosely flowing, hair as free:
Such sweet neglect more taketh me
Than all the adulteries of art:
They strike mine eyes, but not my heart.

TO ALTHEA FROM PRISON

RICHARD LOVELACE

When Love with unconfined wings
  Hovers within my gates,
And my divine Althea brings
  To whisper at the grates;
When I lie tangled in her hair,
  And fetter'd to her eye,
The birds that wanton in the air
  Know no such liberty.

When flowing cups run swiftly round
  With no allaying Thames,
Our careless heads with roses crown'd,
  Our hearts with loyal flames;
When thirsty grief in wine we steep,
  When health and draughts go free,
Fishes that tipple in the deep
  Know no such liberty.

When, linnet-like confined, I
  With shriller throat shall sing
The sweetness, mercy, majesty
  And glories of my King;
When I shall voice aloud how good
  He is, how great should be,
Enlarged winds, that curl the flood,
  Know no such liberty.

Stone walls do not a prison make,
  Nor iron bars a cage;
Minds innocent and quiet take
  That for an hermitage:

If I have freedom in my love
  And in my soul am free,
Angels alone, that soar above,
  Enjoy such liberty.

FATE WITH DEVOTED . . .

ARTHUR DAVISON FICKE

Fate, with devoted and incessant care,
Has showered grotesqueness round us day by day.
If we turn grave, a hurdy-gurdy's air
Is sure to rasp across the words we say.
If we stand tense on brink of perilous choices,
'Tis never where Miltonic headlands loom,
But mid the sound of comic-opera voices
Or the cheap blaze of some hair-dresser's room.
Heaven knows what moonlit turrets, hazed in bliss,
Saw Launcelot and night and Guinevere!—
Or from the cliffs of what great sea-abyss
Tristan and Iseult watched their doom draw near. . . .
I only know our first impassioned kiss
Was in your cellar, rummaging for beer. . . .

EGRETS

MAX EASTMAN

How delicately they are wild,
On their proud wings how slender,
Or resting in the river mild,
Untamable yet tender.

And you, as delicate as they,
Seem kin to their slim hauteur,

Seem gentle and yet far away
As wings upon wild water.

Give beauty when you give your heart,
Give tenderness a river,
Give love which is the giving art,
But give the wild will never.

WOMAN WITHOUT FEAR

GEORGE DILLON

How beautiful is a woman whose avarice is over.
She is content that time should take what it will.
She is proud to have no pride. She asks of her lover
Love only, for good or ill.

She makes of her body a strange bed till morning
Wherein he breathes oblivion better than sleep;
And when he wakes she is nowhere—she has fled without warning,
And left him nothing to keep

But the trace of her tears on the pillow, and a bright strand
Out of her hair, and happiness, and a little grief
That is but the weight of a plum-petal in the hand,
Or heart-shaped mulberry leaf.

WHAT ARE WE FIRST?

GEORGE MEREDITH

What are we first? First, animals; and next
Intelligences at a leap; on whom
Pale lies the distant shadow of the tomb,
And all that draweth on the tomb for text.
Into which state comes Love, the crowning sun:

Beneath whose light the shadow loses form.
We are the lords of life, and life is warm.
Intelligence and instinct now are one.
But nature says: "My children most they seem
When they least know me: therefore I decree
That they shall suffer." Swift doth young Love flee,
And we stand wakened, shivering from our dream.
Then if we study Nature we are wise.
Thus do the few who live but with the day:
The scientific animals are they.—
Lady, this is my sonnet to your eyes.

ORSAMES' SONG

SIR JOHN SUCKLING

Why so pale and wan, fond lover?
  Prithee, why so pale?
Will, when looking well can't move her,
  Looking ill prevail?
  Prithee, why so pale?

Why so dull and mute, young sinner?
  Prithee, why so mute?
Will, when speaking well can't win her,
  Saying nothing do't?
  Prithee, why so mute?

Quit, quit, for shame, this will not move,
  This cannot take her;
If of herself she will not love,
  Nothing can make her:
  The devil take her!

FIE ON LOVE

FRANCIS BEAUMONT

Now fie on foolish love, it not befits
  Or man or woman know it.
Love was not meant for people in their wits,
  And they that fondly show it
Betray the straw, and features in their brain,
And shall have Bedlam for their pain:
If simple love be such a curse,
To marry is to make it ten times worse.

THE MARRIAGE OF TRUE MINDS

WILLIAM SHAKESPEARE

Let me not to the marriage of true minds
Admit impediments. Love is not love
Which alters when it alteration finds,
Or bends with the remover to remove:
O, no! it is an ever-fixed mark,
That looks on tempests and is never shaken;
It is the star to every wandering bark,
Whose worth's unknown, although his height be taken
Love's not Time's fool, though rosy lips and cheeks
Within his bending sickle's compass come;
Love alters not with his brief hours and weeks,
But bears it out even to the edge of doom.
  If this be error and upon me proved,
  I never writ, nor no man ever loved.

NOT MARBLE

WILLIAM SHAKESPEARE

Not marble, nor the gilded monuments
Of princes, shall outlive this powerful rhyme;
But you shall shine more bright in these contents
Than unswept stone, besmear'd with sluttish time
When wasteful war shall statues overturn,
And broils root out the work of masonry,
Nor Mars his sword nor war's quick fire shall burn
The living record of your memory.
'Gainst death and all-oblivious enmity
Shall you pace forth; your praise shall still find room
Even in the eyes of all posterity
That wear this world out to the ending doom.
So, till the judgement that yourself arise,
You live in this, and dwell in lovers' eyes.

LUST

WILLIAM SHAKESPEARE

The expense of spirit in a waste of shame
Is lust in action; and till action, lust
Is perjured, murderous, bloody, full of blame,
Savage, extreme, rude, cruel, not to trust;
Enjoy'd no sooner but despised straight;
Past reason hunted; and no sooner had,
Past reason hated, as a swallowed bait,
On purpose laid to make the taker mad:
Mad in pursuit, and in possession so;
Had, having, and in quest to have, extreme;
A bliss in proof, and proved, a very woe;
Before, a joy proposed; behind, a dream.
All this the world well knows; yet none knows well
To shun the heaven that leads men to this hell.

MEDITATION AT KEW

ANNA WICKHAM

Alas! for all the pretty women who marry dull men,
Go into the suburbs and never come out again,
Who lose their pretty faces, and dim their pretty eyes,
Because no one has skill or courage to organize.

What do these pretty women suffer when they marry?
They bear a boy who is like Uncle Harry,
A girl, who is like Aunt Eliza, and not new.
These old dull races must breed true.

I would enclose a common in the sun,
And let the young wives out to laugh and run;
I would steal their dull clothes and go away,
And leave the pretty naked things to play.

Then I would make a contract with hard Fate
That they see all the men in the world and choose a mate,
And I would summon all the pipers in the town
That they dance with Love at a feast, and dance him down.

From the gay unions of choice
We'd have a race of splendid beauty, and of thrilling voice.
The World whips frank gay love with rods,
But frankly gaily shall be got the gods.

CONFINED LOVE

JOHN DONNE

Some man unworthy to be possessor
Of old or new love, himself being false or weak,
  Thought his pain and shame would be lesser,
If on womankind he might his anger wreak,
    And thence a law did grow,
    One might but one man know;
    But are other creatures so?

Are Sun, Moon, or Stars by law forbidden,
To smile where they list, or lend away their light?
  Are birds divorc'd, or are they chidden
If they leave their mate, or lie abroad a-night?
    Beasts do no jointures lose
    Though they new lovers choose,
    But we are made worse than those.

Who e'er rigg'd fair ship to lie in harbours
And not to seek new lands, or not to deal withal?
  Or built fair houses, set trees, and arbours,
Only to lock up, or else to let them fall?
    Good is not good, unless
    A thousand it possess,
    But doth waste with greediness.

HYMN TO CHRIST, AT THE AUTHOR'S LAST GOING INTO GERMANY

JOHN DONNE

In what torn ship soever I embark,
That ship shall be my emblem of thy ark;
What sea soever swallow me, that flood

Shall be to me an emblem of thy blood;
Though thou with clouds of anger do disguise
Thy face; yet through that mask I know those eyes,
 Which, though they turn away sometimes,
  They never will despise.

I sacrifice this island unto thee,
And all whom I loved there, and who loved me;
When I have put our seas 'twixt them and me,
Put thou thy sea betwixt my sins and thee.
As the tree's sap doth seek the root below
In winter, in my winter now I go
 Where none but thee, the eternal root
  Of true love, I may know.

Nor thou nor thy religion dost control,
The amorousness of an harmonious soul;
But thou wouldst have that love thyself: as thou
Art jealous, Lord, so I am jealous now;
Thou lov'st not, till from loving more, thou free
My soul: whoever gives, takes liberty:
 O, if thou car'st not whom I love,
  Alas, thou lov'st not me.

Seal then this bill of my divorce to all
On whom those fainter beams of love did fall;
Marry those loves, which in youth scattered be
On fame, wit, hopes, (false mistresses,) to thee.
Churches are best for prayer that have least light:
To see God only, I go out of sight;
 And to scape stormy days, I choose
  An everlasting night.

HYMN TO INTELLECTUAL BEAUTY

PERCY BYSSHE SHELLEY

The awful shadow of some unseen Power
  Floats tho' unseen amongst us,—visiting
  This various world with as inconstant wing
As summer winds that creep from flower to flower,—
Like moonbeams that behind some piny mountain shower,
  It visits with inconstant glance
  Each human heart and countenance;
Like hues and harmonies of evening,—
  Like clouds in starlight widely spread,—
  Like memory of music fled,—
  Like aught that for its grace may be
Dear, and yet dearer for its mystery.

II

Spirit of Beauty, that dost consecrate
  With thine own hues all thou dost shine upon
  Of human thought or form,—where art thou gone?
Why dost thou pass away and leave our state,
This dim vast vale of tears, vacant and desolate?
  Ask why the sunlight not forever
  Weaves rainbows o'er yon mountain river,
Why aught should fail and fade that once is shown,
  Why fear and dream and death and birth
  Cast on the daylight of this earth
  Such gloom,—why man has such a scope
For love and hate, despondency and hope?

III

No voice from some sublimer world hath ever
  To sage or poet these responses given—
  Therefore the names of Demon, Ghost, and Heaven,

Remain the records of their vain endeavor,
Frail spells—whose uttered charm might not avail to sever,
  From all we hear and all we see,
  Doubt, chance, and mutability.
Thy light alone—like mist o'er mountains driven,
  Or music by the night wind sent,
  Thro' strings of some still instrument,
  Or moonlight on a midnight stream,
Gives grace and truth to life's unquiet dream.

IV

Love, Hope, and Self-esteem, like clouds depart
  And come, for some uncertain moments lent:
  Man were immortal, and omnipotent,
Didst thou, unknown and awful as thou art,
Keep with thy glorious train firm state within his heart.
  Thou messenger of sympathies,
  That wax and wane in lovers' eyes—
Thou—that to human thought art nourishment,
  Like darkness to a dying flame!
  Depart not as thy shadow came,
  Depart not—lest the grave should be,
Like life and fear, a dark reality.

V

While yet a boy I sought for ghosts, and sped
  Thro' many a listening chamber, cave and ruin,
  And starlight wood, with fearful steps pursuing
Hopes of high talk with the departed dead.
I called on poisonous names with which our youth is fed;
  I was not heard—I saw them not—
  When musing deeply on the lot
Of life, at the sweet time when winds are wooing
  All vital things that wake to bring

News of birds and blossoming,—
Sudden, thy shadow fell on me;
I shriekt, and claspt my hands in ecstasy!

VI

I vowed that I would dedicate my powers
To thee and thine—have I not kept the vow?
With beating heart and streaming eyes, even now
I call the phantoms of a thousand hours
Each from his voiceless grave: they have in visioned bowers
Of studious zeal or love's delight
Outwatcht with me the envious night—
They know that never joy illumed my brow
Unlinkt with hope that thou wouldst free
This world from its dark slavery,
That thou—O awful Loveliness,
Wouldst give whate'er these words cannot express.

VII

The day becomes more solemn and serene
When noon is past—there is a harmony
In autumn, and a lustre in its sky,
Which thro' the summer is not heard or seen,
As if it could not be, as if it had not been!
Thus let thy power, which like the truth
Of nature on my passive youth
Descended, to my onward life supply
Its calm—to one who worships thee,
And every form containing thee,
Whom, Spirit fair, thy spells did bind
To fear himself, and love all human kind.

XCII

EMILY DICKINSON

Drowning is not so pitiful
  As the attempt to rise.
Three times, 'tis said, a sinking man
  Comes up to face the skies,
And then declines forever
  To that abhorred abode

Where hope and he part company,—
  For he is grasped of God.
The Maker's cordial visage,
  However good to see,
Is shunned, we must admit it,
  Like an adversity.

THE PILLAR OF THE CLOUD

JOHN HENRY, CARDINAL NEWMAN

Lead, Kindly Light, amid the encircling gloom,
    Lead Thou me on!
The night is dark, and I am far from home!
    Lead Thou me on.
Keep Thou my feet; I do not ask to see
The distant scene—one step enough for me.

I was not ever thus, nor prayed that Thou
    Shouldst lead me on.
I loved to choose and see my path, but now
    Lead Thou me on!
I loved the garish day, and, spite of fears,
Pride ruled my will: remember not past years.

So long Thy power hath blest me, sure it still
　　　　Will lead me on,
O'er moor and fen, o'er crag and torrent till
　　　　The night is gone,
And with the morn those angel faces smile
Which I have loved long since, and lost awhile.

INVICTUS

WILLIAM ERNEST HENLEY

Out of the night that covers me,
　Black as the Pit from pole to pole,
I thank whatever gods may be
　For my unconquerable soul.

In the fell clutch of circumstance
　I have not winced nor cried aloud.
Under the bludgeonings of chance
　My head is bloody, but unbowed.

Beyond this place of wrath and tears
　Looms but the horror of the shade,
And yet the menace of the years
　Finds, and shall find me, unafraid.

It matters not how strait the gate,
　How charged with punishments the scroll,
I am the master of my fate:
　I am the captain of my soul.

AN APPOINTMENT

W. B. YEATS

Being out of heart with government
I took a broken root to fling
Where the proud, wayward squirrel went,
Taking delight that he could spring;
And he, with that low whinnying sound
That is like laughter, sprang again
And so to the other tree at a bound.
Nor the tame will, nor timid brain,
Nor heavy knitting of the brow
Bred that fierce tooth and cleanly limb
And threw him up to laugh on the bough;
No government appointed him.

AN IRISH AIRMAN FORESEES HIS DEATH

W. B. YEATS

I know that I shall meet my fate
Somewhere among the clouds above;
Those that I fight I do not hate,
Those that I guard I do not love;
My country is Kiltartan Cross,
My countrymen Kiltartan's poor,
No likely end could bring them loss
Or leave them happier than before.
Nor law, nor duty bade me fight,
Nor public men, nor cheering crowds,
A lonely impulse of delight
Drove to this tumult in the clouds;
I balanced all, brought all to mind,

The years to come seemed waste of breath,
A waste of breath the years behind
In balance with this life, this death.

THE RHODORA: ON BEING ASKED, WHENCE IS THE FLOWER?

RALPH WALDO EMERSON

In May, when sea-winds pierced our solitudes,
I found the fresh Rhodora in the woods,
Spreading its leafless blooms in a damp nook,
To please the desert and the sluggish brook.
The purple petals, fallen in the pool,
Made the black water with their beauty gay;
Here might the red-bird come his plumes to cool,
And court the flower that cheapens his array.
Rhodora! if the sages ask thee why
This charm is wasted on the earth and sky,
Tell them, dear, that if eyes were made for seeing,
Then Beauty is its own excuse for being:
Why thou wert there, O rival of the rose!
I never thought to ask, I never knew;
But, in my simple ignorance, suppose
The self-same Power that brought me there brought you.

THE END OF THE WORLD

ARCHIBALD MACLEISH

Quite unexpectedly as Vasserot
The armless ambidextrian was lighting
A match between his great and second toe
And Ralph the lion was engaged in biting
The neck of Madame Sossman while the drum

Pointed, and Teeny was about to cough
In waltz-time swinging Jocko by the thumb—
Quite unexpectedly the top blew off:
And there, there overhead, there, there, hung over
Those thousands of white faces, those dazed eyes,
There in the starless dark, the poise, the hover,
There with vast wings across the canceled skies,
There in the sudden blackness, the black pall
Of nothing, nothing, nothing—nothing at all.

CRITICS AND CONNOISSEURS

MARIANNE MOORE

There is a great amount of poetry in unconscious
  fastidiousness. Certain Ming
    products, imperial floor-coverings of coach
wheel yellow, are well enough in their way but I have seen something
  that I like better—a
    mere childish attempt to make an imperfectly ballasted animal stand up,
    similar determination to make a pup
      eat his meat from the plate.

I remember a swan under the willows in Oxford,
  with flamingo-coloured, maple-
    leaf-like feet. It reconnoitred like a battle-
ship. Disbelief and conscious fastidiousness were the staple ingredients in its
    disinclination to move. Finally its hardihood was not proof against its
    proclivity to more fully appraise such bits
      of food as the stream

bore counter to it; it made away with which I gave it
  to eat. I have seen this swan and
    I have seen you; I have seen ambition without
understanding in a variety of forms. Happening to stand
  by an ant-hill, I have
    seen a fastidious ant carrying a stick north, south, east,
      west, till it turned on
    itself, struck out from the flower-bed into the lawn,
      and returned to the point

from which it had started. Then abandoning the stick as
  useless and overtaxing its
    jaws with a particle of whitewash—pill-like but
heavy, it again went through the same course of procedure.
      What is
    there in being able
      to say that one has dominated the stream in an
      attitude of self-defence;
    in proving that one has had the experience
      of carrying a stick?

ADDRESS TO VENUS

EDMUND SPENSER

(Translated from Lucretius)

Great Venus, Queene of Beautie and of grace,
  The joy of Gods and men, that under skie
  Dost fayrest shine, and most adorne thy place;
  That with thy smyling looke doest pacifie
  The raging seas and makst the stormes to flie:
    Thee, Goddess, thee the winds, the clouds do feare;
  And when thou spredst thy mantle forth on hie
    The waters play, and pleasant lands appear,
And heavens laugh, and all the world shews joyous cheare.

Then doth the daedale earth throw forth to thee
  Out of her fruitfull lap abundant flowres;
And then all living wights, soone as they see
  The Spring break forth out of his lusty bowres,
  They all doe learne to play the Paramours;
    First doe the merry birds, thy prety pages,
  Privily priked with thy lustful powres,
    Chirpe loud to thee out of their leavy cages
And thee their mother call to coole their kindly rages.

Then doe the salvage beasts begin to play
  Their pleasant friskes, and loath their wonted food;
The Lyons rore; the Tygres loudly bray;
  The raging Buls rebellow through the wood,
  And breaking forth dare tempt the deepest flood
    To come where thou doest draw them with desire.
  So all things else, that nourish vitall blood,
    Soone as with fury thou doest them inspire
In generation seeke to quench their inward fire.

So all the world by thee at first was made,
  And dayly yet thou doest the same prepayre:
Ne ought on earth that merry is and glad,
  Ne ought on earth that lovely is and fayre
  But thou the same for pleasure didst prepayre:
    Thou art the root of all that joyous is:
  Great God of men and women, queene of the air,
    Mother of laughter and welspring of blisse,
O graunt that of my love at last I may not misse!

A LECTURE UPON THE SHADOW

JOHN DONNE

Stand still, and I will read to thee
A Lecture, love, in Love's philosophy.
  These three hours that we have spent,
  Walking here, two shadows went
Along with us, which we ourselves produced;
But, now the Sun is just above our head,
  We do those shadows tread;
  And to brave clearness all things are reduc'd.
So whilst our infant loves did grow,
Disguises did, and shadows, flow,
From us, and our cares; but, now 'tis not so.

That love hath not attain'd the high'st degree,
Which is still diligent lest others see.

Except our loves at this noon stay,
We shall new shadows make the other way.
  As the first were made to blind
  Others; these which come behind
Will work upon ourselves, and blind our eyes.
If our loves faint, and westwardly decline;
  To me thou, falsely, thine,
  And I to thee mine actions shall disguise.

The morning shadows wear away,
But these grow longer all the day,
But oh, love's day is short, if love decay.

Love is a growing, or full constant light;
And his first minute, after noon, is night.

LOVE IS ENOUGH

WILLIAM MORRIS

Love is enough: though the World be a-waning,
And the woods have no voice but the voice of complaining,
  Though the skies be too dark for dim eyes to discover
The gold-cups and daisies fair blooming thereunder,
Though the hills be held shadows, and the sea a dark wonder,
  And this day draw a veil over all deeds pass'd over,
Yet their hands shall not tremble, their feet shall not falter:
The void shall not weary, the fear shall not alter
  These lips and these eyes of the loved and the lover.

GIVE ALL TO LOVE

RALPH WALDO EMERSON

Give all to love;
Obey thy heart;
Friends, kindred, days,
Estate, good-fame,
Plans, credit, and the Muse,—
Nothing refuse.

'Tis a brave master;
Let it have scope:
Follow it utterly,
Hope beyond hope:
High and more high
It dives into noon,
With wing unspent,
Untold intent;
But it is a god,
Knows its own path,
And the outlets of the sky.

GIVE ALL TO LOVE

It was never for the mean;
It requireth courage stout,
Souls above doubt,
Valor unbending;
It will reward,—
They shall return
More than they were,
And ever ascending.

Leave all for love;
Yet, hear me, yet,
One word more thy heart behoved,
One pulse more of firm endeavor,—
Keep thee to-day
To-morrow, forever,
Free as an Arab
Of thy beloved.

Cling with life to the maid;
But when the surprise,
First vague shadow of surmise
Flits across her bosom young
Of a joy apart from thee,
Free be she, fancy-free;
Nor thou detain her vesture's hem,
Nor the palest rose she flung
From her summer diadem.

Though thou loved her as thyself,
As a self of purer clay,
Though her parting dims the day,
Stealing grace from all alive;
Heartily know,
When half-gods go,
The gods arrive.

MY SWEETEST LESBIA

THOMAS CAMPION

My sweetest Lesbia, let us live and love.
And though the sager sort our deeds reprove,
Let us not weigh them: heavn's great lamps do dive
Into their west, and straight again revive,
But soon as once set is our little light,
Then must we sleep one ever-during night.

If all would lead their lives in love like me,
Then bloody swords and armour should not be,
No drum nor trumpet peaceful sleeps should move,
Unless alar'm came from the camp of love:
But fools do live, and waste their little light,
And seek with pain their ever-during night.

When timely death my life and fortune ends,
Let not my hearse be vexed with mourning friends,
But let all lovers rich in triumph come,
And with sweet pastimes grace my happy tomb;
And Lesbia close up thou my little light,
And crown with love my ever-during night.

THE SEA-LIMITS

DANTE GABRIEL ROSSETTI

Consider the sea's listless chime:
  Time's self it is, made audible,—
  The murmur of the earth's own shell.
Secret continuance sublime
  Is the sea's end: our sight may pass
  No furlong further. Since time was,
This sound hath told the lapse of time.

No quiet, which is death's,—it hath
  The mournfulness of ancient life,
  Enduring always at dull strife.
As the world's heart of rest and wrath,
  Its painful pulse is in the sands.
  Last utterly, the whole sky stands,
Grey and not known, along its path.

Listen alone beside the sea,
  Listen alone among the woods;
  Those voices of twin solitudes
Shall have one sound alike to thee:
  Hark where the murmurs of thronged men
  Surge and sink back and surge again,—
Still the one voice of wave and tree.

Gather a shell from the strown beach
  And listen at its lips: they sigh
  The same desire and mystery,
The echo of the whole sea's speech.
  And all mankind is thus at heart
  Not anything but what thou art:
And Earth, Sea, Man, are all in each.

THE HIGH MIND

SAMUEL DANIEL

He that of such a height hath built his mind,
And rear'd the dwelling of his thoughts so strong,
As neither fear nor hope can shake the frame
Of his resolvèd powers; nor all the wind
Of vanity or malice pierce to wrong
His settled peace, or to disturb the same,
What a fair seat hath he, from whence he may
The boundless wastes and wilds of man survey!

And with how free an eye doth he look down
Upon these lower regions of turmoil!
Where all the storms of passion mainly beat
On flesh and blood; where honour, power, renown
Are only gay afflictions, golden toil;
Where greatness stands upon as feeble feet
As frailty doth, and only great doth seem
To little minds, who do it so esteem.

He looks upon the mightiest monarch's wars
But only as on stately robberies;
Where evermore the fortune that prevails
Must be the right: the ill-succeeding mars
The fairest and the best-faced enterprise.
Great pirate Pompey lesser pirates quails:
Justice, he sees (as if seduced), still
Conspires with power, whose cause must not be ill.

He sees the face of right t' appear as manifold
As are the passions of uncertain man;
Who puts it in all colours, all attires,
To serve his ends and make his courses hold.
He sees, that let deceit work what it can,
Plot and contrive base ways to high desires,
That the all-guiding Providence doth yet
All disappoint, and mocks this smoke of wit.

Nor is he mov'd with all the thunder cracks
Of tyrants' threats, or with the surly brow
Of Pow'r, that proudly sits on others' crimes,
Charg'd with more crying sins than those he checks.
The storms of sad confusion, that may grow
Up in the present for the coming times,
Appal not him, that hath no side at all
But of himself, and knows the worst can fall.

Although his heart (so near allied to earth)
Cannot but pity the perplexèd state
Of troublous and distress'd mortality,
That thus make way unto the ugly birth
Of their own sorrows, and do still beget
Affliction upon imbecility;
Yet seeing thus the course of things must run
He looks thereon not strange, but as foredone.

And whilst distraught ambition compasses,
And is encompass'd; whilst as craft deceives,
And is deceiv'd; whilst man doth ransack man,
And builds on blood, and rises by distress;
And th' inheritance of desolation leaves
To great-expecting hopes: he looks thereon
As from the shore of peace, with unwet eye,
And bears no venture in impiety.

PRAYER AGAINST INDIFFERENCE

JOY DAVIDMAN

When wars and ruined men shall cease
To vex my body's house of peace,
And bloody children lying dead
Let me lie softly in my bed
To nurse a whole and sacred skin,
Break roof and let the bomb come in.

Knock music at the templed skull
And say the world is beautiful,
But never let the dweller lock
Its house against another knock;
Never shut out the gun, the scream,
Never lie blind within a dream.

Within these walls the brain shall sit
And chew on life surrounding it;
Eat the soft sunlight hour and then
The bitter taste of bleeding men;
But never underneath the sun
Shall it forget the scream, the gun.

Let me have eyes I need not shut;
Let me have truth at my tongue's root;
Let courage and the brain command
The honest fingers of my hand;
And when I wait to save my skin
Break roof and let my death come in.

IN TIME OF "THE BREAKING OF NATIONS"

THOMAS HARDY

Only a man harrowing clods
  In a slow silent walk,
With an old horse that stumbles and nods
  Half asleep as they stalk.

Only thin smoke without flame
  From the heaps of couch grass:
Yet this will go onward the same
  Though Dynasties pass.

Yonder a maid and her wight
  Come whispering by;
War's annals will fade into night
  Ere their story die.

RECONCILIATION

WALT WHITMAN

Word over all, beautiful as the sky,
Beautiful that war and all its deeds of carnage must in time be utterly lost,
That the hands of the sisters Death and Night incessantly softly wash again, and ever again, this soil'd world;
For my enemy is dead, a man divine as myself is dead,
I look where he lies white-faced and still in the coffin—I draw near,
Bend down and touch lightly with my lips the white face in the coffin.

DOVER BEACH

MATTHEW ARNOLD

The sea is calm tonight.
The tide is full, the moon lies fair
Upon the straits;—on the French coast the light
Gleams and is gone; the cliffs of England stand,
Glimmering and vast, out in the tranquil bay.
Come to the window, sweet is the night-air!
Only, from the long line of spray
Where the sea meets the moon-blanch'd land,
Listen! you hear the grating roar
Of pebbles which the waves draw back, and fling,
At their return, up the high strand,
Begin, and cease, and then again begin,
With tremulous cadence slow, and bring
The eternal note of sadness in.

Sophocles long ago
Heard it on the Ægaean, and it brought

Into his mind the turbid ebb and flow
Of human misery; we
Find also in the sound a thought,
Hearing it by this distant northern sea.

The sea of faith
Was once, too, at the full, and round earth's shore
Lay like the folds of a bright girdle furl'd.
But now I only hear
Its melancholy, long, withdrawing roar,
Retreating to the breath
Of the night-wind down the vast edges drear
And naked shingles of the world.

Ah, love, let us be true
To one another! for the world, which seems
To lie before us like a land of dreams,
So various, so beautiful, so new,
Hath really neither joy, nor love, nor light,
Nor certitude, nor peace, nor help for pain;
And we are here as on a darkling plain
Swept with confused alarms of struggle and flight,
Where ignorant armies clash by night.

INDEXES

INDEX OF AUTHORS

INDEX OF AUTHORS

INDEX OF AUTHORS

INDEX OF AUTHORS

INDEX OF FIRST LINES

INDEX OF FIRST LINES

INDEX OF TITLES

INDEX OF TITLES

INDEX OF TITLES

INDEX OF TITLES

INDEX OF TITLES